CW00767570

REASSESSING JOHN BUCHAN:
BEYOND THE THIRTY-NINE STEPS

REASSESSING JOHN BUCHAN: BEYOND THE THIRTY-NINE STEPS

EDITED BY

Kate Macdonald

LONDON
PICKERING & CHATTO
2009

Published by Pickering & Chatto (Publishers) Limited
21 Bloomsbury Way, London WC1A 2TH

2252 Ridge Road, Brookfield, Vermont 05036-9704, USA

www.pickeringchatto.com

All rights reserved.
No part of this publication may be reproduced,
stored in a retrieval system, or transmitted in any form or by any means,
electronic, mechanical, photocopying, recording, or otherwise
without prior permission of the publisher.

© Pickering & Chatto (Publishers) Ltd 2009
© Kate Macdonald 2009

BRITISH LIBRARY CATALOGUING IN PUBLICATION DATA

Reassessing John Buchan : beyond The thirty-nine steps.
1. Buchan, John, 1875–1940 – Criticism and interpretation.
I. Macdonald, Kate.
823.9'12-dc22

ISBN-13: 9781851969982
e: 9781851965861

This publication is printed on acid-free paper that conforms to the American
National Standard for the Permanence of Paper for Printed Library Materials.

Typeset by Pickering & Chatto (Publishers) Limited
Printed in Great Britain by the MPG Books Group, Bodmin and King's Lynn

CONTENTS

LIST OF CONTRIBUTORS

Ahmed al-Rawi is a lecturer at the Faculty of English Language Studies, Majan University College, Muscat, Sultanate of Oman.

Simon Glassock worked in IT before reading history at Oxford. He is now a radiographer.

David Goldie is a senior lecturer in the Department of English Studies at the University of Strathclyde.

Paul Benedict Grant is an assistant professor of English at Memorial University of Newfoundland, Canada.

The Rev. James C. G. Greig is a linguist and former staff member of the World Council of Churches, Geneva.

The late *Isobel Haslett* was a classicist, a barrister and a historian.

Michael Haslett is a retired GP and was a classical scholar.

Peter Henshaw is an analyst of Southern African affairs in Canada's Privy Council Office, and is attached to the Department of History at the University of Western Ontario.

Douglas Kerr is a professor in the School of English, University of Hong Kong.

Kate Macdonald is an assistant professor at the Department of English at the University of Ghent, Belgium, and the author of *John Buchan: A Companion to the Mystery Fiction*.

John Miller is at the Department of English at the University of Glasgow.

Bill Nasson is Professor of History at the University of Stellenbosch, South Africa, and is a Fellow of the Stellenbosch Institute of Advanced Study. His publications include *The South African War 1899–1902*, *Britannia's Empire* and *Springboks on the Somme*.

Michael Redley is an African historian and economist who teaches at the Department of Continuing Education at the University of Oxford.

Alan Riach is a poet and Professor of Scottish Literature at the University of Glasgow. His most recent book of poems is *Clearances* and he is the coauthor, with the artist Alexander Moffat, of *Arts of Resistance: Poets, Portraits and Landscapes of Modern Scotland*.

Hew Strachan is the Chichele Professor of the History of War, All Souls College, University of Oxford.

H. E. Taylor graduated in history from Kings College, London. He has been a shipbroker and is now a commodity trader.

Nathan Waddell is at the Department of English, the University of Birmingham.

Tony Williams is a professor of Film Studies at the University of Southern Illinois, USA.

INTRODUCTION

John Buchan was born in Scotland in 1875 to a Presbyterian family with strong farming connections, and left Glasgow University for Oxford in 1895. He took a First in Greats (classical studies) in 1899, while supporting himself throughout his studies as a writer and a publisher's reader. He tried the Imperial Civil Service, the Bar and journalism, but settled in 1907 into publishing and his lifelong happy marriage, and continued to publish his own fiction, though without wild success. His interest in actively engaging himself in politics was tested in 1911 when he failed to gain a seat in the House of Commons, but by 1914 he was in the thick of wartime publishing, and was developing his skills as a historian, a novelist and as a government propagandist. Buchan emerged from the war famous, with a growing family (his fourth child was born in 1918), and a house in Oxfordshire, but also a sick man and much bereaved. The 1920s were spent in constant writing and publishing, and he won the coveted seat in Parliament. Honours and formal appointments followed, and in 1935 he was ennobled as Baron Tweedsmuir to become Governor-General of Canada. His flow of writing began to slow, and in 1940 he died after suffering a brain haemorrhage. His most well-known novel, *The Thirty-Nine Steps* (1915) has never been out of print, and he published over 100 books in his lifetime, a substantial proportion of them non-fiction.

There have been three biographies of Buchan,[1] three bibliographies[2] and much critical writing. Only two full-length books on Buchan's writing have been published, but a substantial amount of critical research has been done, scattered as book chapters, academic articles, op eds in the public press and book reviews.[3] Only very recently was a comprehensive survey of his fiction published and, shortly after the date of this volume, he will come out of copyright in Britain to an expected surge of new editions of his works.

The impetus for this volume on John Buchan came from the realization that a great many individuals were working on Buchan simultaneously, but that no collection of essays representative of this sustained effort existed. Collections of essays on a single author by a range of authorities examine the subject thoroughly, and have the extra value of tackling the same subjects from different angles. A collection such as this also ensures that the author under discussion is approached from outside a single discipline. In collating this book it became obvious how impossible it is to separate out aspects of the life and work of John Buchan solely in terms of his historical writing or his literary work. Both are inextricably intertwined, and dominate the other genres in which he published (for example, poetry and the law). Interestingly, the contributors to this volume are also divided, roughly equally, between historians and literary scholars: the work of the classicist and theological contributors can also be read predominantly through the lens of history and literary style. It seems clear that to understand Buchan's fiction we must understand his history and his place in history. To understand how he felt about his own times and the events in which he participated we need to look at how he wrote his fiction, and what he chose to put into it.

It will also be apparent that none of the essays presented here are solely historical or solely literary-critical. History washes around the discussions of form and language, and examples from Buchan's fiction inform the historical points being made. With such crossings-over and mutual influencing, organizing the essays seemed to need a different set of criteria, not derived just by historical period or literary concern, but by looking deeper into the essay subjects to determine their underlying links. We have also striven for a certain amount of chronological progression, but this was not always possible, because the thematic approaches taken have ranged over Buchan's entire life and work.

Alan Riach notes in his essay in this volume that 'a comprehensive reassessment of Buchan's achievement must read his work in three ways: intensely and closely as literary art ... in terms of his biography, the divided loyalties he experienced himself very early on ...; and thirdly in the entire political and cultural moment of his era'. I have taken this useful tripartite division as a guide for ordering the essays, because Riach seems to me to have got straight to the heart of the matter. Buchan's cultural roots powered all his writing, and demand reconsideration for the simple fact of their all-pervasiveness in Buchan's work and life. The divisions and loyalties that he developed and experienced are also crucial for an understanding of what he wrote and why he wrote it. Finally, reassessing Buchan as a literary artist has been too long overdue, particularly from such a broad range of specialisms as those represented here.

Opening the section on Buchan's cultural roots, then, the value of J. C. G. Greig's discussion of Buchan's Calvinism lies in the author's long professional engagement with Presbyterian and Calvinist theology. The present generation, and several generations preceding them, simply do not have the intellectual and cultural training to read the religious aspects of Buchan's writing in the way that Buchan intended, or would have expected from his own generation. Greig's exegesis of the Calvinism in Buchan's writing fills an important gap in the literature, and advances our understanding of how Buchan's religious philosophy informed his creative imagination. A similarly important lacuna in modern education, quite different to that expected by Buchan of his readers, is supplied in the essay on Buchan's use of the classics by Michael Haslett and the late Isobel Haslett. Their survey of Buchan's fictional oeuvre unpicks the patterns of his reading and citations, explains his motivations, and shows how his reliance on Jane Harrison and his Oxford tutors influenced his plots and writing style.

Buchan probably started to acquire a notion of his own cultural identity at around the same time that he began untangling Latin conjugations. David Goldie's essay on the Scots and English in Buchan discerns a more subtle relationship than mere opposition. Buchan was not a convert to Englishness, and neither was he a Scots nationalist: somehow he made these two opposites produce a force of twin, parallel loyalties that have rarely been articulated so lucidly in fiction. Simon Glassock also deals with a fundamental force in the life of a male Scot: the passion for sport. He shows how Buchan reflected and shaped ideas of late Victorian and Edwardian masculinity into a philosophy of life and behaviour addressed to his middlebrow male readers. This philosophy informed his response to changing ideas about male culture and literary art, and developed into the Buchan hero, a character who maintained links with masculine ideals of the past and who could be relied upon to re-present these ideals to a postwar readership in the throes of a modernist agenda. Combining these two ideas, of physicality and national identity, Bill Nasson's essay on Buchan's depiction of the South African soldier in the First World War shows how Buchan drew on an idealization of the colonial soldier fighting for the Home Country in his *History of the South African Forces in France* (1920). Buchan's values for the colonial warrior rested on the physical requirements of a successful Imperial settler, but Nasson decodes the rhetoric to show how these contrasted with the values exhibited in the soldiers at the time.

This sense of doublethink, of what Buchan presented as his own view and how this differed from other perspectives, takes us to the second section of the book, on divided loyalties. Staying in South Africa, but going back twenty years to the turn of the twentieth century, Michael Redley examines Buchan's work for Lord Milner in South African land settlement immediately after the Boer War, using hitherto unpublished archive material. He shows how Buchan deployed a ruthless pragmatism that took advantage of the Boers, and drove his political master's policies forward at the expense of the established protocols. Redley shows how, even this early in his career, Buchan used his journalistic connections to advance political propaganda. Revealingly, this pragmatism also convinced Buchan to struggle against the racist prejudices of the Boer farmers, so that Redley presents us with a complex picture of the young Buchan as an early resistor of Apartheid, as well as a man who took advantage of the confusion of post-war conditions to further British government aims.

Moving on to the First World War, historian Hew Strachan explores how Buchan wrote his own war histories, and how he responded to war in his portraits of soldiers and the wounded. Buchan's administrative and political pragmatism, now rather more tempered by time and experience, was matched to the upholding of civilized values, where the truths that Buchan chose to tell, in his fiction and in his official historical accounts, were for the benefit of the British people, not necessarily for the British authorities. Nathan Waddell also addresses Buchan's reportage of the cultural experience of the First World War, by examining his depiction of pacifists and conscientious objectors. Buchan can be seen to have moderated his views on pacifism, and Waddell shows how he divided his loyalties by his principles in acknowledging a personal sympathy for the individual conscientious objector, while disagreeing with pacifist philosophy.

Continuing the investigation of dual perspectives, Peter Henshaw examines Buchan's American-aimed propaganda to find a consistent pattern in Buchan's long-held beliefs about the British Empire and in how Britain and America should continue to do business together. Buchan's depiction of Americans, his use of America as a fictional setting and as a market, and his attachment to Anglo-American relationships are shown to have been a directed insistence from Buchan that Anglo-American understanding was fundamental to how he saw the future of the civilized Western world.

The Iraqi scholar Ahmed al-Rawi also offers a new close reading of Buchan by examining Buchan's use of Islam in his fiction and essays, in terms of how Buchan's Empire writing can be seen to be predicated upon an assumption of Christian authority as well as Western white rule. Using *Greenmantle* (1916) as a starting point, al-Rawi examines the small, fleeting glances in idiom and phrase in Buchan's dialogue and settings, and makes a highly persuasive case for a postcolonial reassessment of Buchan's works that opens up spiritual and cultural rather than racial territory. H. E. Taylor also uses a new lens, that of the world of work, to examine how Buchan dealt with businessmen, showing how the evolution of business methods was reinterpreted in Buchan's fiction by rooting the terrifying Conquistadors of *The Courts of the Morning* and the pawkiness of Mr Craw in *Castle Gay* in a sound appreciation of the role of the entrepreneur in society. The divided loyalties of conscience and money, God and Mammon, are reconciled through an acknowledgment of moral consequences.

Opening the third section to examine Buchan as a literary artist, Douglas Kerr goes to Buchan's earliest publications, and to the heart of creative endeavour, by unearthing an old literary libel. Did Buchan plagiarise Joseph Conrad? Kerr explores the nature of literary borrowing and hypertextuality, and gives Conrad and Buchan a close reading to establish that there are unsettling but perhaps not unbenign coincidences at both ends of Buchan's career. Kate Macdonald gives similarly close attention to Buchan's depiction of women in his fiction, using narrative theory and feminist readings to categorize his female characters in terms of their function in the story, and their relationship to the protagonists. The use of archetypes, of the older, the sexualized and the challenging women, who might also be class infiltrators, is shown to be Buchan's way of expressing disapproval of changing social behaviour.

Alan Riach looks at Buchan's art in terms of a framework from which Buchan engaged with the world through his language and stories. The tension that Buchan employed in his fiction to produce suspense can be read as a motivating force, in the narrative, in Buchan's own life and in the journey that must end. Linguistic choice makes clearer 'the pathos of epic effort', and shows how Buchan reconciled his narratives with form. Paul Grant also explores Buchan's fiction as a mode for reconciliation, in presenting Nature as both benign and malign in his supernatural fiction. Buchan's use of landscape in addressing the nature and origins of fear, and his literary skill in producing an uncanny atmosphere, by the powerful impetus of suggestion, make him a classic writer of horror and the unknown. Contrariwise, John Miller shows how Buchan's depiction of ecology allows him to bypass the horrific in his fiction, by advocating a harmonious integration with nature, rather than a resistant alienation. Using *The Waste Land* and anarchism as exemplars of the negativity that Buchan was striving to overcome, or at least avoid, Miller shows how Buchan's metaphors and metonymy also resist modernist tendencies. Hygiene is correlated with resistance to extremism, in all its forms.

No work on Buchan can avoid *The Thirty-Nine Steps*. As we see below, this single work is dealt with thoroughly in many of the chapters published here, but Tony Williams takes *Thirty-Nine Steps* studies to a new level with a discussion of the first three films of the novel, and reallocates Buchan's original literary tropes across forty years of film history. Intertextuality, hybridization and the demands of a screen audience rather than a readership disembodied the original novel and made it a flickering screen creation in 1935 (Hitchcock), 1954 (Thomas) and 1978 (Sharp). Williams reinterprets the films to show how Buchan cast shadows on them, rather than seeing the films as pale imitations of his book.

Over forty fictional works by Buchan are discussed in this volume, many of them by more than one contributor. The Buchan work cited by the most contributors is, however, Buchan's autobiography, *Memory Hold-the-Door* (1940), showing how it is still considered a valuable key to Buchan's own thought, and as evidence of his interpretation of his life. That which he did not recall in print in this work is also notable: he says little about his relationship with his mother, his early years working with John Lane in the context of decadent aesthetic *Yellow*

Book London, or about exactly how his early First World War journalism turned into official war reportage. Negative data are also indicative in considering how his works of fiction have been discussed. *Mr Standfast* (1919) and *The Three Hostages* (1924) are the novels most often examined by the contributors to this volume, followed by *The Thirty-Nine Steps* (1915) and *The Dancing Floor* (1926). 'The Grove of Ashtaroth' (1910) is the most fruitful short story, discussed in as many essays here as *A Lodge in the Wilderness* (1906), *Greenmantle* (1916), *The Courts of the Morning* (1929), *The Island of Sheep* (1936) and *Sick Heart River* (1940). 'The Moor-Song' (1897), *Prester John* (1910) and *A Prince of the Captivity* (1933) are ahead not only of *Sir Quixote of the Moors* (1895), *Huntingtower* (1922), *John Macnab* (1925), *Witch Wood* (1927), and *The Blanket of the Dark* (1931), but also *Nelson's History of the War* (1915–19). By looking at the works that have not been covered by more than one author we can see how trends of interest are apparent. All the supernatural stories have been looked at, by Grant and the Hasletts, as well as by others, but less obvious works, such as *Salute to Adventurers* (1915) and *The Gap in the Curtain* (1932) have not been covered widely, yet contain much material of importance to, say, the study of the historical novel and the perception of America as a frontier, and the social history of the 1930s. Clearly more work is waiting to be done.

Also used intensively in this volume is Buchan's journalism. His collected editorials and leaders for *The Scottish Review* (1907–9) are usefully available in one volume (ed Gray, 1939), but Buchan's *Spectator* journalism, which lasted for a great deal longer and had the advantage of being anonymous, is a fascinating but underused resource to supplement Buchan's fiction writing and his burgeoning historical and biographical work from the turn of the twentieth century.

It is hoped that the seventeen essays in this volume will advance Buchan studies to a level where the foundations will be seen to have been solidly laid down from 1949 to 1995, and work on Buchan began its second phase in 2009. Buchan is taught now more than ever, either for his place as a great Scottish writer (his works have been on Scottish school and university curricula for decades), or for *The Thirty-Nine Steps* in the context of film history or the genesis of the thriller genre. More recent critical approaches have included his war novels as expressions of reading history, his place in the middlebrow continuum and as an aspect of pre-modernist *fin de siècle* writing. The scope is broad: these essays demonstrate that, with the right viewfinder, Buchan and his writing can be used as a valuable and productive lens for new cultural, historical and literary exploration.

Kate Macdonald
Brussels & Ghent, Belgium
December 2008

1 JOHN BUCHAN AND CALVINISM

The Rev. James C. G. Greig

Home environment contributes to the making of a mindset. A Presbyterian and ostensibly Calvinist Scot, born in Perth, on the east coast of Scotland, but brought up in Presbyterian manses, first in Pathhead (Fife), and then to the west of Scotland in Glasgow, could hardly escape being aware that Calvinism could be doctrinaire and legalistic. John Buchan's thoughts about his parents and other Calvinists he encountered in his early life will be discussed below. As a boy, he intuitively sought to develop a natural literary flair for his imaginative and critical pursuits. Calvinism was an important part of his life. Throughout his life he remained a Presbyterian, but as a liberal Calvinist with distinctly ecumenical leanings.

Most who have heard of Buchan plump for *The Thirty-Nine Steps* (1915), one of his First World War espionage 'shockers'. These and his later novels exemplify his imaginative range, as do his contributions to the short story genre, more than one political symposium and his biographies. His posthumous autobiography *Memory Hold-the-Door* (1940), as his preface indicates, is like a prolegomenon for work on religion and philosophy that he did not live to complete. In this memoir he demonstrates how his formal education as a classicist 'mellowed' his avowed initial 'Calvinism'.[1] This chapter makes an attempt to discern what this change meant in Buchan's life, and when it began.

John Calvin (1509–64) was a classically trained lawyer, intended initially for the Roman Catholic priesthood, but came to accept and develop Luther's Protestant Reformation. Besides writing many commentaries on Scripture his chief work was the *Institutes of the Christian Religion* (1536–59), which fathered a 'presbyterian' form of church order, still the norm in the Church of Scotland and its offshoots. The World Alliance of Reformed Churches embraces similar churches globally.

Along with Calvin's focus on Scripture and the Early Fathers we might note his doctrine of 'double predestination', that is, that some would be damned and some would be saved. This evoked controversy within Calvinist circles. He had accepted it himself because of its ostensible presence in Scripture, but he did not make it the central issue throughout his teaching in practice. Many of his followers did.[2]

Controversies in Calvinism were rooted partly in doctrinal issues and partly in legalism. The latter produced a constitutional problem relating to the spiritual independence of a church. In 1843 this led to the separation of the Free Church of Scotland from the 'Auld Kirk', as the traditional Church of Scotland continued to be called. Doctrinal issues had led sometimes to denominational splits within Calvinism, and to trials for heresy. But towards the latter part of the nineteenth century a major constitutional issue also came to a head, until a union came into being in October 1900, between the small 'United Presbyterian' denomination and much of the membership of the Free Church of Scotland. The strongly conservative congregations (particularly in the Highlands) were not part of this union. The immediate context was Scottish, but the implications were wider and part of a general theological movement that we nowadays recognize as ecumenism.

John Buchan's writings from 1895 to 1900 suggest that his own approach to Calvinism was already more liberal than that of some in his environment, whose understanding of Calvin's Institutes and other writings was both legalistic and doctrinaire. By this time, Buchan had become a student of the classics, which certainly would have encouraged him to see life as involving many checks and balances.

After work as a student at the University of Glasgow, partly under Gilbert Murray, later to be the Regius Professor of Greek at Oxford, Buchan began classical studies at Brasenose College, Oxford in 1895. Already in a small way a writer, in 1898 he published his second novel, *John Burnet of Barns*. This early product reflects the 'Killing Times' towards the end of the seventeenth century, in the conflict between extreme Covenanters and Episcopalians and the Roman Catholicism of James VII and II.[3] The hero moves between Peeblesshire, Glasgow, the Netherlands and London, and in some respects covers ground familiar to the author himself. Buchan gives us a John Burnet whose faith is scarcely that of a religious extremist but who implicitly follows the 'latitudinarianism' of the seventeenth-century Gilbert Burnet, who, having been a probationer of the normatively Calvinist Church of Scotland, ended as a Bishop in the Church of England. If we can assume that the early novels of a very young man may reflect some considerable self-identification with their narrative voice, this may suggest that Buchan's period at Oxford encouraged his incipient tendency towards similar liberalism, in his personal religious life and theological thinking.

We may see *John Burnet of Barns* as the forerunner of *Witch Wood* (1927), which points in the same direction. The period of the later novel is also the seventeenth century, but this time takes in a little of the career of the Marquis of Montrose, the Presbyterian general who remained loyal to Charles I and II, to his own undoing. The substance of *Witch Wood* is located in the fictitious village of Woodilee, based on the countryside around the village of Broughton, near Peebles, where Buchan had holidayed with relatives for years. The well-meaning young minister of Woodilee Kirk in the novel is caught between the legalistic Calvinist authorities, one of whom has a double life close to that of the narrator of James Hogg's *The Private Memoirs and Confessions of a Justified Sinner* (1824). In the latter work we see the persistence of a doctrinal legalism that misinterpreted 'justification by faith' and affected some Calvinists from the seventeenth to the nineteenth century (and marginally today).

Buchan knew that this took 'a long time a-dying'. In his second biography of Montrose (1928) he noted that a more liberal Calvinism also went back into the seventeenth century.[4] He believed that he could show this from Montrose's experience, where he quotes from the cultured fourth-century pagan Roman Symmachus: *uno itinere non potest pervenire ad tam grande secretum* ('One cannot come at such a great secret (or mystery) by one way alone'), clearly implying that no denomination is able to claim it has the whole truth.[5]

Buchan's biography of Oliver Cromwell (1934) provides an English Puritan counterpoise to his Montrose. In the latter we find the conjunction of the compatibility of Calvinism with moderation, in support of the King rather than of the rigorous Covenanters who wanted a Presbyterian church for England and Scotland despite Charles I's interventions through Archbishop Laud's liturgy. Both elements are writ large in the appendix he gives on Montrose's serious political philosophy.[6] In *Oliver Cromwell* (1934), Buchan cites both the Calvinists of the Cambridge Platonists and the younger Isaac Pennington's 'startling words for the seventeenth century': 'All truth is shadow except the last truth. But all truth is substance in its own place, though it be but a shadow in another place. And the shadow is a true shadow, as the substance is a true substance'.[7] We might take this as a counterpart to the Symmachus quotation.

In a later novel, Buchan provides a nineteenth-century picture of two further types of humane Calvinism. The principal character in *The Free Fishers* (1934) is a Scottish clergyman who is also a professor at the University of St Andrews. His forays into state affairs mark him as a 'Moderate', one of a significant group of that period who carried their formal Calvinism lightly. But the fetching second exemplar is of an aging Scottish parish minister, able to work just south of the border in an ill-conditioned English parish. Buchan's depiction marks him as worthy because of his continuing devotion to the classics (he quotes from Epictetus's *Encheiridion*), and because he exhibits a gentle unwillingness to speak ill even of a local squire of dubious repute.

The Free Fishers bears comparison with one of Buchan's early short stories, 'The Song of the Moor'.[8] Both works show the frequent topological shift from Scotland to the south and both have a motif that embraces Calvinism, the later novel lacking the stringency of the early brief tale. The short story has a shepherd consult a 'black-gowned' Presbyterian minister about the distraction of a mystical journey occasioned by an encounter with a talking curlew. Dissatisfied with the minister's aghast reaction, the shepherd takes the road south, rejecting a wise woman's appeal, because of the call to ambition.[9] Considering the date of composition and initial publication we can read the shepherd as Buchan himself at Oxford, another young Calvinist Scot seeking the highroad to England – and looking for an alternative to the stricter aspects of Calvinism. We do not find him objecting to the Anglicanism of his college chapel, despite his mother's concern about the 'house of Rimmon'.[10]

In 1902, in Buchan's short story collection *The Watcher by the Threshold* (1902), the title story is an acute portrayal of Ladlaw suffering from what is now diagnosed as schizophrenia. Mr Oliphant, the local minister of the Kirk is – unusually – a modernist, though still officially a Calvinist.[11] He finds he cannot handle the sufferer, who is too perturbed to be amenable to a merely modernist solution. The minister's notion to deal with the case by working out a radical advance on Nietzsche just does not work, and Oliphant finally has to have recourse to his church's leadership. In this instance the solution does not run wholly counter to a conservative Calvinism. When this story was written Buchan had left Oxford and was just entering the legal profession. He would have been quite aware of the parting of the ways, but was still cautious enough not to let varieties of theological modernist thought go to his head.

A more traditional exposition of Calvinism is also present in the same collection, 'The Outgoing of the Tide'. The theme is the conflict between diabolism, or witchcraft, and Christian faith. The spiritual welfare of a young girl is challenged by her attraction to a dissolute admirer, and compounded by her mother's witchcraft. The environment is seventeenth-century, Scottish, rural and Calvinistic. The girl drowns in an unnaturally swift ebb tide, with the implicit assumption that its source is supernatural. But the lover experiences a belated religious conversion because he is convinced that the girl died in a state of grace, and escaped her mother's pact with the devil. The inherent Calvinism of the plot leaves room for mercy and grace.

Thus far Buchan (then twenty-five) does not offer a total conflict between his inherited background and his Oxford experiences. But Oxford was not as distant from home as South Africa, where Buchan moved in 1901 for two years. There he worked under Lord Milner, and came into close enough contact with many Boers who were to him a prime example of quite old-fashioned Calvinism.[12] His African experience cropped up in later fiction, and his exploration of Calvinism is most apparent in 'The Grove of Ashtaroth' (1910). This is an admixture of biblical Old Testament material applied to a hero with Jewish roots. The narrator could certainly pass as an earnest Calvinist, and has something of the author's own perceptions of sin as found in Calvinism, Old Testament Judaism and simply the power of imagination. This we discern from the narrator's concern to save the chief character from lapsing into ancient Canaanite paganism, while he himself has more than a purely aesthetic appreciation of certain features of that paganism. Buchan also displays competent academic biblical exegesis to supplement his knowledge of the classics.[13]

We have seen how Buchan's preoccupation with the history of the narrower type of Calvinism – which he found uncongenial – remained a live force in his writing. During the First World War he wrote *Salute to Adventurers* (1915), with a seventeenth-century subplot focused on a historical representative of an extreme Scottish Covenanter.[14] Though the war inevitably gave him a wider perspective, much of the Calvinist ethos is retained in his fiction and poetry of the period, in the generally Christian emphases on grace, mercy and peace. We can see some of this after that war in *The Three Hostages* (1924), where the death of the villain, Medina, is not left in Hannay's hands – on the principle that 'Vengeance is mine, saith the Lord; I will repay'.[15]

In Buchan's final novel, *Sick Heart River* (1941), the lawyer Leithen, the hero with distinct Calvinist elements in his personality,[16] dies in the care of the Oblate Fathers after his efforts to help the Hare Indians in northern Canada. Buchan was on friendly terms with the Jesuit Father D'Arcy while he lived at Elsfield in Oxfordshire from 1919 to 1935, but the Roman Catholic Church did not supply a character for his fiction until the very end of his life in Canada. This ecumenism in matters religious is expressed in *Sick Heart River* where the Oblate Father quotes John 10:16 from the Vulgate Bible, which Buchan as a classicist knew well.

Thus far can ecumenism go, but not often farther, as Buchan fully understood, knowing well the difficulties in church unions. In 1937 Buchan gave an important address to the Fifteenth General Council of the 'Alliance of Reformed Churches holding the Presbyterian System', in Montreal.[17] This included a brief reference to Buchan's interest in the theology of Karl Barth, who as a theologian in the nominally Calvinist tradition is given a little more space in *Memory Hold-the-Door*. Barth has importance overall as a director of Buchan's developing thought on Calvinism.

The Greek word *aidōs* occurs frequently in Buchan's writing, from Mary Hannay, in *The Three Hostages* (1923),[18] to Buchan's own memoirs in *Memory Hold-the-Door*. According to the context, this term covers 'a sense of shame', bashfulness, modesty and a sense of honour, or respect, including self-respect. We may therefore regard it as opposed to vanity and to hubris.[19] *Aidōs* is a relatively straightforward key to Buchan's final stance on Calvinism. Writing within a year or so of his death, he explains that

the Calvinism of my boyhood was broadened, mellowed and also confirmed. For if
the classics widened my sense of the joy of life they also taught its littleness and transi-
ence; if they exalted the dignity of human nature they insisted upon its frailties and
the *aidōs* with which the temporal must regard the eternal.

In this specific context, *aidōs* is in effect humility and the opposite of hubris: 'I
became profoundly conscious of the dominion of unalterable law. Prometheus
might be a fine fellow in his way, but Zeus was king of gods and men'.[20]

The literary terminology might be from the classics, but it had to operate
within a mindset already and inevitably conditioned by Buchan's upbringing in
the manse of a Free (later United Free) Church of Scotland minister and that
minister's vigorous wife. That wife, herself very young when John Buchan was
born, had a streak of dominance, whereas his father was, at least in domestic matters, perhaps a little milder for a Calvinist of his day. As an extremely conservative
Calvinist theologically, it was his father's 'delight, when a member of the Annual
Assembly, to stir up all the strife he could by indicting for heresy some popular
preacher or professor'.[21] We may well claim that Buchan was already developing
his less doctrinaire notion of Calvinism at an early age.

Buchan wrote of his father: 'It was odd that he should have been by profession a theologian, for he was wholly lacking in philosophical interest or aptitude'.
Here we have to ask what constituted 'theology' for John Buchan himself. He
must have been aware that it is not confined solely to philosophy. He continues:
'But a stalwart theologian of the old school he certainly was, rejoicing in the
clamped and riveted Calvinistic logic and eager to defend it against all com-
ers'.[22]

This is only part of the reckoning: 'except as regards dogma, [Rev. John
Buchan] had little of the conventional Calvinistic temper. He had no sympathy
with the legalism of that creed, the notion of a contract between God and man
drawn up by some celestial conveyancer'. Here we do have the makings of a paradox. But the younger Buchan does his best to resolve the paradox: 'I could wish
that he had lived to read Karl Barth, for their views had much in common'.

Barth (1886–1968), a Swiss pastor, had become disenchanted, like some
other contemporary theologians, with some aspects of European nineteenth-
century 'liberal' Protestantism, and had also turned to a kind of 'religious'
socialism.[23] His own theological focus was to be on the absolute otherness of
God, seen in his commentary on the Epistle to the Romans. Buchan's speech to
WARC's predecessor in 1937 already shows his live interest in Barth, translated
into English only a few years before.

Buchan's father had been a Liberal in politics but had become a Conservative in reaction to Gladstone's countenance of Irish Home Rule. John, as an
ostensibly latitudinarian Calvinist who became and remained a Conservative
in politics, was never so thirled to his own party label as to ignore the strong

social concern he did learn from both his father and his mother.[24] This concern goes back to the often wrongly maligned Calvin himself, and it found expression in the welfare interests of the best elements of the Free Church of Scotland in the nineteenth and twentieth centuries. John could safely claim that his father 'believed profoundly in the fact of "conversion"'. 'But, the first step having been taken, he would insist on the arduousness of the pilgrimage [...] His religion was tender and humane'.[25]

A further reason for Buchan's interest in Barth was of course the latter's decided stand against the Nazis in 1934, when he played a central part in the Declaration of Barmen. This cost Barth his professorship at Bonn in 1935,[26] but the Declaration became part of the confessional stand of the Evangelical Church of Germany.

A further relevant element in Barth's teaching was the shift he made in handling predestination. Calvin had accepted 'double predestination' because he thus interpreted the appropriate biblical texts,[27] but Barth produced a more subtle approach to the New Testament evidence. For him Jesus Christ could be regarded as the Elect One 'in whom Israel and the church are elected and in whom individuals are elected or rejected'.[28] Perhaps even more precisely, Barth in his commentary on Romans presents what we may call a dogmatic paradox, such as Kierkegaard would have loved. Calvin's 'double predestination' has, paradoxically, become (though ambivalently) a kind of universalistic salvation, in that God is represented in all his absolute otherness as revealing himself 'in' Jesus Christ in an act of grace. Jesus is at once the unique Reprobate for human beings (he was crucified) and (as being resurrected) uniquely the Elect One for them.[29]

Looking at the commentary one can see its relevance for Buchan in the difference between his father's day and the 1930s. Buchan would have seen that his father would have appreciated that the commentary presented an exegesis less legalistic and more 'spiritualized' than that of the theologically 'liberal' Protestants whom Barth disowned, though he did make use of the work of various biblical scholars – to some of whom his mode of exegesis did seem inadequately analytical.

From Buchan's historical stance, one could safely say that Barth's involvement in and after 1934 with the Declaration of Barmen was consistent both with the commentary on Romans and with the permanent state of crisis in Europe which the success of Nazism (1932) in Germany and Italian Fascism (since 1922) had exacerbated.

Buchan's awareness of the dangers in these had a bearing on his 1933 novel, *A Prince of the Captivity* and, in a more comic vein, *The House of the Four Winds* (1935). The former has fairly strong religious undertones. It impinges on the Calvinist ethos, especially in the (superficially unlikely) hero's quest for 'quality' in society. But it also focuses on social concern in England, as seen in an Anglican clergyman's disillusionment at the scope of his opportunities for social work. It also contains backward glances at the First World War in Belgium and the later alarms signalling the onset of Nazism. The quest for quality becomes a watchword for Buchan's serious writing and speaking from this period, whether in public addresses, or, most definitively, in the last chapter of *Memory Hold-the-Door*. This manifestly challenged the European dictators; Hitler's war began in September 1939, six months before Buchan's death.

> Today the quality of our religion is being put to the test. The conflict is not only between the graces of civilisation and the rawness of barbarism. More is being challenged than the system of ethics which we believe to be the basis of our laws and liberties. I am of Blake's view: 'Man must [...] have some religion; if he has not the religion of Jesus he will have the religion of Satan, and will erect a synagogue of Satan [...] Today the Faith is being attacked, and the attack is succeeding [...]'.[30]

Barth's relevance in both religious and social issues, and in his political concern was important to Buchan the public figure: from 1935 till his death in 1940 he was Governor-General of Canada (as the first Lord Tweedsmuir).

Buchan's interest, like Calvin's, in St Augustine's view of predestination suggests that he would not see predestination as excluding free will in practice. Several of Buchan's novels do show some hints of a generally predestinarian approach to the development of a story.[31] But we cannot assume such references are always doctrinally relevant to his personal faith. Sometimes they are no more than the presentiments of a character such as Richard Hannay. But, particularly in *Mr Standfast* (1919), we do have instances of theological content. The emphasis in that novel on sacrifice forewarns us of something that might in human terms be seen as a disaster, but is actually a theological necessity. The references are to the death in action of Launcelot Wake, a conscientious objector (but also a counter-spy), and Peter Pienaar, who is a reader of *The Pilgrim's Progress* (as a Calvinist Boer could be), and who, in a duel with a German air-ace, dies with fortitude as a crippled and over-age Allied airman. The war in pushing civilization to the brink of chaos was calling for theological answers.[32] In Christian circles, one does not normally equate the death of Christ, seen as the 'atonement' for human sins, with other instances of sacrifice, even though the war did reach fever pitch in the German offensive of 21 March 1918 (to which powerful campaign the novel crucially refers).

Buchan was not simply commemorating here his dead brother and friends, killed in action. In the novel, Hannay's words at Peter's funeral are from *The Pilgrim's Progress*, and Buchan had used another reference from that work, as an in memoriam for Alastair, in his *Poems, Scots and English* (1917). The prime force here is as Christian and as Calvinistic as Buchan's father had been, given the popularity at that time of Bunyan's work throughout Scotland.[33] *Mr Stand-fast* can be seen as Buchan's personal confession of faith for that period, at many levels, and *The Pilgrim's Progress* is crucial for understanding the novel.[34]

Poems, Scots and English does mark the distinction in Buchan's writing between the pre-war period and wartime trauma. His Scots poems contain some classical allusions, but these are set in the atmosphere of the Scottish lowlands, whose country people he knew so well. The later poems are pre-eminently harrowing retellings of the stark tragedies these fellow-countrymen and their like had to endure in war. The third element in the collection is the generally ironic assault on the narrow Calvinism that thought it had won through the 'Church Case' of 1904.[35] We find Buchan being most satirical in 'Midian's Evil Day' (1904) and in 'The Shorter Catechism' (1911). This is a masterly and justifiable caricature of some of the 'holy Willies' whom Burns had also outstandingly pilloried in his 'Holy Willie's Prayer' (1786). From all these aspects of the collection one can see Buchan's likely movement in his attitude to Calvinism and to war. Much later, in the thirties, this would make it easy for Buchan to welcome Barth's 'neo-orthodoxy'.[36]

Among the English poems in the volume, we cannot ignore one with special theological and psychological significance: 'Wood Magic' (1911). This poem signals a lifelong appreciation of the sentiment already noted in the quotation from Symmachus. The poem's ninth-century monk knows from the teaching he has received where he can find a temenos (sacred grove) that goes back to classical pagan days. He catches a forbidden glimpse of what he feels could easily mean something of religious value to himself. So, though he does and says all the proper things to please his ecclesiastical superiors, he says to himself:

> likewise I will spare for the lord Apollo a grace,
> And a bow for the lady Venus – as a friend but not as a thrall
> Tis true they are out of heaven, but some day they may win the place;
> For Gods are kittle cattle, and a wise man honours them all.[37]

Buchan makes use of possible positive influences that could have lain behind some features of classical religions, as he did later in *The Dancing Floor* (1926) and *Witch Wood* (1927). This does not mean that he was himself succumbing to such influences, but his creative powers may have conjoined with a perceptiveness of what 'might have been', which he could also analyse in quite different contexts. Fancy is free but can yet be tied to inherited, if also modifiable, perceptions. At all events, instances of his use of the classics occur almost everywhere in his works.[38] But unlike Hölderlin and Nietzsche (who both went mad) Buchan held on to all the most positive elements in Calvinism, in which a kind of capitalism that forbade exploitation[39] is consistent with grace and self-discipline.

These two are keynotes – the last of them similar to ancient Roman gravitas and pietas.

Buchan could count on what he would have called 'whinstone common sense'. He was a strong man spiritually and mentally, and a longstanding duodenal trouble did not conquer his spirit. After he died, his son Alastair wrote of his father's sōphrosunē;[40] that 'right-mindedness', 'moderation', 'self-control', is a New Testament word too. Strangely, Calvinism and the classics can not infrequently work in synergy. Many of us can still go along with his tombstone in Elsfield churchyard as it records in Greek: ΧΡΙΣΤΟΣ ΝΙΚΗΣΕΙ (Christos nikēsei) – Christ will conquer.

2 BUCHAN AND THE CLASSICS

Michael and Isobel Haslett

Buchan's family circumstances delayed his introduction to Latin till after his thirteenth birthday, and to Greek even longer.[1] He was well taught at Hutchesons' School in Glasgow[2] and was later grateful to his teacher James Caddell for inspiring in him a lifelong love of classical, particularly Latin, literature.[3] At Glasgow University his professors Caird, Jones and Gilbert Murray gave him a taste for philosophy and Greek literature, Murray becoming a lifelong friend who kept him in touch with developments in classical scholarship. At Oxford, because of his late start, Buchan had great difficulty with the Mods course,[4] but due to hard work on a heroic scale and excellent one-to-one teaching he got a very good second-class. In his Greats he got a first.

During his Greats course[5] Buchan's writing was particularly influenced by his tutors Dr F. W. Bussell and A. H. J. Greenidge. Bussell was described by Buchan as 'the nearest approach in my acquaintance to a mediaeval polymath,'[6] a comment justified by Bussell's lecture list in the *Oxford University Gazette* of October 1898. In one term he lectured on Lucan, Outlines of Mediaeval Thought, the Epistle to the Romans, Frontiers of the Roman Empire AD 500–1500 and Fragments of Plato. Of greater importance were some lectures 'on an obscure period of Byzantine history'[7] quite irrelevant to Buchan's Greats course. Bussell particularly remembered Buchan's interest in the survival of pre-Christian cults.[8] Buchan was to make use of this knowledge in his novels *The Dancing Floor* (1926) and *Witch Wood* (1927).

A. H. J. Greenidge might have been the best ancient historian of his generation in Britain, his early death being 'a serious blow to Roman studies.'[9] During Buchan's period as a pupil (1897–9) Greenidge was working on his abridgement of Gibbon's *Decline and Fall of the Roman Empire* up to the death of Justinian. It was an important time for tutor and pupil. Greenidge's interest in Roman history was aroused by his work on Gibbon and two years later he turned to Roman history himself, planning a six-volume history from the tribunate of Tiberius Gracchus to the accession of Vespasian as emperor. Had it been completed it would have almost spanned the gap between Mommsen's *History of Rome* and

Gibbon's great work, but he only lived to complete one volume. For Buchan, his Greats course was significant because it left him with an ambition to write biographies of Julius Caesar and Augustus, which he accomplished almost forty years later. It also got Buchan his first-class degree, which opened many doors to him in the years ahead. At the end of his time at Oxford he felt sufficiently confident to turn down a lectureship in philosophy in the hope of something more rewarding.

During his time at Glasgow Buchan had read voraciously to develop his style. It is often assumed that his classical studies played a part in his stylistic develop-ment; if this had been so, it was a minor part. Buchan wrote later 'Faulty though my own practice has always been, I learned sound doctrine – the virtue of a clean bare style, of simplicity, of a hard substance and an austere pattern'.[10] An inflected language such as Latin appears deceptively concise to the student. For example the Latin word *necavi* means 'I killed' or 'I have killed', two or three words being needed to translate one. A fairer conclusion would be that both languages need three syllables. Similarly, Tacitus's judgement of Galba, *omnium consensu capax imperii nisi imperasset*, can be translated 'all would have thought him capable of rule had he not ruled'. Here twelve English words translate six Latin words, but fourteen English syllables translate eighteen Latin syllables. Moreover the styles of ancient authors vary enormously, Livy and Cicero being prolix and complex and Caesar concise and simple. There is no uniform style that dominates Latin or Greek literature, and therefore there is no such thing as a classical style.

Mastery of Latin and Greek also gave mastery in a broad range of literary expression, however. At Oxford, Buchan spent much time translating Latin or Greek into English, and vice versa. He was taught to follow an author's style in his translation, Caesar's simple Latin requiring simple English and Macaulay's and Churchill's English requiring ornate and complex Latin. He was used to varying his style exactly as he advised an audience of young journalists in 1926, when he defined style as 'the exact and adequate expression in words of the author's meaning', which should be varied according to the content of the text and the mood of the author.[11]

Moreover, translation into and out of the classical languages fosters clear thought, and the careful choice and precise use of words, qualities which are found in Buchan's legal, historical and literary writing. He developed his style by reading English and French authors rather than writers of Latin and Greek – espe-cially Pater, Stevenson, Flaubert, Maupassant, Newman, and Thomas Huxley.[12] Pater, Buchan dismissed quickly – he was to be admired, not imitated. 'Pater's style was certainly not a model for other men to follow; it was far too organically knit to his thought.'[13] Stevenson was a different matter: he 'had taught himself to write miraculously, and for those of us who were dabbling clumsily in letters his expertness was a salutary model, for it meant hard and conscientious labour'.[14]

Buchan's early efforts to imitate this model were effective, the Oxford scholarship examiners describing his essay as 'just like a bit of Stevenson'.[15]

Maupassant was recommended to Buchan by a francophile uncle,[16] and his short stories showed Buchan how to achieve a rapidly moving narrative with an economy of words. Another French influence, Flaubert, was famous for the immense pains he took with his style, spending five years of hard work in writing *Madame Bovary*. Every sentence had to have a 'cadence and a harmony of sounding syllables' and, since he insisted that there was no such thing as a synonym, he selected with immense care the correct word ('*le seul mot juste*') to express his meaning.[17] The effect of his classical studies on Buchan's care in choosing his own words was reinforced by Flaubert's example.

Neither Cardinal Newman nor Huxley ever wrote a novel, but both could express complicated ideas in simple English. Newman could justify to the layman the tortuous development of his theological thought in his *Apologia pro Vita Sua* (1864), and Huxley could explain to everyone complex scientific ideas and their consequences for philosophy and religion. From his writing the general public could understand Darwin's theory of evolution. Buchan showed the same ability in his *The Law Relating to the Taxation of Foreign Income*.[18]

Aided by the six stylists and his classical education Buchan evolved a style which was 'vigorous and natural, athletic and spare, running beautifully clear like one of his border streams, with an occasional rare and coloured pebble in it to arrest the attention, some infrequent word that was yet authentic, coming out of the life of the land and the language of its people'.[19] Rowse's simile describes the features of Buchan's style. The stream's smallness emphasizes his preference for short words and sentences. The idea of flow describes how one sentence leads to the next, usually without a conjunction. Because of his careful choice of his verbs and nouns adverbs were seldom needed. The restraint in adjectives ensures that they impress the reader when used. The narrative of a novel was clear in his head when he wrote it down, whereas in his histories and biographies the narrative is less clear-cut and discussion may be needed when there is uncertainty. The stream slows and the course is less clear, but it is clearer and faster than is the case with other historians and biographers. It is here that Buchan owes so much to Thomas Huxley and Newman, the two authors whom he advised the young journalists to imitate.[20]

Throughout his life Buchan read classical authors as a relaxation and embellished his writing with Latin and Greek quotations, the latter in translation. These can be counted and used to detect Buchan's like or dislike of individual authors and to estimate the extent of his classical learning. All his novels, short stories, histories, biographies and collected essays were examined. Only *Julius Caesar* and *Augustus* were omitted, because repeated citations of Cicero and Caesar himself as sources would have distorted the sample. It was decided to exclude classical 'tags', both legal and religious, such as *causa causans* ('primary cause') and *in tuas manus* ('into thy hands'). Similarly, quotations from historical sources in the biographies and quotations from other poetry in the essay on Catullus[21] were disregarded. The reasoning for this was that these quotations were not used because of Buchan's taste for the authors, but were only used to illustrate Buchan's discussion of Catullus in the essay. Finally, the number of uses of each quotation was not recorded in the survey, since the range of quotations used was being studied rather than their frequency.

One tenth of the quotations could not be attributed to numbered lines in named works. Some of these were Buchan's own creations. For instance the Latin poem in chapter 1 of *The House of the Four Winds* (1935) is attributed as 'partly my own or wholly John the Silentiar's'.[22] A 'Paul Silentiarius' is mentioned in Gibbon, but Buchan's silentiar, indicatively named 'John', has left no trace in history.[23] Other quotations found in the survey are from ecclesiastical sources. For instance, *Mea culpa, mea maxima culpa* (my fault, my very great fault) is used in the Roman Catholic Mass, and is well enough known as general knowledge. The remaining five per cent of findings in the survey were never identified, but are statistically insignificant.

Within the rules enunciated above, Buchan's classical studies at university were clearly dominant. Virgil (a set author in Mods) and Horace (a chosen author in Mods) led the field, followed by Homer (a set author) a nose in front of Plato (a set author). A considerable way behind, Theocritus (a chosen author) was bunched with Tacitus (a chosen author) and Catullus, one of many poets who might crop up in the History of Roman Poetry paper. It would also be fair to describe all of these, plus Cicero (set author and a recommended author for an Ancient History paper), Appian and Julius Caesar (recommended ancient historians), as personal enthusiasms as well as examination fodder, particularly Catullus who in the event did not appear in the examination. The remaining writers on the syllabus barely feature in Buchan's writing at all, and poor Demosthenes (a set author) was completely ignored. Buchan must indeed have found him a 'grind' as he complained in a letter to Gilbert Murray.[24]

In the philosophy syllabus for Greats, Plato and Aristotle are more or less equal in importance. One might have expected that Plato, the easier in thought and language, would predominate in Buchan's writing, but the extent to which Plato overwhelms Aristotle indicates a strong personal preference. Moreover Buchan praised Plato as a poet,[25] and even writes a poem about him.[26]

Buchan's translations of poems present problems in the assessment of their importance. Those of Callimachus,[27] Anyte,[28] Leonidas of Tarentum,[29] Horace[30] and Antiphilus of Byzantium[31] do not exceed thirteen lines, but the translations of Theocritus, Idylls 7 and 21[32] are substantial. If classical authors are defined as those writing in Latin or Greek on non-Christian subjects before the dedication of Constantinople in AD 330, in addition to those used frequently, Buchan quotes the following authors who were connected with his examination subjects: Juvenal, both Senecas, Aulus Gellius, Martial, Lucretius, Lucan, Ovid, Petronius Arbiter, Ennius, Herodotus, Xenophon and possibly Hadrian. In addition he quotes Livy, Helvidius Priscus, Cato the Elder, Apuleius, Plautus, Callimachus, Aeschylus, Aristophanes, Pindar, Diogenes Laertius, Sappho and Meleager, who were almost certainly not.

Even more striking than his broad acquaintance with classical authors was the extensive list of early Christian and mediaeval writers from western Europe to the Near East in Latin and Greek who add colour and verisimilitude to his pages, particularly the fiction. Dr Bussell, the 'mediaeval polymath', was the first to arouse his interest in them. Judging by the contents of his lecture list quoted above Bussell was probably the origin of Buchan's knowledge of Antiphilus of Byzantium, St Ambrose, St Clement of Alexandria, Tertullian, Bishop Basil of Caesarea, St Thomas Aquinas, the *Gesta Romanorum* and Meleager at least. Many writers discussed by Helen Waddell and mentioned below may have been brought to Buchan's notice initially by Bussell, but it is impossible to be certain.

In 1927 Helen Waddell published *The Wandering Scholars*, the result of a research scholarship at Lady Margaret Hall at Oxford, and the first of her books on mediaeval literature. Within three months Buchan's novel *Witch Wood* was also published, which quoted four lines from Peter Abelard's hymn *O quanta qualia* ('Oh how great, how wonderful').[33] The following year Buchan published the supernatural short story 'The Wind in the Portico' in the collection *The Runagates Club*, which mentions Ausonius[34] and Sidonius Apollinaris, also a poet, who became Bishop of Clermont,[35] all three being subjects of Helen Waddell. Her influence can also be seen in Buchan's novel *The Blanket of the Dark*, with its references to Priscian,[36] St Augustine,[37] Boethius and to the manuscript at Beauvais containing the poem *O blandos oculos et inquietos* ('O alluring and restless eyes'), all Waddell subjects.[38] Buchan's only children's novel *The Magic Walking Stick* contains a reference to the *Acta Sanctorum* ('the acts of the saints'),[39] which has a place in the bibliography of *The Wandering Scholars*. Bernard of Marlaix is quoted in Buchan's eulogy to King George V, *The King's Grace*,[40] and Bishop Malachi in his essay 'Montrose and Leadership'.[41] Helen Waddell's influence fades after Buchan's departure for Canada, but the use he made of her work is remarkable. His enthusiasm for classical literature, his range of knowledge and the accuracy and aptness of quotations are all astonishing, despite a few unimportant mistakes.[42]

The first of Buchan's stories to be dependent on his classical education was 'The Watcher by the Threshold', first published in 1900 but written when he was a student at Oxford. In it the narrator's friend Robert Ladlaw is possessed by an evil demon and feels an affinity to the emperor Justinian, who was similarly possessed according to the *Anecdota* (Secret History) of Procopius. Buchan must have derived some familiarity with the *Anecdota* from his tutor A. H. J. Greenidge who was then preparing his abridgement of Gibbon. Ladlaw is described as owning a 'French life of Justinian made up of stories from Procopius and tags of Roman Law'.[43] Curiously, the hallucinations described by Procopius and Buchan differ in various ways. Ladlaw was attacked on his left side by a creature separate from himself, 'a kind of amorphous featureless shadow would run from his side into the darkness'.[44] Conversely, Procopius makes no mention of the left side, and the demon replaced Justinian himself, or parts of him, rather than being a separate entity.[45] When Ladlaw spoke of the Empress Theodora, she was but another part of the horror by his side, but Procopius is quite clear that Justinian and Theodora were two separate avenging demons, and the featureless face was part of Justinian and not separate.[46] Buchan may have felt entitled to improve on Procopius because of the wild improbability of his scurrilous tales.

Justinian is used in other stories by Buchan. In 'The Kings of Orion' (first published 1906) there is brief mention of a character who imagines himself to be Emperor of Byzantium.[47] In the same year, in *A Lodge in the Wilderness* there is an anecdote of a character who thinks himself John Chrysaor, General of the Army of the East and subsequently Emperor, with a wife called Theodora like Justinian himself.[48] Justinian even appears in *The Magic Wallking Stick*.[49]

In 1910 Buchan went on an Aegean cruise from Istanbul. During the cruise Buchan wrote a very attractive poem, 'An Echo of Meleager'. Meleager was the initiator of *The Greek Anthology* of which Buchan must have had a copy on the cruise – yet another example of his wide reading. Unusually the ship sailed through the narrow channel between the mainland and Euboea (Evvoia). Buchan took his chance to explore the site of the battle of Thermopylae on foot and lost his way in the hills. A few days later he wrote to Gilbert Murray: 'I have been re-reading your 'Greek Epic' and am filled with admiration. Years ago when I was in your class at Glasgow I remember thinking what a wonderful book might be written about the Ionian migration'.[50] His interest in the migration and his exploration of the site led him to write 'The Lemnian'. In this short story an islander, whose ancestors had been chased from island to island, blunders into the Greek camp and, through masculine pride, decides to fight with the descendants of his ancestors' enemies against the Persians. He fights until he is killed, singing an 'ancient song', printed at the end of the story, and of which part is said to have been stolen by Euripides and put into a chorus in his *Andromache*. Nothing resembling 'Atta's Song' is to be found in the *Andromache*. One can only conclude that Buchan is the author, and that the editors of *John Buchan's Collected Poems* were right to include it, as it is as good as many a chorus from Euripides.

After Thermopylae they cruised onwards to the Petali islands and landed on one of them. There they saw a mysterious house that 'cried out for a tale to fit it'.[51] Buchan's first attempt at such a tale was the short story 'Basilissa', published in 1914. Vernon Milburne dreams every April in his Lake District home of a series of rooms, the last of which contains a mystery. Each year the mystery comes one room nearer. When the great moment arrives he finds himself in a room, which he recognizes, in a large house on a Greek island. A beautiful girl is being menaced by a lustful Greek from whom Milburne rescues her.

In his later novel, *The Dancing Floor*, the initial section of 'Basilissa' is retained, with the addition of the narrator and interpreter, Leithen. A second section, set in southern England, is inserted, in which a much more interesting heroine, Koré Arabin, is introduced and her dangerous position is gradually revealed. She has inherited the Greek island from her father who has antagonized the local inhabitants by his outrageous sexual behaviour. Moreover, there has been a bad harvest and a severe winter, so that the starving islanders are planning to burn Koré as a witch and a sacrifice. Vernon, having learnt from Leithen the local rites, persuades Koré to escape with him from the burning house, dressed as a god and a goddess, and to confront the maddened islanders. The islanders run, terrified, back to their church and homes.

The Dancing Floor is in part a tribute to Buchan's close friend Raymond Asquith, the best classical scholar of his undergraduate generation at Oxford,[52] who had died in the First Battle of the Somme in 1916. Vernon Milburne can be read as being based on Asquith, and has his knowledge of ancient Greek religion to outwit the islanders. His love for Koré is observed rather than described, perhaps to avoid offending Asquith's widow who never recovered fully from his death. The island countryside spoke to Buchan of ancient religion, but instead of writing a historical novel, as Naomi Mitchison was to do with *The Corn King and the Spring Queen* in 1931, which used the same archetypes that Buchan was exploring, Buchan describes a return to ancient religion in modern times. In this he was following the lectures of Dr Bussell on the long survival of paganism in the Christian Byzantine Empire.[53]

He was probably also following the work of Gilbert Murray and of Jane Harrison.[54] In 1924 Murray, then a regular visitor at Buchan's home, was updating his book *Four Stages of Greek Religion* (1912). In its introduction he acknowledges the expertise of Jane Harrison, whose books and articles had changed the accepted views of Greek religion. A classical scholar, she had studied anthropology and contended that the ordinary Greeks had no interest in the Olympian gods, who retained only their literary and artistic importance during the classical period, but were instead far more interested in spring and fertility rites. She had summarized her views in her book *Themis* (1912), which included a chapter by Murray on 'Greek tragedy and its relationship to Greek religion'. This too had to be revised in 1924. Murray's conversation at Buchan's home about his current work and about Harrison's importance may have been the stimulus that Buchan needed to write *The Dancing Floor*, which he started in November 1924.[55]

> If you starve for three months and put your soul into waiting for the voice from heaven, you are in a mood for marvels. Terror and horror perhaps, but beauty too and a wild hope. That was the Greek religion, not the Olympians and their burnt offerings, and it is the kind of religion that never dies.[56]

Here Buchan shows how well he understood Harrison's thesis.[57] In another passage Leithen reads some lines of Greek from a manuscript found with Koré's father's will, translating as follows:

> Io, Kouros most great I give thee hail
> Come, O Dithyrambos, Bromios come and bring with thee
> Holy hours of thy most holy Spring.
> Then will be flung over earth immortal a garland of flowers,
> Voices of song will rise among the pipes,
> The Dancing Floor will be loud with the calling of crowned Semele. [58]

Vernon recognizes this as being a translation of parts of three separate pieces of Greek strung together:[59] the Hymn of the Kouretes (first line), the Paeon to Dionysos (second and third lines) and a fragment of Pindar (the remainder). These are quoted and translated by Harrison as follows:

> Io, Kouros most Great I give thee hail.[60]
> Come O Dithyrambos, Bacchos,
> Come Bromios, and coming
> With thee bring Holy hours of thine own holy spring.[61]
> Then are flung over the immortal
> Earth lovely petals of pansies, and
> Roses are amid our hair; and voices of
> Song are loud among the pipes, the
> dancing floors are loud with the
> calling of crowned Semele.[62]

Although Buchan's translation of the third section is incomplete, he otherwise follows Harrison closely. His intellectual debt is owed to Murray and Harrison rather than to James Frazer, author of *The Golden Bough*, as suggested by contemporary reviewers. His title, to be found in Harrison's third section above, he owes to Harrison alone.

Buchan's classical education also contributed to *The Three Hostages* (1924). The villain, Dominick Medina, gives himself away by quoting a Latin sentence: *Sit vini abstemius qui hermeneuma aut hominum petit dominatum* ('let him not drink wine who tries to interpret or seeks to dominate mankind').[63] Sandy

Arbuthnot, alerted by the rare word *hermeneuma*, traces the sentence to a previously unknown manual of the arts of spiritual control by Michael Scott, the Scottish Border wizard. No such manual exists, and the Latin sentence is a creation of Buchan, or perhaps Murray, the phraseology and word order being most unusual. *Hermeneuma* occurs twice in the extant Latin literature, on both occasions in the *Controversiae* of the Elder Seneca, where it means 'interpretation' in the sense of translation from a foreign language. Originally it was a Greek word meaning 'symbol' or 'interpretation', and was derived from the Greek god Hermes. He had begun as a phallic god and eventually became the messenger of the Olympic gods and therefore the god of interpretation. The English word 'hermeneutics' is the technical word for the study of biblical interpretation – a strange metamorphosis for Hermes.

Moreover, just as Sandy Arbuthnot could detect the villainy of Dominick Medina through his use of a Latin word, so we can learn something about Buchan. In his autobiography he praised Greenidge's legal teaching highly.[64] There is no evidence that he or Greenidge ever formally studied Roman Law, which was only taught at Oxford by the Law faculty. Greenidge, however, displays so much detailed knowledge of Roman legal procedure in his books that he must have attended, at some point in his career, law lectures for undergraduates or had been taught by a law coach. He may, in addition, have been helped by E. Gruber, a fellow of Balliol and University Reader in Roman Law from 1886 to 1893,[65] years during which Greenidge studied Greats at Balliol and wrote *Infamia*. Buchan, although he never studied Roman Law,[66] as a future barrister he may have taken, as his special subject in Greats, 'The procedure in public and private trials under the Republic', the only course given in Buchan's year with legal content. This was a field that interested Greenidge greatly. The *Controversiae*, a textbook on legal oratory of no interest to a historian, would have been a recommended sourcebook for Buchan.

By far the most important memorials of Buchan's enthusiasm for the classical world are his biographies of Julius Caesar (1932) and Augustus (1937). *Julius Caesar* is slighter both in length and scholarship, and was written for schoolboys who, guided by an excellent bibliography, could pursue their interest further. However, the book's reviewer in the *New Statesman* felt that too much detail was provided for schoolboys and too little for scholars, a criticism even more valid today.[67] Moreover, C. G. Stone in *The Classical Review* of 1938 implied that Buchan had attributed too little ambition and ruthlessness to Caesar. Modern scholars make a similar criticism of *Augustus*.

Augustus is on an altogether higher level. It covers an enormous subject at a gallop and its style is a delight. To Buchan, 'Augustus seemed to embody all the virtues of a dictator, when a dictator was needed, and to have tried valiantly to provide against the perils'.[68] As both a politician and administrator Buchan shows real insight into Augustus's achievement: as a governor-general himself at the time, he was able to observe how a modern empire is governed. Buchan had few sources. Velleius Paterculus, the only contemporary source apart from Strabo, was a man of thirty when Augustus died. He wrote a compendium of Roman history treating the reign of Augustus in considerable detail. Buchan's only other sources were Appian, Suetonius, the two Plinys and Dio Cassius, who wrote anything from fifty to two hundred years later and were not reliable historians, let alone reliable judges of Augustus's personality. Buchan had to rely on his own interpretation of Augustus's achievements and character.

The reviewers were kind, and the professional historians praised his insight and style, but felt that he had at times been too uncritical. Prosopography, the study of the careers of individuals and members of individual families through inscriptions, strongly suggested that the old Roman aristocracy never recovered from the civil wars and proscriptions, was excluded permanently from all important administrative posts and military commands, and as a political force was virtually extinct by AD 70. All the research had been done in Germany in 1900–25, so that only British scholars with fluent German would have been aware of it, who did not include Alan Last, the Oxford Professor in Ancient History whom Buchan had asked to point out any errors in his manuscript. Buchan and Last did not understand that Augustus had sidelined and emasculated the old aristocracy, who never forgave him. Buchan also described a cosy relationship between the Imperial civil service and the Senate, but these ideas were questioned and undermined in 1939.[69] *Augustus* ends with a splendid tour of the Empire by a traveller to demonstrate how extensive, safe and prosperous it had become during the decades of peace. Today, seventy years after publication, it remains a good introduction to the early years of the Empire. It is a book of which Buchan was rightly proud and was worthy of the full-time scholar he had once wanted to become.

The influence of Buchan's classical education was lifelong. He took Virgil and Horace to South Africa in 1901,[70] and read Plato, Thucydides and Virgil to escape the horror of the First World War.[71] His classical studies also contributed greatly to his writing as essential background knowledge for his classical biographies, which also fed into his work on the Marquis of Montrose. The plots of 'The Lemnian' and *The Dancing Floor*, respectively one of his best short stories and one of his best novels, are based on classical motifs, and *The Three Hostages*, *Witch Wood*, 'The Wind in the Portico' and 'The Watcher by the Threshold' all include significant plot elements which require an understanding of Latin and/or Greek literature or history to understand their import for the story. Translating Latin and Greek had taught Buchan to vary his style according to the context and content of his writing, and contributed to the clarity of his thought and his careful choice and precise use of words. His scholarly output as well as his literary productions were saturated in the classics to a degree which has rarely been appreciated, the more so as the cultural references of Buchan's era grow more distant in time and understanding. Education in the classics is a dwindling discipline, no longer a norm, and certainly no longer the basis for Western education that it was only a century ago. Parts of Buchan's writing are becoming less and less accessible to new generations of readers, but the clarity of his writing and the careful structure of his works make it still possible, even if no Latin or Greek is known, to feel a powerful force in his use of classical sources.

3 'TWIN LOYALTIES': JOHN BUCHAN'S ENGLAND

David Goldie

In his multifarious roles of poet, anthologist, novelist, journalist, businessman, committee man and politician, John Buchan saw to it that Scotland maintained, and was seen to have maintained, a distinctive cultural identity. His historical fiction and biography were reminders of Scotland's past, as was his active membership of Scottish historical, antiquarian and literary societies and his editorship of the *Scottish Review* (1907–8). His Scottish novels offered explorations of the national psyche, while his work in poetry – in his own writing and as editor of the anthology *The Northern Muse* (1924) – showed his commitment to the Scots language and its traditions. It is hardly surprising, then, that he has been considered an important figure in the foundation of the Scottish literary revival of the interwar years, and that Hugh MacDiarmid, the movement's godfather hailed him as 'the Dean of the Faculty of Contemporary Scottish Letters'.[1]

But to characterize him as a Scottish writer is to tell only half – perhaps less than half – of the story. Buchan's Scottish birth and upbringing would always remain central to his concerns, but his involvement with wider British and imperial issues meant that his attention was often focused elsewhere. In most practical senses this meant England, the nation that provided him with the completion of his formal education and his home as an adult. England properly became a subject in his fiction only after the First World War, in a series of novels from *Mr Standfast* (1919) to *The Free Fishers* (1934) that dealt with the nation at significant moments in its history. Just as he had done in his early Scottish writing, in *Sir Quixote of the Moors* (1895) and *John Burnet of Barns* (1898) and the short stories in *Grey Weather* (1889) and *The Watcher by the Threshold* (1902), in which he had attempted to account for the historical, topographical and religious qualities that combined to form a distinctive Scottish national identity and temperament, so too in his English fiction he set himself to uncovering the elements that made for a specific, independently English, *genius loci*.

What is most interesting about Buchan's engagement with England in these books is the way that he appears to view the country not as a disinterested foreigner but as an enthusiastic convert – as one who is prepared to explore, invest in, and ultimately to identify with its national historical culture. This might in other circumstances be seen as an act of submission – a Scotsman yielding to the hegemonic interests of the larger southern neighbour and senior partner in union. But this is clearly not the case here. Buchan remained a proud, patriotic Scotsman for all his commitment to England, and it is this that makes him particularly interesting: his willingness to acknowledge two distinct literary and cultural traditions and his desire to work within each while furthering the aims of both. In 1935 Buchan chose to take the title Baron Tweedsmuir of Elsfield, a combination of Scottish and English placenames that might be seen as either capitulation or self-contradiction. In the light of his post-war fiction, however, it makes perfect sense, as an example not of divided loyalty but of what Buchan called 'twin loyalties' – a phrase that he used in the dedicatory poem to *Midwinter* (1923), in which he professes, tellingly, to 'love with equal mind / The southern sun, the northern wind, / The lilied lowland water-mead / And the grey hills that cradle Tweed'.[2] It is this sense of equal-mindedness that characterizes Buchan's engagement with England and Scotland: his celebration of their distinctness and independence from, but also accessibility to, the other.

'England' had featured as a place in Buchan's fiction before the war, but it was only with the publication of *Mr Standfast* in 1919 that it became an idea and an ideal. The England of Buchan's earlier fiction had been a series of locations dispersed around the metropolitan centre of power. In *Mr Standfast* it becomes a countryside in which is embedded a national disposition and temperament. This becomes clear to the novel's narrator Richard Hannay as he gazes out over the ancient Fosse Manor from the Cotswold Ridge and experiences a 'kind of revelation'. Used to the wide-open spaces of his native South African veld, he is immediately converted to the subtler, homelier charms of an England characterized by 'little fields enclosed with walls of grey stone and full of dim sheep', streams slipping among water-meadows, church towers that sound the hours 'with a curiously sweet chime', and the 'twitter of small birds and the night wind in the tops of the beeches'. In this landscape, which bears on its light winds more than a little whiff of Rupert Brooke, Hannay awakens not just to a landscape, but to the temper of a people and their sense of purpose:

> now I realized that I had a new home. I understood what a precious thing this little England was, how old and kindly and comforting, how wholly worth striving for. The freedom of an acre of her soil was cheaply bought by the blood of the best of us ... For in that hour I had a prospect as if from a hilltop which made all the present troubles of the road seem of no account. I saw not only victory after war, but a new and happier world after victory, when I should inherit something of this English peace and wrap myself up in it till the end of my days.[3]

The idea of 'home' is important here. This is partly because it iterates a discourse in which the servants of empire in the nineteenth century cultivated an idea of the English countryside as a 'home' that sustained them in their exile – as in Browning's 'Home Thoughts from Abroad' – and to which they aspired to return on retirement.[4] More directly, it can be seen to mark Buchan's own personal identification with a new home, for the writing of this novel coincides with an idyllic holiday in the Cotswolds with his wife in 1917 and his subsequent purchase in 1919 of Elsfield, which lies not far from the fictional Fosse Manor on the other side of Oxford.[5] Mr Standfast moves swiftly in typical Buchan fashion from the Scottish islands to Switzerland and the Western Front, but it has at its heart Hannay's vision of a redeeming English countryside – identified closely with the English rose, Mary Lamington, who will domesticate Hannay in other ways – which stands as a symbol of the qualities of decency, temperateness and tradition, for which the war is being fought. The novel's main structural device is a series of extended comparisons with The Pilgrim's Progress, and Buchan clearly blends Hannay's vision of a home in the English countryside with Bunyan's Land of Beulah, the hard-won earthly paradise of 'orchards and vineyards and gardens' in which weary pilgrims await their call to the Celestial City.

Buchan would never again be quite so ecstatic or so overtly spiritual in his celebrations of the southern landscape, but in several later works his writing ranged over this landscape in which, like Hannay, he had found a resting place and a home, seeking the history and the cultural traditions that had shaped its character. An example is the essay, 'Thoughts on a Distant Prospect of Oxford', first published in Blackwood's Magazine in October 1923, which is written from the perspective of a spectator, viewing from the high ridge of Elsfield the historical development of the city from the times of the Roman occupation. The emphasis is on the domestication and settlement of the land, on the civilizing and educating of the people. The topographical and cultural history here is fundamental, because as Buchan puts it, 'the spiritual Oxford can only be truly understood when considered in regard to her setting – which is the people of England. The people of England have begun to awake to a sense of their heritage'.[6] This sense of heritage is, for Buchan, clearly a good thing and one that, as a Scotsman, he plainly doesn't resent or feel inhibited from exploring. His writing, in historical novels such as Midwinter and The Free Fishers (1934) and stories such as 'Fullcircle' (1920), shows instead a clear commitment to uncovering that heritage, as it is manifested in the relationship, developed over centuries of habitation, between the people and the land.

Buchan's English landscape is characteristically softer, more habitable than his Scottish one. It is not, as his Scottish land tends to be, the site of a hard-won compromise between doughty subsistence farmers and an intractable earth, but is rather a place in which a temperate nature and moderate people coexist more or less in contentment. It offers, in short, a more meliorative psycho-geography. What it lacks is the sense of spiritual malevolence that is often found in his Scottish scenes. While the emphasis in his English writing is on the homely, the *heimisch*, his stress in many of his Scottish stories is on the uncanny, the *unheimlich* – what he described in *Memory-Hold-the-Door* as 'the harsh Gothic of most of the Scots landscape'.[7]

Buchan did occasionally note the 'mellow habitable charm' of Scotland's homelier corners; places like the valley of the Tweed, which might be suitable subjects for traditional pastoral. But in stories such as 'The Watcher by the Threshold' (1900) the historical landscape is experienced mainly as a brooding, unsettling presence; in this case a malign remnant of the Pictish 'Manann', that takes possession of Robert Ladlaw and drives him out of his mind. In 'No-Man's Land' (1899) the presence of a Pictish remnant, literally inhabiting the landscape similarly creates the oppressive sense of 'a *temenos* sacred to some old-world god', and forces the aptly named Graves, an Oxford don and specialist in 'Northern Antiquities', into a fatal madness.[8] The valley of the Fawn in 'The Green Glen' (1912) is another such landscape haunted by an 'ancient *aura*' that 'brooded over its greenness and compelled men's souls'.[9]

The haunted landscapes of Buchan's Scotland can also be found in his other 'primitive' places: in the Africa of 'The Grove of Ashtaroth' (1910) and the Greece of *The Dancing Floor* (1926). But they are seldom present in his England. Where there is a sense of threat in Buchan's England it tends to reside in the built rather than the natural environment – at Brightwell in *Midwinter*, the castle of Minster Lovell in *The Blanket of the Dark* (1931), or the Merry Mouth inn in *The Free Fishers* – and is usually the product of human error rather than supernatural agency.[10] The old gods are not entirely forgotten, but in Buchan's England they are naturalized and their mystery is minimized. The first encounter the reader has with the 'Naked Men', for example, the representatives of old England in *Midwinter*, is at a characteristic Buchan *temenos*. Midwinter informs the Scottish traveller Alastair Maclean that the obelisk at its centre, 'Jacob's Stone', was 'an altar where the Romans sacrificed to fierce gods and pretty goddesses'. It is clear, however, that for the Naked Men it is a trysting spot consecrated merely by use rather than spiritual immanence. Midwinter's feeling for the place is more the respectfulness of the canny pragmatist than the awe of the believer:

> We Christian men have forsworn Apollo, but maybe he still lingers, and the savour of our little cooking fires may please him. I am one that takes no chances with the old gods.[11]

Midwinter's gentle agnosticism is re-emphasized when he introduces Maclean to the song that figures as one the book's leitmotifs, 'Diana and her darling crew'. The song, a gentle hymn to 'Diana, or as some say Proserpina' or 'the Queen of

Elfhame', is a kind of mysterious affirmation in music of what Midwinter calls 'the law' of the greenwood. But its mood is melancholic rather than imperative: its wistfulness a reminder that a once-forceful Proserpina has become tamed and domesticated by the temperate English countryside. As Midwinter puts it: 'over you and me, as baptized souls, she has no spell but persuasion. You can hear her weeping at midnight because her power is gone.'[12]

The 'painted floor', discovered by Peter Pentecost in *The Blanket of the Dark* (1931), is another melancholic reminder of Roman times. Featuring at its centre 'a figure of some goddess – Ceres perhaps or Proserpina', Pentecost imagines it 'a sacred place' and visits it secretly in the hope of discovering there some woodland magic, wishing to wake from drowsiness to see 'the shimmer of a woman's gown and to hear the call of an elfin flageolet'.[13] But he is disappointed. When eventually he does experience something like a moment of sylvan revelation there, witnessing the moonlit dance of Sabine Beauforest, it is clear that his emotions have a profane rather than a sacred source: 'that it was a mortal who danced below him' for whom 'every movement spoke of youth and vivid, throbbing, exultant life'.[14]

In both these examples we find a strong urge towards demystification, manifested in a landscape that is not entirely free of pagan elements but which has an inherent vitality and reasonableness that triumphs over more credulous and terrible forms of folkish supernaturalism – a quality Buchan rarely extends to his Scottish landscapes. This is seen clearly in *Witch Wood*, a novel that was written between *Midwinter* and *The Blanket of the Dark* and in which are found several of their plot elements: notably a young man who encounters a folk culture that shakes his principles and his faith; the man's discovery of an elf-like woman in the wood, for whom he yearns but ultimately loses; and a mysterious Roman ritual site. But where the Oxfordshire Wychwood of *The Blanket of the Dark* is alive with the spirit of a cooperative people, characterized in its parliament of beggars, the Scottish *Witch Wood* is a place of silence and darkness – a vestigial fragment of the ancient Pictish pinewood of Melanudrigill.[15] Such differences in nature and supernature mean that in *Witch Wood*, the folk are fearful and isolated and we are presented with a Roman altar that has not been assimilated and naturalized, as in *Midwinter*, but has rather become the setting for the rituals of black magic.

In exploring the differences between Scottish and English nature, Buchan is working in two distinct traditions. In novels like *Witch Wood* he draws on the supernatural tales heard during his childhood, on the twilit mood of the Celtic revival and the folkloric and psychical researches of the likes of Andrew Lang and J. G. Frazer. Novels like *Midwinter*, on the other hand, can be placed firmly within a distinctive English tradition in which the supernatural is treated more whimsically and where the emphasis is on *Natura Benigna* rather than *Natura*

Maligna. Kenneth Grahame is an influence here, especially his *Pagan Papers* (1893) and 'The Piper at the Gates of Dawn' episode in *The Wind in the Willows* (1908).[16] Rudyard Kipling is plainly another, with his treatment of the Picts in *Puck of Pook's Hill* (1906) being of particular relevance. Like Buchan, Kipling holds a rather dim view of the Picts: they are the 'worm in the wood ... the rot in the root ... the germ in the blood ... the thorn in the foot'.[17] What is interesting, however, is the way Kipling excludes them from historic England. His Picts are part of the wild world from which England has historically separated itself and against which it defines its identity and builds its character – in this case, a part of the savage universe excluded by the civilizing cordon of Hadrian's Wall. The qualities they manifest are thus not repressed within the English character, but are rather forcibly and physically excluded at an early stage in its historical development. England has no place for their malevolence within its pale, just as it has no place for the fairies and 'People o' the Hills' after the Reformation.[18] But if modern English culture can be said to begin with the Romans, what then of Scotland where they never established a firm foothold? In Kipling the consequences are only implicit, but in Buchan they are more overt: never having forcibly excluded the Pictish influence with all its supernatural baggage, the Scots have instead interiorized and repressed it. Such influences remain below the boundaries of the conscious and the visible worlds but require only the slightest jolt to come creeping back into the mind and into view.

This is not the only part of the English tradition that Buchan picks up on in his English writing. One of the animating ideas of *The Blanket of the Dark* is that English values are expressed more profoundly in the quiet wisdom of its folk than the forceful actions of its rulers: an idea that lies at the heart of the debate between Peter Pentecost and Henry VIII and which ultimately prompts Peter, the heir of Bohun, to renounce his claim to power and disappear into the dark blanket of the Greenwood. This draws on a range of English traditions: from the myth of Robin Hood, and the whig tradition in politics, to poems such as Gray's 'Elegy Written in a Country Churchyard' (1751) and Kipling's 'Cities and Thrones and Powers' (1906). But it also chimes with a contemporary mood in the 1920s and 30s, seen in Henry Newbolt's *The Old Country* (1906), H. V. Morton's *In Search of England* (1927), and the pageant histories of Arthur Bryant, which was attempting to impose the perceived values of 'Old England' on the modern political state.[19] Patrick Wright has noted this common strain running through the work of conservative thinkers such as Stanley Baldwin (to whom Buchan was, of course, close in this period), G. K. Chesterton and H. A. L. Fisher, and has characterized it sceptically as a search for 'Deep England': a form of 'invisible heritage' that is shared 'as a kind of sacrament' between 'true members of the ancestral nation'.[20] This conservative 'Deep England' is essentially a flight from the contemporary troubles of strike and slump – an attempt to diminish the realities of the present by placing them in the long, mythical perspectives of the rural nation and its folk. It is this deep England that Richard Hannay stumbles across on the hill above Fosse Manor and decides to make his home, and it is the England to which Buchan dedicates his English historical fiction.

Even when there is something wrong in that deep England, as there is in *The Free Fishers*, it turns out not to controvert the myth but eventually to reinforce it. In this novel, the Northumbrian Yonderdale is immediately identified as a blasted, malign countryside: 'one of "the sour bits in England"'.[21] Buchan paints its landscape with the full Gothic palette; endowing it, as befits a man who had once edited Edgar Allan Poe, with a rain-lashed countryside of ravines and stunted trees, a furtive, surly peasantry, a mysterious inn, and a large house of 'extreme shabbiness': 'a place not of death and emptiness, but crowded with a maleficent life'.[22] It becomes clear, however, that the malignity comes not from some lurking old-world gods but from the politically-inspired actions of the wicked Jacobin landlord, Justin Cranmer. At one time, we are told, the valley 'was the bonniest bit God ever made,' but now it 'is sair defiled by man.'[23] Gabriel Cranmer confirms this, remembering that she had once 'lived in Arcady' there, 'among streams and flowers and country faces' before her husband's true nature had revealed itself.[24] This notion, that it is the presence and influence of a human individual, and not an inherent spirit of place, that has made the valley so unwelcoming, is cemented when Cranmer abandons it for the last time and it returns almost instantaneously to 'a place of running waters and sleeping birds and springing flowers.'[25]

Yonderdale represents an English countryside at the mercy of a man whose views and character have been formed in the shadier corners of continental Europe. Justin Cranmer is an Englishman perverted by exposure to European decadence: a point made by his repeatedly being compared to Byron's Childe Harold. The character who mirrors him in the novel's schema and who is a much healthier, if still somewhat flawed, example of Englishness is Sir Turnour Wyse. Sir Turnour is a type common in Buchan's fiction: intellectually limited and humourless, rather pompous and inflexible in his punctilio, but with an unerring moral compass and an unflappable common decency. He is, tellingly, an accomplished country sportsman who embodies all that is best in the Englishman's easy relationship with his natural environment: a master in the field and an excellent judge equally of sound horses and sound countrymen. It is this skill in the field, particularly as a driver of horses, that saves the day at the narrative's conclusion, winning round his Scottish comrades in arms and prompting one of them, Jock Kinloch, to profess himself 'dumb with admiration' at his exemplary English steadiness and resolution.[26]

Buchan himself was never dumb with admiration for this England, and he makes here two significant claims concerning it. The first is that while the characters of 'Deep England' may sometimes lack the imagination and the passionate fire of their neighbours, they have soaked up from prolonged habitation in a temperate landscape such quantities of reasonableness and sense that they will never be prey to passing political fads or dangerous forms of enthusiasm imported from the continent. England preserves itself from Jacobinism here in much the same way as it saves itself from modernism and Prussianism in *Mr Standfast* and Jacobitism in *Midwinter*. The second claim is that it is in their mutual interests that the Scots and the English maintain their differences from one another, but that they respect those differences. The lesson of *The Free Fishers* is that Scots can admire the qualities they find in an Englishman like Sir Turnour without losing their own distinctive sense of identity: that difference is no bar to cooperation, and that to learn about and respect the Other brings no diminishment to oneself.

This second element is a regular theme in Buchan's literary treatments of historical England. What it suggests is that neither nation has the right to impose its values on the other, whether these are the values of Anglicanism, of Covenanting Presbyterianism, or Jacobite Catholicism. This is what Alastair McLean realizes in his encounters with General Oglethorpe in *Midwinter*, a man whom he resembles closely in everything but his political and national affiliations. In Oglethorpe's steady English neutrality he discovers the impossibility of the Jacobite cause in England: feeling 'himself suddenly and in very truth a stranger and alone' in this foreign country.[27] Maclean shares a kinship with Oglethorpe, as he does with Samuel Johnson, but in both cases he recognizes that it would be an abuse of that commonality to impose the politics of his nation violently upon it. The honourable thing is to respect the values of his English friends and fight his battles inside the border of his own country. The novel closes with his parting from Johnson on his return across that border. 'You offer me Old England', Maclean has told Johnson, 'but I am of another race and land. I must follow the road of my fathers.'[28]

The crossing of national borders is a common feature of Buchan's stories. In his Scottish tales the protagonist is frequently an Englishman or an Anglified Scot whose metropolitan complacencies are shaken by an uncanny countryside, while his English novels often feature Scots who have crossed the border into an equally unfamiliar and disorienting, but ultimately more welcoming and homely, landscape. His heroes, too, are rarely pure in their national backgrounds and affiliations: Richard Hannay, for example, is a South-African Scot who becomes an unequivocal Englishman, while Edward Leithen (like Buchan) is a Scot who spends his working life in England and eventually discovers his life's purpose in Canada. At first glance, this tendency might be seen to be the antithesis of nationalism – a desire on Buchan's part for the perfect integration and homogenization of an imperial identity. And this is certainly one strand of the didactic and polemical elements that creep into his fiction: why, for example, does he bring together in *Mr Standfast* such a nationally-diverse group of allies – South African, American, Ulsterman, Scots and English – if not to show the common heritage, attitudes and purpose of the British empire and its English-speaking friends that can successfully resist the modernism and tyranny of continental Europe?

But if one side of Buchan's work is all about emphasizing union and homogeneity, in the form of the common historical and cultural bonds that hold together the English-speaking peoples, there is another side to his thinking in which national differences and discrete national identities are valued and celebrated. This is a paradox that has sometimes troubled commentators on Buchan: the coexistence of separatist and integrationist tendencies that make him a Conservative and Unionist who can argue powerfully for Scottish national self-determination, or an eager imperialist who actively cultivates Canada's sense of itself as a nation with its own distinct history and culture.

Such apparent double-mindedness might be said to come from Buchan's Scottish formation, from that inherent sense of Scottish dualism, explored by James Hogg in his *Confessions of a Justified Sinner* (1824) and Robert Louis Stevenson in *Dr Jekyll and Mr Hyde* (1886), and defined famously by G. Gregory Smith in 1919 as the 'Caledonian antisyzygy'.[29] Or it may be seen as an instance of what Christopher Smout has identified as 'concentric loyalties': the ability developed by Scots to inhabit and assimilate the sometimes conflicting demands of their various personal, regional, Scottish and British affiliations.[30] It can also be located in Buchan's own time as a particular attitude prevalent in British national and imperial culture. Recent scholarship in Scottish history has identified a paradox in nineteenth-century Scotland in individuals who professed a strong British political nationalism while manifesting a keen Scottish cultural nationalism – most markedly visible in the vigour with which Scottish national monuments were built in the early Victorian period.[31] The term coined for this tendency, 'unionist nationalism', is one that has particular resonance in Buchan's case. For unionist nationalists, British Imperial identity was not a threat to constituent minor nations but was rather a guarantee of their continued vitality: a proper union being one in which partner nations maintain separate identities, combining the strengths of their histories and cultures, rather than one in which differences are subsumed into an undifferentiated group identity. Sir Walter Scott had rehearsed many of these arguments in his fiction, welcoming union and its benefits while fearing its diluting effects on the national culture, and in the *Letters of Malachi Malagrowther* of 1826 had made one of the defining statements for the necessity of the maintenance of strong, distinctive identities within union.[32] Such ideas, of 'a diversity that is held in friendship', were frequently reiterated in the period of unionist nationalism and by later advocates of a distinctive Scottish identity within a strong union.[33]

The term 'unionist nationalism' is one that Buchan would probably not have recognized, although the idea is manifest throughout his work. A term he did know, however, was 'colonial nationalism', which shares many of the same attributes as 'unionist nationalism', offering an extension of its principles into the imperial sphere. Colonial nationalism was a development of, and a movement away from, the ideas of Imperial Federation that had circulated since the 1880s. It is most closely identified with Richard Jebb, a contemporary of Buchan's at Oxford, who crystallized the idea in his influential *Studies in Colonial Nationalism* of 1905.[34] Buchan was certainly familiar with the term – he puts many of its arguments into the mouths of his characters in *A Lodge in the Wilderness* (1906), having his Canadian statesman, Ebenezer Wakefield make a strong case that 'national pride' is not a threat to imperial harmony but rather 'the chief incentive to union'.[35] And, later, he has one of his characters, George Souldern, in 'Tendebant Manus' (1927), write 'a book on the meaning of colonial nationalism'.[36] These examples are significant because they prefigure the kinds of arguments Buchan would go on to make about Canadian nationalism as Governor-General in the late 1930s: arguments in which he strongly defended empire and commonwealth while paradoxically promoting Canadian nationalism – telling Canadians, for example, that their country 'is a sovereign nation and cannot take her attitude to the world docilely from Britain, or from the United States, or from anybody else'.[37]

It is arguable that Buchan was able to understand Canadian aspirations so well, and was thus seen to be a capable and sympathetic Governor-General, because he was the inheritor of a set of beliefs, subsequently given the name of unionist nationalism, according to which he might actively celebrate two distinct cultures with little sense of contradiction. The idea of twin loyalties that he had explored in the fiction he wrote about England was an important part of this: it was a gesture of magnanimity at a time of growing nationalist separatism and an enactment of a desirable multiculturalism within Britain in preference to a unionist or imperialist monoculture. Sir Walter Scott once wrote to an English correspondent that 'if you *unscotch* us, you will find us damned mischievous Englishmen'.[38] Buchan quoted this in a speech in parliament in 1932, using it to support his contention that 'Britain cannot afford, I do not think the world can afford, a de-nationalized Scotland'.[39] The fact that Buchan was never 'unscotched', that he remained an ardent advocate of a 'nationalized' Scotland for all the time that he lived and worked in England, meant that his attitudes to Englishness were far from mischievous. They were instead respectful and often reverential. This was a sign not of weakness but of strength – by being able to explore and celebrate Englishness fully he was not diminishing his Scottish identity but was rather enhancing and strengthening it. His maintenance of twin loyalties meant that he was no North Briton, allowing his native traditions to be watered down in a weak solution of Britishness. He remained instead a proud native Scotsman – and adoptive Englishman.

4 BUCHAN, SPORT AND MASCULINITY

Simon Glassock

In late Victorian and Edwardian society the concept of masculinity was entwined in a series of confusing yet mutually dependent relationships between athleticism, Empire, war and degeneration. John Buchan's life and writings intersected profoundly with this debate. This chapter seeks to elaborate Buchan's beliefs about masculinity by reference to his public life, his biographical and autobiographical writing and in particular the use of sport and the motif of the sportsman in his popular novels. It will suggest that Buchan's adventure stories and his heroes were created in a deliberate attempt to articulate his beliefs to a wider audience. By developing Lowerson's analysis of Buchan's work as presenting a philosophy of life and behaviour to a middle-class readership, light may be shed not only on Buchan's own personal and literary development but also on the broader social and cultural processes which shaped and reflected masculinity in late Victorian and Edwardian Britain. Positioning Buchan and his readership in this way may also contribute to the debate about the reception of modernism in post-war British cultural life.[1]

Athleticism was intimately concerned with codifying the standards of male conduct and behaviour which defined masculinity. Heavily promoted in British public schools, athleticism was predicated on the belief that physical activity, especially team games, inculcated in their pupils the qualities of honesty, fairness, loyalty, cooperation and physical and moral courage.[2] Games were considered to be a valuable social tool which both mirrored and created the norms defining civilized conduct. Success in games, as in life, demanded cooperation, the sublimation of individual desires and the ability to give and take orders. But since success was not simply coterminous with winning, pupils were expected to learn to 'play the game' by accepting victory with grace and facing loss with equanimity. These attributes and attitudes were held to be the essence of 'manliness'.

From at least the last quarter of the nineteenth century an increasingly close connection developed between the public schools and the Empire, as sport and manliness came to be equated with Empire building. The public schools produced a stream of vigorous young men looking for adventurous careers which they often found as soldiers, imperial administrators and settlers in the frontier dominions. Thus, as the energetic homosocial world of the public school extended into the Empire, it both validated the imperial project and emphasized the participants' own worth.[3] But although many proposed a positive link between physical and moral development there had long been criticism that the primacy of athleticism was leading to moral and intellectual deterioration in the public schools and universities.[4] The 'insane athleticism' of the public schools[5] and the general public's adulation of the 'peculiarly futile doings in the football field ' of the 'hired scum of our great provincial towns',[6] which merely glorified without either participation in or understanding of the higher purpose of team games, was a debilitating influence on the nation as a whole. Pleasure and leisure, it was asserted, were turned into new gods to the detriment of more serious matters such as the waging of war and the furtherance of Empire.[7]

Kane has suggested that identification with the nation-state or empire strongly supported the idea that moral regeneration could be achieved by physical interaction with wilderness and the colonial frontier.[8] Alongside this, 'English literary taste turned to the adventure stories of such writers as Sir Rider Haggard and Sir Anthony Hope Hawkins'.[9] Adventure writing was not of course new to English literature. Green has charted the ways in which distinctions were drawn between the serious domestic novel and the non-serious adventure story, a process ultimately attributable to the failure of scholars and clergymen to take empire seriously since at least Daniel Defoe's *Robinson Crusoe*.[10] The poor physical condition of British soldiers in the Boer War combined with *fin de siècle* concerns about moral degeneration contributed to a feeling that an excess of civilization was decaying and feminizing the masculine virtues that had won Britain her empire. Declining physiques were taken as evidence of declining national character, which logic even led to a questioning of the moral validity of British imperialism.[11] A sense of the confusion generated by these issues can be gleaned from the reaction to Kipling's poem 'The Islanders' (1902), whose critical lines about 'muddied oafs' and 'flannelled fools' provoked public praise and ire. This included flatly contradictory letters on the value of sports to soldiering from two masters at well-known athletic public schools, Loretto and Uppingham, which were printed consecutively on the letters page of *The Times*.[12]

However, athletic simpletons were not the only threat to nation and empire. Anxiety surrounding the ending of the nineteenth century itself combined with the rise of modernism and feminism to induce in patriarchal European societies a feeling of dangerous flux destabilizing established values, norms and socio-sexual categories.[13] Victorian visions of virtuous manly love as 'a meeting of souls attracted to each other by moral virtue, a generous simplicity of heart, good manners and conversation',[14] had been rocked by Oscar Wilde's trial, which was both a scandalous setback for the languid aesthete and an indication that traditional notions of 'healthy' masculinity and homosociality were under threat from a 'sick' homosexuality.[15] The Cambridge Apostles under J. M. Keynes and Lytton Strachey did little to dispel this fear.[16] The vision of ancient Greece which had informed Victorian notions of manly love was now used by the Apostles to champion the Higher Sodomy and, although they professed a superior, spiritual love and shied away from physical desires, homosexual or otherwise, they nevertheless asserted the primacy of male–male relationships, and prominent Apostles were indeed homosexual.

The entwined members of the Apostles and the Bloomsbury set of writers and artists not only threatened Victorian concepts of manliness and appropriate sexual and gender relations, but were also prominent in moving away from other Victorian values by promoting modernism in art and literature. Pykett bears witness to the fluidity of the terms 'modern' and 'modernism' but there is broad agreement that modernism was a discernible movement in literature and art that can be dated to the first two decades of the twentieth century and which was self-consciously aesthetic, deliberately intellectual and determined to break with established and familiar conventions in society and the arts.[17] Compared to the narrative forms and emotions of traditional forms of literature, and contrasting with the dominant nineteenth-century realist novel, 'Modernism was taken to stand for artifice, frigidity, intellectualism'.[18] Modernist subject matter included 'figures like the alienated wanderer; problems such as the impermeability of the individual psyche; images of fragmentation and loss (at both personal and cultural levels); an apparent rejection of tradition'.[19] Yet despite the differences between the Apostles and public school athletes, some attitudes remained constant. Modernism was a masculine affair,[20] and, as Taddeo notes, 'while they [the Apostles] claimed to be "immoralists", they advocated a version of male love that further emphasized class privilege, gender difference, and male superiority'.[21] Indeed, the Platonic Apostles asserted a fundamental distinction between their own exalted 'reality' and the 'phenomenal', and therefore unreal, world of women and the masses. Roger Fry went so far as to suggest that women had never and would never exist since they had been denied entry into the real world of the Apostles, and J. M. Keynes experienced violent agitation at having to teach women.[22] Such attitudes led Bertrand Russell, an Apostle of an earlier generation, to accuse the society of attempting to distance itself from ordinary people and of spreading an insidious 'disease' at Cambridge which contributed to what he felt was an Edwardian neglect of duty.[23]

John Buchan is not known for his associations with modernism, or with the philosophies of the Apostles, yet he swam in some of the same waters in his undergraduate days. As a very young man he had been an admirer of the Oxford don Walter Pater, an aesthetic proponent of classical Greece who played a role in helping to link virility with the nation and associated public schools with Sparta, and whose sister studied Greek with Virginia Stephen, the Bloomsbury intimate of Apostles Lytton Strachey and Leonard Woolf.[24] While at Oxford Buchan playfully shocked his tutor with Nietzsche[25] and dabbled in aestheticism with his own contribution to the cult of the scholar gypsy (1896), though this early interest did not continue in later life. On leaving Oxford, Buchan cemented his entry into the homosocial world of the British elite by joining first the Bar and then the Imperial administration as a member of Milner's kindergarten in South Africa.[26] Buchan's main characters in his fiction are predominantly men who remain bachelors or marry only in middle age and who inhabit a world in which adventure and intrigue take precedence over domesticity, and women are welcomed on the basis of their physical and emotional resemblance to public schoolboys. Homosocial groups demonstrating a decent and pure love between men feature strongly in Buchan's novels, and in this we may discern a connection between Buchan's early exposure to alternative, non-traditional ideas about relationships between men. Richard Hannay, Peter Pienaar, Sandy Arbuthnot and John S. Blenkiron form a close-knit band in the Hannay series, Dickson McCunn and the Gorbals Die-Hards populate the Dickson McCunn trilogy, and Sir Edward Leithen is a confirmed bachelor whose circle of friends appears to be limited to old Oxford chums. To twentieth-century readers some relationships appear to verge on the physically homoerotic. For example, Hannay and Peter Pienaar share an intimate friendship built on a foundation of big-game hunting and prospecting in Africa, which is as tender as it is virile, and in *The Three Hostages* Hannay is both attracted to and repelled by the physical person of Dominick Medina. Buchan himself though makes a very clear distinction between 'beastliness' and innocent affection.

Yet even though he was a man of diverse practical skills whose prodigious literary output ranged from serious editorial journalism to well-received historical biography, it was Buchan's commitment to Empire and his talent as an adventure writer that marked him as not quite serious. For his part, Buchan was temperamentally and philosophically opposed to the self-absorbed and deliberately exclusive elitism of modernism, expressing irritation at those intellectuals who 'ran round their cages in vigorous pursuit of their tails'.[27] Thus while there is a strong didactic element in Buchan's popular writing which rises above pure entertainment, much of his fiction nevertheless takes the form of adventurous thrillers determined to appeal to rather than exclude the general reader. His most popular stories are consequently suffused by decent, vigorous masculinity and peopled by 'sportsmen' heroes who are keen exponents of outdoor pursuits and who actively articulate the ideals of athleticism by 'playing the game'.

Buchan's early education offers few clues to his adoption of athleticism. Writing in his autobiography he claimed not to have been to school 'in the conventional sense',[28] by which he intended his audience to understand that he had not gone to a public school. Buchan actually attended Hutcheson's, one of the oldest and most prestigious grammar schools in Glasgow, but he instinctively highlighted the key difference when he said that he would have made a good rugby wing three-quarter had he gone to a 'conventional' school.[29] Regardless of its age or prestige, it was the absence of team games which distinguished Hutcheson's from a public school. However, this appears to have been of little consequence to the schoolboy Buchan, for he added that he and his brothers were never interested in 'running with the pack', preferred 'dares' to organized games and were incapable of the public school spirit.[30] At the age of sixteen Buchan left Hutcheson's to go to Glasgow University and so entered another utilitarian Scottish educational institution with few facilities available to its students beyond the lecture hall.[31] As at Hutcheson's, this seems not to have discomfited the rather austere young undergraduate. In later life Buchan recalled returning home from lectures early in the afternoon and studying until midnight, a routine which rendered his academic terms 'periods of beaver-like toil and monkish seclusion'.[32] During his third year Buchan determined to go to Oxford and decided to apply to Brasenose College because of his admiration for Walter Pater, even though at the time it had a reputation for 'heartiness' rather than academic prowess.[33] Initially, Buchan was deeply disappointed by the immaturity of his fellow students at Oxford and by the lack of intellectual sophistication at the university when compared with Glasgow.[34] Nevertheless he acquired a lasting loyalty to Oxford and his college, recalling with evident gratitude that 'At first I disliked the place intensely, but I ended up by falling most deeply under its spell. It smoothed out the prig and the barbarian in me, and, I hope, gave me a reasonable perspective in life'.[35] Buchan attributed this smoothing out to a 'mellowing of character through friendship'[36] and in spite of his initial antipathy to the 'hearty' undergraduate he gravitated towards a sporty public school set, forming a 'large acquaintance among athletes and sportsmen, chiefly the rowing and rugby football groups'.[37] His friends included Tommy Nelson, captain of the Varsity rugby team in 1898 and Scottish rugby international, Raymond Asquith, captain of the Balliol soccer eleven and member of the college rugby fifteen, Johnnie Jamieson, a boxing Blue, Sandy Gillon, captain of the New College rugby fifteen, Auberon Herbert, rowing Blue, and the Brasenose rowing eight which Buchan cheered on enthusiastically from the towpath.[38] But what impressed Buchan so much about his friends was their breadth of talents and the harmony which existed between their physical and intellectual excellence. Raymond Asquith, Cuthbert Medd, Aubrey Herbert, Harold Baker and Buchan himself won Firsts, Asquith and Medd were elected to All Souls, and Baker took up a fellowship at New College.[39] By the time he was asked to write the history of Brasenose Buchan had curbed his antagonism towards the athletic undergraduate and positively applauded the character of his own college:

The sturdy north country stock from which she drew her members, and the vigorous corporate spirit which was always present, made her name famous in outdoor sports, and, when all has been said, it is likely that this is the highest praise which a College can attain to, for it means that the life within her walls is manly and wholesome, and that, if the minor moralities get scant respect, there is abundant reverence for the greater virtues of pluck, endurance and good temper.[40]

In 1901 Buchan joined Milner's staff in South Africa and the two years he spent there had a lasting impact on him. It is clear from his autobiography and editorials written for the *Scottish Review* between 1907–8 that Buchan had reflected closely on the nature of social and political bonds between men. At Oxford he had learned that corporate identity and solidarity of purpose were based on friendship and mutual respect, and in South Africa he learned that these things might be developed not only by education and team games but also by civil and military service and shared hardship, such as working in the open spaces of the veld alongside the tough, resourceful men of the frontier Dominions. When he returned to London Buchan found that he had lost the desire to write fiction and instead continued his direct involvement with the world through journalism, politics, business and married life. It was only in 1910 that he published *Prester John* and then, in 1913, the first of his real 'shockers', *The Power-House*. It was during the Great War that Buchan produced two of his most famous novels, *The Thirty-Nine Steps* (1915) in which he created Richard Hannay and *Greenmantle* (1916), which introduced the other major characters of the Hannay series.

These novels mark the emergence of the decent, vigorous masculinity which came to be the defining theme of Buchan's popular fiction. However, his books were not simply adventurous escapism. In his exploratory discussion of Buchan's use of field sports Lowerson observed that Buchan asked his reader 'as much to search for self-meaning, like Leithen, as to enjoy a good yarn' and offered 'philosophies of life and action for grown men' by using 'well constructed middlebrow writing to continue a process of value implantation that was by no means limited to the public schools and their aping institutions'.[41] This brief analysis may be usefully developed and extended by a fuller discussion of the role of the 'sportsman' and the sporting man, of team games and field sports, in Buchan's fiction. Indeed, in spite of the high profile of outdoor pursuits in Buchan's writing, it is to rugby football, the game which perhaps best encapsulated the spirit of athleticism and which he once described as 'an image of life',[42] that Buchan turns to telegraph a character's essential qualities of decent manliness. David Crawfurd, a Scottish emigrant to South Africa, says that his 'prowess at Rugby football was renowned'[43] and is thus established as an honest, decent and popular young man. Edward Leithen, the Eton and Oxford educated barrister, relaxes after an attempted kidnap 'as tired as if I had come out of a big game of Rugby football'.[44] Peter Pienaar, the Boer hunter turned First World War air-ace, is discussed by troops in the trenches as if he was a 'crack football-player'[45] and defines bravery as 'playing the game by the right rules without letting it worry you that you may very likely get knocked on the head'.[46] Perhaps the most extensive use of rugby in character delineation occurs in the Dickson McCunn stories *Castle Gay* and *The House of The Four Winds*. The game is fundamental to Jaikie Galt's persona, for although he is originally an orphaned Gorbals boy who remains through-out the McCunn trilogy a curiously detached and individualistic character, his rugby prowess and the personal qualities he derives from the game define him as a gentleman.

These characters hint at the integrative function of Buchan's popular writing. Not every reader had been to public school yet there was clearly an expecta-tion on Buchan's part that his characters would be both comprehensible and sympathetic to his audience. Thus, while Sandy Arbuthnot (more properly Lord Clanroyden), Sir Archie Roylance, Sir Edward Leithen and Sir Walter Bullivant are all products of the Establishment, his other heroes are certainly not. Rich-ard Hannay is an émigré Scot who grew up in southern Africa, Peter Pienaar scouted for the British in the Boer war, Blenkiron is an American businessman, Dickson McCunn is a retired Glasgow grocer and Jaikie Galt and the other Gor-bals Die-Hards appear to be rag-clad orphans left to fend for themselves among the Glasgow tenements. Yet this disparate group does conform to a type. The Die-Hards define themselves as Boy Scouts and resolve to aid the White Rus-sians when they might be expected to have more sympathy with the Communist villains. Hannay, the colonial who saves Britain from cunning foreigners by his instinctual manliness, rises to the rank of Major-General, is knighted and lives in a manor house in the Cotswolds. Dickson McCunn retires from the grocery trade, buys a small country estate, and by virtue of his solid, pragmatic decency becomes the saviour of princes and princesses. Jaikie Galt is a Glaswe-gian orphan who goes to Cambridge University, finds fame as a Scottish rugby player and whose quiet refusal to be bullied helps save a fledgling democracy from the threats of communism and fascism. These characters from vastly dif-ferent backgrounds ultimately all agree that civilized behaviour is defined by moral and physical courage, honesty, a sense of fair play and a commitment to putting the needs of society before those of the individual. This convergence on the same moral ground demonstrates to Buchan's readers that the values his heroes endorse are not only central to a well-ordered society but also universal in their application.

On this reading, outdoor sports act as a complement to athleticism to add greater depth to Buchan's characters and to his message. Whereas games were social, sports were activities which took place in Nature. Buchan believed that mountains, and by implication all wild places, are 'remote and untarnished'[47] and that 'One meets [Nature] on equal terms and matches one's skill and endurance against something which has no care for human life'.[48] Interaction with implacable forces developed a man's hardiness of body and humility of spirit by stripping away excess and pretence, an important corollary of which was the whittling away of false distinctions between men. Buchan had a fondness for the intelligence and forthright honesty of practical men such as shepherds, game-keepers, stalkers and gillies and, as an *intellectuel* (Buchan's word), he believed that mountaineering was essentially democratic: 'Class distinctions do not exist for mountaineers'.[49] He noted that in Austria and Germany mountaineering was a popular activity and was delighted 'to see clerks and shop-boys ... shouldering the pack and wandering about the mountains'.[50] Perhaps unexpectedly therefore, Buchan's message is essentially democratic.

However, Buchan's vision of democracy is not that of a modern, atomized and individualistic liberalism but of the classical world in which the citizen cultivates moral excellence and exercises his virtues through public service.[51] Buchan had returned from South Africa with the conviction that a citizen should do public service, and as a democrat of the outdoors he appears to ally himself with the values and attributes which the public school was capable of producing, yet also to distance himself from the spirit of Welldon's comment that 'Practically the whole governing class of Englishmen is educated in the public schools'.[52] While Buchan recognized the truth in this statement he was also aware that society was weakened if men did not participate in social and political life. His novels high-light the precarious nature of social order and the dangers to 'the thin veneer of civilisation' from both the dilution of responsibility epitomized by complacent suburbanism, created at least in part by preventing almost all but those educated at public schools from creatively engaging with society, and the equally destruc-tive egocentric individualism of those who affected an aloof detachment from their fellow men. Combining the motifs of sporting man and 'sportsman' there-fore served to explain to Buchan's readers the paradox that individuals develop their abilities most fully by willingly submitting to group norms and values and working with their fellow men in the pursuit of mutually beneficial goals. The ideal man is therefore one who recognizes the precarious nature of the individu-al's existence in a hostile world and consequently understands the protection afforded by social rules and the urgent necessity of adherence to them. Buchan's writing thus encouraged all of his readers to hold true to the values of manliness and fair play and to maintain a sincere commitment to society, whether they were the dedicatees of his novels, those 'Gentlemen of Eton', Major Generals and Professors at Oxford, or the more modest readership of an 'educated public with seven and sixpence to spend'.[53]

This aspect of Buchan's novels helps explain the plot device involving the redemption of an individual by socialization. When the reader first meets Lombard in *The Island of Sheep* (1936) he is a middle-aged man emasculated by suburban convention, entirely unrecognizable as the young idealist who had dreamed of 'a spiritual renaissance for England'[54] by completing Rhodes's work in Africa. By the end of the story Lombard has regained his zest for life and determines on 'coming back to the Norlands to make my soul'.[55] In *Mr Standfast* (1919) the young conscientious objector Launcelot Wake is an excellent mountaineer and in *Huntingtower* (1922) John Heritage is a keen walker, but neither are 'sportsmen'. Both are fundamentally decent men but are too self-centred to contribute to society, and therefore cannot be truly happy. Heritage is a cynical young man filled with the latest literary and political fads but by the end of the novel he has transferred his allegiance to McCunn's romantic humanism.[56] Hannay promises to 'break you to harness, Wake, and then you'll be a happy man'[57] and fittingly Wake eventually dies in the voluntary service of his friends and country. In similar fashion, in *The Courts of the Morning* (1929), Sandy Arbuthnot resolves to save Castor's soul and Castor is transformed from a rationalist with an arrogant and manipulative faith only in pure reason into a humbler man alive to humanity, its fallibility and its loves.[58]

The question implicit in this analysis of what Buchan was promoting in his writing is why he chose to continue articulating pre-war ideals of manliness in his post-war novels. The answer can be found by examining Buchan's personal response to the War and his related convictions about how society should recover from the trauma of the conflict. After the Armistice Buchan attempted to come to terms with the losses he and others had suffered by channelling a good deal of his creative energy into regimental and general histories of the War and memoirs of family and friends who had been killed. In his biography of the Grenfell twins and the privately published *These for Remembrance* (1919) Buchan recalled and recorded the essential qualities of men he had admired and loved. He extended these individual memorials to the wider remembrance of his brother's regiment and to a history of the British Empire in the War, which was intended primarily for secondary schools and the older pupils of elementary schools.[59] Alongside these intellectual efforts Buchan received an emotional uplift when he woke again to the joy of Nature during a trip to the Cotswolds in April 1919. Aged forty-three he regained 'something of the exhilaration of youth'[60] and found that he had 'recovered the past, and with it hope for the future'.[61] This sentiment perfectly echoes Buchan's political desire to 'preserve continuity with the past and to keep whatever of the old foundations were sound'.[62] Although Buchan lost one of his brothers and many close friends during the war he refused to succumb to *ennui* or give up hope. His life was informed by the principles of conservation and integration and rather than recreate and preserve the past he sought to encourage a post-war audience to build the world afresh. Buchan's contribution to the future was to articulate the best ideals of the pre-war world.

These personal convictions cannot be divorced from the wider context of social, political and artistic movements, especially the response to the War of what Buchan termed 'the interpreting class'.[63] Modernism, which has been described as 'a wrestling with, and ultimately a discarding of, the past',[64] was criticized by contemporaries as being deliberately obscure intellectual snobbery that was out of touch with the majority of readers.[65] Hilliard, seeking to 'unpick' Rose's claim that working-class autodidacts were especially antagonistic to an exclusive modernism, expands Rose's comment that readers, working and middle class, may simply have been attached to older forms of literature and so unable or unwilling to appreciate newer forms.[66] Buchan's own temperamental and philosophical opposition to modernism seems not to have been based on structure and style so much as on a fundamental disagreement about the proper attitude to life. Contemporaries felt that while modernism may have dealt with new subjects it did so in a way that had little intrinsic beauty and which ultimately propelled one not to a higher but to a lower place. Buchan noted with distaste that 'in literature, especially in fiction, a dull farmyard candour became fashionable', an insistence upon the functions of the body which had rarely artistic value'[67] and was critical of 'sans culottes who sought to deflate majestic reputations, and reduce the great to a drab level of mediocrity'.[68] Modernist concerns with fragmentation and alienation may therefore not have been representative of society at large, and certainly Buchan preferred to put his trust for renewal in 'the plain man who for four years had carried the globe on his shoulders, with no gift of expression, unperplexed by philosophies, but infinitely loyal, enduring and unconquerable'.[69] The war had shown him how men of real character coped with adversity and he was exasperated by those who 'plumed themselves wearily on being hollow men living in a waste land'.[70] He abhorred the failure of some intellectuals to offer anything other than futile, arrogant emptiness, and had little time for the young modernists who 'would admit no absolute values, being by profession atomisers, engaged in reducing the laborious structure of civilised life to a whirling nebula'.[71] As has already been indicated, Buchan consistently expressed his opposition to this paucity of spirit in his popular fiction and continued to do so in public life. As late as 1936 he delivered a speech to the Boy Scouts' Association in Montreal in which he said 'The Scout movement stands firm upon certain great moral principles which no sophistry can undermine, for they are the basis of civilisation. It teaches the personal duties of courage and self-discipline and patience, and the social duties of sacrifice and sympathy'.[72] His heroes are correspondingly virile, decent and powerfully positive men who refuse to decline in mordant reflection and self-analysis but are active participants in life. Buchan's own determination to meet the world head-on defined the character of his popular novels: 'Even a perverse career of action seemed to me better than a tippling of ale in the shade'.[73]

Buchan's education, popular fiction and public life can be seen to demonstrate the development and articulation of his faith in the virtues of manliness grounded in outdoor virility and sporting socialization. The references to sport and games in Buchan's post-war fiction serve not only to delineate character but also to maintain continuity with the past. His recovery from the trauma of the First World War illustrates his remarkable optimism in the resilience of British manhood as he had known it, and it is in the context of the renewal and re-presentation of these ideals to a post-war audience that Buchan's use of the language and motifs of athleticism and the 'sportsman' has been examined. Viewing the life of one individual from this perspective illustrates the tenacity of Victorian and Edwardian notions of masculinity beyond the end of the First World War and demonstrates that in spite of the emphasis which is traditionally given to the rise of modernism there also existed recovery and continuity in British post-war social, political and cultural life.

Acknowledgements
I would like to thank Kate Macdonald for her great help and encouragement. This chapter is dedicated to the memory of my mother.

5 JOHN BUCHAN AND THE CREATION OF THE SPRINGBOK WARRIOR

Bill Nasson

The quintessential, self-cultivated image of John Buchan as an imperial man of action and exponent of subterfuge was embodied nicely in two of his preoccupations during the First World War. These tugged him in very different directions, one secretive, the other showy. Buchan's persistent political energy went into low-level involvement in British war propaganda, while his historical imagination was put to work in launching a scholarly infantry offensive. One thrust was the provision of a multi-volume account of the Great War, serialized from 1915 to 1919 as *Nelson's History of the War*.

This brought on a second thrust, the crafting of a dashing authorized depiction of South Africa at war in Europe.[1] Buchan had the right kind of overseas service pedigree for such an undertaking. An ardent imperialist from the provincial fringe, he had a close association with South Africa through his work in Britain's reconstruction administration after the end of the Anglo-Boer War of 1899–1902.[2] At the outbreak of hostilities, he was a press correspondent, adventure story novelist and informed follower of military affairs. At almost forty years of age and not particularly fit, he spent the initial months of the conflict in bed. But, being Buchan, he was not so indisposed as to be unable to observe, scheme and write. Following a posting to France in 1915 as a war correspondent, he moved up a gear a year later when he joined Sir Douglas Haig's staff complement and got stuck into government war publicity and propaganda assignments.[3] In February 1917 he was put in charge of a new Department of Information by the prime minister, David Lloyd George. This massively increased the propaganda directed at enemy troops, including airborne drops of German-language pamphlets explaining the advantages of surrendering, and assuring anyone who gave up of civilized Allied leniency.

While receptive to the value of new propaganda techniques from art and film to the mass presentation of large-scale war, Lieutenant-Colonel Buchan maintained a balance between flashy opportunism and traditional expertise. Thus, his bookish presence helped to ensure the continuing primacy of written texts to the positive reinforcement of the war effort. A deft hand at running up pen-portraits, he furnished warrior-king descriptions to accompany Francis Dodd's 1917–18 portrayals of commanders, *Generals of the British Army*. The venera-tion of soldiers in these sabre-rattling sketches led the liberal C. E. Montague, probably the leading British correspondent on the Western Front, to wrinkle his nose. They were, he felt, rather too sunny to be credible to the ordinary Tommies idealized in regular press reports.[4]

Buchan's rhetoric was unlikely to win an appreciative audience among those who had come through post-1917 Ypres and the Somme. Still, his role in man-aging war news and in war presentation appears to have remained workaday, constrained by the exigencies of a world that was a far cry from the decisive exploits of his romantic heroes in adventure novels such as *The Three Hostages* (1924) or *The Dancing Floor* (1926). Buchan's government propaganda activities obviously loom larger as an actual war contribution than the military history that he wrote after the First World War. Yet, in its way, this further imperial undertaking may well have been no less notable an achievement in its contribu-tion to Great War representation of South Africa. While in France in 1916 on General Headquarters staff duties, which included assessing the state of troop morale, Buchan was identified by the Pretoria government as the individual best equipped to craft a history of the South African contribution to the Allied war effort. In due course, he was commissioned by Colonel Geoffrey Herbert, chief staff officer of the Union Defence Forces, to produce 'an official History of the South African Forces in Europe'[5] as a national record of the fighting experience of South African volunteers where it was considered to count the most.

Buchan had had only a short stint in South Africa, as private secretary to the High Commissioner, Sir Alfred Milner, augmenting this with land scheme dabbling in the post-war settlement. But these preoccupations were sufficient for him soon to have become a household name in reconstruction circles. He had also found the country to be an arresting personal experience. He not only reviewed books on South Africa, but had also produced a study of his own, *The African Colony: Studies in the Reconstruction* (1903), and fiction, as in his 1910 boys' story about white settler rule and conflicted African worlds, *Prester John*. Even more crucially, Buchan the colonial administrator had forged a close asso-ciation with the Union's pro-imperial military establishment. Following Union, he had taken a close interest in the formation of a national defence force in 1912, and had been drawn into policy discussions of the country's role in imperial defence.[6] Moreover, he had been in regular touch with the South African Infan-try Brigade ever since its arrival in France in 1916, and had paid a series of visits to its base camps and training grounds, if mostly for handshaking.

Predictably, Buchan wanted to get going on his commissioned history right away. But, because of competing demands on his time during the war, he was unable to commence work on his projected volume, *The History of the South African Forces in France*, until the end of hostilities. Then, once given a clear run, in the immediate post-Armistice months he nosed out all available official papers and began concerted lobbying of higher level officials and senior Union Defence Forces officers for a sight of field orders, official journals, battle accounts, registers and other information on the operations of the South African Brigade. His 400-page official history was first published in 1920 and remains available today in facsimile edition.[7]

Publication brought swooning review notices in the main South African English-language press, with reviewers in papers like the *Rand Daily Mail* and the *Natal Witness* applauding the history as 'magisterial' and 'wholly enthralling'.[8] The volume was followed several years later by a leaner, popular-heroic edition aimed at the dormitories of South African boys' collegiate schools, which carried a gushing preface by Douglas Haig. Presiding over civic dinners for white war veterans on his visit to the Union in 1921, Haig had been feted as 'good old Dougie', as he made much of South African battlefield courage, endurance and resourcefulness.[9] Buchan's *South African Forces* was waved like a torch. A controversial field-marshal, Haig could scarcely not promote a book which trumpeted praise for his 'audacious' command, and credited him personally with having salvaged the British Army, turning it 'in two years', into 'the most formidable in the world'.[10] As with the original edition, the slimmer and more visually atmospheric version of *The South African Forces* was acclaimed as compelling, with a *Bloemfontein Sun* reader urging parents with sons in school cadet corps to put it at the top of their Christmas stocking list.[11]

The History of the South African Forces in France was both the first and by far the most readable of official histories of South African First World War involvement.[12] It was more concentrated in focus, more fluent and more crisp in its narrative drive than the First World War accounts of any other contemporary authors on South Africa. At the same time, for all its authoritative title, it was restrictive in its coverage of the range of expeditionary forces. It omitted any reference to the field support role of the South African Native Labour Contingent and the Coloured Cape Corps service battalions, or to the heavy loss of African life in the sinking of the troopship the *Mendi* in the English Channel in 1917, an omission which went largely unnoticed in South African historiography until the 1970s.[13] The *General Staff Official History* at least went to the trouble of devoting an entire page in its appendices to the employment of thousands of black labouring auxiliaries behind the lines along the Western Front.[14] Nor, in this discriminating male creed, was there any recognition of the middle-class South African women who volunteered for European nursing and supply duties. With empire a man's business, 'crisis overseas' required 'the supply of men of a certain type – practical, resourceful and self-reliant … unsqueamish and stoical'.[15] For the masculine imperial project, that now applied to men coming home rather than venturing abroad.

This was not the only blinkered context in which Buchan's account of South Africa has to be set and understood. Throughout the war, the Afrikaner National Party, disdainful of the country's imperial obligations, had favoured neutrality and asserted a more independent and autonomous national interest. This translated into implacable opposition to 'South African forces being used in war, only twelve years after the Anglo-Boer War'.[16] Within white society, pro-war English and Anglo-Afrikaner loyalists remained a minority of a minority, with one scholar estimating that by 1917 well over half of the Afrikaner population was opposed to their government's war policy.[17] Not surprisingly, then, this troubled atmosphere diluted the wider impact of *The South African Forces* as a 'national fiction', in the sense that it could feed into the ideas, images, myths and traditions which were coming to form the imaginative constructions of a manufactured national character and national identity.

Self-evidently, therefore, Buchan's impact on the post-1918 public culture of war history and remembrance was not even remotely comparable to that of Charles Bean, 'the emotional locus of Australian narratives of nation'.[18] Bean's popularizing portrayals of the fighting prowess of heroic diggers in publications like *The Anzac Book* and *Australians in Action* were enormously influential in fashioning mythologies of Anzac manhood and in defining the wartime qualities of Australian nationality in legendary terms. What Buchan did share with Bean was a vision of the war experience as a white national narrative, with black South Africans and Aboriginal Australians considered to be outside the nation, left out of the picture as an unacknowledged shadow. In the South African case, wartime disunity ensured that there was something more. While a national war narrative romanticized loyalist Springbok warriors, on an alienated home front nationalists mocked volunteers as 'Botha's pets' and 'Smuts's sweets'.[19]

Yet, at another level of the dominant discourse of the time, Buchan also knew his beans. He had no intention of considering the achievements 'of South Africans in many British battalions, in cavalry regiments, in the Flying Corps, in every auxiliary service'.[20] Rather, as an imaginative writer, the purpose of his official history was to convey a distinctively personal interpretation of the Union's fighting contribution, and to depict the larger symbolic meaning of the country's role in the British imperial war effort. In this, what mattered above all was appreciation of the eager participation of upright colonial patriots, drawn 'largely from the inhabitants of British blood', whose sacrifice on French soil offered 'incontrovertible proof of manly virtue and civic vigour'.[21]

The South African Forces was a volume loaded with such superlatives, and was no lukewarm armchair history. For its author, what defined the South African Promised Land was its age; an old African region, stirring 'before the birth of

Christ'. Yet, for all its remoteness 'from the main centres of the world', one way or another it had always been affected 'by the great crises of modern history'. No less significantly, in the course of achieving its desirable *pax Britannica*, a turbulent South Africa had formed 'the theatre of many wars'. That accumulated experience of fire, of having passed 'through so many furnaces', had been invaluable in setting rigorous standards of manliness and virility, and had blessed South Africa with no shortage of hardy 'sons' who instinctively preferred action to repose, and who could be counted on not to stand aside should 'the hard-won gains of civilization' ever be menaced.[22]

For the patchwork country which had become the Union of South Africa in 1910, an implanted European cultural heritage of standing firm and fighting for the values of 'civilization' had, in a sense, become almost its defining reality. Or, the rich folklore of its upbringing on frontier fortitude and settler heroism had become that saturating reality. For Buchan, this made it 'right, nay, inevitable' that 'in any war of nations' which represented a clash between high civilization and barbarism, the Dominion of South Africa should 'play a conspicuous part' in ensuring that light prevailed over darkness.[23] As *The South African Forces* stressed, world war in 1914 immediately saddled the Pretoria administration with political difficulties that were fiendishly 'intricate' as well as 'exasperating'. Disaffected nationalist Afrikaners constituted an enemy within, a prowling fifth column plotting 'internal revolution' to bring about the collapse of the imperial order and to turn the land into 'alien' soil. Alongside this was a further insidious threat. This was the duplicitous lip-service paid by the German South West African authorities to local neutrality in any event of war between European colonial powers. Those Prussian degenerates in command in Windhoek 'had been engaged for years in putting temptation in the way of restless spirits within the Union'.[24] All they needed was the impetus provided by the Balkan crisis for an assault on South Africa.

This amounted to advanced paranoia about the dangers to Union security that would not have been out of place in any of John Buchan's potboiling thrillers of the 1920s and 1930s, steeped in conspiracies, espionage, spies, scares and international hostilities. Sure enough, a band of anti-British Afrikaner rebels was set on rising against a Union invasion of German South West Africa at the behest of the War Office, but this muddled 1914–15 insurrection was well short of any revolution. Equally, the spectre of a pre-1914 South Africa having become infiltrated by nests of German agents, plotting darkly with sinister local conspirators, was a breathless Buchan embellishment at its best. The basis of the Union conquest was self-evidently simple. If not quite a new jewel in the Crown, the territory snatched by General Louis Botha in 1915 was an early strategic enemy target that had been marked by London. After that, the British could relax about South Atlantic sea-lanes.[25] Moreover, concluded Buchan, the campaign task had been accomplished with commendable 'firmness and far-sighted humanity', with Botha's invasion columns conducting operations with 'decency' and restraint.[26]

In this, *The South African Forces* was perhaps not being unduly sanguine. After all, captured Afrikaner rebel combatants were treated with considerable latitude for their sedition, with Botha making much of the binding up of wounds. Thereafter, losses on both sides in the short and conclusive German South West Africa action were hardly costly, and capitulating enemies enjoyed liberal peace terms of the very kind to be promised by Buchan in his European propaganda. In the approach to Passchendaele, for instance, leaflets from his Department of Information would emphasize the favourable treatment by the British of their prisoners of war. Trading on charity in victory, when it came to goodwill in war, the Union was a model for the Allies.

For Buchan, at the centre of this was the aura of Louis Botha. His appreciation of the Union's first prime minister as a most loyal of loyal Boers ran deep. In its enthusiastic advocacy of the politician-general, *The South African Forces* painted him as an expansive and fidgety war leader, never one 'to rest on his laurels' because of his sure insight into 'the great war in its true perspective'. The character and speed of his response to hostilities demonstrated that he knew exactly what that was. Cognizant of the enduring indivisibility of the empire family, Botha grasped that there could be no difference between a successful defence of the borders of the Union and prevailing 'on the battlefields of Europe'. For he had perceived the essential truth about his country, 'that the fortunes of that land were indissolubly bound up with the fortunes of the British Commonwealth, and of that civilization which Germany had outraged'.[27] In that sense, Louis Botha, the Afrikaner empire patriot, was leaving history and almost entering an elevated realm of Buchanesque fiction.

So choreographed, in his masterly qualities the tubby general was a mature Buchan hero: fully conscious of personal destiny, alert to the danger of slackness and straying, a man of deft movement in a world beset by murky threats and uncertainties, while perpetually on the brink of ever greater accomplishments. General Botha was the sort of decisive man to immerse himself in high-stakes international struggles of whatever necessary kind to enable Britain to win its wars. Although more lard than lean in appearance, he was, in his way, a real-life Richard Hannay, a case from history where 'the real could be appropriated to serve the truly fantastical'.[28]

Understandably, therefore, Botha would not have countenanced 'inaction after the close of the German South-West campaign'. Committed to oiling British wheels on other war fronts, by July 1915 he had 'persuaded' the imperial government to accept a volunteer contingent of 'seasoned' infantry for European service. 'Inured to the hardships of war' in German South West Africa or earlier in the Anglo–Boer War, these were men spoiling for a bigger European fight.[29]

For Buchan the evangelical historian of South Africa at war, the classy character and military pedigree of the overseas Infantry Brigade was a particularly appealing part of the overall picture. Accordingly, its social background required full and careful delineation in *The South African Forces*.

One tricky problem confronted by the story was that although Dutch-Afrikaners were a clear majority of the minority white population, the author's own estimate of the proportion of Afrikaner volunteers at 1915 enlistment was that they made up at most about 15 per cent of the Brigade complement.[30] This dearth certainly exercised John Buchan. Was it because most Afrikaners were indifferent to the patriotic call? Was it because they were alienated from the imperial cause? For an idealist history, that just would not wash. No, argued its writer, Afrikaners preferred fighting in the saddle to fighting on their feet. Thus, in any local infantry recruitment drive, it was only to be expected that volunteers would be overwhelmingly of British descent. 'The Dutch', after all, were bred to the saddle as instinctive 'light cavalrymen' and, as wheeling sharpshooters, were unrivalled in battle.[31] Yet, sadly for the willing and honest Boers, terrain, climate and Western Front tactics could not provide a mobile arena for their renowned natural aptitudes. So, they stayed away from a war which would not suit their fashion.

As a charitable explanation of tepid Afrikaner responses to recruitment, this was putting a dubious best face on a politically uncomfortable state of affairs. Equally, there was another factor that mattered far more to Buchan's historical imagination. In part, this was his exuberant depiction of the South African Brigade as bronzed, big-boned infantry, outdoor 'men of the right kind of experience', against whom none 'showed a better standard of physical well-being'. With only a miniscule number of Brigade recruits lacking any prior military training or experience with firearms according to *The South African Forces*, Union Springboks were indisputably the praetorian guard of Africa, uniquely adaptable colonial warriors of 'its towns and its veld', who would stick to their nation and its cause through thick and thin.[32]

In another part, what commended the Brigade was that it was not only strong as brandy but smart. The emphatically 'middle-class', well-educated background of its men made them especially suited to the challenging technological and other 'mental demands' and 'slow intricacies of a modern campaign'. These were impressively cultivated and successful individuals from mining, farming, finance, the professions, government office and the armed services, whose 'level of education and breeding was singularly high', banding together unfussily to go off to a distant war. Here, in its way, was the spinning of another strand of *South African Forces* romance, in which men of talent and grit found a shared purpose in a far-flung venture, fortified by the middle-class moorings of independence, duty and resolution. As Buchan put it, these eager Brigade recruits were spoiling for a scrap, 'not only because they like it, but because they have much to fight for, and are determined to get the job finished'.[33] Naturally, this description did little justice to men such as miners and mechanics in an infantry rank-and-file whose motivations for enlistment included rootlessness, boredom and unemployment.[34] Yet, in its way, it also confirmed the author's preoccupation with those who had done well, with whom he wanted dreamily to assert an affinity. As David Cannadine has suggested, John Buchan always 'wanted to be at the centre of things', using 'his books' to convey the illusory 'impression that he was'.[35]

Ultimately, it was perhaps a third perspective on the nature of the expeditionary force which mattered most of all to Buchan, still an ornamental Scot for all that he had by 1920 established himself as an English country gentleman outside Oxford. This was its 'Scottish' military plumage and morale, or its clannish embodiment of an expatriate colonial army Scottishness. On the Brigade's first formation, *The South African Forces* totted up 258 English, 30 Irish, 13 Welsh, 595 South African, 337 Scottish and around 50 other recruits drawn from elsewhere, including local Australian and New Zealand migrants who trooped up as South African Anzacs. Slightly over half the contingent was judged to have been immigrant 'home'-born rather than 'colonial' or South Africa-born. Taking a rounded view which may have been slightly too round, their inspired author piped, 'in nearly every company the Scots were stronger than any other element except the South African born who, of course, included a large proportion of men of Scottish descent'.[36] If, on the face of it, this was largely conjecture, the South Africans' association with kilts, bagpipes and bare knees was still something that could hardly be missed.

In this respect, John Buchan's *South African Forces* had surely captured a pervasive element of identity. The Springbok Jockies and Robs of the 4th Regiment, as well as a fair number in other battalions, had nearly all been absorbed through expatriate Scottish military groupings. At least one of these formations had an imported stag as a regimental mascot, another a stuffed pheasant, a third a Scots terrier and all 'observed some form of Gaelic etiquette'.[37] Other Scottish Springboks were trawled from the membership rolls of a network of wealthy Caledonian societies, or were egged on to enlist at public recruiting fairs presided over by 'prominent Scotsmen throughout South Africa'. In almost every imaginable way, therefore, *The South African Forces* depicted the Union's 'European' contingent as a body steeped in tartan military cachet.[38]

Yet, whether this meant that things in France went swimmingly between the Union's more pushy colonial Scots and starchy Highland regiments officers and men may well remain an open question. After all, a number of those who moored themselves to the military tradition of the Transvaal Scottish were simply non-Afrikaner whites who fancied themselves as upstart Scottish soldiers. Given the fractured Anglo–Afrikaner hinge of white politics, in wartime many non-Afrikaners, including some with a Scots pedigree, also tended to lump themselves together conveniently as patriotic English. At the same time, a good many 'English' Brigade volunteers reinvented themselves as Cape Town, Port Elizabeth and Durban Rob Roys, Yet, being short of family and territorial connections, few South African English in heavily Scottish units would have been left under any illusion that they were anything other than sassenachs.

Nonetheless, the fabricated Scottishness of the Union Brigade which so gripped Buchan formed the underlying symbolic power of his *South African Forces*. At one level, it was an appreciation of the 'overseas' role of Scots migrants in creating the right kind of expeditionary military culture for a settler society grounded in the promise of 'young men in town and country whose eyes turned naturally towards Europe'. Brimful of altruism, in their ferocious prosecution of battlefield objectives South Africa's volunteers would never be confined selfishly to necessary 'frontier wars', nor would their mission be dictated solely by 'the defence of borders' and the primacy of 'local interests'. Secondly, the 'South African Scottish' amounted to a returning rock to which all of the Union's 'sons in France', including 'true patriots' of 'Dutch blood' could cling safely, as they endured, sacrificed and fought 'for that liberal civilization of which the British Commonwealth is the humble guardian'.[39]

While this was Buchan's way of seeing the universe, he was also an uncommonly talented teller of gripping stories, and his self-assured narration made *The South African Forces* an enthralling read. The author's extended account of the contingent's doings started with its clash with Turkish opponents in North Africa (tackling 'the frontier brigandage' of 'a fanatical horde'),[40] before moving to its early 1916 deployment in northern France and subsequently in Flanders. In some respects, it is the case that Buchan's depiction of marches, sweeps and the trivia of water supplies and equipment has such verisimilitude that at times it is hard for an average reader not to yawn.

Equally, every now and then there were arresting flashes of artful perception or lyrical description. Buchan's dismissal of German hopes of taking Cairo with their Bedouin allies was an acknowledgement that trying to 'build up armies from such material was like an attempt to make ropes of desert sand'.[41] Notable, too, was the reflection, in *The South African Forces*, of an acute consciousness of place and a need to find affirming images of national being in the landscape of a war-torn Europe. War had thrown up a bridge between France and South Africa, bringing unexpected encounters with a France that seemed to have an Africanised sheen of familiarity. Thus, the haunting evocation of Pretoria's battalions tramping through serene squares of Picardy countryside early in June 1916 had them 'in 'the heat and dust of midsummer', panting for a canal in which to dip their legs or for a rest in the 'stillness' of a deserted field, beyond which lay a 'horizon of purple'. For infantrymen, the sight of it all 'must have recalled their own country', as 'the Somme, with its acres of swamp and broad lagoons', was suggestive of the 'northern tracts' of South Africa, 'not unlike some river of the bushveld'. The lionized 'tawny ground' through which soldiers were roaming, had 'something of the air of the high veld ... ridges and slopes falling away to an infinite distance ... the kind of spectacle which is common enough beyond the Vaal ... the weather, too, was the soft, shimmering mist which one meets on the edge of the Berg'.[42]

Buchan took the Battle of the Somme as the obvious climax. His *South African Forces* judged the Brigade's July 1916 performance in its Delville Wood clash with crack German forces to have been 'an epoch of terror and glory', and 'a feat of human daring and fortitude' without any known equal on the Western Front. More than this, his portrayal of this Somme 'epic', with its brave and unbending South African 'Jocks' holding out against immense odds, helped to fashion a defining moment of Springbok martial prowess.[43] In turn, that national construction of a Somme legend of blood sacrifice would go on to play its part through the 1920s and later in mythologizing Delville Wood as a South African Gallipoli or Vimy Ridge, the furnace of battle igniting a New World nationhood to match that of Australia and Canada. It was, of course, nationhood under a red, white and blue umbrella. In a tribute to the infantry brigade's many Delville Wood dead and missing at a February 1918 memorial service, Haig declared, to the thin sound of a pipe lament, that 'their gallant death' had not merely 'made desolation glorious', it had also lifted Delville Wood as 'a perpetual witness to the strength of those common ideals which bind together all British people'.[44]

For what remained, by November 1918 Botha's Springboks were where they deserved to be, in the easternmost 'advance guard' of the British Armies, 'finishing the War as the spear-point of the advance to victory'.[45] In those terms, theirs was a transferred identification to a pale Zulu warriorhood. All the while, an overriding aim of *The South African Forces* as a whole was to illuminate what its author saw as the intimidating quality of good colonial 'stock' or 'breeding' when roused. It was, for instance, the depth of their individual initiative, bravery and perseverance that helped infantrymen to get stuck into the perilous business of trench-raiding with such gusto. Indubitably, once blackened up and using 'only the Zulu language' to chill 'the blood of the invading hordes', the guile and ferocity of white Springboks would have matched that of any Cetshwayo war party or impi. As to the latter, in Buchan's view colonial warfare experience was vital for that combined heritage of environmental temperament and combative tradition which had left 'every man of the Brigade ... undismayed by any odds'.[46] They were, after all, 'the kinsfolk of men' who had eventually routed the terrifying Zulu 'hordes', and had had their blood warmed earlier by the Natal imperial fighting tradition of 'the laager at Rorke's Drift', and at 'the Ridge of Delhi' during the 1857 Indian Rebellion.[47] Immersion in war was, then, an idealized male belonging, virtually an art in which colonists of this kind should be expected to excel.

For Buchan the action writer, such adulation of soldiering colonial heroes was a literary process underway well before his shaping of *The South African Forces*. Having 'fought like crusaders', the union of 'British-born' and 'stout Dutchmen' was the finest display yet 'of true race integration', of 'what South Africa may yet become'.[48] That nationhood was to be understood as a version of the author's own island story. There, an early eighteenth-century British Act of Union had extinguished any remaining Anglo–Scottish border conflicts and local national enmities. Accordingly, just as 'the auld enemies of England and Scotland' had transcended their 'shallow' Catholic Highlands and Protestant Lowlands differences, so would the South African Union's white 'race-stocks' develop a love of shared 'liberty' under the wise guardianship of the British Commonwealth.[49] In this respect, the experience of the Great War as a shared conflict had renewed Buchan's earlier optimism and hope of a post-1902 white assimilationist Reconstruction and Union, reflected in his 1902 articles in the British gentleman's magazine, *Blackwood's*.[50]

The 1914–18 War provided just the right kind of heavy ground for John Buchan to thresh out his cherished vision of British imperialism as the fount of a reborn Classical civilization. His pacy story of the Springbok Brigade warriors who 'preferred a rendezvous with death' to a wasting life 'of comfort and ease', amounted to a 'miraculous Odyssey', made all the more astonishing by their small number. Reminiscent of the few hundred of Leonidas, Springboks were nothing if not recognizable as true 'Spartans'. In history-writing 'soaked with legend', they embodied the moral purpose and romantic being which coloured all of Buchan's writings on the wider British war effort as an epic of national survival. Through these, he sought to make his mark as a magisterial scholar, a later Thucydides of the mystical and sacrificial elements of the battlefield.[51] Buchan's approach mirrored that of the British imperial architect, Herbert Baker, who designed the South African National War Memorial at Delville Wood. For both men, in discharging its imperial obligation by falling in with the common calling of English-speaking races and in displaying such fortitude, South Africa had displayed the 'Olympian character' of its pioneering European civilization in Africa.[52]

Here, the soldierly ideals of a young frontier society were matching those of Classical Greece or Rome. So, at Delville Wood, sturdy Union Scots had become reincarnations of infantry hoplites or legionnaires. This hard Graeco-Roman glaze to *The South African Forces* affirmed Buchan's idealization of European South Africa as the masculine personification of a Classical empire in Africa, wreathed in the mythic spirit 'of that secret country', which bore the fleshy seed to 'make fruitful the workaday plains'. In that sense, the productive legacy of

Buchan's *South African Forces* was an assurance that the country would go on to fulfil its national promise as a great British Dominion of 'assimilated European kinsfolk'.[53]

6 JOHN BUCHAN AND THE SOUTH AFRICAN WAR

Michael Redley

On 14 September 1901 John Buchan took ship from Southampton to South Africa. He had worked in his early twenties as a barrister of the Middle Temple, and in journalism as an editorial writer and book reviewer. Now he was embarking on something new. At Cape Town station where he took the train to the north, Buchan caught sight of military guards and the jostling crowds of refugees from the war which had engulfed southern Africa. He wrote to his younger brother, William: 'I liked it, and felt I was at last getting near my work'. The train slowed to a crawl through the Northern Cape where there were rumours of Smuts's commando lying in wait up ahead. Crossing the Karoo Desert Buchan sat at the end of the train smoking his pipe and watching the passing landscape, his Scottish Presbyterian soul thrilling to its 'sabbatical stillness'. At midday on Thursday 3 October the train crossed the Orange River into the Free State, newly under British administration as the Orange River Colony. He wrote to a friend 'It was funny to see the watch-fires and the Kaffir scouts, to hear rifle shots and to see the guard turning out from every blockhouse with fixed bayonets till the train passed'. At the wayside stations, soldiers began to hitch a ride on the train, 'so dusty and ragged that only their white teeth and clean nails distinguished them from tramps'. Near the border between the Orange River Colony and the Transvaal at Kroonstadt a young Lieutenant-Colonel came aboard: Douglas Haig whom Buchan had known at Oxford. They travelled on together discussing the progress of the war and the deeds of mutual friends under arms. On Friday evening Buchan arrived, in serious need of a bath, at his destination, Johannesburg.[1] The following evening he dined with the man whose staff he had come to join, the High Commissioner of South Africa and governor of the occupied republics, Alfred Milner.[2]

His time in South Africa, less than two years, fitted into Buchan's view of his own life as the sort of adventure a hero in his fiction might have had. There is an account of it in his autobiography of 1940, *Memory Hold-the-Door*.[3] The title of the South African chapter, 'Furth Fortune', is the same as the one in *Prester John*

(1910) in which the young hero sets off for his epic encounter with the Ethio-
pianist African missionary priest and proto-nationalist leader, John Laputa. But
Buchan approached his own adventure with immense seriousness. On the voyage to South Africa, as well as lighter reading he ploughed through 'Blue Books',
publications of the British government containing the reports and despatches on
which its policies were based.[4] As one of Milner's private secretaries it was to be
his job to draft the material which found its way into print in this form. 'Was he
writing anything?', a literary friend asked after he had been there a few months.
'Many despatches, Sir', he replied. 'A recent Blue Book was almost entirely my
composition'.[5] The task facing Milner, rebuilding the country after the war and
tying the new colonies in to the imperial system, was seen as one of the great
administrative challenges of its day, compared by Buchan himself in an editorial in the *Spectator* with reconstruction after the American Civil War. Buchan
wrote before he knew that he would be chosen for the work, of 'the years of
work before us, only to be undertaken by responsible and serious men'.[6] He told
a friend, 'I feel it a great honour to be associated with a man I admire in so serious
and difficult a business'.[7]

His time in South Africa was also to be of great importance in Buchan's
later life. The body he now belonged to, Milner's 'kindergarten', a cohort of
able younger public administrators handpicked from their first job after leaving Oxford and sharing a powerful formative experience as Milner's assistants,
remained a force in public life long after Milner had left South African in 1905.[8]
This network was put to use again ten years later by the wartime Prime Minister,
David Lloyd George. Following Milner's appointment to the War Cabinet in
December 1916, several members, including Buchan as Director of Information
responsible for Britain's propaganda effort, secured important posts in the wartime administration. Buchan's experience in South Africa meant that he could
draft Haig's despatches from the Battle of the Somme in 1916 just as he had
drafted Milner's from South Africa a decade earlier.[9] He also discovered in himself an unexpected talent for handling practical information, what he called 'the
plain dealing with facts'.[10] This subsequently provided one of the most distinctive characteristics of his fiction.

Experience in South Africa above all informed Buchan's view of the future
of the British Empire. Many of Milner's younger supporters followed his lead
in hoping for closer political and economic unity for the Empire. But contact
with the independent-minded volunteers from the colonies and Dominions
during the war gave Buchan an inkling that this might not work. He came to see
the Empire instead as a coalition of independent parts united only by a shared
legal tradition, culture and language, with a common allegiance to the British
Crown.[11] As we shall see later, South Africa gave him an antipathy to racist attitudes which also fed into his position on the Empire. As was so often the case,

Buchan understood before many of his contemporaries the direction events would take.

Even at the time, Buchan's relations with the 'kindergarten' were not what they seemed to be. He had been recommended to Milner by Leopold Amery, another young journalist with a brilliant Oxford background. Amery had been Milner's first choice, but had undertaken a monumental multi-volume history of the South African War for his newspaper, *The Times*, and could not be spared. It seems clear that Milner was particularly keen to secure Buchan's services. He offered Buchan £1,200 a year (about £90,000 equivalent in terms of today's purchasing power), which was up to twice what he paid other 'kinder'.[12] Buchan's contacts in the world of political journalism were clearly part of the attraction. John St Loe Strachey, previously editor of the Liberal Unionist *Cornhill Magazine* and now editor and owner of the influential *Spectator*, gave Buchan a personal greeting to carry with him to South Africa pledging the support of the magazine for Milner's policies.[13] But political considerations, and appealing to opinion within the upper reaches of the Liberal Party, were also important to Milner. Buchan noticed on the day he arrived that Milner kept a signed photograph of Herbert Asquith's second wife, Margot, on a shelf beside his desk at Johannesberg.[14] Raymond Asquith, Herbert Asquith's eldest son by his first marriage, had been one of Buchan's closer friends at Oxford. Buchan also had connections through journalism with others on the imperialist wing of the Liberal Party, including the former Prime Minister, Lord Rosebery. Milner valued Buchan for his connections as well as his agility with a pen.

Throughout his time in South Africa, Buchan wrote fortnightly letters to Strachey at Milner's behest offering guidance on the editorial policy of the *Spectator* and seeking its support for Milner's policies. He also penned at least one poem which appeared anonymously in the magazine.[15] 'The Little Englander' was a gentle attack on what he regarded as woolly thinking by opponents on the left of the Liberal Party about Milner's reconstruction project:

> They stand deriding, while the sowers sow –
> Fain would they scatter tares the field to blight
> Yet when the reapers down the furrows go,
> They share the harvest in their own despite.
> No service high of heart and hand they brought
> These spacious courts enduringly to build,
> Yet shall they dwell therein with those that wrought,
> And wear a lustre which they never willed.[16]

Buchan's role as a propagandist for Milner's cause set him apart, but something else marked out his working relationship with Milner. They met most weeks, Milner's desk diaries containing such entries as 'In the afternoon I had Buchan in and did a lot of work with him. This went on 'til nearly dinner time'.[17] As a private secretary, Buchan helped to develop policies for Milner's consideration, drafted his despatches to the Colonial Office and corresponded in his name with senior officials in the administration. He also sifted through the High Commissioner's incoming correspondence and marked letters and memoranda for action. But he rarely attended meetings in which other members of Milner's inner circle were involved. His role was somehow separate and special. Among the people interviewed by Buchan's official biographer, Janet Adam Smith, for her book which appeared in 1965 was another of the 'kinder', Hugh Wyndham, who had been responsible in Milner's office for the affairs of the Orange River Colony.[18] He explained that Buchan's role had been a specific one:

> Milner had to do things in a hurry starting from scratch. John Buchan who had no qualifications at all for administrative work was very good at this extreme privacy improvising kind of work, he 'pushed things through' and 'got things done'. He was very quick at appreciating situations and making decisions. Milner gave him a free hand. But he 'left carcasses in his way'.[19]

Buchan's style as an administrator was ideally suited to situations under martial law when no questions were asked about what was done and why. But it would have made him unsuited for senior administrative posts in more settled times.[20] It is surely no coincidence that his only other substantive experience of public administration, as Director of Information during the First World War, occurred in very similar circumstances.[21]

Buchan was Milner's 'fixer', dealing with difficult operations characterized by political sensitivity bordering on constitutional impropriety. This is not a view of Buchan which many will recognize, but it is borne out by the official records in South Africa. It is well known that the topics Milner gave him to handle; the concentration camps, the immigration of new British settlers and repatriation of the Boers to their farms, were particularly challenging in terms of public relations.[22] What has been less apparent is the way these issues were managed together by Buchan in order to achieve Milner's political objectives.

In late 1901, with guerrilla activities abating and the end of the war in sight, Milner realized that the opportunity to plant British settlers in the occupied republics before the burghers returned to reclaim their land was fast disappearing.[23] In February or March 1902 Buchan was given charge of a clandestine operation employing a string of agents posing as private land dealers to buy up private land for settlement purposes. Information was collected during the last six months of the war on the state of farming in the Transvaal in order to identify where resources would be required to re-establish burghers on their land. This information was also used to identify vulnerable individuals whose land might be acquired for British settlers. Other land agents acting for private clients found their way into the camps, providing the necessary cover for Buchan's agents. Owners of the farms that Buchan identified were checked against the registers of burgher families in the concentration camps, and the agents were then instructed to visit the camps, posing as ordinary private land dealers, to make offers to the owners which would secure options for the government.[24]

The morality if not the legality of this operation was doubtful. With the threat in the air that the victorious British would simply confiscate land from their enemies, frightened burgher-owners, isolated in the camps, could easily be persuaded that any price was better than none. Senior officers in charge of the camps who became aware of what was going on tried to stop what they regarded as a common swindle. But they were told that the order to operate in this way had come from the top.[25] Milner was concerned that land prices would move against the government and the public exchequer would suffer if it became known that he was in the market. But the underlying impetus to the clandestine nature of the operation was political. As Buchan explained to the commandant of the camps in the Orange River Colony, the Boers would not sell to the British government on principle, and it was therefore necessary to forge an identity for the purchaser which eased the way.[26] Foreshadowing techniques used by Buchan in propaganda during the First World War, the land dealers he employed were themselves often unaware that they were acting on behalf of the government.[27]

Milner also applied to London to be given powers of compulsory purchase over agricultural land in the former republics. He told the Colonial Secretary, Joseph Chamberlain, in a despatch which Buchan is likely to have drafted, that 'if we lose the next year or two, we lose the game'.[28] On Milner's instructions Buchan wrote to St Loe Strachey advocating that compulsory purchase powers be given to the colonial authorities. There would be those, he said, who would 'scream confiscation and robbery', although it was 'important to keep telling people that this is a wise policy, a moderate policy and a paying policy ... If you can put it before people in the *Spec.*, Milner will be very grateful'. A leader in the magazine in November bore the marks of Buchan's briefings.[29] Buchan also personally wrote two substantial articles presenting the case for Milner's land policies which he placed anonymously with the help of friends in influential magazines in Britain. He insisted that their authorship should not be traceable back to him.[30]

Buchan also pursued on Milner's behalf a policy of taking back for use by incoming British settlers land in the former republics which had already been leased by their governments to Boer farmers. He drafted terms of reference for commissions appointed to examine land tenure arrangements in different parts of the Transvaal and oversaw their appointment. The threat that leases issued by the previous government might be cancelled was seen as a way to induce loyalty in the new regime.[31] Buchan considered that land should be reclaimed where its occupants paid negligible rents to the state or had done little to develop the land.

Loyalty in the recent conflict was another possible consideration. The Attorney General in the Transvaal Administration, Sir Richard Solomon, refused to play this game. He wrote to Buchan: 'I am quite prepared to go into court and justify the cancellation of any lease where there is direct evidence of the breach of a condition and the lease provides that it can be cancelled for such a breach ... A lease however cannot be cancelled merely because the rent charged by the late government is inadequate; there may have been reasons for making the rent low such as a desire on the part of the government to have the land occupied'.[32]

When the Treaty of Vereeniging, marking the end of the war, was signed on 31 May 1902, demobbed British soldiers descended on the offices of the Land Boards in Pretoria and Bloemfontein demanding the opportunity to settle in the country. Buchan was in the thick of it, buying more land, organizing settlement schemes on land already purchased near to railways, and pledging the government's credit for the supply of seed, agricultural implements and livestock which new settlers needed. In June 1902 he was appointed Acting Secretary of the Department of Lands, effectively its executive head, until a permanent appointment could be made. He travelled widely and frequently alone in the rural areas of the Transvaal examining land for purchase, visiting the Department's settlement schemes and meeting Boer farmers as well as new British settlers. Presumably for personal protection he was issued in May 1902 with two Mauser rifles and 500 rounds of ammunition.[33] He pictured himself to friends at this time as mixing with the lowlife of the settler frontier and thoroughly enjoying it. He wrote to one of them: 'I wish you could see me sitting daily surrounded by any variety of blackguards who want to make contact with me. I am getting a really first class judge of rascality'.[34] Buchan was given his head by Milner who had many other matters to attend to. 'I tried to avoid worrying Milner more than I could help'.[35] Among Buchan's closest associates was a group of colourful colonial characters whom he appointed as District Commissions to be the executive arm of the Land Department operating in the main centres across the Transvaal. Working closely with them, he guided the department during the first crucial months of post-war repatriation and settlement.[36]

When a permanent Commissioner of Lands was appointed in February 1903, Buchan reverted to the regular duties of a Private Secretary.[37] But it was from the period of his intimate involvement with land matters that he gathered the reputation to which Wyndham referred for cutting administrative corners and acting in a cavalier way with public money. In January a weighty complaint reached Milner from a local land company about the government's land policy. No name was attached to the catalogue of criticisms it contained, including the mistaken attempt to settle small farmers on land fit only to be exploited by large enterprises and profligate investment in land at inflated prices. But a reference to policy being 'the plaything of theorists and essay writers' suggests that Buchan was its real target.[38] His land dealings were said to have cost the government over £1,000,000.[39] When rumours of the accusations he faced reached his family in Scotland, he rebutted them indignantly.[40] He had tried to sort out the difficult financial situation he inherited; the government ultimately recouped much of the investment for which Buchan had been only temporarily responsible; and the accusations were levelled by people who had applied to him for jobs and been refused.[41] But Buchan came to epitomize the inexperience and naïvity of the young assistants, 'unbusiness-like, confiding and simple', whom Milner had set over the permanent civil servants in South Africa. Buchan was particularly singled out, 'now in a hole, now out, but always rushing and stumbling, and getting off the track and having to hack back', and blind to the way he was manipulated for financial gain by local interests.[42] It is notable that similar accusations marred the end of Buchan's time as Director of Information in the First World War.[43]

The venom behind the public criticism came as a shock, although it left Buchan in defiant mood. He wrote to his mother: 'I don't think after my experience here I shall ever be afraid of responsibility again'.[44] The atmosphere which now surrounded him surely played a part in his decision to leave South Africa before two years was up. Milner told Buchan that although he would be happy to keep him on his staff, it might be better in his own interest for him to return to his place at the Bar in the London.[45] Buchan told his sister he had set his sights on a 'higher administrative post', the route to which lay, he believed, through London.[46] On 28 July 1903, Milner had a final working lunch with Buchan at the office. A few days later, after a farewell dinner given in his honour by the trout fishermen at the Rand Club in Johannesburg, Buchan slipped quietly back to London.[47]

Prevailing racial attitudes in local white society may also have hastened his departure. Promoting agricultural settlement by British farmers had required Buchan to challenge the prevailing racial order of the day. In a pamphlet for new settlers, he wrote that owing to the shortages of African labour 'it is necessary for the average settler to be prepared to work himself'.[48] But the immigrants, working the land themselves, faced abuse from neighbouring farmers for not acting as white men should.[49] Buchan also encountered opposition in attempting to increase the British population in the towns. He supported a limited experiment to work a gold mine in Johannesburg with a higher proportion of white workers both above and below ground than was the norm. The experiment was discontinued prematurely in late 1903, and Buchan, by now back in London, wrote an eloquent editorial in the *Spectator* denouncing the self-interested racial policy which lay behind the decision: 'The mine owners are afraid of a rise of a great white industrial population which would make the labour element too strong a factor in economic questions, and when representative government is given in political questions.'[50] Buchan also opposed the scheme to import Chinese labour to restore the gold mines to full production, believing that employing whites on slightly higher wages would have better served the wider political purposes of 'Milnerism'.[51]

Relieved of his settlement responsibilities, Buchan turned in the last few months of his time in South Africa to wider questions, including the development of 'native policy'. In the debate within the administration about whether African societies should be required to follow a path of separate development, reflecting beliefs about the economic and social backwardness and 'childlike' mental state of 'the native', Buchan came down firmly in favour of integration. Travelling to the fringes of the Transvaal on land settlement business he had visited tribal locations and talked there to chiefs and to missionaries. He wrote to St Loe Strachey: 'The native is not nearly so unprogressive as people make out. If he is treated wisely, he has considerable capacity for progress ... He is a progressive farmer, more progressive a great deal than the Boer'. He felt particularly strongly about the labour tenancy system by which Africans in the former republics were given subsistence rights on white farms only on the basis that they worked for the farmer without cash payment. This enabled the white farmer 'to exact as much forced labour as he liked and turn them off at a moment's notice'.[52] In a collection of essays written while he was in South Africa and published shortly after his return, Buchan argued the case in terms of white self-interest:

> There are men ... who see no hope in the matter and who would segregate the native in a separate territory under British protection. The chief objection to this policy is that it is impossible. The native is in our midst, and we must face the facts ... If [the Africans] are a portion, however small, of the civic organism, there is hope for the future; but if they are a thing apart, denied the commonest of rights and remaining in their present stagnant condition, they will be a menace, political and moral, which no one can contemplate with equanimity'.[53]

Buchan was clear that in practical terms this meant promising political advancement in due course for Africans. He wrote to Strachey, who also held progressive views on racial matters: 'I thoroughly agree with you that we must do nothing to endanger the chance of the native progressing to equal political rights, as at present he enjoys equal legal rights'.[54] But he realized he was dealing not with reason but with blind prejudice among the white community in which he lived. 'It is impossible to realise the colour prejudice here. People listen to your arguments and even agree with them, but always add "I have my prejudice and nothing can shake it"'. He was equally impatient with the extreme idealism of white racial liberals who knew nothing of local realities. Moreover his own position was based, as he frankly admitted, 'not on the rights of the native but on the duties of the white man'.[55] But it seems unlikely that he could have become reconciled to what he saw and heard around him. In February 1903, he wrote to Strachey: 'The ordinary Johannesburger talks rubbish, abuses Exeter Hall [the Headquarters of the Anti-Slavery Society in London], and declaims about using a strong hand with those d—d niggers. You see I have gone frankly into opposition.'[56]

Perhaps partly as a result of the circumstances under which he left the country, Buchan subsequently had little direct involvement with South Africa affairs. He seems to have returned only once briefly to Cape Town on legal business in May 1905.[57] *The African Colony* (1903), in which Buchan gave a popular account of the reconstruction was his idea, though Milner blessed it as part of his propaganda duties.[58] His political work for pressure groups promoting the Empire in Britain drew on South African experiences, as did *A Lodge in the Wilderness*, which Buchan wrote to rescue Milner's ideas from the wreckage of his South African policy when British politics lurched to the left in January 1906.[59] But while continuing to write about Africa, Buchan located its problems and issues in British East Africa (now Kenya and Uganda), which he never visited, rather than South Africa which he knew well. It was as though he wanted to keep well clear of the situation from which he had made good his escape.[60] Buchan worked in 1904–5 on the outline of a work of fiction set partly in Africa. His notes for the unfinished work 'The Mountain' suggest that its first part was to be a theoretical exploration of the moral and practical dilemmas of imperialism. But the second part in which an African rising against European rule in Portuguese East Africa is defeated, leading to reconciliation between Black and White who coexist thereafter in peace and harmony, would have given him the opportunity to set out his own ideas on race.[61]

Buchan was well placed to accentuate the positive in Milner's reconstruction against its detractors, and did so in numerous reviews written anonymously for *The Spectator* and the *Times Literary Supplement*.[62] On racial issues, he developed his liberal position further, writing in a review of a book by a friend, Violet Markham, in 1913:

> Economic equalisation is needed, the entry of the white man into the ranks of unskilled labour and the entry of the native into the ranks of the skilled. Otherwise the whole labour problem in South Africa is involved in a vicious circle.[63]

He took a particular interest in the development of the Ethiopian Church in which black missionaries from Protestant churches in the United States were involved. This movement had already been identified as a danger to racial equilibrium when Buchan was on Milner's staff. When tribal unrest in Natal early in 1906 grew in to what became known as the Bambatha Rebellion, Buchan considered it to have been 'engineered by American negroes who mix up [with the legitimate aspiration of religious independence] certain political aims of which the ordinary Kaffir is perfectly innocent'.[64] The vulnerability to this sort of exploitation of Africans no longer subject to the disciplines of tribal society and as yet inadequately integrated into modern society was to Buchan another illustration of the need to prepare them to occupy a place 'in our social fabric'. He wrote in the *Spectator*:

> The decaying tribes will not be united by a military genius, but they may come together for a dangerous moment under the influence of some crazy faith. It is our duty to protect the uncivilised against the dangers of their status, and meanwhile to do all in our power to raise it.[65]

In 1909 Buchan took this as his theme for a book to strengthen the children's list of his employers, the Scottish publishers Thomas Nelson and Sons. The resulting novel, *Prester John* (1910), has been considered a founding text for Apartheid.[66] It seems to me very much to reflect the contrary view, which he highlighted in an approving review of a collection of essays by Olive Schreiner, the white South African novelist and campaigner for progressive causes, in 1921:

> We love freedom not only for ourselves, but we desire with a burning passion to spread it broadcast over the earth; to see every human being safeguarded by it and raised to the level at which they may enjoy it.[67]

Buchan's direct involvement with the South African War was slight. Yet the experience of it was to guide his thinking and actions for the rest of his life. Coping with irreconcilable political forces from a position of political weakness in South Africa turned out to be a seminal experience for the British political elite. It explained a pattern which repeated itself in various forms, in which they remained trapped for better or for worse through the long decline of empire for the next fifty years. Milner adapted to the situation in which he found himself with an autocratic and manipulative style of administration. His methods were characterized by the use of propaganda and information derived from espionage, often careless of whether or not it offended against political shibboleths. As an example, a decision had to be made on the treatment of Emily Hobhouse, the humanitarian campaigner who had revealed to the British public the shocking conditions in the concentration camps created during the war. When Hobhouse tried to land at Cape Town on a second visit to South Africa in October 1901, permission was refused. Buchan wrote to St Loe Strachey, 'Miss Hobhouse has been treated in the proper way, and returned home in the boat she came in as an "undesirable" in every sense of the word'.[68] In a letter from the ship, Mrs Hobhouse wrote in anger to Milner: 'Now I recognise the truth of one who told me you had "the Soul of a Spy". That is perhaps necessary in a despot'.[69]

 Buchan's formative experience with Milner in South Africa added to his make-up some small part of that same 'soul of a spy'. But what else did it contribute? Milner's influence on Buchan continued for twenty years more. They corresponded and met from time to time. After the First World War, Milner became chairman of a company Buchan created, Road-Rail Ltd, to develop and supply heavy tractors for land clearance and logging in the colonies.[70] Buchan continued to speak of him as 'my chief', and on Milner's death wrote to a friend, 'You know what it means when someone who has filled a big part of your life suddenly goes out of the world'.[71] Milner was vastly amused at a short story by Buchan, published in early 1910, 'A Lucid Interval'. The story concerns Liberal Ministers who under the influence of a drugged curry at a society dinner party abandon the principles of their party and favour, as Milner had done in 1904–5, the importing of Chinese labourers to work the mines of Africa.[72] Once the antidote is administered, the rampant idealism of their political creed returns and they become blind once again to the merits of empire. Milner wrote to Buchan: 'I think the satire is quite admirable, the idea most marvellous'.[73]

Arguing from facts and the rigorous pursuit of what was deemed a worthy end were what Buchan took from Milner. But there was also a significant difference between them. Buchan was much less of an autocrat and more willing than Milner to acknowledge the contribution of the 'popular voice' in politics.[74] He saw this in places where others didn't, among the contingents from the white dominions fighting for the British Empire in the South African War as well as among the Boers, and in African leaders he met in the backwoods of the Transvaal. When the 'free press' of Johannesburg was re-established in the six months after the end of the war, Milner was wary of its criticism of the process of reconstruction. In contrast Buchan welcomed the change as a step, not just towards greater freedom but also to better government. He wrote to Strachey, 'I cannot help thinking [it] is very natural and a not unwholesome thing – far better at any rate than official subservience'.[75] To political participation by Africans, Buchan also applied without fear or favour the principle of inclusion. He argued that 'the safety of the Commonwealth absolutely demands that no hatches be battened down over the heads of any part of the community'.[76]

In his own South African adventure Buchan felt the contrast between the ruthless pragmatism of Milner's tutelage and the more moral and inclusive approach derived from his own upbringing operating side by side. Their incompatibility, more personally uncomfortable than has generally been recognized, meant that Buchan would not stay in South Africa. The unease created by these unresolved conflicts also made him a less than whole-hearted party politician back in Britain. Armed with a testimonial from Milner, Buchan was adopted as a Conservative candidate in 1911, although he withdrew at the general election in 1918 when he would surely have won.[77] It was not until after Milner died in the mid-1920s that Buchan finally found a way to engage with party politics on his own terms. Yet the dualism of his South African experience was also a source of Buchan's strength. The two factors side by side were the foundation of his Conservatism in the 1920s and 1930s, and enabled him both to direct wartime

propaganda during the First World War and to emerge as one of the main strate-
gist of 'caring Conservatism' under Stanley Baldwin during the interwar years.
What Buchan learned as a young man from Lord Milner, both as exemplar and
foil, shaped the contribution he made to public life in his own time.

A longer version of this paper was presented to a seminar at the History Department of the University of Cape Town in July 2008.

7 JOHN BUCHAN AND THE FIRST WORLD WAR: FACT INTO FICTION

Hew Strachan

On 7 January 1917 the British prime minister, David Lloyd George, had a brief meeting with the new French commander-in-chief, Robert Nivelle. He was told of a plan to break through on the Western Front and achieve victory in forty-eight hours. John Buchan described the meeting at the Gare du Nord as decisive:

> Mr Lloyd George heard of Nivelle's plan – limitless objectives, the end of trench fighting, victory within two days – and naturally fell in love with it. [1]

Lloyd George had backed the wrong horse. The Nivelle offensive failed, and that summer half of the French army would be wracked by mutiny.

In 1933, Lloyd George had his revenge on Buchan's version of events:

> When a brilliant novelist assumes the unaccustomed rôle of a historian it is inevitable that he should now and again forget that he is no longer writing fiction, but that he is engaged on a literary enterprise whose narration is limited in its scope by the rigid bounds of fact ... Three fundamental inaccuracies in a single sentence are not a bad achievement even for a writer who has won fame by inventing his facts. The real explanation is that Mr Buchan found it so much less trouble to repeat War Office gossip than to read War Office documents. [2]

Lloyd George's accusations have, as was often the case, a mote and beam quality about them. His own account of the battle of Passchendaele was described by the official historian of the war as 'entirely fictitious'.[3] However, his response to Buchan's account of the Nivelle affair raises three important issues. Two – the relationship between Lloyd George and John Buchan, and the former's presumption that the latter had access to War Office documents – will be returned to later. The third is more immediate: the idea that John Buchan was a novelist posing as a historian. In 1933–6, when Lloyd George first published his memoirs, he was able to get away with that suggestion, but in 1914 that was less obviously the case. When the First World War broke out, Buchan was more clearly a man of affairs than a novelist. He had served as Alfred Milner's secretary in South Africa and he had stood for parliament in the 1911 elections. Moreover, he could reasonably claim to be a historian: his biography, *The Marquis of Montrose*, had been published in 1913.

Buchan was not yet a household name. The war made him one, and it did so in both capacities – as much as a historian as a novelist. When the war broke out, he was rising thirty-nine, almost too old for military service, and certainly not fit for it. While convalescing he worked on *The Thirty-Nine Steps*, which launched his most famous fictional character, Richard Hannay, and marked the evolution of the writing style which would make his reputation – what he called his 'shockers', fast in pace, and set clearly in the political context of the war. Published in September 1915, *The Thirty-Nine Steps* sold 33,000 copies in three months, and Hannay starred twice more in wartime thrillers – in *Greenmantle*, which sold 34,426 copies in 1916, the year of its publication (and sold even more, 50,409, in 1918), and *Mr Standfast*, written between July 1917 and July 1918, but not published until May 1919.[4]

By the time *The Thirty-Nine Steps* came out Buchan was already well known for a very different literary endeavour, *Nelson's History of the War*, the first volume of which had by then been in the bookshops for seven months. It would eventually extend to twenty-four volumes, each of 50,000 words, or 1.2 million words in all. This was Buchan's war work, and it was the project that ensured his position in the public eye and gave him an entrée to public affairs. He maintained a punishing writing schedule, sustaining it even after he collapsed with a duodenal ulcer in France in October 1916.[5]

Buchan was a private man, who revealed little of his own emotions in his writings, but it may not be fanciful to see here some effort to atone for his frustration at the fact that he could not himself serve as a frontline soldier.[6] Many of his closest friends did so, and many of them, including his youngest brother, were killed in action.[7] John Buchan did not fight but he often wrote as though he had – as though he knew at first hand what combat was all about. He came under fire on the Somme in 1916,[8] and in volume 12 of the *History*, which introduces the events of that year, he devoted a chapter to a discussion of military morale, entitled 'the breaking point in war'.[9]

Buchan's was the first major history of the war in English, written as the war progressed, its outcome uncertain, and its full details unknown. It does not stand academic scrutiny today, and it is easily, if wrongly, typecast as nationalist, patriotic propaganda. When Buchan himself looked back on his achievement in 1921 he compared himself with Thucydides, arguing that the contemporary historian is the greatest sort of historian:

With such a writer, writing in the surge of contemporary passions, and yet with an eye abstracted and ranging over a wide expanse of action and thought, no reconstruction of forgotten ages from books and archives can hope to lie. For the scholar in such a case competes with the creator, the writer of history with one who is also its maker.[10]

His advocacy grew in succeeding years. In 1923, he took on the editorship of a multi-volume history of the world, and his general introduction became a manifesto for a subject not yet deemed worthy of serious study by university history departments. His contributors, he declared

conceive history as a living thing of the most urgent consequence to the men of to-day; they regard the world around us as an organic growth dependent upon a long historic ancestry.

The First World War had itself contributed to that realization. It

brought the meaning of history home to the world. Events which befell long ago suddenly became disruptive forces to shatter a man's ease, and he realised that what had seemed only a phrase in the textbooks became a thing to die for.[11]

Buchan's approach to history was utilitarian and even a cursory glance at the *History* shows what that meant. He compared the events which he and others were passing through with their context; events in the past. He also looked for continuity in those past events, suggesting that humanity had found itself in similar situations and had therefore already devised ways of coping with them. The continuity of military doctrine, the notion of unchanging principles of war, was a case in point.

The success of the Nelson *History* was immediate. In May 1915 Buchan became one of five journalists attached to the British army, and found himself engaged in propaganda-related activities for the rest of the war. The timing of this step confirms the role of the war in enabling his 'arrival' as a literary figure. (When Charles Masterman had organized the War Propaganda Bureau at Wellington House in August 1914, he summoned the leading writers of the day to a conference, and Buchan had not been included.) In June 1916 Lord Newton of the Foreign Office News Department discussed with John Charteris, Haig's Director of Military Intelligence, the need for stories from the front to boost morale. Charteris, responsible for General Headquarters' relations with the press, was anxious to help, provided 'the boosters confine themselves to boosting what has happened and not what they hope may happen'. Newton offered him the assistance of 'a free-lance man from his own department', and on 28 June Buchan arrived at GHQ in France. Charteris told Buchan that 'he can do exactly as he wishes and go where he pleases', and, to aid him in his work, arranged that he should be commissioned into the Intelligence Corps.[12] Ironically, for all his lack of direct frontline service, Buchan would end the war as a colonel. In September he was given the task of preparing weekly communiqués on the fighting, while still continuing work on the Nelson *History* and completing two independent volumes on the battle of the Somme.

British propaganda in the hands of the Foreign Office was seen as too defensive, too cerebral and too divided in its structure. The Department of Information, responsible for propaganda at home and abroad, was created on 9 January 1917 and Buchan was appointed its director. He found himself working (in the words of F. S. Oliver) 'night and day in the interests of Great and Greater Britain with the assistance of Little Britain'.[13] But the criticisms continued, and indeed worsened. Buchan was not exempt from the sniping directed at the Department of Information: he was seen as too close to the Foreign Office, and not a true propagandist in the sense understood by the big-selling newspapers. Wearied by the attacks, and by the realization that journalists commanded the ear of the prime minister more than he did, Buchan sought the appointment of an independent minister responsible for propaganda. Lord Beaverbrook became Minister of Information on 10 February 1918. Buchan's role within the new ministry was Director of Intelligence, a post which he held to the end of the war. Unlike many others in the Lloyd George era, he received no honour for his war work.[14]

The central conundrum posed by Buchan's wartime activities is the one raised by Lloyd George in his memoirs: what was the relationship between Buchan the man of affairs, historian and propagandist, and Buchan the novelist? How far did fact, or knowledge of the facts, affect his fiction? How could a man commissioned in the Intelligence Corps, operating within the Foreign Office and then at General Headquarters, continue to be allowed to write thrillers that were so close to the truth, and that went to the heart of some of the central preoccupations of British wartime intelligence?

Both *Greenmantle* and *Mr Standfast* may appear to be fantasy, but both pivoted on threats that were with good reason regarded as potentially subversive of both Britain and its empire. In November 1914, the Ottoman Empire, prompted by Germany and exploiting its claim to the Caliphate, declared a holy war on Britain, France and Russia. As in *Greenmantle*, German agents actively promoted revolution in the Near East and North Africa. British spies were indeed trying to counter the very conspiracies which Richard Hannay too confronted.[15] More mysterious than John Buchan's familiarity with the world of spies is his knowledge of signals intelligence. A message in code is the launchpad for the story of *Greenmantle*, but Buchan gave no indication in his *The Battle of Jutland* that he knew the secrets of Room 40, that the Admiralty was reading the German naval codes, and that the clash of the two fleets was not the accident that his propaganda suggested. The same was still true of his revised and abbreviated edition of the Nelson *History* published in 1922. In 1927, Buchan's short story 'The Loathly Opposite' is tantalisingly suggestive because its first draft,

'The Post', was clearly written much earlier.[16] In the story, a 'hush' department in March 1918 breaks codes without any consideration of the eventual outcome in the field. Buchan explained the differences between codes and ciphers, the methods by which an enciphered message could 'locked and double-locked', and the challenges of decipherment. The parallels with Room 40 are evident, but the story is set on land, not at sea, the code that is broken is that linking Liman von Sanders, the German commander of the Ottoman forces in Palestine, and the German supreme command, and the decisive battle is Allenby's victory at Megiddo in September 1918.

Buchan may not have known this much during the war itself.[17] In his stories the battle is the pay-off: the fall of Erzurum to the Russians in 1916 in *Greenmantle*, and the defeat of the German spring offensives in 1918 in *Mr Standfast*. Like a general in battle, Buchan was a user of intelligence, not an agent or an analyst. There is no evidence that he was actually privy to its collection, and any intelligent and careful reader of *The Times* and the *Scotsman* could have gleaned the information on jihad contained in *Greenmantle*.[18]

Both *Greenmantle* and *Mr Standfast* show how propaganda and intelligence went hand in hand, how ideas could be spread and how counter-intelligence could prevent their dissemination. For Buchan the pay-off for intelligence was not on the battlefield, but in men's minds – those of the enemy, of neutrals and ultimately of one's own population. As he put it in the preface to his revised history of the war:

> In a contest of whole peoples psychology must be a matter of prime importance; mutations of opinions and the ups and downs of popular moods are themselves weighty historical facts, as much as a battle or a state paper.[19]

The bottom line was that both the Foreign Office and General Headquarters were prepared to let Buchan lead a double life, writing his *Nelson's History* and novels on the one hand, and being on the fringes of intelligence-related activity on the other. From late 1915, when Buchan was at the Foreign Office, he was effectively composing the *History* under official auspices as part of Britain's overseas propaganda effort. In 1916, after Buchan had moved to France, Charteris worried about this, arguing that 'critical words should not come from anyone who has access to such papers as we propose to show Buchan'. The Foreign Office refused to succumb to Charteris's pressure, and a deal was done, under which Buchan was able to continue with the *History*.[20]

Charteris, like the Foreign Office, shared Buchan's view that propaganda should be accurate and honest, and that that was the basis of trust between the communicator and the public. In early 1908 Buchan had used the pages of the *Scottish Review* to condemn what he called the new journalism: 'shrillness and wildness seem to be characteristics of too many leading articles, just as exaggeration is the chief feature of the news'.[21] He saw the sale of *The Times* 'to a manager who has hitherto been chiefly connected with halfpenny papers' as the end of 'the golden age of British journalism'.[22] That manager was Lord Northcliffe, who would be appointed head of the Department of Enemy Propaganda at Crewe House and made answerable directly to the prime minister.

In 1914, therefore, Buchan's approach to propaganda was not that of the popular newspapers but more akin to that of Wellington House or of the Foreign Office.[23] It should tell the truth; it should persuade through moderation and common sense; it should be directed at opinion-makers, and not at opinion itself. Its output was reflected in books and pamphlets more than in headlines and atrocity stories. By 1917 the war itself had evolved and so had the audience for propaganda. Now the target was less opinion-makers, more opinion itself; less in neutral countries like the United States, and more in belligerent states both at home and abroad. In March 1917 Buchan's mistake, according to his critics, was to judge Russia by its leadership and intelligentsia, not by the power of its masses. It was an experience from which he learnt. In May he wrote to the prime minister, stressing the need for what he called 'direct propaganda' in Britain itself. The result was the all-party National War Aims Committee, which organized public meetings throughout the country, designed 'to assist the country during the ensuing months of strain to resist influences of an unpatriotic character'.[24]

Buchan had confidence in the inherent good sense of the common people, but neither Buchan nor the National War Aims Committee was populist in the sense that Beaverbrook and Northcliffe were. For them the story mattered more than its veracity, its effect more than its content. Robert Donald of the *Daily Chronicle*, having castigated the Department of Information for its hesitancy about using uncorroborated and fanciful stories of German atrocities, was then tasked with reporting on the organization of propaganda.[25] Buchan and his ilk were affronted: they saw a significant difference between popular journalism and government propaganda. Writing in 1921, Buchan compared the popular newspapers in wartime with an eighteenth-century mob:

> they conceived violent admirations and violent dislikes; they were often sound in principle and wrong on the facts, sometimes correct on the facts and false in their deductions, rarely right in both; like the old mobs, too, when things went wrong they hunted perseveringly for scapegoats.[26]

But in 1918 they represented a media approach whose time had come.

Buchan's differences with both Beaverbrook and Northcliffe might have been mitigated by his politics. He, like they, was a Conservative – and even more a Unionist. Indeed Beaverbrook and Buchan seem to have cooperated well enough in 1918, but unfortunately for Buchan the principal driver in the direction of propaganda was Lloyd George. Buchan's dislike of Lloyd George was not just political. His real criticism was that the mobilization of Britain for war in 1915 had been botched, and for that Lloyd George took a large measure of responsibility. Buchan's portrait of Lloyd George in the section of the Nelson *History* praised the premier for his courage and energy, but warned that

> It remained to be seen whether this instinct for action was combined with an equal sagacity in counsel and prescience in judgment, for it is a rule of mortality that the considering brain and the active will are not commonly found together in the same being ... There was the risk that his fine ardour might be sometimes wasted through misdirection, and that paths might be chosen in haste which would have to be abandoned later.[27]

These judgements were sharpened in the post-war version of the history. There, Buchan praised Lloyd George for his rhetorical powers, but 'as an administrator he was indeed of small account, touching little of detail that he did not confuse'. In Buchan's view, Lloyd George could assimilate masses of information but not retain it. His vitality made him unconquerable, but 'his mind had nothing of the scientific in it, it was curiously insensitive to guiding principles, and each intellectual act was a new and unrelated effort'.[28]

Lloyd George, for his part, saw Buchan as the mouthpiece not only of Unionism but even more of Haig's General Headquarters, where he had spent so much time in 1915 and 1916. This was not unreasonable. Buchan and Haig were not only both Scots and devout members of the Kirk, they had both been to Brasenose College, Oxford, and they had got to know each other in South Africa. Haig felt that he could trust Buchan.[29] In *Mr Standfast* Richard Hannay finds himself caught up in the German spring offensives of 1918, and is summoned to GHQ, where he has 'half an hour's talk with the greatest British commander'. Hannay goes on:

> I can see yet his patient, kindly face and that steady eye which no vicissitude of fortune could perturb. He took the biggest view, for he was statesman as well as soldier, and knew that the whole world was one battlefield and every man and woman among the combatant nations was in the battle-line. So contradictory is human nature that talk made me wish for a moment to stay where I was. I wanted to go on serving under that man.[30]

Even those who are ready to argue Haig's stronger points probably cannot recognize him from that description, and Buchan did not give the general of the novel a surname. Nothing in the *History* approached this panegyric: in it Buchan could be more critical. He described the third Battle of Ypres as 'strategically a British failure': 'We did not come within measurable distance of our major purpose'.[31] But he blamed the weather, not the generals. 'It would ill become an

Officer attached to Headquarters Staff', he had written in December 1916, 'to criticise or to praise Generals in the field.'[32]

Buchan became one of Haig's most dogged defenders. In 1935 Buchan was invited to write a volume to mark the silver jubilee of the accession of George V to the throne and he asked Basil Liddell Hart to comment on the section of the book which described the war. Liddell Hart's responses contain his most developed and sophisticated criticism of Haig, and drew from Buchan his fullest defence. Buchan acknowledged that he was driven by personal acquaintance, by common institutional affiliations and by the harshness of the posthumous criticism which prompted 'defiant eulogy' in response. But the key issue for Buchan was the tension between Haig's character and his military professionalism, and the struggle of the former to assert itself over the latter:

> I am ready to admit every kind of fault and imperfection, but he seemed to me to have a real greatness of character, which practically nobody else of the time possessed, and he had a power of grasping, in the end, simple truths, and holding to them tenaciously which was the quality most needed for the particular situation.[33]

Although he wrote biographies of great commanders, including Caesar, Montrose and Cromwell, Buchan's war writing was not really populated by generals. Its heroes, particularly in his fiction, are the men of his own age, for whom the war offered challenge and fast promotion, ending, like Richard Hannay, as brigadiers. In *The Dancing Floor*, published in 1926, Leithen's nephew Charles explains why Vernon Milburne had not been promoted:

> He was a first-class battalion officer but he wasn't a first-class soldier. The trouble with him, as I say, is that he wasn't interested in the war. He had no initiative, you understand – always seemed to be thinking about something else. It's like Rugby football. A man can be a fine player according to the rules, but unless his heart is in the business and he can think out new tactics for himself he won't be a great player.[34]

This was Buchan as a Tory interpreter of history: he believed that history was contingent, that an individual could shift its course in reality as much as in fiction. Also implicit in Buchan's interpretation of war history were war memories. In *The Dancing Floor* (1926), Leithen declares:

> There has been a good deal of nonsense talked about the horror of war memories and the passionate desire to bury them. The vocal people were apt to be damaged sensitives, who were scarcely typical of the average man. There were horrors enough, God knows, but in most people's recollections these were overlaid by the fierce interest and excitement, even by the comedy of it.[35]

For Buchan, this was not just fiction. Peter Pienaar, the crippled South African big-game hunter turned pilot, who saves the day in March 1918 in *Mr Standfast* but is killed in the process, had a real counterpart in Auberon Herbert, Lord

Lucas. Bron Lucas had had a leg amputated below the knee in the South African War, nonetheless served in the Royal Flying Corps in the First World War, and was killed over the Somme in November 1916: 'Up in the clouds', Buchan opined, 'he had come to his own and discovered life'.[36] In part this was the cliché of willing sacrifice. Alastair Buchan wrote home just before his death, 'These last two years have been the happiest of my life'.[37] But it went further. When in 1920 Buchan wrote *These for Remembrance*, a volume to commemorate six friends killed in the war, and *Francis and Riversdale Grenfell*, he told their stories so that their deaths in action became the high points of their lives.

After the war, Buchan's characters generally suffer from *ennui*, not from post-traumatic stress disorder. In *A Prince of the Captivity* (1933) the war has created a 'big problem ... for the world [which] is not economic but psychological – how to get men's minds on an even keel again'. Buchan is at pains to stress that he is not talking about shellshock: the case of a Dorset postman is cited, who 'had four of the most hellish years that ever fell to the lot of man – Gallipoli and France – blown-up, buried, dysentery, trench fever, and most varieties of wounds', but contentedly returned to his peacetime job. It is concluded that 'it is not the people who had the roughest time that are the most unsettled', but (by implication) those who continue to need a sense of purpose comparable with that created by the war. 'The brotherhood of the trenches', which is acknowledged to be 'a silly, rhetorical phrase', nonetheless reflects a truth, that 'people who went through the same beastliness together did acquire a sort of common feeling'.[38]

Readers of Buchan's novels, looking at characters such as Archie Roylance and Adam Melfort, who, like Buchan, took their holidays on Scottish sporting estates, compare them with Buchan's real-life friends, the Grenfells, Asquiths and Grosvenors (his wife's family), and conclude that Buchan, a son of the manse from comparatively humble origins, had lost himself in the world of Eton, Oxford and London clubs. More humble individuals who served in the ranks have, at best, walk-on parts in the novels. But Buchan was at pains to refute such assumptions. Throughout the novels the British working man remains potentially decent, loyal and sensible, and the classes more united in mutual respect than divided by political difference. For him, the war has made this vision more immediately realizable, not less. In *A Prince of the Captivity*, Joe Utlaw, trade union leader, member of the Labour party, and a wounded veteran of the western front, describes how the gentry has been changed by the war: 'Their fathers were shy of the working man apart from their own folk, for they knew nothing about him, but this generation has lived four years with him in the trenches, and inclined to make a pal of him'.[39]

Again the fiction is in step with the facts as Buchan saw them. Buchan's repeated refrain as a historian was that the war had been won by the rank and file. His peroration to the 1922 revision of the Nelson *History* ends both with a tribute and with optimism:

> The war was a vindication of the essential greatness of our common nature, for victory was won less by genius in the few than by faithfulness in the many. Every class had its share, and the plain man, born in these latter days of doubt and divided purpose, marched to heights of the heroic unsurpassed in simpler ages. In this revelation democracy found its final justification and civilization its truest hope.[40]

Before the war, in 1907, Buchan had criticized the plans of R. B. Haldane, the secretary of state for war, to create a voluntarily enlisted Territorial Force, as being either too much if Britain were secure from invasion or too little if it were not. He favoured the proposals of the National Service League, which called for compulsory military training in peacetime, and argued that 'In a great war it is the nation that fights, not the army and navy'.[41] Arriving at the front in May 1915, he 'learned that we now had a homogeneous army, in which it was hard to say that one part was better than another'. What followed was a paean to the 'nation that fights':

> The miners of South Wales and North England, the hinds and mechanics of the Scottish Lowlands, the shepherds and gillies of the Highlands, the clerks and shop-boys of London and the provincial cities, were alike in their fighting value. They were led, and often brilliantly led, by men who a little time before had been merchants, and solicitors, and architects.[42]

For Buchan the changes war had wrought were particularly marked for Scots, and especially for his beloved Borderers. The English pastoral tradition, reflected both in so much war poetry and in the idealized rural landscape which recruiting posters suggested that Britain's armies were called to defend, was adapted by Buchan to the hills and burns of the Southern Uplands.

In his short story, 'The King of Ypres', first published during the war in *Allied News*, Buchan made a hero of one of these Scottish private soldiers. It tells the tale of Peter Galbraith, left behind in Ypres when it is abandoned by the British (which they never did). Galbraith modestly saves the day, imposing order, preventing looting, and so sustaining the honour of the army. He is the reliable Tommy, honest and sensible, without pretension, the heir to Rudyard Kipling's 'Soldiers Three'. Even more powerful, and intensely moving, is Buchan's portrayal of the private soldier in his war poetry. Here Borderers dominate, and here too is his most graphic acknowledgement of the horrors of trench warfare:

> For sax weeks hunkerin' in a hole
> We'd kenned the warst a man can thole –
> Nae skirlin' dash frae goal to goal
>   Yellin' like wud,

> But the lang stell that wechts the soul
>   And tooms the bluid.[43]

A soldier writing from his billet to a friend who is in the trenches, tells him that what they are fighting for is not love of nation, defined in terms of patriotism, but love of community, expressed through home and hearth:

> What gaurs us fecht? It's no' the law,
> Nor poaliticians in a raw
> Nor hate o' folk we never saw; -
> Oot in yon hell
> I've killed a wheen – the job wad staw
> Auld Hornie's sel'.
> It's luve, my man, nae less and nae mair, –
> Luve o'auld freends at kirk and fair,
> Auld-farrant sangs that memories bear
> O' but and ben,
> Some wee cot-hoose far up the muir
> Or doun the glen.[44]

Current scholarship endorses the idea that morale at the front was linked to, not separate from, thoughts of home. Citizen soldiers fought in the First World War to protect their families and friends, and longed to return to them; leave and mail were the high points that sustained these links. But could that be all that gave the war meaning? Did Buchan himself really believe that these men were not fighting for the rule of law or in pursuit of policy? The answer is clearly no.

Before the war Buchan had been firm about two issues in international relations. The first was that civilization is constantly under threat, and its continuation, growth and development were not axiomatic. The second was that right-thinking men had to be ready to fight for it. At the individual level, the barrier between the conscious, rational mind and the irrational subconscious figured in his earliest fiction and would come increasingly to preoccupy him in his post-war novels.

Buchan's belief that civilization had to be defended, that it would not survive as of right, meant that he saw war as vital to international order.[45] The outbreak of the First World War confirmed Buchan in his way of seeing the world, and from the outset he saw the conflict as one waged for ideas. Those of the nineteenth century were in decline; in their stead were what he called 'Americanism', a 'craze for luxury', and its opposite, socialism, which appealed to the dispossessed. Both these competing value systems of the twentieth century were materialistic, seeking to 'to master the world's wealth rather than to regenerate the world's spirit'.[46] Germany had recognized these problems but had then drawn conclusions that were irrational and barbaric. Buchan acknowledged the need for Germany, like other nations, to seek a way out of the spiritual malaise of the twentieth century.

He was ready to condone the claims of military necessity as exhibited by the advance into Belgium and northern France in 1914; but he did not accept the use of terror as an instrument of war. 'Civilized war', he wrote, 'respects the non-combatants ... But this was not civilized war'. Belgium made clear why Britain was in the war:

> To massacre a hundred unarmed people because a man fired off a rifle may be enjoined by some half-witted military theorist, but it is fundamentally inhuman and silly. It offends against not only the heart of mankind, but against their common sense. It is not even virilely wicked. It lacks intelligence. It is merely childish.[47]

Germany's sin therefore was not barbarism; it was that having been civilized it became de-civilized. The challenge that confronted Britain in the war was to respond to Germany without itself becoming de-civilized, to counter Prussia without itself becoming Prussian. Buchan was clear that that was possible. In part it was a task for individuals, men like Hannay who fought as sportsmen, honouring the code of fair play. It was a more profound challenge for the state, which had to find a balance between its collective needs in war and its protection of individual freedoms.

The principle to which Buchan remained loyal throughout the war was that it was being waged to defend civilization, by which he 'meant especially the rule of law which gave us freedom to possess our souls'.[48] As the war ended he warned against the dangers of disillusionment in its aftermath. Defeating Prussianism in the field would not itself create 'security for free development'. Peace would not follow automatically from victory but had itself to be worked for: 'It is itself a construction'.[49] In the post-war world, the League of Nations would replace the British Empire as the international agency committed to the maintenance of law and civilization. The League's cornerstone, as Buchan put it in *The Island of Sheep* (1919),[50] would not be blind universalism, but a recognition of independent, robust nations working together.[51]

The continuity that the shift from British empire to American-sponsored League suggests underestimates the impact of the war on Buchan. His life had been irrevocably altered, and he knew that that was true of all those who had participated in it. He also mourned. He felt the loss of his friends: 'each of us has seen his crowded circle become like the stalls of an unpopular play'. He was an early adherent to the idea of the lost generation, that those who were killed were the best and the brightest, 'the flower of their race, the straightest of limb, the keenest of brain, the most eager of spirit'.[52] But, like others in the 1930s, he found the memories hard to dismiss, as Hitler renewed the German threat to civilization, as the League of Nations failed, and then a Second World War broke out. By Christmas 1939, Buchan's three sons were in uniform, and he was writing his last novel, *Sick Heart River* (1941). In it his *alter ego*, Sir Edward Leithen, suffers from terminal tuberculosis, brought on or exacerbated by the effects of being gassed in the previous war. He sets off on a mission in northern Canada, and there hears the news of the war's outbreak. He clothes the Second World War in the 'dimly remembered terrors' of the First:

> Men shot in the stomach and writhing in no man's land; scarecrows that once were human crucified on the barbed wire and bleached by wind and sun; the shamble of a casualty clearing station after a battle.

Memories of 'waste, futile waste, and death, illimitable, futile death' swamp Leithen, as they swamped Buchan: 'Now the same devilment was unloosed again'.[53]

The accusation which Lloyd George levelled against Buchan in his war memoirs was founded on a false premise. For Buchan, fact and fiction were not alternatives, but part of a continuum. His novels were vehicles for his ideas and beliefs, a way of propagating values that he thought important through heroes who were often based on real people. What really divided Lloyd George from Buchan was their different understandings of propaganda. Lloyd George and those whom he appointed to run the propaganda agencies in 1918 saw propaganda as a form of popular journalism; Buchan saw it as a form of truth-telling. Of course he recognized that confidential information should be censored in wartime; of course he appreciated that criticisms which might be legitimately voiced after the war was over had to be silenced while the struggle was in hand. But if the war was a struggle to defend civilization, waged by democracies, then the people on whose behalf it was being fought, and who were bearing the brunt of the fighting, had the right to be apprised of the facts, not fired by unsubstantiated rumour or half-baked opinion. Buchan was accused of speaking to those who shaped public opinion, not to the public itself, but he himself felt that 'he could confide implicitly in the mass of my own people'.[54] To mislead them, to spin fiction posing as fact, was the way to undermine civilization, not to protect it.

Acknowledgements

This chapter began life as a lecture given at a conference on 'Scottish writers and the First World War', held at the University of Glasgow on 11 September 2004; it has also had airings at a meeting of the Historical Association in Oxford on 23 January 2007 and at the annual conference of the John Buchan Society at Brasenose College, Oxford on 24 March 2007. I am grateful for the comments and suggestions I received on all three occasions. Thanks are also due to Dr William Buckingham, whose research on my behalf in the papers of the National Library of Scotland was funded by the Oxford History Faculty. Dr Jim Beach provided me with references covering Buchan's time at General Headquarters in 1916. A much fuller version has been published in *War in History*, 16:3 (2009), pp. 298–324.

8 BUCHAN AND THE PACIFISTS

Nathan Waddell

A key moment in *Mr Standfast* (1919) is the death of Launcelot Wake, a conscientious objector and committed pacifist. Having belatedly signed up as a
non-combatant, Wake's service in a Labour battalion and the Italian Red Cross
pales in comparison to the gallant, patriotic and voluntary act that kills him:
carrying a vital communiqué through enemy fire to prevent a German flank-
ing move at the Battle of Amiens. Despite Wake's heroics, and the ravaging of
his body, his devotion to pacifism stays unrepentantly *intact*: 'Funny thing life.
A year ago I was preaching peace ... I'm still preaching it ... I'm not sorry.'[1] By
presenting pacifism in this way Buchan ensures that it retains an important
otherness which would have been suppressed if he had made Wake shuck his
principles for the aristo-military values against which he is defined. Wake contributes to the war effort but doesn't have to abandon his principles, a loyalty
textually approved by Hannay's reading of events: 'I had never had his troubles
to face, but he had come clean through them, and reached a courage which was
for ever beyond me'.[2]

Mr Standfast marks a key shift in Buchan's views on pacifism. Before the
First World War Buchan had been highly critical of anti-war sentiment, rejecting it in 'Count Tolstoi [*sic*] and the Idealism of War' (1904) as a threat to social
pluralism and as fundamentally unrealistic as politics. His position gradually
moderated, however, after the first Military Service Act, which legislated conscription for most men aged between eighteen and forty-one, was introduced in
January 1916.[3] By 1919, as we will see, Buchan could provide a more detailed critique of pacifism, and he was sympathetic to the sufferings of individual pacifists
and pacifist groups that he felt had been victimized. *Mr Standfast* clearly states
this refined perspective: with its descriptions of Biggleswick, Red Clydeside
and Wake it highlights the diversity of pacifist politics and shows the numerous
spaces that generate them. It refuses the typecasting of objectors as degenerates
by portraying them as complex selves motivated by disparate psychologies;[4] and
if it does not assent to pacifist values it holds a somewhat equivalent view to
Herbert Asquith's claim that non-combatants could bear responsibilities that

exposed them 'to the very same risks as those who go into the trenches to man the guns and use the rifles'.[5] This last point is made emphatically by dint of Wake's flank-running job: 'He knew nothing of military affairs before,' Hannay says, 'but he got the hang of this rough-and-tumble fighting as if he had been born for it. He never fired a shot; he carried no arms; the only weapons he used were his brains. And they were the best conceivable'.[6]

In this chapter I will clarify what I think is Buchan's genuinely significant response to pacifism and explore how *Mr Standfast* problematically features in the dual perspective that that response implies: a basic disagreement with paci- fist *philosophy* and a sympathy towards certain pacifist *individuals*. My discussion moves from Buchan's quarrel with anti-war sentiment to an examination of his symbolic depiction of Wake, and is split into four sections. I explore Buchan's critique of Tolstoyan pacifism and set it alongside William James's account of conflict ethics; I reconstruct Buchan's reactions to pacifism and objectors in his non-fictional First World War writings; I compare and contrast the varieties of pacifism to which Buchan alludes in *Mr Standfast*; and I survey the ambiguous senses in which Wake represents the pacifist cause. Although Wake has variously been read by critics as a heroic, individualist or otherwise alternative figure whose specificity denies wartime stereotyping, what unites these readings is a question- ing faith in the figurative scaffold that underpins Wake himself.[7] This chapter concludes by suggesting that Wake cannot be read accurately without reference to a textual conflict between the form and content of his characterization.

From Russia with Love

Buchan's antipathy towards pacifism is inseparable from his thinking about conflict. In 'Count Tolstoi and the Idealism of War' Buchan criticized Tolstoy's idealist rejection of war and violence as engines of change and his notion that absolute love (*agapē*) signifies a cure for a belligerent modernity.[8] Buchan's objections were several: he accused Tolstoy of a naïve optimism that neglected contemporary realities; he opposed the view that war could be eliminated by appeals to a universal spiritual morality, finding in Tolstoy a potentially ruinous apathy; and he insisted that this denunciation of war rested upon a material- ism solely contrived to alleviate psychological and physical torment. Buchan claimed: 'Pain, on this theory, is the one great evil; to avoid pain any sacrifice of honour, self-respect, and wholesome ambition is justifiable. It is a repulsive doctrine when set down explicitly in words, but it underlies much of the so- called "humanity" of the apostles of peace'.[9] Whether Buchan was justified in his objections, especially on the count of apathy, is a moot point, but it is from these perspectives that his wartime attack on pacifism emerges.[10]

Buchan countered Tolstoy's idealism by suggesting that conflict contains its own ennobling qualities, and he claimed that the fitting way to conceptualize warfare is not through the language of atrocity but 'to emphasise the spiritual and idealist element which it contains'.[11] Buchan stressed that war accentuates human dignity (shades of Ruskin) by highlighting mankind's capacity for self-sacrifice on behalf of non-material values. He argued that 'to prohibit men to fight for a cause in which they believe – that is, to devote to it their most valuable possessions, their lives – is to strike at the root of faith', and to deny this fight 'between the real and the ideal' is 'to cast doubt upon the highest instinct of our mortal nature'.[12] William James admitted rather ambiguously, in a variant of this argument, that 'so far as the central essence of this feeling goes, no healthy minded person, it seems to me, can help to some degree partaking of it', and he decried the supposed 'absolute good' he felt customarily had been attributed to such a view, in which 'the militarily patriotic and romantic-minded everywhere, and especially the professional military class, refuse to admit for a moment that war may be a transitory phenomenon in social evolution'.[13]

Even if Buchan's argument roughly equates to James's view that 'militarist authors' defend war as 'a biological or sociological necessity', it would be inadvisable to claim a congruency between them here.[14] Although Buchan notes that the idealism of war is 'rooted in the foundations of human nature',[15] and so argues that pacifist attempts to eradicate war *debase* that humanity,[16] neither caveat necessitates that his views are ahistorical.[17] Indeed, Buchan admits that wars may cease if and when ideals become non-significant, but he chose to emphasize that 'while they are living creeds to their followers war is inevitable'.[18] Buchan contended that what matters is what *kind* of war one means. Wars waged for, say, seventeenth-century Republicanism received Buchan's approval, as they represented 'battles not of the flesh but of the spirit', while wars fought for base interests (greed, plunder) signified ignominy.[19] Buchan acknowledged the trouble in determining which side in such conflicts fought righteously, if such determinations are in fact possible, and he noted that 'common ideals held with a difference are, unhappily, as strong disruptive forces as clear opposites'.[20]

Buchan's vision is essentially pluralist, and it contends that while difference exists interested selves will necessarily fall into conflict.[21] He maintained that a pacifism like Tolstoy's aimed for peace at the cost of variation across cultures and between moral selves, and he refused to permit an outlook which silenced difference by appeasement: 'The truth of the matter is that until nationality and national ideals are abolished, and all the races and States are fused into one, to make war impossible you must destroy, not the baser desires of man, but his essential idealism'.[22] While this indicates that Buchan was neither indifferent to the precariousness of a passionate, multi-ideological world, nor that he was uninterested in efforts to defend humankind from global hostilities, it emphasizes the centrality of variation within Buchan's thinking, a mindset convinced that a monochrome humanity symbolized nothing less than a victorious decadence.[23]

Resisting the Machine

Germany's ambitions during the First World War intensified these concerns. While Buchan was no crude Germanophobe, and carefully distinguished between Germany's Establishment and its citizenry, Andrew Bonar Law's claim that 'blinded by Imperialistic visions of success, by *Realpolitik*, the great German people have turned their *Kultur*, sciences and economic organization into instruments of wrong, crime, and ruthless disregard of common morality and Christianity' is fairly indicative of Buchan's attitude towards a nation which, he thought, had succumbed to ruling-class demagoguery.[24] His speech for Francis Younghusband's 'Fight for Right' campaign in December 1915 (published in 1916 as *The Purpose of War*) attacked German expansionism, militarism, and race pride, and rejected Germany's coldness towards the ideals of other nations and its conquest-lust, which Buchan attributed to a vulgar materialism. Likewise, in *Greenmantle* (1916) Hannay sees Germany as a 'monstrous bloody Juggernaut that was crushing the life out of the little heroic nations', and Sandy Arbuthnot fears a neurotic industrial machine intolerant of difference aiming to 'destroy and simplify' by reducing 'all the contrivances of civilisation to a featureless monotony'.[25]

In *The Purpose of War* Buchan outlines two kinds of men: those who will resist such an enemy and the 'intellectuals' for whom 'there is nothing in the world worth fighting for, nothing certainly worth the risk of pain and death'.[26] It is hard to miss the links here with Buchan's critique of Tolstoy, but even if his sympathies at this point overwhelmingly sided with soldiers and those willing to actively resist the violations of *Machtpolitik*, he was critical of how their resistance was institutionally organized. Although he backed National Service and conscription, in his *Nelson's History of the War* (1915–19) he condemned the turmoil that preceded the authorization of enforced enlistment in 1916, regarded industrial compulsion (a key issue in *Mr Standfast*) as 'neither more nor less than a vicious type of class legislation', and slated Lord Derby's 1915 recruitment drives, the machinery of which he saw as 'that familiar under conscription, save that it was a little more cumbrous and lacked the driving power of legal compulsion'.[27] Moreover, he criticized on two grounds the protracted setting-up of an impartial conscription of all men of appropriate age: he argued that the delay had been another element in the wearying of the national spirit; and for Buchan this reflected a misalignment between the desires of the populace and those supposedly representing their interests: 'Had the rulers been a little closer to the nation many heart-breaking delays would have been saved, and much needless waste in money and men'.[28]

Indeed, Buchan took the relatively unusual step of suggesting that the problems caused by the status of married men in Derby's proposals eclipsed those caused by conscientious objection.[29] But he remained a sceptic. He avowed that the stance of 'that typical British product, the conscientious objector' was logically impossible: 'He claimed the rights and declined the most urgent duty of citizenship'.[30] In this view, objectors were mistaken not only because they urged a double standard but also because they misread the extent to which Germany could be reconciled. They protested against a war organized on Germany's part to assimilate other nations and yet invoked those values that were so endangered to justify their dissent. Nevertheless, Buchan accepted that most objectors were sincere protestors. As he noted, 'it was no easy task to riddle out from such claimants the *bonâ fide* objectors and the charlatans', but he remembered the process as 'performed on the whole with tact and fairness'.[31] Hindsight has shown this to be a distortion of the sufferings experienced by objectors during this period, but it does indicate that by 1916 Buchan had a more refined overview of the relationship between pacifists and their society than that evidenced by his earlier writings, one that would become, in turn, far more perceptive.[32]

As the War progressed Buchan revealed himself as an insistent localist with regard to conscription. Although he disagreed with the varied reasoning of the pacifists against an enforced mobilization of the nation's manhood, he did not unthinkingly valorize the soldier's life. Discussing the War Office tribunals in 1917, Buchan argued that the notionally sound theory of sending every man fit enough to fight to the Front, unless his particular capacities could be better employed at home, ran aground due to an insufficiently precise application of its own precepts. '[T]he word "fit" was far too loosely construed: men were drafted into the line who retired to hospital after the first week of service, and thereby increased the cost of our army without adding one atom to its strength.'[33] Buchan was also in tune with the pacifist Fenner Brockway, who contended that Britain's provisions for war had created an automated society of 'efficient machines for industrial and military purposes'.[34] One of Buchan's recurring tropes in describing the First World War is 'mechanization', and in his autobiography he depicts his own involvement in the War as that of 'a minor cog ... in the operations of a huge impersonal machine which seemed to move with little intelligent purpose'.[35]

Buchan had shown himself as not unconcerned with the afflictions of those against military service. He contributed to the group effort to grant Jacob Epstein immunity from conscription, organized by the sculptor's wife Margaret, which succeeded in obtaining several passing deferments, and Buchan was also involved in Epstein's attempts to have his status upgraded to that of a War Artist immediately before his call-up in September 1917.[36] A year later Buchan co-signed a letter written by the No-Conscription Fellowship to the Prime Minister demanding the release of the remaining 1,500 conscientious objectors who had yet to be released from prison.[37] In both cases it is clear that if Buchan could not accept pacifism *qua* pacifism, he was responsive to the sufferings of *individual* pacifists whom he felt had been needlessly wronged.

Garden Cities, the Shapeshifter and Glaswegian Dissidents

The local aspects of pacifism, and the specific politics of its representatives, are important features of *Mr Standfast*. Like Rose Macaulay, who criticized the tendency to lump pacifists 'together in masses and groups, setting one group against another, when really people are individual temperaments and brains and souls, and unclassifiable', Buchan used precision.[38] In the opening chapter of *Mr Standfast* Hannay discusses the armchair critics of the War after encountering an old man 'who, if he had been under fifty, would have crawled on his belly to his tribunal to get exempted, but being over age was able to pose as a patriot'.[39] In chapter 2 Hannay enumerates an assortment of objectors, from the son of the Weekes family, 'who had refused to do any sort of work whatever, and had got quodded [imprisoned] for his pains', to the intellectual Letchford, who, if Britain had avoided war, 'would have been a raving militarist, but since she was in it he had got to find reasons why she was wrong'.[40] As Hannay notes, 'they shut out the war from their lives, some out of funk, some out of pure levity of mind, and some because they were really convinced that the thing was all wrong'.[41]

Pacifists in *Mr Standfast* are socialist critics of a beleaguered Liberal state, the least threatening of whom live in the garden city community at Biggleswick (most probably based on Letchworth in Hertfordshire, founded in 1903).[42] An article in *The Race-Builder* suggested that 'the revolutionist may regard [Letchworth] as a last ditch for the hard-pressed forces of capitalism, but the evolutionists should surely see in it an effort to find a way out of the competitive chaos towards a well-ordered society'.[43] Biggleswick represents a similar convergence of the utopian-minded. Ursula Jimson, though chided by her husband Tancred for her dismissive attitude towards the European situation, and in what is possibly a hostile reference to D. H. Lawrence's *The Rainbow* (1915), describes the War as '"a remote and secondary affair"' compared to '"the great fights of the world"' which are '"fought in the mind"'.[44] Biggleswick ignores the War except insofar as it offers a haunt for pacifists, and is populated by corpulent greenhorns and those dabbling in the 'new' who are prone to describing themselves through the images of post-Impressionism. The key exception here is Wake, who, although not a Biggleswickian himself, visits to speak 'at Moot': 'He was jolly good at the job', Hannay says, 'and put up as clear an argument as a first-class lawyer'.[45] But overall, for Hannay spiritual pride and vanity 'were at the bottom of most of them, and, try as I might, I could find nothing very dangerous in it all' – although he is enraged by the jejune grumblings of the inhabitants, he 'found it impossible to be angry with them for long, they were so babyishly innocent'.[46]

Biggleswick indicates a fear that greater dangers than its speculatively anarchist residents might be smuggled in beneath its harmless façade. The first danger is Moxon Ivery, who immediately looms above his fellow pacifists in Hannay's eyes by virtue of his silver tongue: 'He had a sort of man-of-the-world manner, treating his opponents with condescending geniality, deprecating all passion and exaggeration, and making you feel that his urbane statement must be right, for if he had wanted he could have put the case so much higher'.[47] Not only is Ivery not the genuine article (he is, we discover, Hannay's old foe, the German spymaster Graf Otto von Schwabing), but the genuine article he claims himself to be is, in turn, yet another fraud in a long series of chameleonic deceptions. Alone with Mary Lamington, Hannay's beloved, Ivery misleadingly presents himself as a pacifist inspired by radically alternative compulsions: 'He claimed the same purpose as hers, a hatred of war and a passion to rebuild the world into decency. But now he drew a different moral. He was a German: it was through Germany alone that peace and regeneration could come'.[48] This turns out to be false, but, thinking himself victorious, Ivery declares: '"My country has conquered. You and your friends will be dragged at the chariot wheels of a triumph such as Rome never saw"'.[49] Once again, Buchan's fear of a reductive German uniformity rears its head: what is finally most insidious about Ivery is that, despite his shifts and literal about-faces, he steadfastly *coheres*. His disguises are simply attitudes of mind rather than different physical configurations, and his devotion to his fatherland, even when tormented by his state-imposed exile, never wavers.

The second threat, hinted at in Biggleswick but properly located in '"the big industrial districts"', is labour unrest.[50] Buchan moves the story to Red Clydeside, which figures here as a linkage to Glasgow radicals such as John Maclean and James Maxton, who had disapproved of the War on the grounds that those running it 'had their own axes to grind and were marching to oligarchy through the blood of the workers'.[51] Buchan had argued in 'The True Danger of Socialism' (1907) that while socialism was 'a doctrinaire's dream', one of its problems was to incite an extreme reaction in proportion to its own excessiveness.[52] This finds physical outlets in *Mr Standfast*. The first is in Hannay's punch-up with Wake, who is earlier described as having '"the makings of a fanatic"'.[53] The second is in Glasgow, where the double agent Abel Gresson is attacked by a Scots Fusilier enraged by the anti-serviceman ranting of 'a noted agitator, who had already been deported'.[54] In the latter case Hannay observes that such an agitator 'would soon cease to exist but for the protection of the law which he would abolish'.[55]

Buchan's inclusion of the Red Clyde episode is noteworthy both for its class-war implications, a social rupture he abhorred,[56] and for its implied references offstage to figures such as John Bruce Glasier, a founding member of the Independent Labour Party and a leading Red Clyde campaigner. Glasier argued in 'The Peril of Conscription' (1915) that Britain's conscription policies equated to a home-reared Prussianism, something with which Buchan, though critical of certain aspects of conscription, would have passionately disagreed.[57] Although Buchan ensures that the 'explosive material'[58] of the Red Clyde retains its scandal by leaving its controversies largely uncontested, this is problematized by the character of Andrew Amos, a Border radical who by his own admission speaks '"for ninety per cent in ony ballot"'[59] and whom is described as '"a red-hot agitator who chooses that way of doing his bit for his country"'.[60] There is a certain doubleness with regard to Buchan's (not Hannay's) assigning to Amos an internally-fissured role. He is a sympathetic spokesman for Scottish working-class revolt whose critique of its radicalism underlines its complexities, but which simultaneously devalues the rebelliousness *produced* by that revolt. A shop steward, Amos represents '"the rank and file against office-bearers that have lost the confidence o' the workin'-man"' and differentiates himself from a socialism he thinks has infected the world '"like the measles"'.[61] Buchan's uneasy views on pacifist politics become apparent here: if Buchan permits labour unrest its own chapter ('Andrew Amos'), a tolerance played out at the textual level, then Amos's views, which Hannay nowhere denies, imply a limit to that tolerance which never crosses the margins of humanitarian 'understanding'.

Objectors, Knights, a Horse and the Great Mother

The most problematic socialist in *Mr Standfast* is the character with whom this chapter started, the Fabian pacifist Launcelot Wake. Several ambiguities in the text that thwart *Mr Standfast*'s 'well-disposed' view of pacifism and conscientious objection need to be explained more precisely. As Janet Adam Smith notes, Buchan introduces Wake in a series of deliberately insensitive encounters to facilitate his redemption in later scenes that 'show him in a situation where he behaves as well as the hero'.[62] Thus, though exempted from conscription owing to his civil service, and disliked and pitied by Hannay because of this, Wake proves himself not only a more accomplished mountaineer than Hannay but also an invaluable military asset. *Mr Standfast* clearly challenges Bertrand Russell's view that 'advocates of war are very partial in their recognition of courage', tolerating neither 'those who stand out against popular clamour' nor those who try 'to bring men to reason in times of excitement', and finally unable to recognize that such forms of courage are 'far less common, and far more indubitably of value to mankind'.[63] On the contrary, Buchan permits his conscientious objector to be courageous, but differs from Russell in precisely what that courage is. It is even more laudable that Wake's 'portrait is a perceptive and penetrating study, and his analysis of himself a piece of acute psychology'.[64] By marking Wake as motivated by detailed psychological stimuli, Buchan avoids the reductionism of those too willing to stereotype pacifists and objectors on their particular instances of insurgency alone.

Mr Standfast follows A. V. Dicey's contention, made in 1918, that

> the attention paid to the claims of the conscientious objector is in reality a sign of the extent to which, even where war and possible invasion have excited English patriotism, the country desires to give fair play to the opinions of men who think that peace is preferable to national safety, or even ought to be put before national honour.[65]

Even if Wake's politics remain 'othered', their right to exist beyond the field of acceptance of Hannay, Buchan's representative soldier, is recognized: "'Soldiering in the Salient isn't the softest of jobs, but I don't believe it's as tough as yours is for you. D'you know, Wake, I wish I had you in my brigade. Trained or untrained, you're a dashed stout-hearted fellow'".[66] This extends to Hannay's integration of Wake into the allegorical infrastructure *Mr Standfast* borrows from *The Pilgrim's Progress* (1678): 'He was the Faithful among us pilgrims, who had finished his journey before the rest'.[67] As a martyr executed for his thinking, Faithful's journey into Heaven vindicates those beliefs as enabling the journey from the Destructive City to Paradise. Likewise, the link between Hannay – who sees himself as a foil to Bunyan's Christian[68] – and Wake instantiates the latter's pacifism as a feasible creed among others which can, and does, help in leading the pilgrims of *Mr Standfast* from European war to the paradise-like Armistice in 1918.

Buchan goes to some lengths in *Mr Standfast* to establish the simultaneous difference and viability of Wake's pacifism and, at the level of plot at least, I agree with Lois Bibbings's view that Wake 'is distinct from other fictionalized conchies of the period'.[69] However, what complicates her reading – which is roughly indicative of scholarship to date on this text – is that at the level of symbolism and imagery Wake's 'meaning' is not aligned with the narrative processes that enable us as readers to see him in a favourable context. So, although Pilvi Rajamäe has recently mapped out how closely Wake's actions conform to his Arthurian prototypes, this is in itself of secondary importance, in my view, to how the framework that triggers those correspondences problematizes its own sense-making procedures.[70] Nowhere is this better implied than in Wake's name. 'Launcelot Wake' implies the kindling of a chivalric spirit (Lancelot, awake) that will create a renewed valuing of objectors as men and as human beings. But 'wake' also means 'turbulence' (the disturbance caused by movement through water) and 'death' (a funereal vigil), homonyms that signify with regard to Wake's chivalric becoming in two ways. While they can be seen as denoting the madness that precedes Wake's heroism and his death (a further link to his namesake), they also connote processes of dissolution which oppose the Arthurian awakening they concurrently imply.[71] I do not claim that Buchan rejects the pacifism that Wake's knightliness entails, simply that *Mr Standfast* cannot be read as an *unproblematic* dramatizing of the clearly sympathetic attitude Buchan had in 1919 towards pacifists themselves.

Two further examples must suffice. First, there is Hannay's description of Wake's transferral from a Labour battalion into the Red Cross (and ultimately the Front) as a shift from 'unruliness' to 'conformity'. '"We're going to break you to harness, Wake, and then you'll be a happy man"', says Hannay.[72] The equestrian metaphor of 'breaking to harness' (the taming of a horse so that it can be saddled and reined), is quite clearly equivocal in this instance, suggesting both the indifferent calm Wake finds in his front line employment, about which Hannay has serious misgivings,[73] but also a containment, and thus in some measure an *erasing*, of an alternative philosophy which seems at odds with the pluralism Buchan had previously shown elsewhere and would preserve in later texts.[74] This implication of 'containment' is reinforced by Hannay's closing obituary of Wake: 'he was the first of our little confederacy to go. But what an ending he had made, and how happy he had been in that mad time when he had come down from his pedestal and become one of the crowd!'[75] This comment does not necessarily authorize the ambiguity of Wake's heroic becoming, since in uttering it Hannay merely provides a subjective view of that process, but it doesn't weaken the force of the harnessing metaphor either, which is not contradicted anywhere or by anyone in the text, not even the individual to whom it is addressed. Thus, and rather contradictorily, an instrumentalized pacifism here becomes the 'steed' of the war machine against which it has hitherto been arrayed.

Wake articulates the second ambiguity himself. Shortly before his death, he feyly alludes to the devotional bloodbaths of the pre-Christian *Magna Mater* sects: 'I think I am passing through that bath. I think that like the initiate I shall be *renatus in aeternum* – reborn into the eternal'.[76] However, Buchan's use of a mother-cult metaphor in Wake's anticipation of his death lacks the detail of the historical context from which that imagery is drawn. Wake (or Buchan?) excludes any mention of the ritual castrations used in the *Magna Mater* ceremonies, in which the initially Anatolian goddess Cybele was worshipped as a deification of Mother Earth. These mutilations historically meant a removal of 'oneself permanently from the temptations of the flesh so as to be able to devote oneself to one's religious vows'.[77] Buchan had already used this imagery in 'The Grove of Ashtaroth' (1910), a short story in which Lawson, a British colonial, worships the Semitic fertility goddess Ashtaroth by maiming himself with a knife, and screaming 'such as a maenad may have uttered in the train of Bacchus'.[78] This simile, in which Lawson is compared to the banshee-like, female worshippers of Bacchus-Dionysus, apportions to him an uncertain sexual identity, and it is precisely this ambiguousness which is at work in *Mr Standfast*. The veiled presence of such deeper knowledge in this text maintains Wake's self-sacrifice as both an act of unbroken patriotism and commitment to his cause, *and* corroborates his view of himself, and of pacifists generally, as emasculated carriers of "'ladylike nerves'".[79] But this does not square with Bibbings's view of the text as contradicting a dominant objector stereotype during the period, what Mr Blackwood in Rose Allatini's *Despised and Rejected* (1918) sees as an "'unnatural'", implicitly feminized passivity.[80] If Wake's notion of himself as 'feminized' represents for Hannay an abased humility, that notion is not ultimately *replaced* by Hannay's not necessarily reliable rereading of it.

However, Buchan strongly implies that Wake is literally emasculated, since he dies from a groin injury.[81] It is a curious end result, but whether Buchan wanted this textual element, and its associated imagery, to be taken in an ironic sense is ultimately un-decidable (and, with a nod to Barthes, irrelevant). The text speaks definitively neither way. There must, however, be a last pejorative element present (intended or not) in having Wake argue that pacifism is a negatively-defined philosophy adhered to by individuals with hatred (inwardly- and outwardly-trained) as their psychological wellspring.[82] Yet, as I have already claimed, I don't think this fact prevents the text from being analysed in a favourable light as a symptom of Buchan's increasingly benevolent relationship to the pacifist cause. What it does imply is that this link is not, on the evidence of *Mr Standfast* at least, unreservedly obliging (itself a common enough critical view), but that its expression in this fiction is at odds with itself.

9 JOHN BUCHAN, AMERICA AND THE 'BRITISH WORLD', 1904–40

Peter Henshaw

For much of John Buchan's life he was a champion of closer ties between Britain and the United States. During and after the First World War he played an influential role in shaping Anglo-American relations, through journalism, history, popular fiction and professional diplomacy. His work included leading the British government's wartime propaganda effort, a centrepiece of which was encouraging active American support for the Allies against Germany. His overarching objective was to encourage broad, popular, and mutual understanding between the American and British peoples, including those overseas in the settler dominions. From 1914 onwards, this was a leading personal concern, evident in the subjects he wrote about, the stories and characters he created, and the themes he emphasized – not least in some of his bestselling novels, notably *The Thirty-Nine Steps*, *Greenmantle* and *Mr Standfast*. It was also evident in his direct involvement in international diplomacy. Perhaps most striking was the extent to which his conceptualization of America and its relationship with Britain was shaped by the same ideas that underpinned his enthusiasm for the British Empire.[1]

America was, to Buchan, the epitome of a successful encounter between European pioneers and the wilderness frontier, an encounter Buchan thought was essential for the vitality of the British people. Similarly, the American federal union was seen by Buchan (and many other co-enthusiasts of empire) as a validation of his belief in imperial unity and in the value of the bigger international unit. Buchan also saw America as another example of how fierce local loyalties and differences in outlook (even those strong enough to provoke a civil war) need not be an impediment to successful union, just as he thought national differences within the British Isles or British Empire need not force those groupings apart. Indeed, Buchan sought to resolve the problem of reconciling ethnic, cultural or national differences by proclaiming such differences to be a source of strength rather than weakness. Unity could spring just as effectively from shared heritage and ideals, and from shared experience of tackling common national or international problems. As this chapter will explain, these big linking ideas show up with surprising frequency and salience in nearly everything Buchan did in connection with America, including his most memorable fictional characters, each artfully constructed to embody the diverse spirits of America, Britain and the imperial frontier.

First World War Propaganda

It might be imagined that Buchan only really engaged with the problem of propaganda in relation to the United States in 1916 when – as an intelligence officer on the Western Front – he used to give regular briefings to American journalists about the war; or in 1917 when – as director of Britain's new propaganda arm – he took charge of British efforts to influence opinion in America and elsewhere. When the war broke out, Buchan had had no firsthand experience of America, yet a number of his early wartime activities make clear that he was fully aware of the importance of building a close understanding between America and the 'British world', and that this involved explaining the empire to America and America to the empire. It also involved explaining how differences, as much as commonalities, should be accepted both as inescapable facts and as sources of strength for the English-speaking peoples.[2]

One set of pointers to Buchan's interest in fostering a closer Anglo-American understanding lies in his work as a contemporary historian of the First World War.[3] The chief monument to this work was *Nelson's History of the War*, which Buchan championed and largely wrote. *Nelson's History* was published from January 1915, and eventually ran to twenty-four volumes and more than one million words.[4] It was intended to be a readable, factually-reliable and up-to-date account of the war, but a further important purpose of the *History* was that it should explain the war – and the British Empire's role in it – to Americans in a way that would give them a sense of unity with the British world, a unity of identity and purpose of the sort that Buchan also hoped to foster within the British Empire.

The salience of influencing American opinion is evident from the preface of the first volume of the *History* and from the efforts made to market it in the United States. Buchan invited Lord Rosebery to write the preface, which asserted that a 'world-wide British influence … will be a guarantee of liberty and peace', and that such influence, backed by 'our allies in Europe and … our kindred in the United States, should go far to make another war such as this impossible'.[5] When, in January 1915, the *New York Times* received an advance copy of *Nelson's History*, it reproduced a large part of the preface, including this assertion, without questioning any part of it. The *New York Times* also reproduced Rosebery's observation that 'War is an accursed thing … but our chroniclers cannot fail to enlarge upon the incalculable blessing which the damnable invasion of Belgium has revealed to the world – the enthusiastic and weatherproof unity of the British Empire'.[6] The value of the empire as a globe-spanning bastion of civilization and liberty and the voluntary aspect of the imperial union were highlighted in *Nelson's History*, as in Buchan's other wartime writing, partly to sing the praises the empire for all readers, but also to defuse American anti-imperial predilections. Also prominent was the assertion that 'Blood shed in common is the cement of nations'.[7] This too was a deeply-held belief of Buchan's. It informed much of his writing not only about national identity but also about identities shared between nations.

Buchan was too subtle a writer, and too conscious of the counterproductive perils of being too didactic to advance his underlying messages as explicitly as Rosebery in the *History*'s preface. Commonly his key messages were implicit in the *History*'s content. He conveyed the diversity of the empire by doing no more than taking care to describe the geographically specific origins of British or empire regiments – be they English, Scottish, Australian, South African or Canadian. He also expressed his belief in the moral and physical value of the frontier experience by ascribing particular virtues to men and units from the imperial frontier. Finally, in a more deliberate effort to draw the Anglo-American world together, he drew comparisons between the American experience of the Civil War and the British experience in the European conflict, equating not only the battlefield experience but also British and American leaders and national motives.[8]

The *New York Times* praised *Nelson's History* both for its quality and reliability: 'This compact volume, though the work of a British author, is free from any marked bias, and combines evident accuracy of fact with unusual zest of style'.[9] In January 1917, another review recorded that 'John Buchan is writing Nelson's "History of the War" in a series of small volumes that cover the entire field of operations all over the world. It is high tribute to the author's ability simply to state that his narrative does not become confused'.[10] The following month, *The Times* recorded that 'it is generally believed that the best records of the war are those made by Hilaire Belloc and John Buchan'.[11]

Buchan's transatlantic reputation was such that American newspapers sometimes reported on his important articles in the British press or his public lectures. The *Christian Science Monitor* started doing this in October 1915, with reference to Buchan's articles on the Western Front,[12] and his lecture to the National Liberal Club in March 1916.[13] In another significant speech to the National Liberal Club late in November 1917, some seven months after America's entry into the war, Buchan spoke directly on the subject of Anglo-American relations. He insisted that the shared experience of war would bring new sympathy and understanding between America and Britain. All barriers of prejudice will go down before the whirlwind of war, and the two peoples will stand revealed to each other as sharing common ideals and common instincts, as well as common traditions. After the destruction of Prussianism the alliance of America and Britain will be the greatest safeguard for the peaceful ordering of the world.[14]

But he also warned that Britain had to take care not to alienate America and prompt its return to isolationism: 'let us see that we do nothing by parochialism on our own account' to weaken President Wilson's hands in his efforts to make America 'permanently responsible, as one of the world's greatest powers, for the world's good governance'.[15] Thus did Buchan encapsulate the tension between the latent attraction and repulsion of America and the British world.

Buchan's historical works on the First World War were marketed actively to American readers: an early piece of official propaganda by Buchan was the pamphlet *Britain's War by Land* (1915), published in New York by Oxford University Press. Thomas Nelson's was firmly established in the United States, having had a New York office since 1854.[16] It distributed in America not only *Nelson's History* but also a number of shorter works based on the *History*: *The Battle of Jutland* (1916), *The Battle of the Somme, First Phase* (1916), *The Battle of the Somme, Second Phase* (1917). A fourth work, *A History of the British Navy during the War* (1918) was adapted from *Nelson's History*, by H. C. O'Neill, who worked for Buchan in the Department of Information.[17] These books were 'official' propaganda in the sense that they formed part of the work of 'Wellington House', a British government organization officially sanctioned to use literature to promote the Allied war effort.[18] This was also true of *The Battle of the Somme* (1917), a one-volume version of this battle history produced for the American market and published in New York by George H. Doran Company. Starting in 1917, Nelson's also began to market Buchan's work to the growing number of American troops in France, doing so through the Nelson's office in Paris.[19] By February 1917, 'the war book' had 'had its day',[20] but Buchan's sales of fiction to American readers more than made up for any declining interest in war histories.

Buchan sometimes gave himself freer rein in his fiction to express and promote his big ideas about nationalism, empire and Anglo-American relations than he did in his other writings. The fiction that he published during the war was highly important in shaping American opinion and drawing America and the British world more closely together. *The Thirty-Nine Steps* (1915), *Greenmantle* (1916), *The Power-House* (1916) and *Mr Standfast* (1919), all published in New York by the George H. Doran Company, were widely read in America during and immediately following the war. So was his American-set historical novel *Salute to Adventurers* (1917).[21] All were actively advertised and well received by reviewers in America.[22] *The Thirty-Nine Steps* and *Mr Standfast* were also serialized in the United States.[23] *Greenmantle* acquired the status of 'best-seller'.[24]

The Thirty-Nine Steps, *Greenmantle* and *Mr Standfast* have two noteworthy aspects from the perspective of Buchan's desire to link America and the British world. The first is their heroes' connections with either the imperial frontier or America. The second is their heroes' cultural distinctiveness: each protagonist looks at the world differently, yet works effectively with the others in foiling a common enemy. Richard Hannay is British but his formative experiences were gained as a soldier and mining engineer on the imperial frontier in southern Africa, thus symbolizing the value to Britain of the settler frontier. Peter Pienaar, an expert hunter and an African settler of Dutch ancestry, is loyal to the British Empire even though Britain had gone to war against Boer ascendancy in the Transvaal in 1899. His strength of character and physical talents derived from his experiences in the African wilderness, and his commitment to the common cause of defeating Germany affirms the value and cultural diversity of the empire. Sandy Arbuthnot, educated at Eton and Oxford, is 'the wandering Scot carried to the pitch of genius',[25] a master of disguise able to pass for a Muslim prophet. His mastery of Eastern languages and ways were gained through epic adventures in Arabia and Asia, and – like Hannay and Pienaar – stands as an example of the strength Britain derived from the challenges of sustaining a far-flung empire.

All three novels also feature important American characters who look at the world's problems differently from the British characters. In *The Thirty-Nine Steps* Franklin P. Scudder, a semi-official secret agent, makes only a brief appearance early in the novel before being killed off, yet he is indispensable in putting Hannay on the trail of a murky, middle-European plot to foment war. While Hannay and Scudder share the objective of peace in Europe, they differ sharply in their understanding of the European situation and the sources of conflict there. Scudder is convinced that behind everything is a conspiracy of Jewish capitalists seeking war for profit and to exact revenge on Russia for the pogroms. The British side is highly sceptical of Scudder's theory and soon realizes that elements of the German government are the chief instigators of war. But it is only because of the American red herring that the British are alerted to the German threat.

In *Greenmantle* and *Mr Standfast*, the chief American protagonist has a more indestructible role. John Scantlebury Blenkiron takes a central part in foiling German plans to raise an Islamic jihad against the British Empire, and makes it clear that Americans have no interest in saving the British Empire, or even in European peace per se. Their principal objective is a peaceful international order, governed by the rule of law and free from undemocratic rogue states. He addresses head-on the differences between the British and American approaches to the war:

Say, Major, what are you lot fighting for? For your own skins and your Empire and the peace of the world. Waal, those ideals don't concern us one cent. We're not Europeans, and there aren't any German trenches on Long Island yet ... As I follow events, there's a slunk let been let loose in the world ... [and] we've got to take a hand in disinfecting the planet.[26]

Instead of denying the existence of difference, Buchan demonstrates through the unfolding of his stories that such differences are no impediment to working together in a common cause.

In these three Hannay novels Buchan sought to draw the Anglo-American world together by explaining that working together towards a common goal was the best way to foster closer understanding between peoples and countries. Just as Buchan thought it a mistake to try and foster a single, common identity for the British world, so he thought it a mistake to do so in relation to the English-speaking world. Cultural links could be taken for granted. What needed to be emphasized were the cultural differences, which were the source of so much frustration and misunderstanding. In the Hannay novels Buchan fostered myths of common endeavour and shared ideals, while at the same time defusing latent antagonisms by explaining that differences in outlook and approach were natural and should be welcomed.

Salute to Adventurers was actually written just before the war and before the Hannay novels, and gives full play to the author's preoccupation with the frontier and with ancestral links between Britain and America.[27] *Salute* is the story of Andrew Garvald, a young Scots merchant on the frontier of late seventeenth-century Virginia who discovers and foils a 'native rising'. With its hero leaving urban Scotland, finding himself on the edge of civilization, and saving a colony of British settlement from disaster, Buchan produced a book that proclaimed the value of empire and the historical depth of Anglo-American ties. In many ways, this story was a reworking of *Prester John* (1910): David Crawfurd, a young Scots merchant on a frontier in early twentieth-century southern Africa, discovers and foils a black African uprising. In both colonies the settlers are compelled by frontier challenges to rise above metropolitan tendencies to slip into complacency or moral decay, and are led to realize their true potential and moral purpose. That both novels use Scots protagonists reminds the reader that these far-flung frontiers are closely connected through the ancestry of the British people who settled there. Moreover, in both stories the heroes are men of humble origin who rise to the occasion, find greatness, and in so doing help to steer their nations away from decadence and weakness. *Salute to Adventurers* thus encourages its readers to see not only that America and the British Empire were linked by the common ancestry of many settlers, but also that they faced similar challenges on their frontiers, where individuals and nations develop to their full potential.

By the end of the First World War, Buchan had exerted considerable effort to promote Anglo-American understanding and unity. Most of what he published during these years was infused with his ideas on how to foster a closer understanding of English-speaking peoples and to underpin their vitality as individuals and nations. He continued to emphasize these in the 1920s and 1930s. But they were also ideas that had already taken definite shape in the years before the outbreak of war in August 1914, in the context of Buchan's efforts to promote greater unity within the British world.

Imperial background to Buchan's Anglo-American Ideas

Buchan's ideas about America took firm shape well before he crossed the north Atlantic for the first time in 1924. He developed them in the preceding decades when he was preoccupied with the development of the British Empire as an integrated international system. In common with other leading Edwardian enthusiasts of imperial unity, Buchan saw America as a model of how to create a functional, large-scale federation which balanced central authority with local autonomy.[28] This interest in America was magnified by the fact that in geopolitical terms, an alliance with America was obviously invaluable to Britain. Given this background, Buchan's early ideas about America were naturally influenced by his own evolving ideas about the place of blood ties, cultural links, shared ideals and the frontier experience in holding together the British settler world.

Most of Buchan's early knowledge about America was derived from books.[29] While he was a student at Oxford, Buchan read and was deeply attracted by Thoreau and Whitman, writers who – like Buchan – were preoccupied with rural life and with the relationship between man and nature. Buchan also developed a deep interest in the American Civil War, which was intensified by talks with his wife's uncle, Sir Reginald Talbot, who had been attached to the staff of a Civil War general.[30] Buchan's reviews for the *Spectator* provide insights into the evolution of his ideas about America, revealing that Buchan often displayed a strong bias towards viewing America as an imperial project comparable to the British empire. These reviews also indicate that from an early date Buchan took it upon himself to interpret each side to the other.

One book of special significance for its connections to America and the British Empire was F. S. Oliver's life of Alexander Hamilton,[31] which Buchan reviewed for the *Spectator* in 1906. The subject was an American of Scottish ancestry, a leading politician in revolutionary America who played a pivotal role in drawing the fractious American colonies together in a federal union. For Buchan, Hamilton's story demonstrated the value of the colonial frontier as a place where Scots or other Britons could find new opportunities and build new countries. Secondly, F. S. Oliver was also an ardent proponent of a closer union of Britain and the settler dominions. Published at the height of British interest in imperial federation, Oliver's book was written to encourage both imperial federation and a union of Britain's settler colonies in southern Africa. At the time, Buchan noted how the ambition of Hamilton (and later Abraham Lincoln) to build and defend the American union closely matched the aims of the proponents of imperial federation. Later he noted that the book 'became a text-book for all those up and down the Empire who were giving their minds to Imperial reconstruction'.[32] Buchan was deeply attached to the idea that the United States and the British Empire were comparable grand political structures inspired by common ideals. The fact that far-wandering Scots were closely involved in both political projects made those projects that much more attractive.

Buchan's writing for the *Spectator* also drew attention to America's own status a colonial power in the Caribbean and Pacific, and sought to make sense of America's contradictory attitudes towards empire and the rule of less developed peoples. He was well aware of the contradictory impulses shaping American imperial policy,[33] and noted the strong American dislike of paternalist rule of subject peoples and the equally strong American desire to spread democracy. He saw that there was a strong American impulse to expand its influence overseas, but he acknowledged that Americans generally were ill at ease with overseas colonial empires. Some of what Buchan wrote about America's imperial experiences was more an encouragement to Americans (as Kipling had enjoined) to 'Take up the white man's burden', than a hard look at the realities of the situation. By drawing explicit parallels between British policy in post-Boer War South Africa and American successes in reconstruction in Cuba and the Philippines, Buchan sometimes seems to be encouraging his readers to look more favourably upon recent British imperial policy.[34]

Buchan's belief that Anglo-American unity rested on a combination of common ancestry and ideals as well as shared experience of the frontier is also evident in some of his pre-1914 writings for the *Spectator*. In 1907, he wrote about a recent disagreement between London and Washington over an American intervention in Jamaica. He argued that there 'is an impulse among men brought up in the same traditions to quarrel violently over small matters, but in a crisis to draw instinctively together'. He went on to say that 'Blood, after all, is thicker than water', that the two peoples shared the same 'principles of liberty and justice', and that their pioneers had 'grappled with the same problems' on their respective frontiers.[35] The significance of shared principles and of confronting common problems in distinctive ways were things that Buchan would return to again and again.

In 1914, not long before the outbreak of war, Buchan gave particular intellectual attention to America by reviewing books about the American Civil War and Abraham Lincoln. In February 1914 he described the Civil War as 'the most desperate war in the history of the Anglo-Saxon race', and thereby took the unity of the Anglo-American world largely for granted.[36] So too with his labelling of Abraham Lincoln as 'probably the greatest product of the Anglo-Saxon race in the last century', and his equating of Lincoln and Cromwell.[37] Buchan also implicitly equated Lincoln's Civil War struggle to defend the integrity of the Union with the efforts of imperialists like himself to hold the British Empire together. As Buchan put it: 'The South fought for the particularism of the smaller units, the North for the bigger social battalions, and it is the latter creed towards which the world is moving'.[38]

The persistence and intensity of Buchan's interest in Lincoln and the Civil War are in many ways explained by their significance for his vision of empire and the future of the Anglo-American world. When Buchan insisted that Lincoln, 'with Cromwell and Chatham, Washington and Hamilton ... must live among the *Di majors* of our common race',[39] it was above all because Lincoln (like Hamilton before him) worked for the integrity of the American federal union, which Buchan equated with the idea of British imperial unity. There was also the fact that Lincoln was a 'Backwoods-boy, rail-splitter, storekeeper, country lawyer, politician President'.[40] Lincoln thus conformed with Buchan's thesis that a nation's best men sprang from humble origins and were the product of hard struggle on the frontier, with part of their greatness linked perhaps to heroic ancestors. Buchan's early identification of the American Civil War as being a decisive struggle for the future of the world was rooted in the belief that the war had been fought to defend an expansive and expanding political union, a geopolitical process which Buchan saw as being essential to the future of the British world and the English-speaking peoples.

Buchan's Post-1918 Promotion of Anglo-American Solidarity

Between the end of the First World War and his installation as governor-general of Canada in 1935, Buchan only periodically made explicit efforts to promote Anglo-American solidarity. His ideas about culture, identity, nationalism and international relations evolved after the war, and the key shift in his thinking was that he moved away from the idea of race and 'Anglo-Saxonism' as the principal underpinning of Anglo-American unity. Instead he placed increasing emphasis on the persistence of cultural bonds and the mysterious working of ancestry as unifying forces; on the capacity of people to have multiple identities, in which local, ethnic, national and transnational identities could happily coexist; and on the power of shared experience (refracted and reinforced through literature, history and myth) to produce new identities. All of this meshed positively with the problem of encouraging a closer understanding between America and the British world, not least because his new approach was more broadly inclusive than a simple appeal to Anglo-Saxon unity. Buchan's post-war efforts to promote Anglo-American solidarity focused on the ideas that this solidarity was rooted in a shared heritage, that its real strength lay in common ideals of the British and American peoples, and in their shared experience of struggle on the frontier and in war.

In the 1920s, in his two main books relating to the United States, Buchan returned to the subjects of Lincoln and the Civil War, with the implicit purpose of fostering Anglo-American unity. In *The Path of the King* (1921), the aim was to build up Lincoln as a shared hero of the British and American people. Buchan did this by creating a fictional account of Lincoln's ancestry, with tales of European forbears going back to the son of a Norse king. One obvious message was that some of the great figures of British and American history were linked by ancestry. A second was the idea that the frontier was where a leader like Lincoln could emerge from seemingly humble origins in the midst of great national struggles. The book concludes with another rehearsal of the view that Lincoln's highest achievement was his defence the American Union, a grand geopolitical association comparable in Buchan's mind to the British Empire.

In *Two Ordeals of Democracy* (1925), Buchan once again examined the Civil War and drew parallels with the British experience of the First World War. This short book is the text of a speech delivered at Milton Academy in America in 1924.[41] Buchan's thesis was that these wars were terrible ordeals because they obliged freedom-loving peoples – both British and American – to militarize and curtail civil liberties in order to preserve their respective democracies. One notable feature of this speech is the care Buchan took not to overstate the bonds between America and the British world. He relied on the metaphor of the British and American people having become part of 'one household' when they fought together in the First World War.[42] Ties of race and blood were only briefly mentioned in connection with Lincoln, when Buchan praised him as being 'one of the two or three greatest men ever born of our blood'.[43] The main message of the Milton Academy address was that the essential bond between the British and American peoples lay in their parallel ordeals of having to fight all-out wars to defend their democracies.

When Buchan visited America in 1934, he did more to foster closer Anglo-American understanding than simply make public speeches. Before he left London in November 1934, the British prime minister entrusted Buchan, then a member of Parliament, with some 'some very confidential things to say to the President of the USA',[44] Franklin D. Roosevelt. This marked the start of the close and partly secretive relationship between Buchan and the president, which grew in strength while Buchan was Canada's governor-general. Buchan's main public speech during this trip to America was given at the opening of Columbia University's new library and was broadcast on American radio.[45] Here, Buchan largely bypassed the question of Anglo-American relations, no doubt following his own later advice to Americans not to get self-conscious about the relationship.[46] Instead, he focused on the role of universities in strengthening nations by training students to think critically and rationally. This practice of saying little in public about the theory of Anglo-American relations and instead talking about practical problems which the two peoples confronted, and of working actively in private to foster closer relations with America, was something he would continue for the remainder of the 1930s.

The most obvious constructive outcome of Buchan's partly secret, partly public approach was a series of high-level meetings and state visits involving Buchan and President Roosevelt during the late 1930s. From Washington, Roosevelt made active use of Buchan as an informal – but high-level – channel of communication with British political leaders in London, doing so, it seems, to circumvent the influence of the American State Department and British Foreign Office. Buchan, as focused as Roosevelt on the vital issue of peace in Europe, was only too happy to oblige the president by acting in this way, even though he should not (as governor-general) have engaged in this subterfuge.[47]

Buchan played such a direct and unauthorized role as intermediary between Britain and America during his 1937 visit to Washington. 'The important point was my private conversations on international questions with the President, which was the real object of my visit'. Roosevelt wanted Buchan to sound out the British government informally on the American president's idea to 'appeal for a Conference to deal with the fundamental economic problems, which are behind all the unrest' in Europe and internationally.[48] No real hint of these activities by Buchan and Roosevelt was revealed in public. They merely indicated to the press that the visit was in return for the one made by Roosevelt to Canada the previous year, and that there would be 'opportunity in the intervals of official engagements for personal conversations'.[49]

Throughout 1937, Buchan continued to act as an unofficial channel of communication between the Roosevelt administration and the British prime minister; by this time Neville Chamberlain.

> I keep in very close touch with Roosevelt, and his recent speech in Chicago [in which he proposed an international 'quarantine' of all aggressor states] was the culmination of a long conspiracy between us. (This must be kept secret!) I think there is just a chance of America now coming back into the fold of the European democracies. I have many domestic troubles to face here [in Canada], but I feel that the most useful work I can do is in connection with the U.S.A. I have Cordell Hull [the US secretary of state] coming up to stay with me in a fortnight for some serious talks.[50]

Chamberlain, though, was not impressed either by Buchan's interventions in British foreign policy or by Roosevelt's proposal for an international conference to deal with international tensions. The British prime minister first warned Buchan off further such interventions, and later blocked Roosevelt's proposal.[51]

Despite this setback, Buchan continued to do what he could to strengthen relations with America, both through public speeches and behind-the-scenes activities. When, in June 1938, he spoke at Yale, he refused to

> talk the usual platitudes about how closely related the United States and the British Empire are, and what good friend they should be. I believe most profoundly in that friendship, but don't let's go get self-conscious about it. Don't let's be pulling up the plant to see how the roots are getting on. I think the best way for Americans and Britons to understand each other is not by analysing their feelings, but by doing things together.[52]

Here, once more, was Buchan's idea that unity should be found through common endeavour.

Buchan's last major contribution to strengthening relations with America was his effort to initiate and organize the first ever visit to Canada and the United States by a reigning British monarch. From the start, Buchan and Roosevelt both strongly favoured a visit by the King and Queen to the United States (and not just to Canada – ostensibly the principal destination), seeing the visit as a way to strengthen American support for Britain as the threat of a European war grew: a key reason why the tour proceeded in May 1939, despite the real risk that war might break out while the King was away. Though Buchan drafted all but one of the King's and Queen's main Canadian speeches, he seems not to have had any direct influence over royal speeches on the American portion of the tour, which the British government regarded as its responsibility. Yet, to Buchan must go an important part of the credit for the fact that the American portion of the tour took place at all.[53]

Foundations of the 'Special Relationship'?

While it would be difficult to document specific cause and effect with respect to Buchan's work and the development of the wartime and post-war Anglo-American 'special relationship', it is hard not to see him as having played a small but significant part in its creation. After all, he devoted considerable energy to the problem of fostering a closer understanding between the British and American peoples from 1914 onwards, doing so from positions of not inconsiderable influence when he was a director of official propaganda and later governor-general of Canada. No less importantly, he infused many of his most widely read books with a set of messages designed to foster a closer understanding between America and both Britain and the British Empire. Foremost amongst these were that the American and British people were linked by shared ancestry and ideals, by a common experience of the frontier, and of fighting together in war. This is the perspective from which the characters and plot of a novel like *Greenmantle* take on such significance, with its abiding image of the dyspeptic Indianan, the Boer big-game hunter, the Scots-Rhodesian mining engineer, and the old-Etonian master of disguise conspiring in Constantinople to foil a German-inspired jihad. Indeed, it might not be too much to say that Buchan's 'shockers' had as big an impact on the way the American and British peoples viewed and understood one another as anything else he wrote or did, not least because they continued to enjoy a wide readership in the decades after his death. In this sense, *Greenmantle* and the other Hannay novels can perhaps lay claim to being small additions to the early foundations of the 'special relationship'.

10 ISLAM AND THE EAST IN JOHN BUCHAN'S NOVELS

Ahmed K. al-Rawi

Introduction

By 1900 the British Empire had spread into many continents and controlled many different nations, hoping to make use of their unexploited wealth and to 'secure to Great Britain the freedom to sell all over the world the products of her growing interests'.[1] The British politicians and intelligentsia who theorized the ideologies of the Empire, played a major role in maintaining, expanding and strengthening the British Empire as well as managing the affairs of the colonized peoples. John Buchan, a prominent empire commentator in the Edwardian period, was strongly influenced by the ethos of Empire in his early fiction and polemics.[2] In the 1916 'Preface' to the third edition of *A Lodge in the Wilderness* (1906), Buchan said that 'our Empire is a mystic whole which no enemy may part asunder, and our wisest minds are not given to the task of devising a mechanism of union adequate to this spiritual unity'.[3] Hence, the 'wisest minds' had to have a duty towards the Empire, impelling them to 'devise' methods and 'mechanisms' to strengthen it.

This emphasis on a spiritual dimension to the British people's 'duty' to maintain the Empire can be connected to the other important forces, beside the pursuit of free trade, that determined the makeup of the British Empire. These were 'the impulses of evangelical religion' and the 'missionary societies'.[4] It was claimed at the time that Britain had a divine message that must be achieved because it was God's will. In the 1920s Edward Byers made a comparison between the Israelites and the British, in the sense that both were chosen by God and had 'the temporal blessings' of 'the possession of certain land'. Byers argued that Britain must be 'the greatest on earth' and that 'the greatest race on earth is the Anglo-Saxon'.[5] In brief, Christianity and commerce were the decisive factors and forceful motives that shaped the British Empire.

Giving weight to the religious, pro-Christian impetus was Victorian Britain's inheritance of an old prejudice against Muslims that could be traced back to before the Crusades. The British journalist Grace Ellison, who travelled through-out the Middle East in the early twentieth century, referred to the deep-rooted 'hatred [*sic*] which have become almost part of the British national "attitude" towards Turkey' or the Muslim Turks.[6] This old stereotype was mixed with the snobbish Victorian values of the ruling classes that encouraged contemptuous attitudes toward foreigners and the lower classes.[7]

As a result of the empire's expansion, the British were encountering various cultures and religions that were different from its own. The East, and Islam in particular, were seen as exotic, unstable and in many cases decadent because the civilizations of the colonized countries did not match Western and European norms and values. The 'imperial attitude meant thinking of people – encoun-tered in daily business – as being of a different and inferior kind; thinking of them as agreeable or disagreeable, but always as different'.[8]

John Buchan did not have direct knowledge of Islam and the Easterners, although he frequently depicted them in his works. To get his information Buchan depended entirely on books, newspaper coverage, accounts from friends and contacts and, during the war, intelligence reports: these accounts were not always accurate. His single visit to the East was to Turkey, in the spring of 1910. Buchan visited Constantinople with 'his wife and Gerard Craig-Sellar', and reported taking lunch with the 'Sultan's brother and dinning at embassies',[9] where he found a 'pure Arabian Nights' atmosphere, and visited some places further east near Erzerum.[10] Later, Constantinople was depicted in his novel *Greenmantle* (1916), before and during its capture by the Russians in the First World War. Buchan's view of 'the East', and specifically Muslims, as a medieval and superstitious people, while being also mysterious and exotic, produces a powerful, subliminal dynamic in his fiction which uses the East. This chapter investigates Buchan's view of Islam, of Muslims and the East in his fiction, and tries to understand the origins of his attitudes, which embody some of the popu-lar beliefs of British society of his time.

Buchan's Fiction

In his early work on South Africa, *The African Colony*, Buchan revealed his ideas on the disparity that existed between the British people and the other races, and set criteria for distinguishing between the two:

> Between the most ignorant white man and the black man there is fixed for the present an impassable gulf, not of colour but of mind. The native ...lives and moves in a men-tal world incredibly distant from ours. The medium of his thought, so to speak, is so unique that the results are out of all relation to ourselves. Mentally he is as crude and naive as a child, with a child's curiosity and ingenuity, and a child's practical incon-sequence. Morally he has none of the traditions of self-discipline and order, which are implicit ... in white people ... With all his merits, this instability of character and

intellectual childishness make him politically far more impossible than even the low-
est class of Europeans.[11]

Gertrude Bell (1868–1926), on her journey into Arabia in 1891, expressed a
similar popular claim by saying that the 'Oriental is like a very old child ... He is
not practical in our acceptation of the word, any more than a child is practical,
and his utility is not ours'.[12] In other words, the African or the Easterner was seen
in Britain as an uncultivated child because he lacked 'proper' education and did
not conceive the world through Western eyes.

Such an imperialist view is echoed by some of Buchan's fictional characters,
such as the imperialist magnate Francis Carey in the fictionalized debate *A Lodge
in the Wilderness* (1906). Carey says that the concept and pursuit of imperialism
is 'the destiny of England'.[13] In the same novel, Mr Wakefield defines the term
'Imperialism' as

> the closer organic connection under one Crown of a number of autonomous nations
> of the same blood, who can spare something of their vitality for the administration of
> vast tracts inhabited by lower races, a racial aristocracy considered in their relation to
> the subject peoples, a democracy in their relation to each other.[14]

The notion of the 'lesser races' refers to any African or Asian race as long as they
do not look Western or follow Western cultural norms. Similarly, the idea of the
White Man's burden was emphasized by David Crawfurd in Buchan's later novel
Prester John (1910):

> I knew then the meaning of the white man's duty. He has to take all risks, recking
> nothing of his life or fortunes, and well content to find his reward in the fulfillment
> of his task. That is the difference between white and black, the gift of responsibility,
> the power of being in a little way a king; and so long as we know this and practise it,
> we will rule not in Africa alone but wherever there are dark men who live only for the
> day and their own bellies.[15]

Such concepts in Buchan's imagination survived the changing times. Lombard,
for instance, in *The Island of Sheep* (1936) follows Crawfurd's view on the superiority of the white race and the destiny of the British Empire. He dreams of
establishing an empire, that he calls the 'British Equatoria' or the 'new kingdom
of Prester John', to contain 'the highlands of the East and South as the white
man's base ... It was to link up South Africa with Egypt and the Sudan'.[16]

With the idea of empire in his mind, Buchan treated the East as an entity
that was entirely different from the civilized West. In his first attempt at a 'novel
of Empire', *The Half-Hearted* (1900), Buchan described the East during the
'closing years of the nineteenth century'. Lewis Haystoun has written a book
about Kashmir, and is standing for Parliament. His friend Winterham speaks in
support of Lewis at a public meeting, saying: 'I should back Lewis if he were a

Mohammedan or an Anarchist. The man is sound metal, I tell you, and that's all I ask'.[17] As can be seen from this casual assigning of 'a Mohammedan or Muslim' to the most extreme contrast to a white Scottish laird, Victorian Britain perceived these groups negatively because they were linked historically with a residual fear of 'the Turk' and were a reminder of the Ottoman threat against Western interests.[18] As a result, there was a great deal of prejudice against Muslims in Victorian Britain and in the Empire. For example, the Muslim scholar Jamal al-Adeen al-Afghani mentioned the condition of Muslims living under British rule in Ceylon in the late nineteenth century:

> If you look at this island, you will find it filled with innocent Muslims. The British Government judges its Muslim citizens according to its whims and to what is whispered among themselves. No wonder it finds the word 'Islam' if mentioned in a newspaper enough to prohibit it from entering a country ... It considers the Muslim its most hated enemy.[19]

To return to *The Half-Hearted*, Lewis makes another visit to the East, to Bardur, a ragged land with a harsh climate separating Russia and the areas now surrounding Pakistan and India. The place is also 'abundant [with] savage tribes with a particularly effective crooked kind of knife'.[20] While Lewis is travelling on the beautiful road to Forza, he has a new revelation, for he 'felt the East. Hitherto he had been unable to see anything in his errand but its futility'.[21] He also 'felt the mystery of a strange world'.[22] Suddenly, Lewis was able to perceive again the place that was so different from his Scottish homeland. 'He had his eyes turned to a new land, and the smell of dry mountain sand and scrub, and the vault-like, imperial sky were the earnest of his inheritance. This was the East, the gorgeous, the impenetrable'.[23] Buchan uses a romantic image, clearly influenced by the *Arabian Nights*, where the reader is taken

> beyond the mountains ... holy mosques, shady cities of palm trees, great walled towns to which north and west and south brought their merchandise. And to the east were latitudes more wonderful, the uplands of the world, the impassable borders of the oldest of human cultures. Names rang in his head like tunes – Khiva, Bokhara, Samarkand, the goal of many boyish dreams born of clandestine suppers and the Arabian Nights.[24]

Even in later novels such as *The Thirty-Nine Steps* (1915), Buchan presents the *Arabian Nights* as a sourcebook for wonders. Richard Hannay, for instance, saw England as 'a sort of Arabian Nights',[25] because it was the land of his family that he, a South African, had never visited. In *The Path of the King* (1921), Buchan refers to the *Nights* as a book 'full of wilder doings than any ... could imagine ... but beautiful, too, and delicious to muse over'.[26]

However, in the earlier *The Half-Hearted*, Buchan is making a clear point that this East is 'an old fierce world' where he stands on its 'brink ... and the nervous frontier civilization fell a thousand miles behind him'.[27] The East remains backward in Buchan's mind, despite its exotic beauty and charming mystery, and unlike the civilized and organized West. In *The Dancing Floor* (1926), Folliot wonders about the strange French Bluebeard, Gilles de Rais. Someone in the club replies: 'the type was fairly common in the East, and mentioned some Indian potentate'.[28]

Finally, in *The Half-Hearted*, predating Kipling's novel *Kim* by a year,[29] we can see an expression of British imperialist anxiety over a Russian military threat against its interests in the region. At Bardur, Lewis speaks with a Scot who says:

> It is assumed that Russia has but to find Britain napping, buy a passage from the more northerly tribes, and sweep down on the Punjab ... It is a mere matter of time till Persia is the Tsar's territory, and then they may begin to think about invasion.[30]

Buchan notes that Russia is the 'step-daughter of the East'; therefore, 'some day when the leader arrives they will push beyond their boundaries and sweep down on Western Europe, as their ancestors did thirteen hundred years ago. And you have no walls of Rome to resist them, and I do not think you will find a Charlemagne'.[31] Buchan uses the theme of a foreign invasion against Britain, or the destruction of its interests abroad, in many of his novels, particularly in *The Thirty-Nine Steps* (1915) and *Greenmantle* (1916). In these, Germany, instead of Russia, becomes the disturber of the geopolitical system dominated by the British. If the system breaks down, a regression to barbarism will surely occur, which is an expression of Buchan's principal theme of the thin line between civilization and chaos.[32] The necessary barrier separating East and West will be destroyed if Russia sweeps through Europe. 'When that day comes, my masters, we shall have a new empire, the Holy Eastern Empire, and this rotten surface civilization of ours will be swept off'.[33]

Turning away from the East, Buchan depicts South Africa in *Prester John* (1910) as a response to his experience working there in 1901–3.[34] Critics have discussed at length his treatment of Africans in that work,[35] but there is a racial comment, in Buchan's depiction of the Reverend John Laputa, the Christian leader of the black rebellion:

> [The] man's face was as commanding as his figure, and his voice was the most wonderful thing that ever came out of human mouth. It was full and rich, and gentle, with the tones of a great organ. He had none of the squat and preposterous negro lineaments, but a hawk nose like an Arab, dark flashing eyes, and a cruel and resolute mouth.[36]

Buchan distinguishes Laputa from other Africans, indirectly suggesting that he has become a leader because of his different racial origins. Such classification of races can also be seen in Charles Darwin's *The Descent of Man* (1871).[37] In amalgamating the African and the Arabic with Laputa's Christianity Buchan is making a complex statement about the danger within the Empire. The plot of *Prester John* has as its basis the medieval story of Prester John who was believed in the West of the Middle Ages to be a strong oriental king from Ethiopia. He was thought to possess the ability 'to break the power of Islam and restore Jerusalem to Christendom ... The rumour gained so much credence in Europe that messengers and letters were sent to the East in search of the non-existent King'.[38] As Buchan himself noted, Prester John became 'a generic' name for 'any supposed Christian monarch in unknown countries'.[39] In fact, Buchan's use of this Christian legend came at a time when many writers viewed the war in the East as a new crusade due to the efforts of the British government. British Orientalists like Sir Mark Sykes and Sir Stephen Gaselee were influenced by these crusading ideas that were 'central to the way in which the Great War was anticipated, imagined and understood'.[40] Buchan's revival of this mythical Christian figure can be seen as a reminder of the possibility of weakening the Muslim Ottoman bloc. His Christian sense of duty was not foreign to him because it was 'part of his Calvinist training' and his observation of the 'Free Church',[41] although he himself had no leanings towards missionary activity, or to supporting missionary work.

Moving from Muslims to Hindus, but still considering both religions as aspects of the Eastern 'Other' that Buchan incorporated so consistently in his fiction, his short story 'A Lucid Interval' (like *Prester John*, also first published in 1910),[42] deals with the intrigues of Ram Singh, an Indian Hindu landlord from the Nepal border, who tries fruitlessly to regain his land, lost by a government reorganization of boundaries, by travelling to Britain to ask for a judgment from the British government. He is sent to a former Indian viceroy, Lord Caerlaverock, as his last hope. Lord Caerlaverock is fond of curry, and has an Indian cook at his London home. His second footman, James, does not 'hold with the Orient in the kitchen', calls the cook a 'nigger' and has clearly 'expressed profound distrust of his ways'.[43] Buchan's text reads as social history, showing that popular opinion equated Indians with black Africans. Both represent races subject to British colonialism, and both stand in contrast to the white ruling race.

Ram Singh plans revenge on the Caerlaverock household, and uses the Indian cook, Lal Muhammad, to add a secret Hindu drug to the food, that was 'capable of altering a man's whole temperament ... It would turn a coward into a bravo, a miser into a spendthrift, a rake into a fakir'.[44] The drug works, three eminent politicians are affected and their 'reformed' political activities cause consternation for a week. The social comedy that ensues satirizes extreme political views, and the dangers of taking an independent, radical line without due consultation.[45] Colonial and foreign relations are the target of the satire.

'We slaughter our black fellow-citizens, we fill South Africa with yellow slaves, we crowd the Indian prisons with the noblest and most enlightened of the Indian race, and we call it Empire building!' ...

'No, we don't ... we call it commonsense'.[46]

Buchan presents conflicting views in an attempt to give a complete picture of the political debate of the time, while satirizing their extremist views. One of the results is that the Secretary of State for India devises a plan for transferring a great number of Indians to work in South Africa.

'The peoples of the Empire ... must be mobile, shifting about to suit economic conditions. But if this was true of the white man, it was equally true for the dark races under our tutelage'.[47]

The scheme has to be stopped, and Ram Singh applies an antidote to bring British colonial plans back to normal.

In a similar treatment of Indians, *The Three Hostages* (1923) introduces a mysterious character who influences people by unusual eastern methods. Dominick Medina, a representative of another minority race much oppressed by the British, the Irish,[48] is the criminal mastermind of the novel. Instead of using a drug, he practises hypnotism to make his victims forget their pasts.

'There's such a thing ... as spiriting away a man's recollection of his past, and starting him out as a waif in a new world. I've heard in the East of such performances, and of course it means that the memory-less being is at the mercy of the man who has stolen his memory'.[49]

The source of this secret power is an enigmatic and holy Indian guru named Kharáma. Like Ram Singh in 'A Lucid Interval', Kharáma is shown as a mysterious man, whose name is reverenced by 'millions in the East ... like that of a god'.[50] Medina's mother, who taught him mind control, regards the Eastern methods with apprehension:

'Dominick, be careful. I would rather you confined yourself to your old knowledge. I fear these new things from the East'.[51]

Medina wants to combine different kinds of learning to become a modern Dr Faustus. He claims that the

'East has the secret knowledge, but, though it can lay down the practice, it cannot provide the practitioners. The West has the tools, but not the science of their use. There has never ... been a true marriage of East and West, but when there is, its seed will rule the world'.[52]

Medina's idea is that such a marriage could only be achieved with the help of Kharáma. Hannay's first impression of Kharáma is of a man with 'the thin, high-boned, high-bred face of the hillman; not the Mongolian type, but that other which is like an Arab, the kind of thing you can see in Pathan troops ... I had rarely seen a human being at once so handsome and so repulsive'.[53] When his friend Turpin sees Kharáma for the first time, he sees

> an Eastern face, a lean high-boned Arab face, with the eyes set in a strange slant ... He felt in every bone a thing he had almost forgotten, the spell and the terror of the desert. It was a cruel and inhuman face, hiding God knows what of ancient horror and sin, but wise as the Sphinx and eternal as the rocks.[54]

Kharáma's face is also 'as hard as flint and as fierce as Satan'.[55] Like John Laputa, Kharáma has Arabic facial features, which distinguish him from others and increase his dreadful charisma. But this is all play-acting. At the end of the novel, the reader is surprised to find that this Kharáma is Sandy in disguise, since the original Kharáma is safely dead, unknown to Medina. Unbeknown to the reader, this is a safe Kharáma, but Buchan still insists on using that character as an inspirer of fear and as a locus for distrust. Hannay in particular, as the narrative voice and the focus for the reader's self-identification with the story, must be fooled completely.

Hannay is also able to use his own prejudices for his own ends. When he pretends to Medina that he and Sandy have fallen out, Hannay criticizes Sandy in British racist terms:

> 'He has forgotten his manners, his breeding, and everything he once possessed. He has lived so long among cringing Orientals that his head is swollen like a pumpkin ... He's gone back to the East, which is the only place for him'.[56]

Once more, Buchan presents the East as a place of mystery and secrecy, with a degrading and debasing effect. In 'A Lucid Interval' and *The Three Hostages*, Buchan mainly concentrates on the characters of Indian Hindus who have their own secret ways of dealing with Westerners, despite their apparent powerlessness. The writer suggests, though in an undeniably tongue-in-cheek way, that if the peoples of the East have no reasonable or logical ways by which they can persuade the West to take their part, they may have to resort to unexpected and underhand practices. In addition, the East is shown to have mysterious powers that can threaten Imperial powers without necessarily overcoming them at the end.

Leaving Buchan's treatment of Indians, we can return to his lengthy engagement with Arab and Turkish Muslims in *Greenmantle* and to a lesser extent in *The Three Hostages*. Buchan wrote *Greenmantle* during the First World War when the Ottomans, with the help of the Germans, were fighting the British. Hence, the writer used his novel as a work of propaganda that aided the war effort. Before discussing the work in detail, it is important to examine the original meaning of the title.

Despite the fact that the term 'Greenmantle' appears to be closely linked to Islam, as the colour green has a particular significance in that religion, the expression itself is not used by Muslims.[57] The earliest reference to such a phrase comes from the Scottish royal tradition, the Order of the Thistle, established in 1687. Holders of this honour would wear a green mantle as a sign of their noble descent;[58] thus, the phrase's use in Buchan's 1916 novel as the name for the most important imam in Turkey makes a suggestive and entirely positive connection between nobility and the Muslim who 'must be of the Koreish, the tribe of the Prophet himself'.[59]

Far more probable as an influence is Sir Walter Scott, whom Buchan began to read 'early in [his] teens'.[60] In Scott's *The Talisman* (1825), wearing a green turban denotes a pious and distinguished Muslim. For instance, Saladin, the 'Soldan', sent an ambassador to the court of King Richard I:

> This new envoy was an Emir much respected by the Soldan, whose name was Abdallah el Hadgi. He derived his descent from the family of the Prophet, and the race or tribe of Hashem, in witness of which genealogy he wore a green turban of large dimensions. He had also three times performed the journey to Mecca, from which he derived his epithet of El Hadgi, or the Pilgrim.[61]

A year earlier, in his *Redgauntlet* (1824), Scott presented the character of Lilias, a mysterious girl who wears a 'green mantle'.[62] The plot concerns how her uncle Redgauntlet, 'a political enthusiast of the most dangerous character', tries to restore the House of Stuart to the English monarchy.[63] As well as the idea of green signifying purity and truth, there are connections between the unlawful and even treasonable nature of Redgauntlet's plans, and the German plot fomented by Hilda von Einem and von Stumm in Buchan's *Greenmantle*.[64]

In this novel, Buchan tries to show that Islam itself is a threat because the Ottoman sultan had declared a jihad and called all Muslims to participate in the Great War against Britain. In fact, Buchan may have been directly influenced by the Dutch orientalist C. Snouck Hurgronje whose works were translated into English. The titles most relevant to the period of *Greenmantle*'s composition include *The Holy War: 'Made in Germany'* (1915) and *Mohammedanism* (1916).[65]

In *Greenmantle*, Sir Walter says that 'Islam is a fighting creed, and the mullah still stands in the pulpit with the Koran in one hand and a drawn sword in the other'.[66] This terrifying image suggests that even the religious man has a duty to fight the 'Kaffirs' or the infidels. Islam is shown as an uncontrollable force in the British Empire, exemplified by historical events, particularly the Mahdist revolt in the Sudan in the 1870s. If the British tried to interfere, then Muslims 'would be like dried grasses to catch fire ... Look what the English suffered from a crazy Mullah who ruled only a dozen villages'.[67]

The Germans played a major role in creating this prophet; hence the British wanted to interfere before their enemy gained a serious advantage with their Muslim tool. Sir Walter says that containing the Islamic threat is a 'life and death' matter. 'I can put it no higher and no lower'.[68] The only way to counter the Islamic jihad is by controlling its leader, Greenmantle, because 'you can't have a crusade without a prophet'.[69] After the original Greenmantle had died, Sandy Arbuthnot was forced to agree to impersonate him, and the final scene of the novel shows that 'the prophecy had been true, and that their prophet had not failed them. The long-looked for revelation had come. Greenmantle had appeared at last to an awaiting people'.[70] This act suggests that the Turkish Muslims are highly credulous as they have not questioned the identity of the new prophet. It also shows that a Christian white man can lead Muslims to their own advantage: an extension of the Empire's own logic.

Buchan continued to use the character of Sandy as an orientalist in *The Three Hostages* to retain the idea of a Scottish force in Empire, and to voice dissatisfaction with the British government's mishandling of its foreign affairs:

> 'How I loathe our new manners in foreign policy. The old English way was to regard all foreigners as slightly childish and rather idiotic and ourselves as the only grown-ups in a kindergarten world'.[71]

In giving a favoured character such a retrogressive point of view for the post-war world, Buchan is expressing a resistance to change held by conservative society in general. He also demonstrates a disparity between the occupier and the occupied that still exists in the mentality of the British governing elite. Presenting the colonized as a child is emphasized by Buchan to express the popular attitude held at the time.

Sandy was also 'furious about the muddle in the Near East and the mishandling of Turkey'. Because it had remained a major military power after the First World War, Britain set the new borders between Arab countries, but Sandy, or Buchan, believed that the British were doing their 'best to hammer a much-divided Orient into a hostile unanimity'.[72] Sandy's discontent is a continuation of his rhetoric in *Greenmantle* in which he points out the common fallacies held by the British. 'The West knows nothing of the true Oriental. It pictures him as lapped in colour and idleness and luxury and gorgeous dreams. But it is all wrong. The Kâf he yearns for is an austere thing. It is the austerity of the East that is its beauty and its terror'.[73]

Sandy's character is closely drawn from T. E. Lawrence, particularly in relation to the latter's dissatisfaction with British policy in the Middle East and to the assistance he offered to the Arabs in 1914 to rebel against the Turks. In *Greenmantle*, Sandy is described as a well-known figure among Muslims:

> If you struck a Mecca pilgrimage the odds are you would meet a dozen of Sandy's friends in it. In shepherds' huts in the Caucasus you will find bits of his cast-off clothing, for he has a knack of shedding garments as he goes. In the caravanserais of Bokhara and Samarkand he is known, and there are shikaris in the Pamirs who still speak of him round their fires. If you were going to visit Petrograd or Rome or Cairo it would be no use asking him for introductions; if he gave them, they would lead you into strange haunts. But if Fate compelled you to go to Llasa or Yarkand or Seistan he could map out your road for you and pass the word to potent friends.[74]

As a Briton who feels responsible for all Muslims, Sandy visits Egypt and Palestine in *The Three Hostages* to become the organizer of the holy pilgrimage to Mecca. This time, he talks of preparing aeroplanes to take Muslim pilgrims to their destination. He says:

> 'I'm a hamelidari on a big scale. I am prepared to bring the rank of hadji within reach of the poorest and feeblest. I'm going to be the great benefactor of the democracy of Islam, by means of a fleet of patched-up 'planes and a few kindred spirits that know the East'.[75]

As with *Greenmantle* in which he becomes the chosen prophet, Buchan sets up a fictional world where Sandy makes pilgrimage possible, the most important religious act for a Muslim. This implies a colonial attitude because it suggests such inefficiency and economic dependency on the part of Muslims to take charge of their affairs and act independently. Sandy's role in Buchan's novels is to be a mediating contrast with the Western and Muslim characters. By inflating his intellectual abilities and infinite intrigues, Sandy's character confirms Buchan's idea of the superiority of the British, particularly the Scottish, over other races and indicates the writer's continuous imperialist belief that the British are destined to participate in the most intricate matters of other nations and religions.

In conclusion, Buchan was not uniquely prejudiced or racist, but sincerely wanted to give an accurate picture of his time and the beliefs of his generation. He introduces a mixture of portrayals of the East, but emphasizes that the East is backward and decadent, and its people are mostly corrupt and childish. In being different from the civilized and modern Christian West, there has to be a demarcation line separating the East and West, or chaos will overwhelm the whole system. Buchan's Indian Hindu characters are dignified, but they possess mysterious powers that stem from magical practices; their irrational hidden nature is contrasted with the British characters' openness and rationality. In his treatment of Islam and Muslims, Buchan expresses the anxiety of the British Empire by stressing the fearful, unstable and uncontrollable nature of this religion and its 'fanatical' adherents. When he designs a world where the British organize and control the affairs of Muslims, Buchan clearly shows the real aspiration of this Empire and truthfully conveys the popular views of British society.

Acknowledgements

I would like to express my gratitude to the editor, Kate Macdonald, for her valuable remarks, which greatly enriched the arguments in this paper.

11 CONQUISTADORS: BUCHAN'S BUSINESSMEN

H. E. Taylor

The fictional British businessman of the twentieth century has received an uneven level of attention from historians debating the impact of cultural attitudes on economic performance.

Martin J. Wiener, who is most closely associated with the theory that the widespread propagation of an anti-industrial culture was a major factor in Britain's relative decline from its mid-Victorian economic peak, makes almost no analysis of the work of British novelists active in the early decades of the twentieth century.[1] Given the spread of mass literacy that followed the 1870 Education Act, leading to an era in which written entertainment became increasingly central to national culture, this is an unexpected omission if the rural myth and the gentility creed were as pervasive as is claimed.

The literature of this period plays a greater part in the arguments of Professor Wiener's opponents. But in refuting the idea that culture is a key determinant of economic outcomes, W. D. Rubinstein concentrates on the anti-business literary virulence generated in economically triumphant America.[2]

It is possible that a British analysis has been frustrated by a shortage of material. Neil McKendrick, who has paid closer attention to the fictional treatment of the British businessman, cites some eighty British writers who to a greater or lesser extent take business as a theme.[3] Of these, however, only five were active in the first half of the twentieth century.[4]

There is a sense that at a creative level the image of the businessman was fixed before the close of the Victorian period. Positive literary role models were then cancelled out not so much by continued artistic opposition as by the secondary effects of twentieth century literary criticism favourable to the negative school.[5] Despite thematic outliers such as D. H. Lawrence and H. G. Wells, British novelists of the twentieth century increasingly disengaged from business.[6] Even what McKendrick calls 'Literary Luddism' becomes less visible in their work, and in terms of theme the literature of the early twentieth century is just a brief stop on the line that starts with *Hard Times* in Coketown and ends in self-absorption *On Chesil Beach.*[7]

This apparent scarcity of material encourages the study of a politically active writer of the interwar period who was concerned with the consequences of business activity and who responded in his fiction to evolving methods of business organization. John Buchan was an establishment insider whose work was generated from a unique vantage point within the social and political elite. Alert from his wartime service with the Ministry of Information to the didactic possibilities of mass communication, he freighted his books with as much authorial opinion as a thriller-reader could tolerate. And since his books received wide circulation, they may be of greater relevance than those of less popular if more critically acclaimed writers.

Buchan's examination of businessmen is a constant thread running through his adventure fiction. This marks him out as unusual among popular novelists, since the low profile of the British businessman in serious fiction is as nothing compared to his wretched fate in romance. As business activity relates to the means by which sustenance is obtained, it is a point at which fiction touches the real world. As such it is potential anathema to the escapist genre. Among the creatures of Buchan's contemporaries, Sapper's Bulldog Drummond has inherited wealth, while the Dornford Yates crowd are either living off the rents or recovering buried treasure. Perhaps as a consequence of Buchan's background his characters inhabit a more realistic environment than these pure fantasy types. His upbringing was rooted in a Calvinist faith that emphasized the virtues of hard work, and might typically have led to a career in industry or commerce. And although Buchan reached an elevated social position by the more gentlemanly routes of scholarship, public service, the law, publishing, politics and a good marriage, his origins, from which he was never deracinated, were more expressive of practical economic values.

Predisposed by this background to the worship of success, Buchan was drawn to romantic, über-entrepreneurial characters who exemplified the virtues of heart and guts and moral courage as much as the skills of the counting house. Francis Carey, who hosts at his African residence a spectacularly tedious convocation of imperial chatterers, is an idealized version of Cecil Rhodes.[8] A Great Man, he has 'stood by the cradle of great industries', above and beyond the urge to gentrification. Indeed 'the feudal manors of impoverished English squires, the castles of impecunious Highland chiefs held for him no charms'.[9] The momentum of business success has swept Carey into public service on the grand scale. For Buchan there is nothing wrong with business activity that permits this vast agglomeration of capital, so long as it is matched in the application of funds by an equivalent grandeur of vision. There is something touchingly fantastic in the way that English settlers and African tribesmen alike pay Carey the sort of fealty that would not have been out of place at the court of King Arthur. It is as well that he is blessed with a ridiculous squeaking alto.[10] Otherwise he might be mistaken for a god.

But as Buchan evolved from a novelizing political theorist to a genre thriller writer with a political undertow, a withdrawal from the rarefied heights of Carey's talking-shop was indicated. Buchan found a more appropriate level in the engineer. Buchan's conception of civil engineering is mid-Victorian, rooted in the portraits of Samuel Smiles. All the physical facilities of progress are the outcome of the engineer's activity, and in Buchan's implicit view, such things are good. In fact, for Buchan, the word 'engineer' is shorthand for industrious goodness, a positive tag to be attached to characters of which he particularly approved. Herr Gaudian, the 'Good German' who Buchan quite daringly introduced in 1916, is a leader of the profession.[11]

Buchan's first example is Richard Hannay, a mining engineer who has 'made his pile' in South Africa.[12] There is no question of gentrification for Hannay in *The Thirty-Nine Steps* (1915).[13] His practical working background as much as his great outdoorsmanship sets him above the effete specimens of the social elite. The contrast between Hannay and the 'blood stockbroker' Marmaduke Jopley, is telling.[14] In subsequent adventures Hannay is joined by the American John Scantlebury Blenkiron, another mining engineer, who also moves boldly through the world of great affairs and high finance.[15] In fact Blenkiron is at home in any milieu. To drive a taxi, keep a bookshop or impersonate a Mexican while bossing the biggest copper concern on the planet, are all within his repertoire.[16] For such a one as this, to bring off significant Wall Street coups is mere child's play.[17] Blenkiron is Carey come down from his mountain and gone about in the world. It is not money that moves him. It is the love of the game.

Although a foreigner, Blenkiron is very much a businessman in British fiction. Buchan may have felt more comfortable delineating a positive business character as a foreign national who, by reason of his absurd pastiche accent and diction, could not in any case aspire to gentrification. And it is to Blenkiron that Buchan turns when he wants to express a philosophy of business.

> Blenkiron, I remember, got very hurt about being called a business man ... 'Cut it out,' he said. 'It is a word that's gone bad with me. There's just two kind of men, those who've gotten sense and those who haven't. A big percentage of us Americans make our living by trading, but we don't think because a man's in business or even because he's made big money that he's any natural good at every job.'[18]

Blenkiron owes a debt to Samuel Smiles, adhering to his belief that 'the path of success in business is usually the path of common sense.'[19] And in keeping with his Smilesian outlook Blenkiron does not express a cultural contempt for business. Instead he seeks to place it in perspective as one among other important functions in society.

> And don't go confusing real business with the ordinary gift of raking in the dollars. Any man with sense could make money if he wanted to, but he mayn't want. He may prefer the fun of the job and let other people do the looting.[20]

Even Presidents, as Blenkiron generously allows, are hardly inferior to business-men, despite the disparity in pay scales.[21] But nor is it disputed that business efficiency is the mark by which all other efforts are increasingly measured. It is, after all, only Blenkiron's triumphs that allow him to criticize his first calling with such authority.

Blenkiron, whether running a one-man intelligence show, or serving as an 'industrial dictator', is an improbable figure.[22] Buchan's next significant business-men bear a more convincing shape. The Claybodys *père et fils* are set into the plot-landscape of *John Macnab* (1925) as totemic philistine magnates, and in his treatment of them Buchan comes closest to an active propagation of the gentility creed.[23]

The narrative suggests a snobbish anti-industrial cultural ambience. With only Lord Claybody's name, title, residence and referral of John Macnab's challenge to his lawyers to go on, the reader is presumed to recognize (and disap-prove of) a recently ennobled businessman of great wealth and no background. Buchan, however, always sees the other fellow's point of view. The fact that he does not labour Claybody's origins suggests that he is unwilling to demonize him as an irreconcilable outsider. Buchan finds nothing objectionable in Claybody having risen in the world by his own efforts, and accepts that his money has earned him the entrée to society.

Nevertheless Claybody's industrial spirit is strong and has passed undiluted to the succeeding generation: his son, Johnson, is a formidable businessman in his own right. And despite Claybody's social aspirations there is no sugges-tion that his economic vitality is endangered by contact with uncommercial elements. Indeed, as F. M. L. Thompson demonstrates, several scores 'of success-ful businessmen acquired the trappings of estates and country houses' with 'no harmful effects on their immediate or longer-term entrepreneurial capacities'.[24] Equally, it is clear that there is no contradiction in principle between the Clay-bodys' business activities and the material or moral interests of society. Instead Buchan directs his criticism at aspects of Johnson's methods, specifically his cal-lous attitude to the workforce.

Buchan demonstrates that there is no fundamental difference of interest between the business magnates and the well-bred poachers masquerading as 'John Macnab'. They are all bound together in the common cause of property rights. They have a shared interest in social stability. The professionals and aristocrats actually depend on people like the Claybodys for their careers. The banker and the lawyer are employed on Claybody business. The politicians benefit from Claybody contributions to party funds.

There is no question of crying out for a world that excludes the Claybodys. All that Buchan suggests is that if they want to assure the security of property rights, they could do worse than learn from the inherited wisdom of the aristocracy. Acceptance of a self-imposed obligation to treat all men decently will contribute to an integrated and stable society. It is an appeal to common sense. The older generation of Claybodys are already halfway there, and even brash young Johnson is quick to grasp the rudiments.

Buchan's examination of the parvenu Claybodys marks a reversal of his approach. Instead of larding plot-device characters such as Blenkiron with business attributes, he introduces businessmen into the crucibles of his plots for scrutiny and reform. It is not now the fictional businessman of the Blenkiron type who saves society. It is fictional society which saves, and saves itself from, the antisocial businessman.

In developing this approach, Buchan was again drawn to larger than life figures. The Napoleonic mining engineer, Castor, and the newspaper magnate Craw are both engaged in big affairs. And the books in which they appear, *The Courts of the Morning* (1929) and *Castle Gay* (1930) bear, in different keys, a common theme. Central to each is the rediscovery by a great man of long-lost elements of his human nature. Although this idea is more dramatically evolved in the case of Castor, Buchan is equally, if somewhat frivolously, concerned for the soul of Thomas Carlyle Craw.

Unlike the amateur poachers of *John Macnab* Craw has displacement therapy thrust upon him. In this sense he is not particularly interesting as a businessman. He is simply an important personage cut loose from his milieu, and might just as well be a general or a bishop. However, Buchan's treatment of Craw is the closest he comes to examining in any detail the professional activities of one of his businessmen characters. As a newspaper magnate Craw stands at the head of a media world with which Buchan, as writer and publisher, was intimately familiar, and for once the reader learns how the businessman has got his pile. Craw's rise from obscurity to the top of a great combine is outlined in detail, and in a tone that, unusually for Buchan, crosses into satire. Craw is a composite. The unctuous indoorsman Sir William Robertson Nicoll provides his character, while Lord Rothermere's enthusiasm for the Hungarian cause is the model for his 'Evallonian' thunderings.[25] Buchan doesn't think much of his creature. Without diminishing Craw's business achievements, he mocks the commonplace spirit behind them and belittles the man himself.

In emphasizing the unreality behind the 'uplift' themes of the Craw press, Buchan suggests that the purveyor of these fantasies would be even more out of his place in a real-world adventure than his military or religious peers. Craw's business success has been achieved in an isolated sphere. While he professes to guide the opinion and, indeed, the actions of the world, he himself is lost in real life. He contributes nothing to his deliverance, which is accomplished by more practical men.

At the same time Craw does not threaten society. He aggregates vulgar opinion and markets it back to the masses in a circular process. There is no need to upgrade his manners, and to emphasize this point his polished private secretary proves a blackguard. Instead the danger is to Craw's inner self, and Buchan decides on an infusion of adventure. He deflates Craw very quickly, but he does not act out of malice. Rather it is to give himself scope for breathing some human life back into the soggy titan.

Unlike the Claybodys, Craw has no aspirations towards the aristocratic life. His (rented) country house is not an entry point to society – it is a bolt-hole from society in all its forms. Buchan does not criticize this. Yet there is a sense that outdoor training on salmon-river and grouse moor is precisely what Craw lacks. His failure to round himself out suggests that he can never accomplish his potential as a human being, and personal absurdity will always be a pendant to his business success.

Buchan's lighthearted treatment of Craw stands in reaction to his examination of the more complex figure of Castor.[26] Big, black-bearded, literally high-browed, Castor is President of the Gran Seco Company, a world-scale copper-mining operation located in the South American republic of Olifa. He has all the professional virtues, being not only 'a first class man of business' but also 'a very great practical engineer and chemist ... the greatest in the world'.[27] These attributes are admirable to Buchan, although he still considers it advisable to cloak the prodigy in agreeable liberal virtues. So Castor is also a flawless linguist, an ornithologist and a skilled conversationalist whose table talk includes Lord Balfour and Marcel Proust.

In short Castor is a superman in the Carey mould. But whereas Carey has worked his way upward within the context of an expanding and beneficent empire, Castor is the product of imperial collapse. An Austrian émigré, he has devoted his intellectual and organizational abilities to working out the logic of national defeat on the global stage. He is motivated by a progressive megalomania that seeks the destruction of liberty as a step towards his personal assumption of world power.

Castor transcends human vanity – he is a leadership freak on the Presidential scale. His intermediate goal, ambitious enough by conventional standards, is the downfall of the USA, and he runs the Gran Seco Company to provide the necessary funds. Had he not appointed John S. Blenkiron, *incognito* as Sr. Rosas, to the Vice Presidency of the company it is impossible to say what he might not have achieved.

Buchan affords few insights into Castor's business methods, but the materialistic focus necessary to the successful administration of a major industrial concern is apparent.

> His world is a narrow cell with the big dynamo of his brain purring in it ... He is a master over things, and over men so long as he can treat them as things.[28]

Buchan has sensed a new world in which individuals might be smelted into blocks of 'human resource', to be treated as tangible assets in the balance sheet. His disapproval is clear.

Despite his inhumanity, Castor, as scientist, philosopher and megalomaniac, exists at the opposite extreme from Craw. Castor's soullessness stems not from a lack but from an excess of individual potency. The danger is not to himself but to humanity as a whole. There is no call for personal development through adventure training – instead Castor must be withdrawn to a more moderate balance. To this end Buchan applies a well-tried cure – the love of a good woman. But there is no place in the world for an evil superman reformed, and he dies by the hand of a disaffected employee.

At first glance Castor is an old-fashioned entrepreneurial titan, *espèce de Rockefeller*. But on closer inspection he emerges as a businessman of the most advanced contemporary type. The shares of the Gran Seco Company are held by shadowy European interests and by the Government of the Republic of Olifa. Castor is a salaried executive, accountable to shareholders. He exemplifies the progression from personal to managerial capitalism, in which ownership of the company is divorced from control.

In a pre-industrialized model, the interaction of a multitude of independent small-scale activities determined the allocation of resources for the production and distribution of goods. But under the weight of technological development this market mechanism struggled to cope. Transactions were increasingly internalized within ever larger individual firms, and Adam Smith's 'invisible hand' gave way to what Alfred D. Chandler has termed the visible hand of managerial capitalism.[29]

The flow of materials through the modern industrial enterprise called for salaried professionals to manage the process, and for their organization into functional hierarchies. From the 1880s firms raced to evolve managerial structures capable of implementing the growth strategies necessary to realizing efficiencies of scale.[30] The result was the creation of a managerial class that began to assert itself over the swashbuckling heroes of earlier capitalist models. First individual entrepreneurs, and then financiers, were squeezed out of the day-to-day management of the great corporations they had created.[31]

One of Buchan's strengths is an alertness to the zeitgeist. The aeroplane makes an early appearance in *The Thirty-Nine Steps* (1915). In *Mr Standfast* (1919) he picks up on the garden suburb of Biggleswick as a factory of new ideas, however absurd. In the same book the fictional possibilities of an air raid are exploited for perhaps the first time. *The Three Hostages* (1924) sounds an early warning against media manipulation. So although Britain lagged behind America in the shift to managerial capitalism, when a homegrown rationalization movement evolved in the 1920s, engendering a merger wave and the creation of larger business units, Buchan caught the organizational straw in the wind.[32]

In exploring this theme Buchan staffed the Gran Seco Company with a cadre of professional managers, devoted only to the affairs of the enterprise itself. They have no response to wider social concerns. They have lost all connection with general humanity and their individual personalities have been leached away. They enjoy great ability, and are infused with professional pride, but all their energies are internalized. Every noble or romantic emotion has been discarded as inutile. They have not become brutes. (There is an inferior management grade, The Bodyguard, assigned to that function.) But their only communication can be with others of their own, niche, totem. Their only loyalty is to the corporation and its CEO.

> They have a name for their brotherhood. They call themselves the new Conquistadors – conquerors, you see, over all the old standards and decencies of human nature.[33]

The explanation for the Conquistadors' behaviour, for the purposes of the novel, is that they have been addicted to a remarkable drug, *astura*. It is

> a most potent mental stimulant, and its addicts tend to live for the next dose ... Those who once take to it can never free themselves, and they are the slaves of him who can supply it.[34]

This is a device which allows an explanation for conduct that Buchan did not readily comprehend. He was not a student of managerial theory, and used the simple tools of the thriller genre in making his critique. In consequence he presents his readers with the startling concept of the zombie-businessman, an image of the professional manager indoctrinated by the ethos of the extra-national, extra-social corporation that he ever more loyally, ever more moronically, serves.

The picture Buchan paints is vivid:

> They look like robots, with their pallid faces and soft voices and small, precise gestures. All their individuality seems to have been smoothed away, so that they conform to one pattern ... their characters have been stereotyped, and they have surrendered their wills into the hand of their master.[35]

Although the polished and well-mannered Conquistadors are agents of social destruction the greater damage falls upon their selves. Outward refinement of form has been preserved, but inner humanity has been utterly lost.

The Conquistadors meet as an executive board of the Gran Seco Company, and we can infer that these early masters of business administration are senior managers with separate functional specializations forming a head office general staff. The mechanics of what they actually get up to are not explored in any detail, but the broad outline of the organization is sufficiently clear to encourage speculation concerning the models on which Buchan drew. The cadre of European expatriate managers suggests the international oil companies of the period, Anglo-Iranian and Shell.[36] As Chandler points out, these companies were among those at the forefront of British corporate organizational development in the 1920s and 1930s.[37] If we strip off the gaudy trappings of adventure fiction it is possible to discern the outline of Sir Henri Deterding (the Napoleon of Oil), in his office at St Helen's Court, served by a cadre of professional managers whose loyalty is less and less to their national groups, more and more to the globalized entity Royal Dutch Shell.[38]

It is only when faced with the soul-destroying managerial innovation of redundancy that the Conquistadors rediscover their human spirit.

> You have used us, and I think we have given good service ... Now you have changed your plans and would fling us on the scrap-heap. You have different ambitions now, and your old tools are no longer required. But the tools may have something to say to that.[39]

Not for these pioneers of salaried management the self-pitying clearance of their personal effects into a bin-liner before being shuffled off the premises. Instead they shoot the boss.

Buchan's band of idealistic heroes and heroines who oppose the Gran Seco Company in a ludicrously improbable feat of asymmetric warfare take particular objection to the method of the enterprise. This is an extreme variant of the Claybody approach, a system in which the workers are, quite literally, dispensable brutes. It is the *astura* again, and Buchan makes a subtle use of the device, for the drug is isomeric, and comes in two preparations. The managerial isomer is an addictive intellectual stimulant. The substance given to the native workers (iso-*astura*?) is a stamina enhancer, wringing out prodigies of labour until its users collapse as husks. In this way, both managers and workers are used up by a common corporate ethos, equally the victims of the system they serve. In the final analysis, between the drugged and brutalized workers and the drugged and etiolated managers, there is very little to choose.

Irrespective of the fate of the Conquistadors, the development of managerial capitalism continued apace, and before long Buchan was again worrying at its skirts. In *The Island of Sheep* (1936) the focus of his critique was Lombard, a companion of Hannay's stirring early manhood.[40] Here was a man who had stood on scarp and veldt, staring purposefully across Africa, spinning not altogether fantastical dreams of *Lombardy*. And then he went into oil. From a second Rhodes to, as his surname so crudely indicates, a City businessman. *How art thou fallen from heaven, O Lucifer, son of the morning!* When Hannay bumps into his old companion some twenty-five years later, Lombard is a commuter, a golfer, a gardener. He has taken 'a full blown peony' for his wife, and her name is Beryl.[41] In short Lombard has been suburbanized. His vital humanity has drained from him. And to make matters worse he does not regret it a bit.

Unlike the Conquistadors Lombard is not an agent of conscious destruction, but he has answered to the same managerial calling, and has risen by internal promotions to the top of his firm. He makes no obvious contribution to wider society, and is as divorced from it in the preserve of his rock garden as the Conquistadors in the Gran Seco. But Buchan does not give up on the idea of reforming the backslider, and he gives Lombard the most characteristically Buchanesque passage in the book: an exciting car chase up the Great North Road. The fact that this star turn was allowed to someone other than Hannay is a clear indication of Buchan's didactic purpose. It is Lombard who must be re-romanticized and, through action away from the counting house, restored to his essential humanity.

The treatment is yet another a variant of Saki's 'unrest cure'. And having made a full recovery from the success of his business career and the domestic contentment of his private life, Lombard effectively vanishes from the narrative for the final third of the book. A smaller man than his predecessor Castor, his redemption is of less moment. It does not prove fatal to him, and he is permitted a further lease of hopefully more adventurous life.

The Island of Sheep is curiously unsatisfying for a Hannay adventure. There is a sense that Buchan has gone to the well once too often. However, his next, and final, piece of contemporary fiction was an altogether more serious work. *Sick Heart River* (1941) gets under way in a business-friendly environment. In depicting an elite American dinner party, every man a high achiever, Buchan goes out of his way to suggest that financiers and industrialists are as important to society as surgeons, diplomats, scholars and explorers.[42] It is an inverted reprise of Blenkiron's philosophy, twenty years on. For now, in the aftermath of the Great Crash and the Depression, it is business, chastened by these traumas, which must measure its worth against less lucrative pursuits.

The action of the novel is constructed around the search for a missing businessman. Francis Galliard has made a terrific success of his career. His business acumen is vital to his country in its 'present state of precarious balance', and the threat to society lies in the suspension of his activities.[43] But at the personal level it has all gone wrong. He has cut himself off from his ancient Québécois background. He has Anglicized his name. He has married an American woman. He never speaks French. He has deracinated himself, an action incompatible with a balanced approach to life.

Galliard's specific business function is significant. He is an investment banker, at the opposite end of the business spectrum from the 'hands-on' engineer. His activities are far removed from the heavily capitalized companies whose operations he facilitates. And yet his involvement is critical to their success. He is there at the birth of mighty things, and he cannot be insulated from a share of responsibility for the outcomes. The utter despoliation of his childhood home by a new pulp mill is a case in point.[44]

Eventually it all becomes too much, and the confused banker cuts and runs for the wilderness. Galliard is clearly suffering from a nervous breakdown, triggered by tensions between in his new life, and the roots that he has betrayed.

Galliard, even more than Craw, lies at the opposite extreme from Castor. His business success does not project itself externally as a threat to society. Instead it implodes within his individual self. As a result Galliard derives no benefit from the Lombard treatment. He is suffering from something much worse than complacency, and the romantic prescription leads him not into boyish adventure, but into adult madness and terror.

Unable or unwilling to develop the ideas suggested by Galliard's predicament, Buchan loses interest in the runaway. The focus switches to other characters, and Galliard's malaise is transmuted into a terror of the North. The examination of business activity is aborted. The contradictions between material progress, environmental damage and human happiness are suggested, but never resolved. Despite Galliard's sufferings, Buchan's romantic ideal for the life of the individual remains at war with the goal of a stable and prosperous society.

Buchan's early businessmen are hero-figures rooted in the Victorian age. Carey, Hannay and Blenkiron contribute to society. Their images are positive, and go against the idea of a cultural antipathy to business. Followers of Samuel Smiles, they worship at the altar of common sense.

Buchan's later examples are more complicated. The Claybodys, Craw, Castor, the Conquistadors, Lombard and Galliard – all have deviated from the totem of common humanity. These misguided businessmen threaten either society, their own selves, or both.

As a moralist Buchan is not content to observe: he must attempt a cure. Like *astura* his solutions come in two forms. When the negative impact of a businessman's activities falls on his individual spirit, Buchan prescribes romance. Craw and Lombard benefit from the treatment. Galliard suffers complications, but even he manages a recovery of sorts.

Where a businessman threatens society, Buchan recommends gentry values. In the case of the Claybodys he recognizes that poor treatment of labour can be a key factor in business success. But it is a vice, and unless corrected society will be threatened by a challenge to property rights. The correction is simple: a willingness to borrow from the inherited wisdom of an idealized social aristocracy. This is where best practice in labour relations is to be found. Gentrification is not the objective of a business life, but a necessary addition to an active businessman's skill-set.[45]

This utilitarian view of good manners is explored from the reverse angle in *The Courts of the Morning*. The damage wreaked on the workers under personal capitalism is seen in a managerial system to fall also on the upper echelons. It is noteworthy that the Conquistadors display a broad range of elite cultural values. As with their clothes, so also their manners are flawless, at least until the *astura* runs out. Refined behaviour is a salvage from their past lives. But it is not used as a basis for improved labour relations. It is disconnected from a wider social context, existing as a mere form, and its practical benefits are lost. The Conquistadors have failed to remember the lesson which the *arriviste* Claybodys have taken to heart.

The Conquistadors are object lessons for study, but are not themselves subjects for treatment.[46] Castor is a different matter. The ultimate problem businessman, he has lost his soul and consciously threatens civilization. As such he merits the supreme intervention, love. It is an intensification of all other treatments combined.

Even when his early uncritical appreciation of businessmen gives way to a more negative awareness, Buchan avoids direct opposition. Instead he seeks to constrain and redirect unacceptable behaviour within constructive social and individual forms. Although this aligns Buchan with aspects of the Wiener thesis, he does not reject material progress.[47] He accepts the centrality of business in modern society, and he is interested in businessmen. He does not come at them with fixed opinions, and he attempts a balanced appraisal that addresses serious concerns.

Over a period of thirty-five years the intensity of Buchan's critique fluctuates, reaching a peak in his treatment of the Conquistadors. But even here Buchan finds grounds for hope. Rather than stamping out the Gran Seco Company he reforms it into a socially useful enterprise, a New Lanark of the Andes perhaps, with Blenkiron engaged as its homespun Philosopher-CEO.[48]

12 'A FRAUD CALLED JOHN BUCHAN': BUCHAN, JOSEPH CONRAD AND LITERARY THEFT

Douglas Kerr

Which novel is being described here? A reclusive and unworldly Scandinavian, the self-doubting son of a domineering father who was a writer, is content to live a life of obscurity on his remote island. But his sanctuary on the margins of civilization is invaded by a piratical gang led by a gentlemanly villain, bent on getting their hands on what they believe is a great treasure in his possession. There ensues a desperate struggle, reaching a bloody conclusion in which the invaders are finally destroyed by the defence mounted by the islander and those who are pledged to help him.

Admirers of Joseph Conrad will have no trouble recognizing this as the story told in his novel *Victory*, completed just before the outbreak of the First World War and published in 1915. Enthusiasts for the work of John Buchan, meanwhile, will find this account equally familiar, pointing out that it summarizes the main plot of Buchan's novel *The Island of Sheep*, a book published in 1936, a dozen years after Conrad's death. The congruence of these two novels, hitherto unremarked as far as I know, is the starting point for this investigation. It is the scene of the crime, if you will, though it is not clear just what crime – or whether any crime – has actually been committed.

There is clearly a *prima facie* case for bringing a charge of theft against Buchan. Yet in many respects *The Island of Sheep* could hardly be further removed from Conrad's *Victory*. The story of *Victory* unfolds in Eastern waters, and it plays to its climax on Samburan, the 'Round Island', apparently between Java and south-eastern Borneo, where the Swede Axel Heyst has taken refuge from a disappointing world. There he brings the bedraggled Lena, whom he has chivalrously rescued, and when the island is invaded by the villainous Mr Jones and his two henchmen, it is Lena who brings about their defeat, though at the cost of her own life. Heyst, having lost her, dies in a fire at the end of the story, presumably by his own hand. None of these elements of Conrad's story are taken up in *The Island of Sheep*.

Buchan's novel is as Northern a tale as *Victory* was Eastern. Buchan's embattled islander, Valdemar Haraldsen, is a Dane, but his island refuge is in the Norlands, an archipelago very like the Faroes to the north of the British Isles, and at the other end of the earth from *Victory*'s Samburan. Much of Buchan's story takes place in England and Scotland and recounts the persecution of Haraldsen and his daughter by a gang of his father's enemies as well as more opportunistic and sinister villains. But Haraldsen is lucky in his allies, who include the resourceful Richard Hannay and Sandy Arbuthnot (Lord Clanroyden), veterans of earlier Buchan adventures, including *The Thirty-Nine Steps* (1915) and *Greenmantle* (1916). With their help Haraldsen defeats his enemies in a showdown on his island in the Norlands, and may be supposed to live happily ever after.

In spite of these manifold differences, however, it is difficult to dismiss the similarities between the stories as simply coincidental. Nor can it be sufficient to assign the similarities to both writers producing an adventure story from a common box of stage properties. They share elements with *Treasure Island* (1881–2) and *Peter Pan* (1902–4), as well as *Lord Jim* (1899–1900) and *The Three Hostages* (1924). Besides generic parameters of romance adventure, there are other properties which the Buchan story shares with its Conradian predecessor that cannot really be explained as being drawn from the common stock. The Scandinavian provenance of the islander, the unworldly diffidence and anti-sociability that isolate him and make him vulnerable, so carefully mapped to his relationship with a difficult father, departed but still felt to be exigent in his demands – the psychological centre of Heyst's story as it interested Conrad – is reproduced in Buchan's Haraldsen with a completeness hard to justify as mere coincidence.

Then there are the invading villains, both gangs under the leadership of a denationalized gentleman with a history of crime in South America. *The Island of Sheep*'s desperadoes are described in terms that recall Mr Jones and his henchmen in *Victory*: 'D'Ingraville was a fallen angel, Carreras a common desperado, but Martel seemed to be *apache*, sewer-rat, and sneak-thief all in one'.[1] This suggests the taxonomy, or class system, of the invaders of Samburan as Axel Heyst defines them for Lena's benefit, the envoys of the outer world. 'Here they are before you – evil intelligence, instinctive savagery, arm in arm. The brute force is at the back'.[2] The fact that, in both books, villains like this gang up to attack a victim like that, on his island home beyond the reach of the law, in the mistaken belief that he possesses a great treasure, adds up, I suggest, to circumstantial evidence; enough to justify a declaration that the game is afoot. The game becomes more intriguing, if not necessarily clearer, with the introduction of a further item of evidence, which is that Conrad once accused Buchan of plagiarism.

Buchan and Borrowing

In November 1899, William Blackwood sought Conrad's opinion about a story by a young writer, John Buchan, which the proprietor of *Blackwood's Magazine* had accepted for publication in that month's instalment. Conrad's reply, in a letter to Blackwood of 8 November 1899, allows that the story is grammatically written, but then unleashes the following missile:

> There is one thing (though hardly pertaining to criticism proper) which ought to be said of that – production. It is this: it's [sic] idea, its feeling, its suggestion and even *the most subtly significant details* have been wrenched alive out of Kipling's tale '*The Finest Story in the World*'. What becomes of the idea, of the feeling, of the suggestion and of the incidents, in the process of that wrenching I leave it for the pronouncement not of posterity but of any contemporary mind that would be brought (for less than ten minutes) to the consideration of Mr. Buchan's story. The thing is patent – it is the only impression that remains after reading the last words – it argues naiveness of an appalling kind or else a most serene impudence. I write strongly – because I feel strongly. [emphasis in original]
>
> One does not expect style, construction, or even common intelligence in the fabrication of a story; but one has the right to demand some sort of sincerity and to expect common honesty. When that fails – what remains?[3]

The following day Conrad told Edward Garnett all about it, with a little embroidery.

> Bwood is fussing now over a fraud called John Buchan. Asked me to give him my opinion of that unspeakable impostor's story in the last *Maga*. And I did give it to him too. I said it was too contemptible to be thought about and moreover that it was stolen from Kipling as to matter and imitated from Munro as to style. I *couldn't* keep my temper.[4]

It is worth examining the basis of Conrad's accusation. Rudyard Kipling's 'The Finest Story in the World', which appeared in the *Contemporary Review* in July 1891 and later in his collection *Many Inventions* (1893), is about a bank clerk, Charlie Mears, who has a narrative in his head, about the experience of a Greek galley slave and, later, one about a member of a Viking expedition sailing across the Atlantic to the American continent. These stories come in the sort of vivid and convincing detail that a bank clerk, it is assumed, would not have the education to have learned about nor the imagination to invent. Charlie seeks the help of a friend of his, the narrator, a professional writer, who recognizes that the stories are the memories of Charlie's past lives. Realizing their value as authentic historical witness, he determines to buy his friend's stories, transcribe them from Charlie's dictation, and publish them for his own profit. But Charlie falls in love with a tobacconist's assistant and is thereafter interested only in writing dreadful Swinburnean love poems: the finest story in the world will never be written.

It is the trope of ancestral memory that links this Kipling tale to the Buchan story, 'The Far Islands', that so unexpectedly enraged Conrad. 'The Far Islands' begins by noting Colin Raden's ancestry through hereditary Scottish aristocrats to a companion of Bran the Blessed, the giant king of Celtic legend. Colin, a healthy young man with no particular attachment to his national traditions, has recurring reveries about a westward journey across the sea through the mists towards – but never reaching – a group of islands. Scraps of Latin come to him; he gets them translated, and they appear to refer to the Hesperides, islands of apple trees in the western ocean. Colin goes with his regiment to a desert war, presumably in the Sudan: 'He found fragments of the Other world straying into his common life'.[5] His reverie about the Rim of the Mist, an increasing refuge on the campaign, comes clearest to him when he is shot and dying, and now at last in his imagination he makes landfall: '[w]ith a passionate joy he leaped on the beach, his arms outstretched to this new earth, this light of the world, this old desire of the heart – youth, rapture, immortality'.[6] With the attainment of this vision at the moment of his death, the story ends.

The scraps of Latin, not understood by Colin, echo a motif in the Kipling story – Charlie seems to remember graffiti scrawled by the galley slaves in ancient Greek, a language he does not understand. Beyond this it is hard to see any other incidents 'wrenched alive out of Kipling's tale' as Conrad complained, or to make a general case of plagiarism against Buchan. The trope of a recovered memory of earlier incarnations was not original to either story; it had been the premise of Rider Haggard's novel *She* (1887) and would be elaborated in the sequel *Ayesha* (1905).[7] Ancestral memory is quite frequently encountered in late Victorian fiction, and accompanies the epoch's scientific fascination with all kinds of inheritance – the cultural inheritance explored in the anthropology of myth and folklore, the narratives of physical inheritance for which Darwin had provided an explanation, and the psychic legacies assumed in the idea of tendencies – to crime, for example – transmitted with physiological features from one generation to the next within a family or a people.[8] Ancestral memory was no casual romance device, but an important topic related to contemporary understandings of race, a theme of great importance in Buchan's work as Alan Sandison and Juanita Kruse have shown.[9] Buchan was, after all, an exact con-temporary of C. G. Jung (both born 1875), the propounder of inherited psychic archetypes and the 'collective unconscious'. Buchan was unlikely to have needed the Kipling story to inform him about ancestral memory.

Apart from this, the Buchan story has little in common with the Kipling one. Buchan has no equivalent to Kipling's sardonic interest in the relationship between the naive rememberer and his amanuensis. In Kipling, Charlie's descent from an earlier incarnation as a Greek galley slave is arbitrary. For Buchan, the whole point about Colin's visionary gift is that it is the sign and proof of an impressive ancestry going way back to the Celtic origins of Britain, and an authentication of his status as bearer of an unbroken national heroic tradition. Colin's visions, meanwhile, are of a distinctly Celtic Twilight kind; they are of mists and romantic shorelines, and they feature no people, whereas the memories in the Kipling tale are characteristically novelistic, realistic and technical.

Why then Conrad's outrage? He had no particular love for Kipling, his younger contemporary approaching national institution status, whereas he himself was not well-known as an author, and was financially insecure. He may well have felt some hostility towards the upstart Buchan, who was some eighteen years his junior but very much a Scotsman on the make, an undergraduate at Oxford who wrote to pay his way through university. During his time at Oxford, Buchan had published five books in addition to numerous short stories and articles, with a facility unlikely to endear him to Conrad, for whom writing was always a slow and sometimes an agonizing business. Conrad had laboriously secured the trust of Blackwood, and with it a precious outlet for the serialization of his fiction; the second instalment of *Lord Jim* was in the same number that carried 'The Far Islands'. Buchan, who had already published more than a dozen tales, had had his first story in *Blackwood's* earlier that year (January 1899), a preposterous enough tale called 'No-Man's Land', about a young Oxford Fellow in Celtic Studies who stumbles upon a semi-feral tribe of Picts living in the Galloway hills. In the next twenty years *Blackwood's* became Buchan's favourite periodical outlet: he published fourteen pieces in its pages, and Blackwood was also the publisher of Buchan's lightly fictionalized debate on the future of the empire, *A Lodge in the Wilderness* (1906). Almost overwhelmed by his own struggles in 1899, Conrad could not be expected to warm to a young man whom he may have thought of as a facile upstart. Buchan, however, admired Conrad, and as literary advisor to the publisher Thomas Nelson, he was later to be responsible for issuing Conrad's *A Personal Record* and the Conrad–Hueffer collaboration *Romance* in a series of popular reprints.

We risk missing an important point if we put Conrad's vehemence down to in-house rivalries among Blackwood's writers. There is another dimension to the matter: 'To scold others for the sins we are inclined to commit is not commendable, but it is quite common'.[10] Indeed, while Conrad's attack on Buchan as a plagiarist is not especially convincing, Conrad's own propensity to borrow without due acknowledgement is a matter of record.

Conrad and Borrowing

Like any other writer, Conrad's principal indebtedness is to his own work, and is manifold. *Victory* in particular, as Edward Said observed, is 'a novel full of reminiscences' and 'full of self-quotation'.[11] The invasion of the gentlemanly pirate has its prototype in *Lord Jim*, for example, and the story of a man who burns down his house after losing the woman he loves had already been told in Conrad's first novel, *Almayer's Folly* (1895). A good deal of detective work has been done on the question of Conrad's indebtedness to others.[12] Watt notes that Conrad had a remarkable but erratic memory, and suggests he probably forgot that he was remembering; besides, most of his borrowings 'seem more curious than important'.[13]

'Why did Conrad borrow so extensively?', asks Yves Hervouet, who is unwilling to see these borrowings explained away, by Watt and others, as unconscious. This view cannot account, Hervouet says, for the extent and detail of Conrad's purloinings: '[b]ut the number, the length, and the obvious nature of the borrowings ... make it abundantly clear that Conrad knew exactly what he was doing, and that we are faced with a deliberate method of composition'.[14] There may be practical, psychological and literary-historical explanations for this phenomenon. Frederick R. Karl usefully identified 'the dependency pattern that seems intrinsic to Conrad's way of working and surviving'.[15]

The literary-historical account Hervouet advances for Conrad's borrowings has to do with the centrality to literary modernism of borrowing, allusion and imitation. Conrad's novels with their borrowings do not stand out conspicuously. Their intertextual connections 'contribute considerably to the density and complexity of the stories', Hervouet claims, as well as lifting them to that level of generality and universality characteristic of all great art.[16]

Yet the honorific ascription of writerly borrowing to modernism seems both inaccurate and oddly unfair. It is hard to see why this imbrication in 'the network of the already written' should be seen as a quality of modernist (and of course postmodernist) writing, a category that excludes work like Buchan's thrillers on the grounds of genre, as much as it excludes specifically parasitic work like *Hamlet* or *Joseph Andrews* on chronological grounds.[17] Indeed for the classic author, tradition was a shared collection of paradigms, a prestigious neighbourhood in which writers were proud to situate their own new-built work, citing the masters to lay claim to their own role in the tradition. Linda Hutcheon points out, 'perhaps only in a Romantic (and capitalist?) context where individuality and originality define art can the "borrowing" from other texts be considered plagiarism – or "stealing"'.[18] Thus, I exist in and through the network of the already written (goes the modernist conjugation): you borrow; he is a plagiaristic fraud.

Gérard Genette named everything that sets the text in a relationship, whether obvious or concealed, with other texts, 'transtextuality'. He recognizes five types, of which two seem germane to the case of Buchan and Conrad: 'intertextuality', which comprises quoting, plagiarism and allusion, and 'hypertextuality' which, Genette explains, refers to 'any relationship uniting a text B (... the *hypertext*) to an earlier text A (... the *hypotext*), upon which it is grafted in a manner that is not that of commentary'.[19] Both Virgil's *Aeneid* and James Joyce's *Ulysses* are hypertexts of the same hypotext, Homer's *Odyssey*. Virgil and Joyce do not comment on the Homeric precursor, but neither the *Aeneid* nor *Ulysses* could exist without it. Both cases, the simple transformative appropriation of a pattern of actions and relationships, and the more complex imitative appropriation of a style, involve a degree of 'mastery', to use Genette's word, over the hypotextual precursor.[20] They also involve a deference to the original, a recognition of its primacy and generative power even in the act of consuming it. Harold Bloom's account of poetic misprision in terms of tropes and defences offers a different way of looking at such relationships.[21] As we shall see, there is a poignant doubleness – an assertion of mastery, and an admission of belatedness – to what Buchan does with the work of his precursor Conrad.

Buchan and Conrad

The relation between Buchan's fictional world and Conrad's needs to take into account an earlier and yet more awkward pairing. Buchan's novel *The Courts of the Morning* (1929) features a number of his recurrent characters, including John S. Blenkiron and Lord Clanroyden. Most of the action takes place in Olifa, an imaginary republic on the Pacific seaboard of South America, at first sight 'a decadent blend of ancient Spain and second-rate modern Europe', rich in silver and copper and increasingly prosperous, and consequently politically unstable, as the result of the activities of the Gran Seco Company, a mining concern (one of its properties is called the San Tomé mine), with an ambitious European director.[22] A revolution is fomented, a civil war breaks out, there are acts of individual bravery and loyalty, adventures and escapes, an army arrives just in time, and at the end of the story the Gran Seco, with its mineral riches, becomes an independent province, firmly tied by commercial and political partnership with the United States.

While there are not, as far as I can see, any verbal echoes of Joseph Conrad's *Nostromo* (1904) other than the name of the mine, the setting and events of *The Courts of the Morning* are quite startlingly reminiscent of Conrad's South American novel, and there is a good case for saying that the Buchan book is a *Nostromo* hypertext. And yet, just as we saw that *The Island of Sheep* is in significant respects a book hugely different from Conrad's *Victory*, the point I want to make now is that *The Courts of the Morning* is in most important ways nothing like *Nostromo*. For one thing, although the topography, ethnography, history and economics of Olifa are all expounded with scrupulous realism, the improbable plot of *The Courts of the Morning* is far removed from anything that could happen in a Conrad story.

Castor, the denationalized *gobernador* of the province of the Gran Seco and the head of the company, belongs to the anarchist strain of Buchan villains, discussed by Philip Ray, and by Kruse.[23] He is persuaded to lead the revolution after being converted to the cause of goodness, democracy and the American alliance. As a result of this conversion Castor, who had wanted to be 'a Napoleon to shape the world', declares himself now 'quite content if [he] can help to make an inconsiderable Latin republic a more wholesome state'.[24] He dies in the violent climax of the story, but his death only serves to cement the beginnings of a new world order.

No doubt it is possible to read Conrad's *Nostromo* in many different ways, and it could be argued at least that for the Occidental Republic of Sulaco, the story has a happy ending. But even in the most sanguine interpretation, *Nostromo* is far removed from the relentless closures of *The Courts of the Morning*. The brilliant and dangerous Castor is converted through association with Anglo-Saxon womanhood to something like sainthood; the rootless cosmopolitan is humanized by developing attachments for people, place and nation, and becomes even lovable himself. There is never any suggestion that there might be anything questionable in the actions of Blenkiron and Clanroyden, who subvert a state and start a bloody war. Their activities are presented as an irreproachable and completely successful exercise in nation building. Everything that in *Nostromo* might be ambiguous, compromised, insoluble, variously modalized and ironic – modernist, in a word – in *The Courts of the Morning* is straightforward, above-board, settled.

Since, then, the two novels appear to be so radically different in temperament, how to account for the scandalous echoes from one to the other in setting, situation and motif, whether these echoes are deliberate or unconscious? In my mind is an image of a person who closes a door left open and tidies up the bits, after a disruptive guest has blown in and out again. *The Courts of the Morning* closes or restores the matter of *Nostromo* in something like an act of rehabilitation. Buchan's recapitulation of material from *Nostromo* may be an acknowledgment of a half-buried dependence, an act of respect, but it is also an act of redress, the kind of ideological reversal that Genette calls 'thematic transformation'.[25] This could be the accusation levelled at Buchan in the dock, but it might equally be his defence.

Let me illustrate this point with two contrasting examples of borrowing. The first example (itself borrowed from Hervouet) is a sentence of Conrad's in *Almayer's Folly*. "'It has set at last," said Nina to her mother, pointing towards the hills behind which the sun had sunk'.[26] This echoes the words of Mickiewicz's poem *Konrad Wallenrod* (1828): "'It has set at last," said Alf to Halban, / Pointing to the sun from the window of his crenelle'.[27] This is an example of intertextuality, specifically plagiarism. We may wonder at the triviality of the misdemeanour, but there seems to be nothing more mysterious or consequential about it. The second example is Buchan's naming of the San Tomé mine in the Gran Seco in Olifa in *The Courts of the Morning*. San Tomé was the name of the great silver mine at the heart of all the action in *Nostromo*. The borrowing in this case is even less rational; Buchan had an almost unlimited choice of nomenclature for this mine and need not have named it at all. I take the borrowing as something like a symptom, the trace or acknowledgment of a hypertextual dialogue in which the troubling implications (aesthetic and ideological) of the Conradian precursor text are reprocessed to serve the purposes of Buchan's quite different, more sturdy and confident picture of the world.

It is with this understanding of the process that I return to *The Island of Sheep*, approaching Buchan's debt in that novel to *Victory* not as an act of theft but as one of redress, in the sense of a restoration, a return to propriety, the righting of a wrong. At the back of the word is also (by way of a useful false etymology) the idea of reclothing. The novel can be interpreted as a critical activity performed upon Conrad's fiction; I cannot resist describing it as snatching *Victory* from the jaws of its own defeatism. In *The Island of Sheep* we can observe motifs from *Victory* being rehabilitated to offer deep reassurance to its readers living in the increasingly beleaguered 1930s. Motifs from the Conrad story may return, but the shaky moral compass of *Victory* is stabilized, the worryingly open questions of the earlier novel are answered and closed in the later one. Nobody arrived in time to help Conrad's Heyst and Lena when Samburan was invaded, and they perished. Those same Buchan characters and qualities that always prevailed in the end at the time of the Kaiser, in *The Three Hostages* (1923) and against anarchists in *A Prince of the Captivity* (1933), can still pull it off in the Norlands in the age of Stalin and Hitler.

Meanwhile at the level of genre we may begin to understand *The Island of Sheep* as restoring fictional motifs that Conrad had used for his own aesthetically radical purposes in *Victory*, back to their original function as the vocabulary of the conservative genre of romance. Northrop Frye suggested long ago that the basic myth of romance is one of redemption.[28] Lena in *Victory* may in a sense redeem Heyst but she cannot save him, nor can she turn her story into romance of a conventional kind. But in *The Island of Sheep* redemption seems to be offered not only to several of the characters, but also to the hypotextual ghost of Conrad's *Victory*.

Both novels are launched from a similar structure of feeling, an elected withdrawal from the world into forms of passive isolation which in turn are experienced as untenable or insufficient. Conrad's Axel Heyst has withdrawn to Samburan from the world from which nothing can be expected. In the first chapter of *The Island of Sheep*, titled 'Lost Gods', Richard Hannay too is dissatisfied, and we find him living the life of a country gentleman at Fosse, with his adventures in the theatres of empire and war behind him. His old comrade in arms, Lombard, once the idealistic 'young knight-errant', is now almost unrecognizable as a stout bald man on a commuter train.[29] Heyst's story might be described as that of a man who finds again something to have faith in, though this does not save him. The case of Hannay and Lombard, and of Haraldsen, is simpler. They are restored, in a thoroughly Buchanesque phrase, to 'a decent vigour of spirit' and regenerated by the romance of their adventure on the Island of Sheep.[30] For Lombard in particular, the danger successfully undergone 'had brought back ... something of his youth and his youth's dreams'.[31] Heyst's island becomes a crematorium where his story ends in ashes, but Haraldsen's island turns out to be a place of birth and restoration. Paradise restored is a quasi-feudal sense of people belonging to a place and the place belonging to them, the restoration of a youthful purpose and rootedness.

Buchan's novel reaccentuates, in a sort of narrative anagram, motifs from Conrad's *Victory* to its own purposes. Some of the borrowings are arbitrary and seem pointless; these I would class as merely symptomatic. Others are exploited in different ways, and among these the Scandinavian provenance of the victim is an interesting example.

Conrad's Heyst is Swedish. This helps to explain why his temperament is gloomy, possibly accounts for his aristocratic courtesy, and marks him as a solitary even among the other Europeans out East. But although Buchan's Haraldsen is not actually a native of the Norlands, his Nordic provenance gives him a particular legitimacy as a landowner there which means, crucially, that the local whaling folk rally to his side in the crisis of the invasion. Much is made of the cultural theories of the elder Haraldsen who has educated his son in the belief that 'the Northern culture was as great a contribution to civilization as the Greek and Roman, and that the Scandinavian peoples were destined to be the true leaders in Europe'.[32] Ethnic inheritance continues to be important to Buchan, as we saw it was in 'The Far Islands'. Meanwhile the senior Haraldsen's Danish parentage is some explanation of the junior Haraldsen's morbidity and Hamlet-like melancholy.[33]

Nordic heritage is also crucially the warrant for Haraldsen's berserk fit in the crisis of the action, when he reverts to ancestral type, and destroys his principal antagonist unarmed and single-handed in a fit of blind rage. The local whalers who come to help – 'men with conical caps, and beards like trolls and wild eyes and blood-stained whale spears' – go into battle in (or out of) the same state of mind, and the whole scene is enacted in a Nordic atavism, again evidence of something like a racial unconscious.[34] 'Like Haraldsen they had gone back to type – they were their forebears of a thousand years ago making short work of a pirate crew'.[35] We might recall that 'instinctive savagery' and 'brute force' were embodied in Ricardo and Pedro, the invaders of Samburan, in *Victory*,[36] as if in confirmation of Lombrosan ideas of the link between criminality and primitive atavism. The same instinctive aggression emerges from the Nordic past in *The Island of Sheep*, but significantly only to support the forces of law and order and property, and then it subsides again, under proper control. It has served its purpose in the defeat of the villainous D'Ingraville, 'the outlaw at war with society'.[37]

The Island of Sheep, then, does for *Victory* what *The Courts of the Morning* had done for *Nostromo*, activating a memory of reading that may be deliberately recalled, or could be as unconscious as the deep memories of Kipling's Charlie Mears. Leaving behind as clues or symptoms a cluster of similarities, many of which seem too arbitrary to be counted as thefts, the later text pays a kind of homage to the earlier by redressing it, simplifying its theme, reaccentuating it in a more traditional and popular genre, and at the same time reinscribing, in apparently bold and confident characters, ideological positions – on property, family, locality and nation in one case, and on capitalism, the world order, and human nature in the other – which the earlier text had worked to question, or erase.

The Island of Sheep uses the standard scenario of much of Buchan's fiction. The stability of civilization is threatened by traitors within, and by ideological outcasts, a stock of 'all kinds of geniuses and desperadoes'.[38] Against these enemies, the forces of good are ranged in an always defensive war. Buchan's basic chronotope is that of the stockade, where a beleaguered resistance is mounted, and the attackers eventually defeated.[39] This image has its psychological roots in Buchan's deep conservatism, and in *The Island of Sheep* the defensive forces are recruited from an established social order that consists of the hereditary aristocracy (Clanroyden), the white dominions and the army (Hannay), the City (Lombard), and the police (the trusty Macgillivray). The continuity of this vision of society – it is really a utopia – is further guaranteed by the part played in the victory by a resourceful new generation, Hannay's son and Haraldsen's daughter. The warrant of this social order, fantasy though it may be, has no equivalent at all in Conrad, who simply had no such vision of Britain, or of anywhere else. Unlike Buchan, Conrad had little faith in the ability of society to come to its own defence against the forces of darkness. Consequently Buchan's release of these social and ideological resources into a scenario repeated from Conrad's *Victory*, and played out to a more desirable ending, is something like a social reconstruction.

Meanwhile Buchan's hypertextual transformation of the matter of *Victory* tropes the hypothesis of the earlier book, redressing it with an infusion of thoroughly Buchanesque values that enables it to resist its own potential for problem and tragedy, and to close upon a simple conclusion conforming to the desire of the principal characters, and of the generic reader of romance – a reader whom

Conrad was never able to satisfy in the same way. In this rather strange respect at least, Buchan has no case to answer, for he was serving the ghost of Joseph Conrad not with a theft, but with a gift.

Acknowledgements

This is a revised and expanded version of 'Stealing *Victory*?: The Strange Case of Conrad and Buchan', *Conradiana* 40:2 (Summer 2008), pp. 147–63.

13 APHRODITE REJECTED: ARCHETYPAL WOMEN IN BUCHAN'S FICTION

Kate Macdonald

Introduction

Women characters are not principal protagonists in the fiction of John Buchan, but are cast in supporting roles that limit their possibilities. Buchan had also, most obviously in his earliest work, a tendency to be stereotypical and wooden when he wrote women characters.[1] From the outset he cast them as subordinate individuals. His first heroine, Anne of *Sir Quixote of the Moors* (1895), was not even given a surname, an omission which can be read as a metonym for her dependency on her father and her betrothed, who have abandoned her. When she begins to exhibit signs of independence towards the end of the novel she is also abandoned by the hero.[2] In treating women characters as secondary in almost all respects Buchan was simply reflecting his own society, but was also participating in the Victorian literary tradition of the male romance, by, for example, H. Rider Haggard, Arthur Conan Doyle and even Joseph Conrad, which had little room for women protagonists.[3] Buchan was eventually able to write women well, but he continued to resist using them as principal characters, or to tell their stories. He did not focalize a woman character, allowing her to tell her own story in her own words, until he wrote Janet Raden, in *John Macnab* in 1923, when he was nearly fifty years old. This chapter explores how Buchan wrote women, and how his depiction of women characters reflected the changing lives of modern Western women. In looking at how Buchan's attitude changed towards his women characters, we may also arrive at an understanding of the kind of fiction he was writing.

Buchan began his writing career in a period where literary production, and innovation, was closely connected to the main social developments of the age.[4] He was contemporaneous with the Fabians, the New Woman and with feminist political ferment,[5] but Buchan was simply not of that world.[6] The women with whom he populated his fiction were, like him, not 'sociologically-minded',[7] but conventional Conservative Edwardians and Georgians. Present-day accounts of literary activity at the time emphasize the visibility of the New Woman, and the dominance of women in publishing and periodicals, for example,[8] but the New Woman does not appear in Buchan. Current critical opinion holds that 'by 1895 ... British fiction had reached a point of crisis ... fiction was dominated by women and feminism'.[9] If this state of affairs existed, there is no evidence of it in Buchan's early fiction, and neither did it percolate into his writing over time. The 'influence of feminism upon fiction' in this period produced a 'large number of novels by women and men which place modern women and their particular concerns at the center of their narratives'.[10] Again, Buchan was not part of such a response. 'The rebellious woman' who was commonplace in Edwardian fiction[11] has no place in Buchan's writing; his fiction resisted change, rather than sought for it. After the First World War he was best known for his 'purified form of masculine quest romance'[12] which became the modern thriller, a form which had a masculine viewpoint, and told men's stories.

It may be helpful to consider why Buchan deployed his women characters as he did by exploring female archetypes. Archetypes are a useful way to classify character types, particularly in fiction deriving from traditional forms, and may lead to a better understanding of how Buchan wrote. As a classicist with a first in Greats, classical myth was a strong influence on Buchan's fiction, especially at a time when the study of the classics had been given a fresh boost by Frazerian anthropology.[13] I also want to consider how Buchan's female characters can be described in terms of A. J. Greimas's actants,[14] which derive from the work of Vladimir Propp on the morphology of the tale.[15] A further source of archetype, deriving from Jungian analysis, adds a more recent set of variants to the pool of interpretations.

Actants and Archetypes

Greimas's model of actantial roles was derived from stock characters in the traditional tale, and can be used to analyse relationships between characters, as well as to identify character functions.[16] Six actants are used in the original model, although variants are of course possible: the subject (the hero), the object (that which is sought), the sender (who gives the subject his task), the receiver (who is helped by the subject), the helper (who assists the subject), and the opponent (who hinders). Using actants to describe the characters in a rudimentary and non-realist genre like myth makes it possible to discern patterns in the structure of such tales' narratives, but the method has obvious limitations when applied to the novel, which works with characters rather than types. However, such a taxonomy of types for Buchan's women characters shows that, although his work is generally too complex for the reductive actantial approach, his fiction does display strong myth-based characteristics. A more sophisticated tool is the use of archetypal roles to analyse narrative and story. Where actants offer a simplistic signposting of the character types in a tale, archetypes also present behavioural characteristics and established relationships with other archetypes. Incorporating female archetypes into such a taxonomy will also reveal Buchan's 'theory' of gender, in that it will indicate more clearly how Buchan used women as protagonists in his fiction.

Classical religion offers a limited range of female archetypes. Apart from goddesses, J. G. Frazer's *The Golden Bough* (1890–1915) suggests only generic female functions, in the context of primitive religion, that 'are limited to certain well-defined departments of nature: their names are general, like the Barley-Mother, the Old Woman, the Maiden'.[17] Jane Harrison's work on early Greek religion in *Themis* (1912), which identifies a matriarchal society, also produced only a few female archetypes. Themis herself is 'the Mother, the supreme social fact and focus'.[18] The Bride is also important, in her varying representations as a Maenaed, Aphrodite and Koré the Earth-Maiden.

In *The Morphology of the Folk Tale* (1928) the Russian anthropologist Vladimir Propp identified sixteen female character types. Those identifiable in Buchan include the wise maiden, the bride, the wife, the witch, the mother, the princess, the widow, the old woman and the servant.[19] A modern, feminist discussion on female archetypes in myth by Pinkola Estés, drawing on Jungian interpretations, suggests three others that can also be recognized in Buchan: the wise woman, the wild woman and the untrustworthy stranger.[20]

The eighty-nine significant female roles in Buchan's fiction are listed in Table 1 (p. 156), in order of publication, and have been assigned to actantial and archetypal roles. Table 2 (p. 159) shows that three of the actantial roles were found to be absent or severely under-represented, that of the subject, the sender and the receiver. Significantly, these are the roles with power of action and the power of responsibility. The three actantial roles in which the majority of Buchan's women characters play their parts are the object, the helper and the opponent: the first two commonly interpreted as subordinate roles, and the last, significantly, opposing the subject. These may also be recognized as traditional patterns of female roles, and Buchan's compliance with the traditional mode extends to assigning his 'object' roles to the younger women characters, while the older women were mainly in the 'helper' category. The female 'opponent' actants demonstrate a more complex pattern, in that in Buchan's stories they could be of any age. Actantial syncretism can also be observed, where some characters have multiple functions and, therefore, more complex roles.[21]

Table 1: Women characters in Buchan's fiction, ordered by date actantial role and archetype

A Lodge in the Wilderness (1906) has not been included, since this is not a quest tale, but a philosophical symposium with very few traditional story elements or characters in it. Characters who have no obvious archetype, and who are background characters only also, do not appear.

Name of character	Appearing in book/story	Actant	Archetype
Anne	*Sir Quixote of the Moors* (1895)	Object	Princess *
			Daughter
girl in garden	'Afternoon' (1896)	Receiver	Wise Maiden
Sal the prostitute	'A Captain of Salvation' (1896)	Opponent	Aphrodite
old woman	'The Moor-Song' (1897)	Background	Wise Woman
Marjory Veitch	*John Burnet of Barns* (1898)	Object	Princess
Miss Phyllis	'Comedy in the Full Moon' (1899)	Object	Maiden *
Mrs Murray	*A Lost Lady of Old Years* (1899)	Object	Aphrodite
		Sender	Wife
Gaelic girl	*A Lost Lady of Old Years* (1899)	Helper	Maiden
Mrs Birkenshaw	*A Lost Lady of Old Years* (1899)	Background	Mother
			Widow
shepherd's sister	'No-Man's Land' (1899)	Object	Old Woman
Alice Wishart	*The Half-Hearted* (1900)	Object	Wise Maiden
		Sender	
Lady Manorwater	*The Half-Hearted* (1900)	Helper	Mother
Mrs Andrews	*The Half-Hearted* (1900)	Background	Untrustworthy
			Stranger
Sybil Ladlaw	'The Watcher by the Threshold' (1900)	Sender	Wife
		Receiver	
Katherine	'The Mountain' (1990–1)	Object	Princess?
Lady Peggy	'The Mountain' (1990–1)	Object	Aphrodite?
		Opponent	
Clara Etheridge	'Fountainblue' (1901)	Object	Princess
Ailie Sempill	'The Outgoing of the Tide' (1902)	Object	Princess
Alison Sempill	'The Outgoing of the Tide' (1902)	Opponent	Witch
Mrs Crawfurd	*Prester John* (1910)	Background	Widow
			Mother
Zeeta	*Prester John* (1910)	Background	Maiden
			Servant
The Duchess	'The Company of the Marjolaine' (1909)	Receiver	Wise Maiden
Cristina	'The Company of the Marjolaine' (1909)	Background	Servant
Claudia Barriton	'A Lucid Interval' (1910)	Object	Princess
Lady Caerlaverock	'A Lucid Interval' (1910)	Background	Old Woman
			Wife
Mrs Cargill	'A Lucid Interval' (1910)	Background	Old Woman
			Wife

Name of character	Appearing in book/story	Actant	Archetype
Lady Lavinia Dobson	'A Lucid Interval' (1910)	Background	Old Woman
goddess	'The Grove of Ashtaroth' (1910)	Opponent	Aphrodite Artemis
dying wife	'The Riding of Ninemileburn' (1912)	Sender	Wife Mother
Virginia Dasent	'The Green Glen' (1912)	Object	Princess
Ethel Pitt-Heron	*The Power-House* (1913)	Sender	Bride
'Andromeda'	'Basilissa' (1914)	Object	Princess
Elise	'Basilissa' (1914) & *The Dancing Floor* (1926)	Helper	Servant
Elspeth Blair	*Salute to Adventurers* (1915)	Object	Princess
'Julia Czechenyi'	*The Thirty-Nine Steps* (1915)	Helper	Aphrodite
herd's wife	*The Thirty-Nine Steps* (1915)	Helper	Mother
Mlle Omèrine	'The King of Ypres' (1915)	Object	Princess
German peasant	*Greenmantle* (1916)	Opponent Helper	Mother
Hilda von Einem	*Greenmantle* (1916)	Opponent	Aphrodite Wild Woman
Mary Lamington	*Mr Standfast* (1919), *The Three Hostages* (1924) & *The Island of Sheep* (1936)	Object Helper	Princess Mother Wise Woman
the Misses Wymondham	*Mr Standfast* (1919)	Background	Old Women
Ursula Giffen	'Fullcircle' (1920)	Background	Wife
Princess Saskia	*Huntingtower* (1922)	Object Sender	Princess Wise Maiden Artemis
Eugenie	*Huntingtower* (1922)	Background	Old Woman
Mrs Morran	*Huntingtower* (1922)	Helper	Old Woman Mother
Claudia Grevel	*Midwinter* (1923)	Object	Bride
Duchess of Queensberry	*Midwinter* (1923)	Helper	Mother Queen
Adela Victor	*The Three Hostages* (1924)	Object	Princess Daughter
Mrs Medina	*The Three Hostages* (1924)	Opponent	Mother Witch
Madame Breda	*The Three Hostages* (1924)	Opponent	Witch
Janet Raden	*John Macnab* (1925), *The Courts of the Morning* (1929) & *The House of the Four Winds* (1935)	Object Sender	Wise Maiden Artemis
Agatha Raden	*John Macnab* (1925)	Background	Maiden
Lady Claybody	*John Macnab* (1925)	Background	Wife Mother
Mildred Lamancha	*John Macnab* (1925) & *A Prince of the Captivity* (1933)	Background	Wife
Mollie Nantley	*The Dancing Floor* (1926) & *The Gap in the Curtain* (1932)	Background	Mother

Name of character	Appearing in book/story	Actant	Archetype
Koré Arabin	*The Dancing Floor* (1926)	Object	Princess
			Artemis
Katrine Yester	*Witch Wood* (1927)	Object	Princess
Grizel Saintserf	*Witch Wood* (1927)	Helper	Mother
			Queen
Isobel Veitch	*Witch Wood* (1927)	Helper	Mother
			Servant
'Reinmar'	'The Loathly Opposite' (1927)	Opponent	Aphrodite
the Hallward great-aunts	'Ship to Tarshish' (1927)	Background	Old Women
Aunt Letitia	'The Frying-Pan and the Fire' (1928)	Helper	Mother
Miss Cis	'Nemesis' (1928)	Helper	Wise Maiden
Barbara Dasent	*The Courts of the Morning* (1929) & *The Island of Sheep* (1936)	Object	Wise Maiden Princess
Alison Westwater	*Castle Gay* (1930) & *The House of the Four Winds* (1935)	Object	Wise Maiden Princess Artemis
Harriet Westwater	*Castle Gay* (1930)	Helper	Mother
Mrs Johnston	*Castle Gay* (1930)	Helper	Old Woman
Mrs Catterick	*Castle Gay* (1930)	Helper	Mother
Sabine Beauforest	*The Blanket of the Dark* (1930)	Object	Princess Aphrodite Artemis
Mother Sweetbread	*The Blanket of the Dark* (1930)	Helper	Mother Old Woman
Pamela Brune	*The Gap in the Curtain* (1932)	Object	Wise Maiden Princess
Verona Cortal	*The Gap in the Curtain* (1932)	Opponent	Wise Maiden Witch
Jacqueline Armine	*A Prince of the Captivity* (1933)	Helper Opponent	Wife Wise Woman
Camilla Considine	*A Prince of the Captivity* (1933)	Opponent	Bride
Florence Covert	*A Prince of the Captivity* (1933)	Opponent	Wife
Lilah Pomfrey	*A Prince of the Captivity* (1933)	Opponent	Witch Untrustworthy Stranger
Christian Evandale	*The Free Fishers* (1934)	Object	Princess Aphrodite
Gabriel Cranmer	*The Free Fishers* (1934)	Object	Princess Artemis
Georgina Kinethmont	*The Free Fishers* (1934)	Background	Mother
Countess Araminta Troyos	*The House of the Four Winds* (1935)	Helper Opponent	Wild Woman Maiden
Anna Haraldsen	*The Island of Sheep* (1936)	Object	Wise Maiden
two *compagnons de voyage*	*The Island of Sheep* (1936)	background	Aphrodite
Miss Margesson	*The Island of Sheep* (1936)	Helper	Wise Maiden

Name of character	Appearing in book/story	Actant	Archetype
Miss Barlock	*The Island of Sheep* (1936)	Opponent	Mother
Lydia Ludlow	*The Island of Sheep* (1936)	Opponent	Witch
Beryl Lombard	*The Island of Sheep* (1936)	Background	Wife
Felicity Galliard	*Sick Heart River* (1940)	Helper	Wife
Mrs Simon Ravelstone	*Sick Heart River* (1940)	Helper	Wise Woman
Simone Martel	*The Long Traverse* (1941)	Background	Maiden

* The difference between the Maiden and the Princess archetypes, as Buchan used them, is that the Princess is the desired object of the hero, the focus of his desires. The Maiden is a girl, an unmarried woman, who may or may not also be desired, but who is not the focus of the quest.

Table 2 : Female actants in Buchan's fiction

The total does not correspond to the total number of characters in Table 1, as several characters exhibit actantial syncretism, with doubling of roles. 'Background' was added to Greimas's model to accommodate the large number of characters who did not fit his limited range of actants.

object (29)	Anne, Marjory Veitch, Miss Phyllis, Mrs Murray, shepherd's sister, Alice Wishart, Katherine, Lady Peggy, Clara Etheridge, Ailie Sempill, Claudia Barriton, Virginia Dasent, 'Andromeda', Elspeth Blair, Mlle. Omérine, Mary Lamington, Princess Saskia, Claudia Grevel, Adela Victor, Janet Raden, Koré Arabin, Katrine Yester, Barbara Dasent, Alison Westwater, Sabine Beauforest, Pamela Brune, Christian Evandale, Gabriel Cranmer, Anna Haraldsen
helper (22)	Gaelic girl, Lady Manorwater, Elise, 'Julia Czechenyi', herd's wife, German peasant, Mary Lamington, Mrs Morran, Grizel Saintserf, Isobel Veitch, Aunt Letitia, Miss Cis, Harriet Westwater, Mrs Johnston, Mrs Catterick, Mother Sweetbread, the Duchess of Queensberry, Jacqueline Armine, Araminta Troyos, Miss Margesson, Felicity Galliard, Mrs Simon Ravelstone
background (21)	*old woman, Mrs Birkinshaw, Mrs Andrews, Mrs Crawfurd, Zeeta, Lady Caerlaverock, Mrs Cargill, Lady Lavinia Dobson, Cristina, the Misses Wymondham, Ursula Giffen, Eugenie, Agatha Raden, Lady Claybody, Mildred Lamancha, Mollie Nantley, the Hallward great-aunts, Georgina Kinethmont, two* compagnons de voyage, *Beryl Lombard, Simone Martel*
opponent (17)	Sal, Lady Peggy, Alison Sempill, goddess, German peasant, Hilda von Einem, Mrs Medina, Madame Breda, 'Reinmar', Verona Cortal, Jacqueline Armine, Camilla Considine, Florence Covert, Lilah Pomfrey, Araminta Troyos, Miss Barlock, Lydia Ludlow
sender (7)	Mrs Murray, Alice Wishart, Sybil Ladlaw, dying wife, Ethel Pitt-Heron, Princess Saskia, Janet Raden
receiver (3)	girl in garden, Sybil Ladlaw, the Duchess
Subject (0)	—

A considerable number of women characters do not fit into Greimas's model, and were assigned to a seventh role, called 'background'. This need to modify Greimas's model by the large numbers of 'extra' characters indicates that Buchan's fiction is too complex for the simple patterns of the quest tale. However, the classification performed by the actantial model does indicate the parameters of Buchan's female roles: largely powerless, and normally subordinate.

Table 3, below, shows that Buchan's women characters can be assigned to a very few classically-derived archetypes. The archetypes from the domestic hearth and fertility do not appear, and neither do the Frazerian figures of the pregnant woman or the barren woman. Of all the goddesses available, Buchan's characters can be aligned only with Aphrodite and Artemis. A good example of their use is in Buchan's short story 'The Grove of Ashtaroth' (1910), where the male protagonists are tormented by the almost irresistibly lethal appeal of the goddess Astarte (the Phoenician name for Aphrodite).[22] But the goddess in this story also has characteristics of Artemis, with her moon insignia and virginal purity, indicating that Buchan seems to be working with two goddess archetypes at once: seduction and chastity. From Harrison we can see how Buchan has explicitly equated a heroine with a goddess, in *The Dancing Floor* (1926)[23] and in *The Blanket of the Dark* (1930), where the Aphroditic aspects of the heroines Koré and Sabine make them dangerous women. Buchan neutralizes them by privileging the rival feminine values of Artemis, preferring purity over sensuality, and giving chastity primacy as a feminine virtue.

Table 3: Female archetypes in Buchan's fiction

The total does not correspond to the total number of characters in Table 1, as many characters inhabit more than one archetype.
Archetype: classically derived, from Frazer and Harrison
Archetype: from Propp
Archetype: from Estes

Princess (21)	Anne, Marjory Veitch, Katherine, Clara Etheridge, Ailie Sempill, Claudia Barriton, Virgina Dasent, 'Andromeda', Elspeth Blair, Mlle. Omerine, Mary Lamington, Princess Saskia, Adela Victor, Kore Arabin, Katrine Yester, Barbara Dasent, Alison Westwater, Sabine Beauforest, Pamela Brune, Christian Evandale, Gabriel Cranmer,
Mother (20)	Mrs Birkenshaw, Lady Manorwater, Mrs Crawfurd, dying wife, herd's wife, German peasant, Mary Lamington, Mrs Morran, Duchess of Queensberry, Mrs Medina, Lady Claybody, Mollie Nantley, Grizel Saintserf, Isobel Veitch, Aunt Letitia, Harriet Westwater, Mrs Catterick, Mother Sweetbread, Georgina Kinethmont, Miss Barlock,

Wise maiden (12)	Girl in garden, Alice Wishart, the Duchess, Princess Saskia, Janet Raden, Miss Cis, Barbara Dasent, Alison Westwater, Pamela Brune, Verona Cortal, Anna Haraldsen, Miss Margesson
Wife (12)	Mrs Murray, Sybil Ladlaw, Lady Caerlaverock, Mrs Cargill, dying wife, Ursula Giffen, Lady Claybody, Mildred Lamancha, Jacqueline Armine, Florence Covert, Beryl Lombard, Felicity Galliard
old woman (10)	Shepherd's sister, Lady Caerlaverock, Mrs Cargill, Lady Lavinia Dobson, the Misses Wymondham, Eugenie, Mrs Morran, the Hallward great-aunts, Mrs Johnston, Mother Sweetbread
Aphrodite (10)	Sal, Mrs Murray, Lady Peggy, goddess, 'Julia Czechenyi', Hilda von Einem, 'Reinmar', Sabine Beauforest, Christian Evandale, two *compagnons de voyage*
Artemis (7)	goddess, Princess Saskia, Janet Raden, Kore Arabin, Alison Westwater, Sabine Beauforest, Gabriel Cranmer
Witch (6)	Alison Sempill, Mrs Medina, Madame Breda, Verona Cortal, Lilah Pomfrey, Lydia Ludlow
Maiden (6)	Miss Phyllis, Gaelic girl, Zeeta, Agatha Raden, Araminta Troyos, Simone Martel
<u>Wise woman</u> (4)	Old woman, Mary Lamington, Jacqueline Armine, Mrs Simon Ravelstone
Servant (4)	Zeeta, Cristina, Elise, Isobel Veitch
Bride (3)	Ethel Pitt-Heron, Claudia Grevel, Camilla Considine
Widow (2)	Mrs Birkenshaw, Mrs Crawfurd
<u>Untrustworthy stranger</u> (2)	Mrs Andrews, Lilah Pomfrey
<u>Wild woman</u> (2)	Hilda von Einem, Araminta Troyos
Queen (2)	Duchess of Queensberry, Grizel Saintserf
Daughter (2)	Anne, Adela Victor

Mapping Buchan's women characters onto certain, repeated, female archetypes builds on the analysis of their actantial roles. We have already seen that Buchan's writing shows a tendency to place women in powerless and subordinate roles. It is also apparent that Buchan wrote female roles predicated on their relationships with the male characters, rather than as characters in their own right: most of his women characters can be read as object and helper actants. However, his overt use of the goddess archetypes indicates that Buchan's fiction did occasionally need powerful women, and this is supported by the presence in his fiction of those ambivalent female archetypes from traditional myth and dream analysis who could not be controlled by men. There is a duality in Buchan's depiction of women in his fiction: of power and powerlessness, of action and inactivity, and of danger and safety. The subordinate women are balanced by the subversives, but it is not yet clear why this is so.

Of the eighty-nine women characters in Buchan's fiction, most are present in one work only; only a few carry their roles over several linked novels. Some characters exist for no more than a few sentences, but have structural and symbolic importance.[24] A little over half are single women, most are marriageable prizes (the 'object' actant), and most achieve the promise of marriage by the end of the story. Of the married women, their husbands are, interestingly, either dead, temporarily absent, silent or subordinate: a married couple where husband and wife are equally active in the plot is rare in Buchan. Seven older, married, women function principally as chaperones.[25] Very few women in Buchan's fiction earn their own living, which makes those who do of interest as indicators of social change, and as a commentary on his attitudes to working women.

Four groups of characters move in and out of actantial and archetypal roles, with common characteristics in terms of how they interact with Buchan's heroes, and in their function in the stories. The sexualized heroine is allowed, unusually for Buchan, to remain Aphrodite rather than revert to Artemis. The older woman multi-tasks as a chaperone, servant, mother and wise adviser. The women who question challenge the Buchan hero directly by not accepting his authority. The class infiltrators also challenge Buchan's fictional society by breaking society's rules and showing how it is changing. Buchan's treatment of these women is negative and resistant: these are not the types of women that he prefers.

The Sexualized Heroine

In general, Buchan the Victorian drew his sexualized heroines as aspects of Aphrodite, who were thus inevitably bad, whereas those women who personified aspects of Artemis, in purity, innocence and chastity, were good. A review of various new novels in 1933 noted that 'after all this preoccupation with sex at its earthiest it is a joy to open John Buchan's new book'.[26] This tells us that by the 1930s a Buchan novel guaranteed an absence of sex, but in Buchan's early writing there are some stirrings which did achieve expression. The prostitute Sal from 'A Captain of Salvation' (1896) is a one-dimensional symbol of a dissolute past: Aphrodite defeated. The novel that Buchan never completed, 'The Mountain' (1900–1),[27] was to be based on a love affair between Hugh[28] and the married Lady Peggy. The extant fragments of this novel have not been published, but its description by Buchan's first biographer makes it clear that Lady Peggy was to have been bad, and dangerous to know, and the memory of her embraces would have blighted Hugh's life when he returned to find his childhood sweetheart married to someone else.[29] Richard Hannay experiences a few sexualized moments in *Greenmantle* (1916) by standing up to Hilda von Einem, but as an enemy she is out of bounds, and Sandy Arbuthnot torments himself for weeks for having (we are led to believe) succumbed to her seduction. Only when she is killed can Sandy admit to having had feelings for her.

It was not until Sabine Beauforest in *The Blanket of the Dark* (1930) that Buchan was able to submit his hero, Peter Pentecost, to an attempted seduction by an Aphroditic heroine, and to condemn her for being willing to barter her body for a crown. This loose behaviour occurred safely in the Tudor age, indicating that such physicality was probably not possible for Buchan in a novel set in his own time, and could only be expressed with any degree of comfort in the past. Sexuality was not something that came naturally to Buchan in characterization, and for most of his women characters it simply was not part of their function. Its relative infrequency is as interesting as where it does appear, in characters who can be classified as object or opponent actants. There is a strong indication here that for Buchan, sexuality in his women characters was desirable but also dangerous, to be resisted and neutralized where possible.

Mothers and Older Women

Buchan's mother figures generally appear in his fiction solely to help the hero: even Mrs Medina exists only to help her son in *The Three Hostages*, though both are 'opponent' actants to the hero. A potential 'opponent' may turn into a 'helper', as when the nameless peasant woman looks after Richard Hannay when he keels over in the German forest in *Greenmantle* (1916). A combination of the servant and mother archetypes could be intensely practical. Elise, the servant in the short story 'Basilissa' (1914) and in *The Dancing Floor* (1926), is the epitome of common sense: she will not let her mistress die because of pride and *noblesse oblige*. A further layer of archetype, making the servant-mother a wise woman produced Buchan's most redoubtable and powerful characters. Isobel Veitch, who is only the housekeeper in *Witch Wood* (1927), also has the right solutions for all her master's problems. She is connected with Buchan's two modern Scots countrywomen, Euphemia Morran of *Huntingtower* (1922) and Mrs Catterick of *Castle Gay* (1930). These middle-aged women enter into the heroes' troubles with problem-solving gusto, and provide meals, carry messages, lend bicycles and make soft beds for tired travellers. Another wise woman/mother archetype in *Witch Wood*, the aristocratic Grizel Saintserf, has a non-domestic function in the narrative. She is also a great lady and, as the 'mother' of that novel's 'princess', Katrine Yester, embodies the rare 'queen' archetype in Buchan. She represents the rights of Juno rather than of Aphrodite, overseeing marriage rather than lust. In this sense she has a similar function to the Duchess of Queensberry in *Midwinter*, who acts as mother-chaperone, and arbiter of justice.

The helper actants in this group of women outnumber the other actantial functions by three to one, demonstrating that Buchan was predisposed to consider older women as mainly benign, and mostly at the service of others. However, these older women, and mothers, are described by the narrator in a male authorial voice, which has the effect of containing them and their potential. The few moments when an older woman is active alone, as with Mrs Morran in *Hunt-*

ingtower, have a curious resonance, as if some new force is being released into the story, or as if a woman character is telling her own story: a very rare event in Buchan. This sense of contained power can be seen in Mary Lamington's characterization. As the 'object' and as a princess archetype in *Mr Standfast* (1919), Mary is dull, because we rarely see her at work as a secret service agent. Apart from a rare moment of resolute feminism, when she demands to be allowed to work on the same terms as her male colleagues, in *Mr Standfast* (1919),[30] we only hear of her strength and courage through Hannay's doting reportage, but do not often witness it. In *The Three Hostages*, as Hannay's wife and the placid mother of their son, she is still uninteresting, until she is able to return to her secret service surveillance work. Again, her undercover work, particularly female in its manipulation of the domestic routine of suburban houses, is reported through her husband's narrative voice. The fact that Mary rescues two of the three hostages single-handedly is glossed over by Buchan in favour of narrating Hannay's dramatic failures and misunderstandings.[31] Just when Hannay feels that everything has been lost, Mary forces a spectacular surrender by inverting the mother archetype into a figure of implacable vengeance. Her aggression is shocking: she calmly offers to scar Medina for life with acid that she carries in her handbag, and the great criminal mastermind capitulates.[32] Such a formidable demonstration of power, and a quite unconventional refusal to behave like a feminine stereotype, fools all the men, and returns this detective novel to the non-realistic territory of magical reversal and transformation. Mary was never to act so powerfully again, and it is striking that this release of potential occurs when she is most clearly enacting the mother archetype, attempting to rescue a little boy not much older than her own son.

The Women who Question

Buchan women occasionally ask awkward and challenging questions. The old woman from 'The Moor-Song'(1897)[33] appears only in the last paragraphs of that short story, but her intervention is a return to reality for Sim, the protagonist. He has had his faith shaken and destroyed by an Arnoldian vision of a gypsy's life on the open road, and now has no patience for the mundane business of earning a living or fulfilling his duties in church. His exalted attitude is demolished when the seemingly insignificant background character of an anonymous woman at the roadside notes grimly that this is typical male behaviour which she has seen before. She also makes it clear to Sim that it is all very well for him to take the road when he feels the urge: for a woman there is no such escape. The contrast between (irresponsible) male freedom and (dutiful) female servitude may also be discerned in Buchan's own life. At the time that he wrote this story, he was enjoying increasing economic and social freedom at Oxford, whereas his sister Anna had a foreseeable future of no more than being a companion to her parents.[34]

Three years later, Buchan wrote *The Half-Hearted* (1900), his first novel set in his own time and an oblique discussion of class and politics. The Tory hero Lewis has his attitudes questioned by Alice Wishart, the girl he ought to have proposed to, and eventually lost to his successful, Liberal, rival in the local elections. In creating the questioning Alice, who resisted the upper-class values that Buchan was to embrace himself later in life, it is likely that Buchan was using her voice to express his own doubts about the glittering anglicized society that he was seeing himself for the first time. This period marked a significant point of decision in Buchan's life: what to do with himself after Oxford. He was experiencing a clubland existence while reading for the Bar, which is a contrast to his own provincial upbringing and, in the novel, to Alice's nonconformist, urban manufacturing background.[35]

Janet Raden, who is another rarity in Buchan, a reoccurring woman character across novels in leading roles, is a personification of the wise maiden archetype. In *John Macnab* (1925) she is a spirited foil for Archie Roylance, the cheerful but callow Parliamentary aspirant. Janet challenges his views, and Archie uses her words in the ex tempore speech that wins him local supporters. She has the 'best brain in the family',[36] and as a clear thinker is easily Archie's superior. However, she remains inactive, as far as we are told, as the wife of a politician: Buchan did not take the chance of writing a woman character who would stand for parliament herself.[37] Instead, Janet is given a passive, redemptive role in *The Courts of the Morning*, where she challenges Castor's emotions sufficiently to enable him to return to humanity.

Jacqueline Armine, in *A Prince of the Captivity* (1933), challenges Adam Melfort's determination to suborn her husband Kenneth from what she considers to be his rightful role as a Tory grandee, and deliberately sabotages Adam's efforts to keep Kenneth working for the proletariat, outwith his class. Jacqueline would also like to be Adam's 'object', as she has fallen in love with him. Adam respects Jacqueline's reasons for opposing his plans, and acknowledges her bravery and candour by treating her like a man, but he refuses to accept her overtures. He will not see her as the Aphrodite that she has cast herself as, and, in fact, hardly seems to think of her at all. This may be why there are four women 'opponents' to Adam in this novel, a remarkably high number for any Buchan novel, because his robotic, even adamantine resolve, cannot be defeated by just one.

It would seem that, with these post-war women who question his heroes, Buchan had not been able to take Alice Wishart's independent values any further forward. They cross several age and archetypal groups, but are the only characters in those groups who question at all. Further, Janet and Jacqueline are restricted to questioning the hero's motives with only his advancement, or defeat in mind.

There is no development of women's independence here, only an ossification of conservative views with women in subordinate roles. The striking use of four women[38] who not only question but oppose the hero in *A Prince of the Captivity* is also indicative. At the time that Buchan was writing this most political of his novels he was heavily involved with British politics as a Member of Parliament and advisor to successive prime ministers Stanley Baldwin (Conservative) and Ramsay MacDonald (Labour). Buchan was working out his understanding of Depression politics in this novel of thriller episodes, but by using women to represent the forces opposed to his hero's mission to save Britain, and Europe, from catastrophe, we can also discern a possible unease in Buchan with the changing role, and numbers, of women in society.

The Class Infiltrators

In his fiction Buchan depicted as the norm the prejudices and assumptions of the English ruling classes in whose hierarchies he had recently arrived. In *The Half-Hearted* (1900) he drew a portrait of a social climber, Mrs Andrews, who appalls Alice Wishart with her blatant eagerness to be accepted in Lady Manorwater's house. Mrs Andrews' function in the story is that of the untrustworthy stranger, an unsettling element acting as a foil for Alice's own values. Despite Alice's middle-class background she holds to the social codes of the upper classes, and can thus be accepted into their ranks as a potential wife for the novel's upper-class hero. Mrs Andrews is a piercing satirical portrait, but in her depiction Buchan was criticizing a woman attempting to do through female acquaintances and tea-party friendships what a man would do (as Buchan was doing himself) through clubs and college connections.

Ursula Giffen of 'Fullcircle' (1920) is also a climber out of one class into another. This is a story of supernatural manipulation by a house, which quietly turns its new, Bloomsburyite owners, who are atheists, socially concerned and Left, into Roman Catholics and Tory squires. Interestingly symbolic of the brief period of Buchan's 'anti-Bloomsbury' fiction, Ursula has nothing but good intentions and an honest appreciation of her own 'mistakes': to turn the house's chapel into a committee room, to attempt to educate the locals by lectures, and to install a home for unmarried mothers in the local village ('the wrong kind of charity'), all of which goes against established English country rules.[39] By admitting she was wrong, and conforming to a different type by wearing cosmetics and losing her scrawniness in 'comely' plumpness, Ursula is thus admirable, and admissable to county ranks. Buchan's own prejudices are clear in his depiction of Ursula through the remarks of her obtuse husband or the narrative voice of Leithen, the character closest to Buchan's alter ego. Ursula hardly gets a chance to speak for herself. Buchan's use of a supernatural force to produce the change may also be an admission that natural integration may not work fast enough for him.[40]

Lady Claybody of *John Macnab* (1925) is a similar satirical portrait admitting the changing times. She is part of the nouveaux class of what the formidably county Jacqueline Armine of the later *A Prince of the Captivity* (1933) would dismiss as 'war knights, you know'.[41] Lady Claybody is trying hard to be accepted into Scottish county society, with little guidance, but also, mercifully, not much of an audience. Buchan is not kind about her attempts at gentility, but this is her role, to shine weakly next to Janet and Agatha Raden. They are the daughters of the laird and know exactly how to behave and dress. Aside from being mocked, Lady Claybody's additional function is that she demonstrates differing interpretations of 'property', and its value, which is the theme of the novel. Buchan undermines his readers' initial, intended, impression of the unfortunate Lady Claybody by suggesting that her views and those of her class must be taken into account in order for the new post-war world to progress in a healthy fashion.

Florence Covert of *A Prince of the Captivity* has roots in the upper classes, but works as a welfare worker in a factory because of her Left politics. She resigns from her job when she marries trade-union leader Joe Utlaw, because 'Joe had insisted'.[42] This compliance with convention, and patriarchal authority, is also clearly part of her plan to move from circles where independent women had to work to survive, and to climb to moneyed, married leisure. She changes her hairstyle, clothes, political adherences, personal loyalties and even her husband's first name, all to propel his upward political journey. Like Buchan's other political wife, the caricature Mrs Lamington from *The Dancing Floor* (1926) and *The Gap in the Curtain* (1932), Florence is 'devouringly ambitious, first for her man, and then for herself'.[43] The crashingly snobbish Jacqueline Armine observes her with interest, providing revealing reports on Florence's journey up the social ladder. 'In a year she will be so smart she will scarcely be able to see out of her eyes.'[44] Florence is always on the lookout for the chances of her less-observant husband. He is focused on his job, but Florence keeps an eye on the bigger picture, for his career advancement, and for her own security. She is also practical, finding work as a freelance journalist when Joe is out of a job. Once Florence has become socially respectable to the upper middle classes Buchan allows her to revert to type, since, conveniently, and typically for Buchan, we find that she comes from an old county family. Her family connections underwrite and consolidate the Utlaws' trajectory by political maneuvering.

The class infiltrators are women who have not done anything wrong by their own lights, but who by their very existence are a threat to Buchan's society. He was not a malicious writer, but these portraits, mild as they are, are sufficiently unkind, in contrast with his normal practice, to signal that Buchan's passions were aroused by the values they represent. Three are 'background' actants, and all four are wives, suggesting that their ability to challenge society may have come from their adherence to conventional societal groupings, but that the impetus to infiltrate further came from their low social status. They had a foot in the door, and Buchan was alarmed at the strength behind their pushing.

Conclusion

In exploring how Buchan wrote women, it seems clear that chronology affected his depiction of women characters to reflect women's changing lives. Social changes made Mary Lamington, Verona Cortal and Florence Covert possible after the First World War. Buchan's own development as a writer is also apparent: his interest in Artemis as an alternative to Aphrodite did not appear until his mid-thirties, but he remained strongly attached to the 'object'/princess combination for his heroines throughout his career. The kind of fiction he was writing also becomes apparent by studying the archetypes that can be mapped onto his characters: classical derivatives and archetypes from the tale are particularly common, whereas the Jungian sources are rare. A strong classical input is expected from Buchan's background,[45] yet he appears to have been more comfortable with female archetypes from the traditional folk tale, particularly the princess, the wise maiden and the wife. Yet the dependency of these characters is strongly accented when considering their actantial roles: there are no 'subject' heroines at all in Buchan. Mary and Janet do not lead the narratives as Hannay leads his. This is not unexpected in a male writer producing adventures in the mode of the male quest romance.[46] Yet there are small but significant signs in his fiction that Buchan was unsettled. There are an unexpectedly high number of women 'opponents' in Buchan's fiction as a whole, which suggests that he favoured a sex opposition as well as a moral one in structuring his battles for good against evil. The four categories described above show that he exhibited repulsion, disapproval, criticism and rejection towards certain types of female characters.

Buchan's women characters also embody interesting consequences of Buchan's negative feelings. By venting his prejudices, fears and dislikes he added emotional energy to characterization that has remained present after the original causes have disappeared into history. He went through an anti-Bloomsbury phase, in *Mr Standfast* (1919) as well as in 'Fullcircle' (1920), where Bloomsbury types are mocked and dismissed. Buchan had no interest in modernism, and in 1932 he claimed not to read modern fiction at all.[47] In *Mr Standfast*, as well as inventing a modernist novel that is passed around and then abandoned by right-thinking soldiers in the trenches, Buchan creates the Misses Wymondham, two laughably gullible maiden ladies,[48] who provide token chaperonage for Mary Lamington, and who gush about modern art. These women are satirized mercilessly: Buchan does not share their values, and he does not want, at this stage in the novel, his readers to share their embarrassing approval of the conscientious objector Launcelot Wake. No other women in Buchan are ridiculed so unkindly for deviating from his views, but he had the solution for that kind of transgressor. A year later in 'Fullcircle', Ursula Giffen, another Bloomsbury type, is transformed into the right kind of Buchan woman by supernatural means, and all is right with the Buchan world.

Intellectual women also attracted disapproval. Verona Cortal's takeover of Reggie Daker's life and business is treated as the devouring of his soul by an intellectual succubus. Buchan did not like the 'several young women who had been with her at Oxford'[49] who would sort out and shake up Daker's peaceful, bachelor, dilettante occupations. Verona's head for figures is similarly condemned. It is possible that Buchan preferred the limp young ladies who had populated his fiction before the war, who had no interest in business (Ethel Pitt-Heron, who needs Leithen to tell her what to do about her money), and confined themselves at most to politics as the proper sphere for a adult woman's advice (Alice Wishart, and the female symposium participants of *A Lodge in the Wilderness*, based on Buchan's friends and not included in this study). But Claudia Barriton's foolish passion for Abinger Vennard in 'A Lucid Interval' (1910) is based on misguided hero-worship, not political nous: if a woman could be laughed at for trespassing in a man's intellectual world, she was. Buchan was kinder to intellectual women who knew their place, even a working woman like Anna Haraldsen's teacher Miss Margesson. She is accorded dignity, her game conduct is approved of, and she represents a wider tendency in Buchan's women characters that goes back to archetypal mapping. This woman is a 'wise maiden', and her wisdom is derived from her actantial role of 'helper'. She does not challenge, she does not oppose and she nurtures, and as such she represents Buchan's approved archetypal woman character.

Acknowledgements
Parts of this chapter are drawn from Macdonald, *John Buchan*. Thanks are due to Douglas Kerr for reading advice and H. E. Taylor for logic patrol.

14 JOHN BUCHAN: POLITICS, LANGUAGE AND SUSPENSE

Alan Riach

John Buchan's fiction is continuingly popular arguably because of a quality of suspense in his writing; its power to grip and hold the reader's attention. This is perhaps not exceptional: genre fiction flourishes on the basis of the fulfilment of the promise of delivery of particular expectations. In thrillers, crime fiction, 'police procedural' stories, murder mysteries, novels of espionage and 'international intrigue', suspense is a common factor. Whether the narrative involves events unknown to the narrator that must be discovered and pieced together to solve a conspiracy puzzle, or whether a strictly linear narrative brings characters together who are supremely villainous in situations that are life-threatening, the formulae are familiar enough. But Buchan is different.

Almost by definition, commercially successful genre fiction must balance the fulfilment of a prediction (genre expectation) and the maintenance of novelty. The unusual (novelty) cannot be allowed to jeopardize the satisfaction of fulfilment, but the delivery of fulfilment must not lapse into complacency. In Buchan's writing something very different is at stake. Buchan made money from his writing but the commercial imperative was not his major motive. Therefore he did not have to subscribe to the rules of genre. He wrote what he called his 'shockers' for pleasure, because he enjoyed reading this kind of fiction and he thought he could write as well as the authors he was reading.

Buchan's success could hardly have been predicted. One hundred years after they were written, his thrillers are still reprinted, widely available and read with general appetite. Arthur Conan Doyle's Sherlock Holmes stories, aided by a much more extensive representation through film, television and radio, have an international, immense popularity, but they evoke a particular nostalgia, a world that is significantly late Victorian or Edwardian, very firmly set before the First World War. In later stories, though, Holmes is not the same. His era ended with the First World War, and his afterlife as a retired beekeeper on the Sussex downs, withdrawn from London, seems apt. Buchan's first commercially successful writing begins where Conan Doyle's leaves off. *The Thirty-Nine Steps* (1915) is set on the cusp of the First World War, *Mr Standfast* (1919) is set within it, and the later novels move through the period and into the post-war world, always on the edge of things, on borderlands between nations, in remote valleys giving rare access to different political states, led by characters who change their identity but maintain their loyalty to an Empire that is itself no longer what it was before the war that began as *The Thirty-Nine Steps* and Doyle's *His Last Bow* (1917) had ended.

There is a quality in Buchan's writing that intrinsically exploits his pre-film, pre-mass media age. It is also there in Conan Doyle and, most masterfully, in Robert Louis Stevenson. Some indication of it is given in Louis MacNeice's poem, 'To posterity':

> When books have all seized up like the books in graveyards
> And reading and even speaking have been replaced
> By other, less difficult, media, we wonder if you
> Will find in flowers and fruit the same colour and taste
> They held for us for whom they were framed in words[1]

MacNeice is not merely exploiting nostalgia here, but rather indicating a quality of attention that depends on words, a tension between words and things, a propensity to engage with the world one inhabits directly through the 'framing' of words. The word 'framed' in the poem may not simply refer to a border, as in the frame of a painting, but rather to a vertebrate structure, which allows for internal support, balance, poise and movement. This sense of the word applies in painting not so much to the visible frame around the painting as to the wooden stretcher upon which the canvas is mounted, which literally supplies the canvas with tension. On that canvas, the dynamics of pigment and colour create their own tensions and suspense. It is precisely this quality of suspense in Buchan's writing that I'd like to identify and examine more closely.

There is a stylistic aspect of narrative tension that is peculiarly the property of writing and that cannot be represented in any other medium. Perhaps the best example is the ending of *The Thirty-Nine Steps*, which each film version has avoided and which may be unfilmable. As I write, the fourth version is being completed by the BBC for broadcast on 28 December 2008. In a newspaper interview, the actor playing Richard Hannay, Rupert Penry-Jones, in response to the question whether he found the previous films intimidating, said: 'No, they're all dreadful. Well, the Hitchcock is rather wonderful, but of its time. Robert Donat was superb and I don't think I've matched him but our ending's better – better even than the book'.[2]

The entire impact of Buchan's ending depends upon visual recognition, but in such a way that can only be conveyed through words, and not through visual images of literal representation. Richard Hannay, having identified the villains and tracked them down to a house overlooking the sea on the south coast of Kent, finds himself in their company, playing cards with them, but on a knife-edge of indecision. Because the villains are playing innocent characters, pretending to be harmless, Hannay is hesitant about making explicit his declaration of their evil intent. Everything in this final confrontation is about the distance between the experiences Hannay is trying to process and the language Buchan uses to convey his situation. The narration is in the first person, from Hannay's viewpoint, effectively an interior monologue:

> The light from the dinner-table candlesticks was not very good, and to cover my confusion I got up, walked to the door and switched on the electric light. The sudden glare made them blink, and I stood scanning the three faces.
>   … I simply can't explain why I who, as a roadman, had looked into two pairs of eyes, and as Ned Ainslie into another pair, why I, who have a good memory and reasonable powers of observation, could find no satisfaction.[3]

This passage highlights some of the qualities I have noted: Hannay himself has been in disguise, but his capacity for seeing clearly through whatever appearance is something he has maintained as a matter of principle. Nevertheless, in this situation it is radically challenged by the apparently superior skills of dissimulation exploited by the villains. The writing is descriptive of exterior things: the (nineteenth-century) candlesticks and the (more contemporary) electric light switch, the physical, outward appearance of the men; but it is also interior monologue, most evidently in the penultimate sentence quoted. To whom is Hannay trying to explain things? It is as if he is writing the experience up as an account for a judicial or military debriefing. Hannay himself is on trial, being tested, by this encounter. The syntax itself dramatizes the moment. The grammatical structure of the sentences, the qualifying clauses, apologetic or firm, determined or uncertain, counterpoint each other and propel the reader further into the conflict. The point of resolution comes two pages later. Buchan keeps the situation tense by increasing Hannay's uncertainty, escalating the drama by having the characters sit down to a game of cards, and by having Hannay recollect the essential advice given him by his friend Peter Pienaar: 'If you are playing a part, you will never keep it up unless you convince yourself that you are *it*'.[4] Hannay observes that the villains 'didn't need to act, they just turned a handle and passed into another life'.[5] But even with this in mind, Hannay cannot decide:

> I felt mesmerized by the whole place, by the air of obvious innocence – not innocence merely, but frank honest bewilderment and concern in the three faces …
>   'Meantime I vote we have a game of bridge,' said the plump one. 'It will give Mr Hannay time to think over things, and you know we have been wanting a fourth player. Do you play, sir?'[6]

Despite the suspicious shift to playing a card game, when clearly the villains are trying to buy time and confuse Hannay, and despite the self-conscious entrapment suggested by the provision of time for Hannay 'to think over things', Hannay seems genuinely bewildered. It is the novel's equivalent to the pantomime moment when the audience is encouraged to call out, 'Watch out behind you!' We know, now, that these are the villains, and Hannay's 'mesmerized' state makes him a sympathetic victim of the ruse. The deliberately arch, gentlemanly diction of "'Do you play, sir?'" resonates with the frisson of writerly knowingness. This is, after all, a game taking place as part of a much larger game. To be in the game, one must play. The word means not only, take part (take 'a part' or act in the sense of pretend to be something you are not), but also means to take part in an action, to intervene, to attempt to change things actually. Hannay's acceptance offers a reflexive allusion to clubland London and a social context of privilege, but in its automatic response to ostensible 'ordinariness' it may prove to be another kind of effective disguise. Hannay is genuinely mesmerized, but his insistent observation is maintained. And it pays off. He finally recognizes his adversary by the slight tapping of his fingers on his knees.[7]

Finally, after playing on for another half hour, the old man's eyelids fall in a hawk-like hood that confirms Hannay's recognition and he blows his whistle. The villains make a break for it, one escapes for the ship *Ariadne* moored nearby and the others are captured but in the closing sentences we learn that the *Ariadne* has been in British hands for the last hour. Nevertheless, the final paragraph of the novel informs us, three weeks later, the First World War begins.

The ending of *The Thirty-Nine Steps* is astonishingly abrupt and apparently inconclusive. If all the effort of the book has been expended in fierce games of disguise and counter-disguise, what benefit has this been to anyone, when war breaks out in any case? Buchan is careful to keep things tight and unexplained at the end. After the last chapter's long period of suspense the closing action is momentary, quickly over, and heavily overshadowed by the knowledge that war is about to come and that Hannay himself will be caught up in a far less intimate conflict.

Published in 1915, the novel was dedicated to Thomas Arthur Nelson, Buchan's friend from Oxford and a partner in the Edinburgh publishers Nelson (Buchan's employer), who was killed in 1917 at the Battle of Arras, where Buchan's youngest brother was also fatally wounded. In other words, the specific historical moment of the publication of the book became intimately connected to the dramatic impact of the events it describes and portends. The quality of suspense in Buchan's narrative links the fiction with the actual political world his writings evoke, and the political context in which they were written.

Christopher Harvie points out that the entitling of individual chapters, 'The Adventure of ...' ('... the Literary Innkeeper' or '... the Radical Candidate' for example) suggests the form of a Robert Louis Stevenson picaresque romance rather than the tighter structure of the thriller.[8] Chapters entitled 'The Adventure of the Bald Archaeologist', 'The Dry-Fly Fisherman' or 'The Coming of the Black Stone' might also suggest the kind of self-contained stories of Conan Doyle's *The Adventures of Sherlock Holmes* (1892). Buchan's first two chapter titles, though – 'The Man who Died' and 'The Milkman Sets Out on his Travels' – seem self-consciously ironic reflections on the beginning of Stevenson's *Kidnapped* (1886). The opening sentence seems to prefigure David Balfour's journey, both around and across Scotland and into his own inheritance: 'I will begin the story of my adventures with a certain morning early in the month of June, the year of grace 1751, when I took the key for the last time out of the door of my father's house'.

Buchan is deliberately 'setting out' to manipulate expectations made familiar by both Stevenson and Conan Doyle, but partly perhaps because of his own character and partly too because of his different historical moment – the experience of Scotland, Glasgow and Oxford, the experience of the First World War, what preceded it – Buchan's writing occupies a very different place. Distinct from Stevenson, Conan Doyle and Buchan's immediate contemporary the socialist and Scottish nationalist R. B. Cunninghame Graham (1852–1936), Buchan's writing as a whole is characterized by a quality of heightened tension that is not resolved by action but rather by a kind of wise acceptance, that only comes with a sense of dedication beyond the immediate situation by which stories of action are generically confined. We will come to this when we reach Buchan's most poignant works, the less reassuring adventure story *A Prince of the Captivity* (1933) and his late, elegiac novel *Sick Heart River* (1941).

Perhaps the best way to summarize this is to recollect a key phrase from *The Last Secrets* (1923), a book of descriptions of major expeditions of exploration. The book gives various accounts of, for example, the exploration of the North and South Poles, the Holy Cities of Islam, New Guinea, Mount McKinley and Mount Everest. In the first chapter, Buchan describes the approach to the forbidden city of Lhasa:

> Once on the north bank Lhasa was but a short way off, and in growing excitement the expedition covered the last stages. It was one of the great moments of life, and we can all understand and envy the final hurried miles, till through the haze the eye caught the gleam of the golden roofs and white terraces.[9]

What I would like to emphasize here is 'It was one of the great moments of life' and to suggest that, for Buchan, these moments are unrepeatable, and there are literally fewer of them. Buchan's younger contemporary, Lewis Grassic Gibbon (James Leslie Mitchell, 1901–35), in his first published book, *Hanno: or, The Future of Exploration* (1928), ends his account with the speculation that interstellar space travel or expeditions into the deeps of oceans might yield further discoveries generically similar to those of Mungo Park or Nansen, and he did go on to write further biographies of explorers, and science fiction.[10] But there seems to be a profounder, more bitter truth in Buchan's observation.

What that truth confers is a twofold sense of an unrepeatable exhilaration associated with youth, and an unreclaimable loss of aspiration, the sense that adulthood confirms a trajectory of choice or chance that has fulfilled itself, closing itself off from other possible choices – roads not taken – which in youth might seem to have been endlessly open. In the immediate political context of *The Last Secrets*, Buchan himself was at the centre of understanding the significance of that twofold sense and the trajectory which saw the end of major explorations, the understanding of a comprehensive, globalized, earthly identity, the end of empire. In his 'Preface' to *The Last Secrets*, he makes no mention of the two recent events which, along with the First World War, signalled possibilities for complete change in possible social self-determination, different from the British Imperial ethos and opposed to it: the Easter Rising in Ireland in 1916 and the Communist Revolution in Russia in 1917. Different social ideals, different political identities were being asserted in defiance of imperialism, British or Tsarist. But for Buchan, the last efforts towards exploration of the earth's last secret places, as recorded in the book, confirm an imperial ethos even as they record its ending and the ensuing sense of loss. What is central to that sense of loss is an understanding of the cost involved, the waste of human life, the human potential for destructiveness, and the pathos of the epic effort.

One valuable point of comparison is Cunninghame Graham's sketch 'Might, Majesty and Dominion', first published in *Success and Other Sketches* (1902). Cunninghame Graham's writing normally has none of the suspense of Buchan's. It is as if his engagement with social change was untouched by the pathos and edge that Buchan so clearly caught. Cunninghame Graham never wrote extended narrative fiction and his stories and sketches are often ambiguous works between genres, part fiction, part historical account, part reflective essay, part journalistic reportage. There is a constant quality and interest in his work and, like Buchan, he should be considered in relation to Joseph Conrad's work on the cusp between imperial and colonial or 'postcolonial' worlds. 'Majesty, Might and Dominion' – the title itself seems to evoke Buchan's world – is a description of the funeral of Queen Victoria and combines an enormously impressive appreciation of the scale and grandeur of Empire with a totally sceptical, politically progressive socialist intelligence, whose sympathies are predominantly with the labouring class, not the aristocracy, and whose view of society is multifaceted, varying in perspective, and not constrained into a single point. After the vivid descriptions of the funeral cortège, the mourning period in which not only are the newspapers 'all diapered in black' but even the clouds are 'dark-grey and sullen', after noting that the moment marks the end of the period which saw 'England advancing towards universal Empire', after then describing the pomp of the occasion and the circumstance of its industrialized context, factories humming, machinery heaving and jumping, coal mines, blast furnaces and smelting works, the reader begins to question the extent of irony Cunninghame Graham is employing in his description of Queen Victoria as the 'mother of her people' while acknowledging the 'material instances of the great change in human life' characteristic of her era. At the end of the sketch, a couple of well-bred, well-fed dogs roam through the detritus, sniffing disdainfully at rejected scraps. In turn, they are followed by 'a man grown old in the long reign of the much-mourned ruler' who feeds ravenously on the scraps of food the dogs have spurned, and 'whistling a snatch from a forgotten opera', is 'swallowed by the gloom'.[11]

Cunninghame Graham's genius in a short piece of writing like this is to anatomize clearly the ambiguity in the moment, its historical significance and human cost. The tramp, musically sophisticated as he may be, is at the lower end of the social order, reminding us of human worth not accommodated by the Empire. But the contrast with Buchan's style is significant. As the episodes unfold in Cunninghame Graham's sketch, irony, ambiguity, revelation and adult, tempered wisdom develop steadily. There is a sad yet optimistic knowingness about his writing. In Buchan, the quality of suspense in not knowing what actions follow consequently creates a much greater tension in extended narrative fiction. This is also partly to do with the intensity of Buchan's depiction of a single narrative point-of-view. Cunninghame Graham's is an overview. The constraint of perspective in Buchan's writing generates suspense and tension – certainly this is the case with Hannay, as we have seen in *The Thirty-Nine Steps* and it is equally true of Buchan's other novels.

The childhood wonder of David Crawfurd as he sees the great John Laputa's massive, shadowy figure on the Kirkcaple shore at the opening of *Prester John* (1910) is a vision of awe and fear which is gradually matured into an adult sensibility that finds itself in contest with the black man's revolutionary drive in Africa. If that novel reconfigures the conflict between Imperial authority and atavistic self-determination at the heart of Walter Scott's *Waverley*, *Rob Roy* and *Redgauntlet*, it is the intimacy of Buchan's sense of childish and adult sensibilities, the persuasive aspect of the vision aspiring towards liberation, that haunts the memory. The 'return of the native' is a theme that never really goes away forever. It gives his last great novel, *Sick Heart River*, its final resolution and affirmation. In *The Path of the King* (1921), various characters through history, sometimes very obscure characters in almost unrecorded historical moments, are given as evidence of an inimitable quality of aristocratic authority. The implication is at once both élitist – these are the elect, the leaders, the true 'kings' – and democratic – they might be found anywhere, in almost any circumstance.

If there is a divinity at work in their lineage, it has nothing to do with recorded primogeniture.

One of the most moving of Buchan's novels in which this theme is developed is *A Prince of the Captivity* (1933). In some ways it is a reprise of one of his earliest novels, *The Half-Hearted* (1900), which also concludes with the hero's self-sacrifice. But the later novel develops the theme to far greater depth, both in personal, novelistic, fictional terms, and in terms of its precise historical moment. The fine mesh between the work as fiction and as active intervention in contemporary ideology supports its tension and 'frame', as Adam Melfort sacrifices himself first on behalf of his wife, in a domestic cover-up which leads to him taking the blame for a forgery and accepting social disgrace. This makes him an outsider and available for the kind of subterfuge work his government requires. The greater adventure then follows, finally leading to his self-sacrifice on an international, rather than a domestic and metropolitan, scale. Buchan has been accused of anti-Semitism, sometimes because of comments made by fictional characters, but this novel, according to Owen Dudley Edwards, is 'a celebration of Jewish integrity culminating in the death of the hero at the hands of the Nazis'. *A Prince of the Captivity*, Edwards points out, is 'almost certainly the first major anti-Nazi popular novel'.[12] It therefore plays a distinct and important part in a propaganda opposed to Nazism, and in 1933 this was a radical, deeply humanist thing to do.

Murray Pittock succinctly appraises the novel's importance:

> The prescience of the book in its defence of small nations, cosmopolitans and displaced persons against Nazi racial purity and tyranny is not generally appreciated. Adam Melfort becomes a Belgian, a Dane, a man of many nationalities – as a Scot must do, as a Jew must do without a country – he is the hero, the old and new Adam who becomes all things to all men so that they may be saved [...] In 1933, many quite respectable politicians and writers in western Europe were still prepared to think well of the Nazis; but Buchan knew exactly what they were about.[13]

In *The Three Hostages* (chapter 5), Sandy Arbuthnot reports on an opinion of propaganda held by the hypnotist, Ram Dass: 'He said that the great offensives of the future would be psychological, and he thought the Governments should get busy about it and prepare their defence ... He considered that the most deadly weapon in the world was the power of mass-persuasion'.[14] Buchan's novels, especially his popular novels, should be noted as taking part pre-emptively in a war that was to advance on a massive scale after Buchan's death. This also animates them with a quality of tension that retains dynamic resonance. Buchan's world may resemble the late imperial world of Rudyard Kipling, where the fragility of civilization needs to be protected by imperial authority. Marshall Walker memorably suggests that Buchan's cast of favourites – Hannay, Leithen, Sandy

Arbuthnot and the others – 'now seem like humanoid editions of Kenneth Grahame's Mole, Ratty, Badger and Toad at play on a *Boy's Own Paper* riverbank,' yet
Walker insists, rightly, that if they are in a sense 'puppets' they became, for both
Buchan and the English-reading world 'very real flesh and blood'.[15] But these
connections miss the prophetic aspect of Buchan's writing, and this, too, I think,
generates a tension in the novels.

Buchan implicitly endorses imperial authority. This is why the clubland London and home counties comforts are never resisted by the central characters. Yet
there are other ways of reading Buchan. The love his writing shows for Scotland,
for the Scottish borders in *The Thirty-Nine Steps* and for what may be Perthshire
in *Witch Wood* (1927), his commitment to the Scots language in his anthology
The Northern Muse (1924) and his important lecture and essay on the cultural
and political significance of that language, 'Some Scottish Characteristics'[16] suggest different loyalties, deeper connections to an earth he knew he could never
completely leave behind. In other words, Buchan's propaganda is not simply for
an imperialism which now seems inextricably racist and politically reactionary, but is a much more complex thing. As a writer, his fictional creations open
up the imagination to the exploration of possibilities, loyalties that sometimes
pull against the centralizing authorities of imperial command, loyalties that are
always vulnerable to the technologies of mass-persuasion – never more so than
in the twenty-first century.

For Edwin Morgan, *Sick Heart River* (1941) was 'a sombre but finally courageous and encouraging book which has a claim to be Buchan's best'.[17] In it we
can find all the qualities I have been describing fully developed and movingly
deployed in a way that links back, finally, to a tension at the heart of Buchan's
life, his era and his fiction generally. This, finally, is what I am arguing for: a
comprehensive reassessment of Buchan's achievement must read his work in
three ways: intensely and closely as literary art, of varying quality but always curious engagement; specifically in terms of his biography, the divided loyalties he
experienced himself very early on, when he recognized the authority of Oxford
University as something he needed to acquire and endorse, even if this was at
the expense of the authority of Glasgow University, where he had first studied;
and thirdly in the entire political and cultural moment of his era, not only as a
culmination of British imperialism but also as prophetic of mass-media ideology, an era of political persuasion with which the twenty-first century western
world is saturated. Buchan's writing is a defence or resistance against the numb-
ing or mortmain – the dead hand – of such mass-persuasion, precisely because
it was accomplished in its unique moment, when things that matter – intimate
things like an apple you might eat, the colour of flowers or the taste of fruit in
MacNeice's poem, or public things like treaties of government – were framed in
words, and the words held meaning.

This is what makes *Sick Heart River* such an important novel. Ostensibly, the plot is a classic thriller quest narrative: when Sir Edward Leithen is diagnosed with terminal tuberculosis and told he has a year to live, an old friend turns up at his club to tell him about a mysterious man named Galliard who, because of his successful position in American society may be essential for the continued ascendancy of the western world. Galliard has gone missing in the frozen wastes of Canada, north of the Arctic circle. Leithen undertakes to spend his last months usefully, and die on his feet if need be, trying to find and bring, or send, Galliard back. But the novel becomes increasingly layered and complex, exploring deeper and more intricate themes of connection, affinity and kinship across cultural, racial and political difference. Leithen's quest is a search for meaning, for value in life at the moment when all life's values are put in question. Galliard's departure for the north seems to have been precipitated by the same mad urge to go into the chaos of inhuman wilderness to find an answer, if there is one. Galliard has hired a guide, Lew Frizel, whose brother Johnny is hired by Leithen to track their quarry. But Lew himself has gone further, suddenly embarking on an intense quest to find the legendary valley of the Sick Heart River, and has abandoned Galliard. So as the book unfolds, unpredictably, three men on their own individual quests meet and combine forces, as if Leithen is bringing them together to work with each other and not in competitive or ignorant isolation. When they discover the valley it turns out to be a place from which they must return, not a place to reside in, and on the journey back, Leithen's health begins to return. But on their return to a secure camp, they are told about a group of Hare Indians who are suffering from 'accidie' – depression, self-doubt, suicidal ennui, indifference to the world – and Leithen understands something more profound about the value of life, and decides to give his own life to let this value continue. Hare Indians have accompanied the adventurers, carrying packs and doing the menial work. In the final part of the novel the identity of these almost invisible but essential people is the cause to which Leithen is dedicated at a time when the news of a greater threat, another world war, is filtering through. As Douglas Gifford puts it, Leithen makes the discovery 'that humble Indian (or Scottish) tribes matter more than the affairs of the Great Ones'.[18] The elision in parenthesis is important. As the layered characters and motives in the book and its memorable landscapes and depictions of the wilderness make clear, this is a deeply metaphoric novel: ostensibly a thrilling quest narrative written in fluent, accessible prose, it is making profound points about human value, and values that can be passed on to future generations. That it was Buchan's last book and was published posthumously needs no emphasis.

We have considered aspects of Buchan's writing which illustrate unique qualities of tension and suspense in a context where distraction was a political liability and was becoming a tool for mass-persuasion, portending its further development. The suspense in his writing is intrinsic to his literary art, but it is not to be understood simply as a priority of genre, a narrative technique heightened in the context of a particular type of fiction, but rather as a motivating force in three different but integrated areas of his life and work. The first of these is the suspense in the narrative itself, animating every sentence, giving a dynamic stretch to the adventure of each syntactic development, an agility, a muscle tone – and this applies not only to the 'hurried journey' thrillers like *The Thirty-Nine Steps* but also to the more expansively argued novels, including *Witch Wood*, *A Prince of the Captivity* and *Sick Heart River*. The second is in Buchan's biography. We have raised the ambiguous question of Buchan's deepest loyalties, on the one hand, to the Anglocentric and latterly Anglo-American Imperial ideal, and on the other hand, to the small nations of the world, from the Hare Indians to his native Scotland. While these loyalties could be reconciled by a commitment to 'patriotic unionism' there is nonetheless a tension between them, and Buchan felt it keenly. The reconciliation experienced through the final dedication of Edward Leithen in *Sick Heart River* expresses Buchan's resolution and prospective hopes. Finally, there is a tangible quality of suspense in Buchan's understanding of the 'great moments' of life, the discovery of 'last secrets' of the world. There is pathos here too. We have considered the aspects of loss his novels describe, the sacrifices his characters are so often called upon to make, the cost of empire. And yet we should emphasize also the exhilaration of his work, the attractiveness of his writing, the sheer pleasure of the escapade each of his novels takes us on. It would be to enhance that sense of adventure and aspiration, the attraction of the hurried journey, the satisfaction of just resolution towards provision for an unfinished future, if we emphasize the context in which they take place, for that context is not only that of Buchan and his world, but also of the world we now inhabit. And that context – most perfectly depicted in *Sick Heart River* – is the pathos of the epic effort.

15 BUCHAN'S SUPERNATURAL FICTION

Paul Benedict Grant

John Buchan, known principally for a series of espionage thrillers, is also the author of a large number of supernatural stories. His attraction to the genre, while indicating his eclectic interests, was both aesthetic and pragmatic. From the point of view of style, supernatural fiction contains the same essential ingredients as his 'shockers': excitement, mystery, suspense. Secondly, Buchan 'wrote to be read',[1] and in his day, supernatural stories habitually drew a large audience. Modern ignorance of Buchan's contribution to this genre may be the result of the popularity of his other books: the nearest he came to a collection of supernatural stories was *The Watcher by the Threshold* (1902), but this book has 'constantly been overshadowed by his other work'.[2] While novels like *Prester John* (1910), *The Dancing Floor* (1926), *Witch Wood* (1927) and *The Gap in the Curtain* (1932) contain supernatural elements, Buchan's most consistent work in the genre is to be found in his short fiction.[3] He wrote around twenty supernatural short stories, from the 1890s to the 1930s, proving that he had 'an abiding interest in the supernatural'.[4] But because the stories appeared over many years and in various publications, they have not been considered as a contained body of work worthy of serious study.

Buchan's supernatural stories have been included in anthologies, but they have only recently been collected in single-author volumes. To date (to the best of my knowledge), five such collections have appeared.[5] Many of the selections are confusing, however, because a number of the stories have no supernatural content. This reflects the difficulties some editors have in defining the supernatural, a difficulty compounded by the fact that Buchan's stories are variously presented as examples of supernatural, horror, and of fantasy fiction, categories which many specialists working in the field regard as mutually exclusive. Defining the term 'supernatural' as it applies to literature is, in fact, a doomed enterprise, for the supernatural resists precise definition. Nevertheless, in his seminal study, *Supernatural Horror in Literature* (1927), H. P. Lovecraft, an acknowledged authority on the subject, provides a useful theoretical model. He conflates the supernatural with what he terms the 'weird tale':

The true weird tale has something more than secret murder, bloody bones, or a sheeted form clanking chains according to rule. A certain atmosphere of breathless and unexplainable dread of outer, unknown forces must be present; and there must be a hint, expressed with a seriousness and portentousness becoming its subject, of that most terrible conception of the human brain – a malign and particular suspension or defeat of those fixed laws of Nature which are our only safeguard against the assaults of chaos and the daemons of unplumbed space.[6]

For Lovecraft, 'atmosphere is the all-important thing ... the final criterion of authenticity', and its skilful evocation may atone for other, less forgivable faults:

a weird story ... in which the horrors are finally explained away by natural means, is not a genuine tale of cosmic fear; but ... such narratives often possess, in isolated sections, atmospheric touches which fulfil every condition of true supernatural horror-literature. Therefore we must judge a weird tale ... by the emotional level which it attains at its least mundane point. ... The one test of the really weird is simply this – whether or not there be excited in the reader a profound sense of dread, and of contact with unknown spheres or powers.[7]

How do Buchan's supernatural fictions measure against Lovecraft's criteria? Some idea is given by Lovecraft's own brief analysis of Buchan in his study. Of the novels, he praises *Witch Wood*'s 'tremendous force', 'the description of the black forest with the evil stone, and of the terrible cosmic adumbrations when the horror is finally extirpated', though he views these as compensation 'for wading through the very gradual action and plethora of Scottish dialect'.[8] He is also impressed by Buchan's short stories, finding them 'extremely vivid in their spectral intimations', singling out 'The Green Wildebeest', 'The Wind in the Portico', and 'Skule Skerry', 'with its touches of sub-arctic fright', as 'being especially remarkable'.[9] Lovecraft's comments are particularly valuable since, aside from contemporary reviews, passing remarks in critical works, and introductions, criticism on Buchan's supernatural fiction is scarce.[10] That said, it is notable that the critics agree on where Buchan's strengths lie, and that these coincide with those Lovecraft deems essential for a writer who aspires to produce a 'genuine tale of cosmic fear'.

Foremost among these strengths is Buchan's sensitivity to the haunted qualities of landscape and his related skill in evoking uncanny atmospheres. Both have their roots in his childhood in Scotland, as described in his memoir, *Memory Hold-the-Door* (1940). The title of the first chapter, 'Wood, Water and Hill', signals the importance of landscape to Buchan, a fact confirmed in the second sentence: 'my earliest recollections are not of myself, but my environment'.[11] That environment inspired an impressionable mind already primed by his father's storytelling. Entering the woods near his first home in Fife, Buchan felt that he was 'stepping into the veritable world of faery', full of 'witches and warlocks'.[12] However, 'a second imaginative world overshadowed the woods' and proved 'more potent':[13] Calvinism joined forces with landscape and made him see Nature according to moral divisions. He 'came to identify abstractions with special localities', grafting religious concepts and Biblical passages to particular places. In this manner, Nature, for Buchan, became a place of inherent dualities, 'the home both of heavenly beauty and hellish malevolence'.[14] For the rest of his life, he remained sensitive to its twofold potential.

In adulthood, Buchan had 'a passion for landscapes in many parts of the globe',[15] South Africa in particular. The Wood Bush assumed the same sort of supernatural qualities as the woods of his childhood: 'I seemed to be crossing the border of a *temenos*, a place enchanted and consecrate'.[16] As some critics have noted, in a large number of his supernatural stories this *temenos* takes the form of a moor, grove, glen, cave, island or house.[17] These places often function as thresholds or portals between worlds, entrances to what Buchan called, in a Scottish context, 'the back-world of Scotland ... the land behind the mist'.[18] They are spots or shrines where pagan rites were once practised, where gods and spirits (benign and malevolent) may still manifest themselves in response to incantation or worship, and where 'modern Christian gentlem[e]n' may find themselves 'in the presence of some hoary mystery of sin far older than creeds or Christendom'.[19] For the rational man – and Buchan's protagonists are always eminently rational men, scholars, lawyers and scientists – they are frontiers of reason beyond which lie irrationality, madness and, sometimes, death.

The themes of Buchan's supernatural stories have a direct influence on the settings:

> In much of his fiction, Buchan explores borderland areas where civilization is at its most tenuous. In the thrillers the rational, everyday world is threatened by social instability and chaos ... In Buchan's fantasy fiction we also find ourselves at the extremities of rationality but in this case the threat originates not with criminal masterminds bent on domination, but instead, the remnants of the past where primordial, barely suppressed evil still lurks. It is a territory occupied by forgotten gods and dark forces where Christian civilization holds little sway. Accordingly, most of Buchan's short fantasy fiction is set ... in rural areas far from urban centres of commerce and empire, in places like the Scottish countryside or South African veld where the old mysteries persist.[20]

Some of Buchan's best supernatural stories are set in rural Scotland, in the wilds of which one can feel 'the desolation of solitude which can slide into panic'.[21] This can be seen to good effect in stories like 'No-Man's-Land', where the narrator finds himself lost among a remote range of hills called the Scarts of the Muneraw, and 'Skule Skerry', where the protagonist spends a terrifying time alone on a small island off the west coast of Scotland. In the stories set in South Africa – 'The Grove of Ashtaroth' and 'The Green Wildebeest' – Buchan also uses isolated settings to enhance the uncanny elements.

Other elements, such as diction and dialogue, contribute to a story's atmosphere, and the use of local dialect is an effective way of authenticating a tale steeped in uncanny events. Lovecraft's criticism of Buchan's use of seventeenth-century Scots in *Witch Wood* (the 'plethora of Scottish dialect') seems odd in this regard, because the historically precise, idiomatic speech adds to the story's power by carrying the freight of a past and all-but-forgotten culture fuelled on folklore. Indeed, Lovecraft implicitly contradicts his comment on *Witch Wood* earlier in his essay, when, commenting on Sir Walter Scott's 'Wandering Willie's Tale', he argues that 'the force of the spectral and the diabolic is enhanced by a grotesque homeliness of speech and atmosphere'.[22] This applies equally well to some of Buchan's own supernatural stories based in Scotland, 'The Outgoing of the Tide' in particular.[23]

Linked to Buchan's use of setting is his skill in evoking what Lovecraft refers to as 'cosmic adumbrations' and 'spectral intimations': hints and suggestions of supernatural forces. Since a supernatural story depends on these for its emotional effects, it will usually suffer if their source is made explicit (e.g., if a hitherto unseen demon is described in detail), if spectral phenomena are revealed to be mere figments of the imagination or if supposedly supernatural events can be rationalized. Buchan is sometimes guilty of this. When the Devil takes human form in 'A Journey of Little Profit', for example, the effect is droll, not frightening: the narrator finds Satan 'no' a bad sort'.[24] In 'No-Man's-Land', the tribe of Picts are scarier as a rumour than when actually encountered, becoming 'no more shapeless things of terror, but objects of research and experiment';[25] and the 'visible cloud' that appears at the end of 'The Watcher by the Threshold' to cause mayhem on the moors of More is far less frightening than the invisible demon that dogs Ladlaw. An additional detraction is that Buchan's characters often experience supernatural events while suffering from nightmares, fever or hallucinations caused by fatigue, stress, pain or drunkenness.[26] This introduces an element of ambiguity: are the events supernatural, or the result of physiological and/or psychological maladies? By rights, these features should rob the stories of their fear factor and render their status as authentic supernatural fictions questionable, but Buchan's ability to create an atmosphere charged with dread in 'isolated sections' of otherwise flawed stories, sometimes compensates for their faults and enables them to 'fulfil every condition of true supernatural horror-literature'.[27] 'Skule Skerry' is a good example: it should fail on all of the above counts, but it is genuinely chilling in parts. All of Buchan's strengths are on show: his understanding of the duality of landscape, simultaneously banal and threatening; his ability to convey an acute sense of isolation; his use of the *temenos* as a frontier or border vulnerable to things beyond the ken of rational, scientific minds; and his use of legend and folklore to fuel fright in a beleaguered consciousness. These elements act on the susceptible mind of the narrator to produce what Lovecraft calls an 'atmosphere of breathless and unexplainable dread'. But Buchan goes a step further, by exploring the origins and nature of fear itself.

Intrigued by references in an eleventh-century Icelandic saga, ornithologist Anthony Hurrell travels to the remote Scottish island of Skule Skerry to investigate whether it is one of the 'alighting places' for migrating birds. The chronicler, Adam of Bremen, has left a cryptic note in Latin: *ultima insula et proximo Abysso*. Unperturbed by this reference, which situates the island next to a biblical hell, Hurrell travels north, persuades an unwilling and superstitious Scot to ferry him out to Skule Skerry – 'the last bit of solid earth between me and Greenland' – and proceeds to set up camp 'in a curious mood of happy loneliness and curious expectation'.[28] Initially, the place seems to be 'the last word in forgotten peace' and the local warnings absurd. But Hurrell passes an uneasy night. The next day he finds himself 'in the centre of a maelstrom'; his supplies are ruined, and his boat is swept out to sea. Soon after, the wind abates and dead calm descends, disturbing in its suddenness:

> As I sat there I became conscious of an odd sensation. I seemed to be more alone, more cut off, not only from my fellows but from the habitable earth, than I had ever been before. It was like being in a small boat in mid-Atlantic – but worse, if you understand me, for that would have been loneliness in the midst of a waste which was nevertheless surrounded and traversed by the works of man, whereas now I felt that I was clean outside man's ken. I had come somehow to the edge of that world where life is, and was very close to the world which has only death in it.[29]

At first Hurrell does not feel fear, but this soon changes. Stretching his legs, he slips into the water and finds it 'so cold that it seemed to sear and bleach the skin'. This triggers terror such as he has never known:

> One thing I saw clearly – the meaning of Skule Skerry. By some alchemy of nature, at which I could only guess, it was on the track by which the North exercised its spell, a cableway for the magnetism of that cruel frozen Uttermost, which man might penetrate but could never subdue or understand. Though the latitude was only 61°, there were folds or tucks in space, and this isle was the edge of the world. Birds knew it, and the old Northmen, who were primitive beings like the birds, knew it.[30]

Rationality and fancy fight for precedence: although Hurrell feels himself to be 'a reasonable modern man trying to keep sane and scornfully rejecting the fancies which the other, a cast-back to something elemental, was furiously spinning', he becomes convinced that 'down the avenue from the North something terrible and strange might come', a monstrous migratory beast from another dimension which will alight on the island.[31] In his frantic state of mind he envisages the legendary Black Silkie, a ghoul that 'can on occasion don a seal's skin and come to land to play havoc with mortals'.[32] He realises that he is suffering from panic, 'a physical affection produced by natural causes', but he cannot drag his eyes from the waters:

> And then my knees gave under me and my heart shrank like a pea, for I saw that the someone had come ... He drew himself heavily out of the sea, wallowed for a second, and then raised his head and, from a distance of five yards, looked me blindly in the face ... I saw a great dark head like a bull's – an old face wrinkled as if in pain – a gleam of enormous broken teeth – a dripping beard – all formed on other lines than God has made mortal creatures.[33]

Hurrell faints, and three hours later is rescued. Lying in his sick bed, he attempts to account for his experience:

> If that awful thing was a mere figment of my brain then I had better be certified at once as a lunatic. No sane man could get into such a state as to see such portents with the certainty with which I had seen that creature come out of the night. If, on the other hand, the thing was a real presence, then I had looked on something outside natural law, and my intellectual world was broken in pieces. I was a scientist, and a scientist cannot admit the supernatural. If with my eyes I had beheld the monster in which Adam of Bremen believed, which holy men had exorcised, which even the shrewd Norlanders shuddered at as the Black Silkie, then I must burn my books and revise my creed.[34]

Hurrell is presented with a rational explanation for the monster: it was not the Black Silkie, but a wounded walrus. To his relief, he 'need not forswear science'. According to the internal logic of the story, this news should be deflationary, but it is anticipated at the very beginning of the tale, where Hurrell admits that what occurred on the island happened 'inside [his] head' – the result, most probably, of a combination of fear, cold, lack of food, and perhaps a little too much brandy. This fact does not detract from the power of the narrative, however: Buchan manages to evoke a 'profound sense of dread' and produce 'a penetrating study in psychology', showing an acute understanding of the origins of fear.[35]

Buchan weds landscape and metaphysics just as successfully in another of his more powerful stories, 'Space'. Like 'Skule Skerry', this story's strengths lie in its evocation of unknown supernatural forces – what Lovecraft calls the 'daemons of unplumbed space'[36] – and offers acute insights into the nature of fear. It tells of a scientist named Hollond who discovers that Space is actually an 'invisible world ... made up of corridors and alleys'.[37] Animals and savages are sensitive to its non-material landmarks, hence their ability to find their way home from great distances. Humans were once able to perceive it, too, and Hollond wants to see 'whether the civilised mind could not recreate for itself this lost gift'.[38] He manages to restore the 'old instinct' and begins 'living his daily life with a foot in each world'.[39] Initially, there is 'no suspicion of horror or fright or anything unpleasant' about this second world, only an intense loneliness: he spends 'hours travelling those eerie shifting corridors of Space with no hint of another human soul', and comes to regard it as the biblical Abomination of the Desolation.[40] Over time, however, Hollond realizes 'that there are other beings – other minds – moving in Space besides [his]'.[41] These 'Presences' inspire 'intellectual fear', a 'fear so sublimated and transmuted as to be the tension of pure spirit', and Hollond feels himself 'on the edge of a terror ... that no mortal can think of and live'.[42] He seeks to identify the nature of these Presences, and succeeds, but the knowledge drives him to death, for he commits suicide by flinging himself from a mountain in the Alps: 'he had seen the something more, the little bit too much, which plucks a man from his moorings. He had gone so far into the land of pure spirit that he must needs go further and shed the fleshly envelope that cumbered him'.[43] We are left to guess as to what Hollond encountered, because Buchan - wisely - does not provide us with an explicit description of the Presences. We are told only that Hollond threw himself from the 'steepest cliff' to ensure disfigurement, so that those who recovered his body would not be able to see the look on his face.

'Skule Skerry' and 'Space' deal with the same subject, but offer different responses to that subject on the part of the characters. The stories betray Buchan's preoccupation with metaphysics, and speculate on the nature of the cosmos and our place within that cosmos: whether we are alone, or whether we share the universe with other forces or presences; if the latter, what form those presences take, whether they are good or evil; and what the consequences would be of encountering them. While Hurrell rationalizes his experience and ascribes his condition to temporary madness, and while his sanity is in a sense saved by science, Hollond discovers something that cannot be explained by science, something with which the human mind cannot cope, and kills himself as a consequence; moreover, he does so in such a way that the knowledge he has gained has no way of being passed on, presumably because it is a truth too terrible to live with. On Skule Skerry, Hurrell believes himself to be clinging to the edge of the 'Valley of the Shadow of Death'; Hollond finds himself in the Abomination of the Desolation. Hurrell expects a visitor from that Valley; Hollond is a trespasser, and fears being found. In both tales, Buchan suggests that terror can take tangible form, but he does not describe those forms. As a result, these stories are among his best in the genre.

Lovecraft opens his study by stating that fear is the oldest, most deeply rooted of all emotions, and that the strongest type of fear is fear of the unknown.[44] 'Skule Skerry' and 'Space' show that Buchan was acutely aware of this, and his more successful supernatural stories (i.e., his most frightening) are successful precisely because of what they withhold. 'The Green Wildebeest', also praised by Lovecraft, further illustrates this principle. What is most intriguing about the story is that the totemic beast of the title does not appear; it is only experienced second-hand, through Andrew Du Preez's description to Richard Hannay: 'a wildebeest as big as a house – an old brute, grey in the nozzle and the rest of it green'.[45] It is precisely this lack of information that elevates the story above others of its ilk. In deliberately suppressing information and resisting delineation, Buchan demonstrates his understanding that fear does not depend on tangibles; that, on the contrary, it derives from what is left unseen and imagined. This is also the case in his other African-based supernatural short story, 'The Grove of Ashtaroth'. At no point does the eponymous goddess of the Zidonians appear in person; only her pleading, bodiless voice is heard, and this is to the story's advantage. Likewise, in 'The Green Glen': the power that resides in the titular locale and causes history to repeat itself with fatal results is not made explicit. 'The Wind in the Portico', the third and final short story that Lovecraft picks out for praise, further illustrates this principle: Vaunus, the pagan god that wreaks vengeance on Dubellay for attempting to rededicate his altar to the Christian god, does not appear in person: the only signs of his presence are the uncanny wind, a Gorgon's head glowing 'like a sun in hell', and his victim's dead body.[46]

All of these tales benefit from Buchan's restraint with respect to definition and delineation. Unfortunately, however, he did not always play to his strengths. 'Basilissa', for example, has great potential, but is fatally flawed by an explicit and underwhelming reveal at its climax. It begins promisingly. From childhood, Vernon Milburne is plagued by a terrifying dream that reoccurs on the first Monday of every April. In it, he finds himself in a strange room, oppressed by unknown forces: 'There was danger in the place; something was going to happen in that big room, and if by that time he was not gone there would be mischief. But it was quite clear to him that he could not go. He must stop there ... and await the advent of a terrible Something'.[47] As Vernon grows older, the lineaments of the dream, and the room, sharpen:

> In one corner was a door which led to the outer world, and through this he knew
> that he might on no account pass. Another door faced him, and he knew that he had
> only to turn the handle and enter it. But he did not want to, for he understood quite
> clearly what was beyond. There was another room like the first one, but he knew
> nothing about it, except that opposite the entrance another door led out of it. Beyond
> was a third chamber, and so on interminably. There seemed to the boy no end to this
> fantastic suite ... but there was an end. Somewhere far away in one of the rooms was
> a terror waiting on him, or, as he feared, coming towards him. Even now it might be
> flitting from room to room, every minute bringing its soft tread nearer to the chamber.[48]

This 'unmitigated horror' is more terrifying for being 'a Fear which transcended word and thought'. Because Vernon is unable to articulate and give shape to this fear, it is almost unbearable. In his teenage years, he discovers that with each passing year the entity moves one room nearer. One would imagine that this would make matters worse, but his fear begins to fade because 'it was no indefinite fear that lay beyond': 'Hitherto the nightmare had left him in gross terror ... now, though his nerves were tense with fright, he perceived that there was a limit to the mystery. Some day it must declare itself, and fight on equal terms ... The notion exhilarated as much as it frightened him'.[49] Vernon's fear becomes manageable because he is finally able to flesh it out – or at the very least, perceive that it may have a fleshly envelope: 'terror, I think, must have largely departed from the nightmare as he grew older. Fear, indeed, remained, and awe and disquiet, but these are human things, whereas terror is of hell'.[50] This distinction is revealing; fear is human, and therefore bearable, whereas terror is unworldly, and therefore intolerable; the response depends on the difference between the known and the unknown.

In his twenties, Vernon finds himself on a Greek island where he is asked to aid the eponymous heroine. He is taken to her home and left in a room. It is identical to the one in his dream, but has none of the terror it once held: 'in the old days he had regarded it with vague terror in his soul. Now he looked at it with ... hungry gladness ... The hour of his destiny had struck. The thing for which he had trained himself in body and spirit was about to reveal itself in that doorway'.[51] The door opens, Basilissa enters, and proceeds to talk in childish terms of a 'Monster' who had nearly 'gobbled' her up. It is an anticlimax of the first order, and it deteriorates further. The terrible 'Something' which caused Vernon so much terror turns out to be an ordinary, flesh-and-blood rogue who intends to ravish the heroine. When he walks through the dreaded door, the edifice of fear Buchan has been building collapses completely, as does our investment in the story. Predictably, Vernon vanquishes his foe, and he and Basilissa sail off into the night, wrapped in each other's arms. It is a terribly disappointing end to a tale that began with such promise. The solution, which Buchan used to great effect elsewhere, is simple: if one wishes to sustain fear, one should conceal, not reveal.

Haining's assessment of Buchan as 'an outstanding writer of supernatural fiction'[52] is extravagant. Buchan's work is sometimes highly effective, but it is not consistent. The atmospheric and emotional effects which inspire the 'cosmic fear' that Lovecraft deems to be the mark of the authentic supernatural story are used too sparingly. His pacing is poor at times, his stories sometimes lack uniformity of tone, his narratives are hampered by unnecessary details, and his characters are often stereotypes drawn from a uniform batch of stiff-upper-lip Brits. However, these reservations aside, it is only fair to judge Buchan by his best work in the genre, where his strengths are dominant: his sensitivity to the spirit of landscape, his skill in creating uncanny atmospheres, and his instinctive grasp of the nature and origins of fear. His best supernatural fictions include those that Lovecraft singles out for special praise, as well as stories such as 'The Outgoing of the Tide' and 'Space'. If these stories do not reach the heights of Hogg and Stevenson, they can comfortably take their place alongside the supernatural fiction of Scott, of whom Buchan was so fond. All testify to Buchan's lifelong fascination with the supernatural, one of the most critically underworked aspects of his literary legacy.

16 THE ANARCHIST'S GARDEN: POLITICS AND ECOLOGY IN JOHN BUCHAN'S WASTELANDS

John Miller

Two years after T. S. Eliot had opened *The Waste Land* (1922) with the mordant judgement that 'April is the cruellest month',[1] John Buchan's novel of struggle against anarchist conspiracy, *The Three Hostages*, began with a more upbeat reflection on the seasons:

> It was still mid-March, one of those spring days when the noon is like May ... The season was absurdly early, for the blackthorn was in flower and the hedge roots were full of primroses ... [I]n the bracken in Stern Wood I thought I saw a woodcock, and hoped that the birds might nest with us this year, as they used to long ago. It was jolly to see the world coming to life again, and to remember that this patch of England was my own, and all these wild things, so to speak, members of my little household.[2]

Spring at Hannay's Oxfordshire home, Fosse Manor, bought, like Buchan's own Oxfordshire manor, 'just after the war',[3] contrasts sharply with the bleak ecology of Eliot's poem. Organic growth in *The Waste Land* is paradoxically a sign of death as much as the embodiment of life, imaging a post-war world simultaneously sterile and corrupt. Voices in the opening section ask ominously: 'What are the roots that clutch, what branches grow / Out of this stony rubbish';[4] 'That corpse you planted last year in your garden, / Has it begun to sprout? Will it bloom this year?'.[5] Hannay's 'patch of England', on the other hand, figures an optimistic renewal that reads as an antidote to this, and to the chaos of 1914–18, a theme repeated by Buchan in his 1940 autobiography *Memory Hold-the-Door*:

> The war left me with an intense craving for a country life. It was partly that I wanted quiet after turmoil ... But it was also a new-found delight in the rhythm of nature, and in small homely things after so many alien immensities.[6]

Where Eliot sees a corpse in the garden, Buchan enjoys instead retirement into rustic peace after years of global war. Fosse suggests a literal *oikos*, the Greek root of ecology that might be translated as Hannay's 'household'. The 'wild things' that belong to it illustrate his harmonious integration into his environment, in opposition to the alienation revealed by Eliot's voices.

Landscape is a prominent feature of Buchan's writing; indeed, his 'earliest recollections', he writes in *Memory Hold-the-Door*, were 'not of myself, but of my environment'.[7] His childhood in Fife and the Scottish Borders 'induced a love of nature in general' that later generated 'a passion for landscapes in many parts of the globe'.[8] His depictions of British countryside are notable for their attention to locality, to botanical and ornithological detail (like Fosse's blackthorn, prim-roses and woodcock) as well as a romantic aesthetic of place. Many of Buchan's characters are enthusiastic amateur naturalists. In *The Three Hostages* alone, Dr Greenslade is 'mad about botany'[9] and Archie Roylance, before being recruited into Hannay's quest, is keen to get back to Scotland to 'watch a pair of nesting greenshanks'.[10] The ten-year-old Davie Warcliff, one of the three hostages, offers perhaps the most poignant incarnation of an ecological sensibility. Possessed of a 'kind of genius for animals', he knows 'the habits of birds by instinct, and used to talk of them as other people talk of their friends'.[11] Set against this background of ecological harmony are a series of darker and more ambiguous environments encountered as the novel progresses: abandoned yards and derelict gardens in odd corners of London, both overgrown with fecundity and shrivelling towards barrenness. If Fosse produces a comfortable glow of familiarity, these other sites, reminiscent of Eliot's eerie terrain of 'dead land',[12] evoke a shudder as Buchan engages with the unsettling urban inverse of Hannay's rural idyll.

Buchan's relationship with Eliot's imagining of post-war degeneration through environmental decay is not straightforward, and makes ecology in Buchan's work a rich field of enquiry, connected intricately with seismic cultural and political change. Eliot's poem, along with *Ulysses* (1922), was the centre-piece of literary modernism's *annus mirabilis*, a year of such radical upheaval Ezra Pound announced the end of the Christian era and proposed a new calendar starting with 1922 as year 1.[13] Alongside artistic innovation, the post-war years were also marked by political turmoil. The Russian Revolution was the most dramatic embodiment of an extremism fostered by the First World War that shadowed the political establishments of Western Europe. The 1916 Easter Ris-ing in Ireland and the subsequent 1922 inception of the Irish Free State marked a significant change in British domestic politics that, in conjunction with compa-rable developments in Egypt, 'looks like the beginning of the postcolonial era'.[14] Consequently, in 1922, Buchan, as a mainstream, middlebrow novelist who had served his country as a colonial administrator in South Africa from 1901–3, and during the war in the Department of Information, could be seen to be fighting a battle on two fronts, his literary ethos and ideological commitments both belea-guered in a transforming world.

In this context Buchan's post-war political 'shockers' invest ecology with ideological significance. As they narrate the victory of the British state over agents bent on its destruction, environment is a metonym for nation; the dichotomy of unkempt urban wilderness with wholesome, husbanded land conveying the contest of subversion and the status quo. Attached to this reactionary political ecology is a signification of landscape and environment within the literary genres that Buchan draws on and defends against the modernist injunction to 'make it new'.[15] The contrast of wasteland and pastoral is a key aspect of the structure of Buchan's adventures, a textual chiaroscuro of ruined and managed land that adds texture to the classic romance narrative. Inseparable from these symbolic usages of environment is a materialist discourse of ecological damage in Buchan's writing that also reveals an environmentalist at work, bemoaning the impact of industrial capitalism on the natural world. Buchan's wastelands, then, are multifaceted arenas that, read in conjunction with a broader interest in landscape, depict a deep-rooted and complex human habitation of space.

Buchan's Political Ecology

While Eliot and Joyce's masterpieces were ushering in an artistic revolution, Buchan's contribution to the literary scene of 1922 was what he described simply as a 'Glasgow fairy tale'.[16] *Huntingtower*, initially serialized in 1921 in the *Popular Magazine*, is the first Dickson McCunn novel and an archetypically romantic story of Saskia, an exiled Russian princess and her attempts to keep a collection of jewels from Bolshevik conspirators. In the novel's opening chapter the reader is taken on a tour of McCunn's modest library, the volumes of Defoe, Hazlitt and Stevenson testifying to a literary taste inclined more to the classics than to contemporary innovation, and informed, importantly, by McCunn's own 'incurable' romanticism. Reading Scott he imagines 'fantastic journeys', while his enjoyment of Dickens's works stems from their atmosphere of 'hoofs on a frosty road' as the romance trope of the journey appears as the key ingredient of McCunn's readerly pleasure.[17] If 1922 marked 'a larger, more general separation of the avant-garde from the backward', McCunn's colours are clearly nailed to the mast.[18] Accordingly, embarking on a walking holiday in the Carrick hills, he discovers a traditional countryside that evokes pastoral harmony. His companion John Heritage, a modern English poet, exclaims with delight as they discover the remote village of Dalquharter:

> 'Ye gods! What a village!' ... There were not more than a dozen whitewashed houses, all set in little gardens of wallflower and daffodil and early fruit blossom. A triangle of green filled the intervening space, and in it stood an ancient wood pump. There was no schoolhouse or kirk; not even a post office ...

> The Poet became lyrical. 'At last!' he cried. 'The village of my dreams! Not a sign
> of commerce! No church or school or beastly recreation hall! Nothing but these
> divine little cottages and an ancient pub!'[19]

Heritage delights in nostalgia. The 'ancient wood pump' and 'pub' are a time-
honoured backdrop for the village's fertility: the 'early fruit blossom', like Fosse's
'absurdly early' spring growth correlating nature's easy productiveness with the
well-established social setting. Moreover, as the poet seizes on the absence of any
signs of commerce from the landscape as an aspect of its charm, pastoral perfec-
tion is opposed to economic development, illustrating a reassuring conservative
resistance to change in uncertain times.

Buchan's later depiction of Fosse is a similar idealisation of age-old rural life
and of a harmonious balance between human and environment, emphasised
when Hannay qualifies his rapt description of his estate with a reminder of the
labour involved:

> [T]he place wanted a lot of looking to, for it had run wild during the war, and the
> woods had to be thinned, gates and fences repaired, new drains laid, a ram put in to
> supplement the wells, a heap of thatching to be done, and the garden borders to be
> brought back to cultivation ... [A]s I came out of the Home Wood on to the lower
> lawns and saw the old stone gables that the monks had built, I felt I was anchored at
> last in the pleasantest kind of harbour.[20]

Here Buchan presents a landscape as rich in symbolism as it is in biodiversity. The
war caused manmade structures to fall into decay, as nature escaped its segrega-
tions, returning to a wild state that must be 'brought back to cultivation'. Nature's
unruliness chimes with a wider sense of the political and cultural results of war.
Over the preceding years a 'large part of the world had gone mad ... and all the
old sanctities had been weakened'.[21] Fosse's wartime disarray is the environmental equivalent of this collapse of values so that Hannay's diligent labours embody
a reassertion of political stability that gives 'Home Wood' a wider resonance: the
national as much as the local home. In this context, Fosse represents Hannay's
dwelling in residential terms and also by a philosophical usage originating in
Heidegger's thought. Dwelling 'implies the long-term imbrication of humans in
a landscape of memory, ancestry and death, of ritual, life and work'; a relation
of 'duty and responsibility' that encapsulates Hannay's sense of his investment in
the land.[22] The memory of monks in the old stone gables sanctifies a space that
Hannay likes to think has been 'continuously inhabited for a thousand years', a
past he excavates on 'evenings *digging* into county history' [emphasis added], his
researches pointedly metaphorized as entry into the earth.[23]

Hannay's pastoral domain also exists as a network of social relations. Bringing the estate back to order requires people with specific roles in the estate's
management:

> The gardeners were digging in sulphates about the fig trees on the south wall, and wanted directions about the young chestnuts in the nursery; the keeper was lying in wait for me in the stable-yard for instructions about a new batch of pheasant eggs, and the groom wanted me to look at the hocks of Mary's cob.[24]

Fosse's political ecology, then, incorporates a clear sense of class hierarchies that have often been associated with Buchan.[25] Ecological concord emerges through social stasis, a conflict-free society of clearly demarcated class roles with Hannay as the benevolent landowner, providing 'instructions' to his employees. Fosse is a microcosm of beneficent state control that propagandizes the fertile, traditional Britain the war was fought for.

These embattled traditional landscapes are the background to the narrative dynamic of Buchan's political thrillers. Fosse's wartime decay and Heritage's gleeful discovery of a commerce-free village hint at the exposure of rural Britain to destructive influences. This vulnerability is emphasized by the etymology of Fosse as a moat, and is explicitly foreshadowed by Mary Hannay's worries that their peaceful life at Fosse is 'too good and beloved to last'.[26] Mary's foreboding is quickly realized with the discovery of an anarchist plot to disturb the nation's quiet. Apart from Buchan's detailed portrayal of the villain, Medina, this extremist faction is amorphous and only vaguely imagined, with uncertain political objectives. Medina's motives seem to go little beyond nihilist subversion, the desire to 'win everything that civilisation would give him and then wreck it'.[27] Accordingly, Buchan depicts an anarchism devoid of political philosophy, and consisting of two elements: a new breed of 'moral imbeciles' thriving since the war and without devotion to 'any movement, good or bad' and then a few evil, clever men who have profit as their main objective.[28] *Huntingtower's* Bolshevik conspirators strike a similar note. These are 'madmen and degenerates' aiming to purloin royal Russian jewels to turn them into 'guns and armies' that would threaten Europe's eastern edge.[29] In both texts, then, Buchan imagines a generalized destructive force intent on poisoning Britain's peace and stability. Significantly, the environmental implications of these gangs for Buchan's political ecology are disclosed in the metaphors Hannay uses to describe the attitude of the conspirators: 'a wild hatred of something or other' connected to 'dreary wastes of half-baked craziness'.[30] Anarchy is a wild wasteland that contrasts pointedly with the well-manicured nature of Fosse and Dalquharter. As Buchan's heroes track their adversaries across Britain they encounter this ideological wilderness at close quarters in desolate and unsettling micro-environments that illustrate the potential shape of a Britain that does not guard itself against political malevolence and look, as Hannay does at Fosse, to its gates and borders.

Anarchist (and Bolshevik) Gardening

Arriving at Dalquharter's solitary inn, McCunn and Heritage discover it contrasts sharply with the otherwise snug village: 'The cobbles of the yard were weedy
... a pane in the window was broken, and the blinds hung tattered. The garden
was a wilderness, and the doorstep had not been scoured for weeks'.[31] Hardly
surprisingly, the inn is revealed to be a Bolshevik hideout, the weedy garden and
slovenly doorstep a warning image of what a Bolshevik Britain might turn out to
be. The house of Huntingtower itself, where the Princess is held captive, is no less
run down. Once-tended garden borders are now 'rank and wild'; inside a dilapi-
dated verandah 'untended shrubs sprawled in broken plaster vases';[32] a 'dying
magnolia' meanwhile adds the taint of death to ungoverned botanical life.[33] The
estate's degeneration is further signalled by scattered remnants of previous diligent land management: 'below the parapet the verandah floor was heaped with
old garden litter, rotten matting, dead or derelict bulbs'.[34] The accumulation of
debris represents a Bolshevik disinterest in the natural world that marks their
alienation from it, and provides an image of the opposition of political extremism and georgic tranquillity that Buchan was to develop in *The Three Hostages*.

Just as the Bolshevik influence stands out in Dalquharter, so Hannay's coun-
ter-insurgent quest takes him to some strikingly anarchic places. Palmyra Square,
a fictional address in north London's Gospel Oak, is the location of both Medina's mother and one of the hostages. Buchan's description of the house and its
environs pointedly differs from Fosse:

> The place seemed to have been dead and decaying for centuries, seen in that windy
> moonless dark, and No. 4 was a shuttered tomb ... There were some dilapidated out-
> houses, and the back garden with rank grasses and obscene clothes-posts, looking like
> nothing so much as a neglected graveyard.[35]

Fosse's continuous habitation is a marked difference to No. 4 Palmyra Square's
image of desolation and neglect in a plot of land unsanctified by labour or ritual.
Its tumbledown scrub is an anti-garden, a moribund 'tomb' or 'graveyard' rather
than a place of flourishing life. The 'rank' grasses, like Huntingtower's garden
borders, indicate morbid and excessive growth; the 'obscene clothes-posts' offer
a bizarre image of the colonization of the human world by this inhuman force, as
domestic order is gradually lost in the swell of organic matter.

'Palmyra', the name of a Syrian city, adds a further element to the discom-
fiting aura of the anarchist base that chimes with Medina's own name with its
evocation of the Arabic burial place of the prophet Mohammed.[36] If Fosse's
centrality to Britain's political ecology is signposted by the 'Home wood', the
random association of anarchy with Islam and the Middle East tinges the conspiracy with an exoticism that also carries an ecological significance. The Middle

East's desert landscapes conspire at the edges of British fertility. Palmyra Square thus constitutes a curious mixture of organic abundance and destitution, an almost apocalyptic death-in-life. Consequently, recalling Huntingtower's 'dying magnolia', unfruitful grasses thrive at the expense of more productive, and familiar, species as Britain's native flora withers in a general air of desuetude:

> The houses stood apart, each in a patch of garden, which may at one time have had lawns and flowers. Now these gardens were mere dusty yards, the refuse of tin cans and bits of paper, and only a blackened elm, an ill-grown privet hedge, and some stunted lilacs told of the more cheerful past.[37]

With the 'refuse of tin cans and bits of paper' among the 'stunted' and 'blackened' suburban plants, Buchan introduces another element of his wastelands, an economic chain of consumption and waste that accompanies the organic overflow of the 'rank grasses' and indicates the antipathy of Buchan's rural ideal to a commercial culture of mass production. Indeed, suburbia in general awoke Buchan's disapproval, becoming 'a synonym for a dreadful life of commercial drudgery without daylight or hope'.[38] The mistrust of commerce signalled by Buchan in London and Dalquharter is an aspect of a wider dismay at the impact of industrialism on the natural environment. Buchan described the condition of the streams in the Fifeshire of his childhood:

> One was foul with the discards of the bleaching works. There must have been a time when sea-trout in a spate ran up them from the Firth, but now in their lower courses they were like sewers and finished their degraded life in a drain in the town harbour. There was no beauty in those perverted valleys.[39]

The indignation at the effects of pollution revealed by this 'degraded' and 'perverted' space also features in Buchan's final novel *Sick Heart River* when the narrator Leithen describes a Canadian valley overtaken by pulp mills with 'all [its] loveliness ... butchered to enable some shoddy newspaper to debauch the public soul'.[40] Corruption in both these regions takes the place of natural beauty and suggests an aesthetic and moral component to Buchan's environmental enthusiasm: aspiring to keep the harmonious composition of rural areas as much as preserving their ecological health.

In *Huntingtower* and *The Three Hostages*, then, there are two types of garbage: the rubble of environmental neglect and the jetsam of the mercantile city that illustrate a national ecology beleaguered by the harmful impetus of economic, political and cultural foment. The interplay of gardens and waste, of growth and infertility, is given a further metaphorical layer when Hannay imagines another landscape in the urban degeneration around Palmyra Square:

> I passed yards which not so long ago had been patches of market-garden and terraces, sometime pretentious, and now sinking into slums; for London is like the tropical

bush – if you don't exercise constant care the jungle in the shape of the slums, will break in.[41]

On a literal level, the urban jungle provides a geographically confused contrast with the suggestion of desert.[42] Tropical bush, however, has a similar metaphorical function to arid terrain, suggesting a wild and alien presence, like the grasses consuming the civilized space of Palmyra Square's neglected plot. The urban jungle intimates the potential for reverse colonization, the colonial periphery immigrating to the imperial metropolis, 'breaking in' with any lull in Britain's 'constant care'.[43] This vision of environmental menace enacts Buchan's idea of the fragility of the civilised world order: 'you think that a wall as solid as the earth separates civilisation from barbarism. I tell you the division is a thread, a sheet of glass. A touch here, a push there, and you bring back the reign of Saturn'.[44] An echo of this famous phrase occurs in *Huntingtower* when Heritage tells McCunn, 'I learnt in the war that civilisation anywhere has a very thin crust',[45] while the same sentiment is behind Greenslade's judgement in *The Three Hostages* that, 'Original sin is always there, but the meaning of civilisation was that we had got it battened down under hatches, whereas now it's getting its head up'.[46] Saturn is also a Roman god associated with fertility, and so is used to set this peril in ecological terms, an anarchic growth that signals the collapse of western values. Saturnalia, furthermore, temporarily inverted societal roles, emphasising the carnivalesque socio-political dimension of Saturn's reign that Buchan's heroes fear.[47]

Nature in this guise constitutes for Buchan what he describes in *Memory Hold-the-Door* as *natura maligna*, an aggressively alien force typified by overwhelming excess and often associated with tropical vegetation.[48] An example he gives of this trope in *Memory Hold-the-Door*, following Aldous Huxley, is the 'cruel, obscene superabundance of a tropical forest',[49] a designation that corresponds particularly with Buchan's rhetoric of anarchy in the earlier *The Power-House*. Just as tropical bush is a *super*abundance, so Lumley's intended destruction of civilized values is not just anarchy but 'super-anarchy';[50] similarly, the sinister butler, Tuke, is described rather oddly as a 'super-butler'.[51] The problems facing Buchan's heroes as they confront this Saturnine force might be characterized as inversion and excess, an overturning and overflowing of boundaries that is negotiated through a recurrent, and perhaps surprising, interest in the processes of municipal waste management that aims to stem such unseemly growths at the source.

Drains

As Hannay sets about diligently repairing the wartime decay of his estate at the beginning of *The Three Hostages*, he is called upon to look to the drains. While this task was low down on his list ('the woods had to be thinned, gates and fences repaired, new drains laid'), it introduces a striking motif in the novel. Hannay later plans, with the help of the police, to break into an antique shop at night, only to find an obstacle in his path:

> [T]o my disgust I saw opposite the door of the curiosity shop a brazier of hot coals and the absurd little shelter which means that part of the street is up. There was the usual roped-in enclosure, decorated with red lamps, a heap of debris, and a hole where some of the setts had been lifted. Here was bad luck with a vengeance, that the Borough council should have chosen this place and moment ... for investigating the drains.[52]

These council drainage technicians are cover provided by Scotland Yard for their expert housebreaker, Mr Abel, who will help Hannay get into, and out of, the suspect building. Waste management is thus aligned with political hygiene, and indeed, throughout the novel, the metaphors that Hannay uses to condemn the anarchist plot are redolent with unsavoury investigations underground, beneath the street's crust of civilization. In fact, Hannay's metaphors unfold the processes of sewerage sequentially through the narrative. At his first apprehension of the anarchist conspiracy he feels that a 'hideous, muddy wave from the outer world had come to disturb my little sheltered pool'.[53] This unwanted, uncontrollable menace is developed next into a more strictly contained metaphorization of anarchy: the conspiracy becomes a 'hideous underworld',[54] or a 'subterranean movement'.[55] After the disruptive wave has been channelled through this network of metaphorical sewers, anarchy is then discharged as 'an abominable *hinterland* of mystery and crime',[56] [emphasis added] as Hannay locates anarchy in the regions of a sea or estuary and indicates the successful transport of this anarchic substance from its starting point to its final outflow.

The Three Hostages, then, correlates hygiene with a political order besieged by extremism.[57] This association of public health and national stability is buttressed by a wider, and by the 1920s well-established, symbolic register. 'Throughout nineteenth century literature, the representation of dirt in towns – ranging from slums to contagious diseases to pestiferous rivers – was mapped onto traditional themes of moral, social, economic and spiritual decay'.[58] Buchan's anarchic world of wastes evidently reproduces this identification of material degeneration with an erosion of human values. The sewer, in particular, is loaded with significance. It 'retained a strong symbolic resonance as a stubbornly irrational space, the most organic, primitive and uncontrollable part of the modern city'.[59] This designation fits neatly with Buchan's imagination of anarchy as a mad and dangerous force and also connects with the novel's symbolic ecological cycles. Sewers carry the unsavoury matter that nourishes the 'reign of Saturn' and the 'rank grasses' that spontaneously multiply in the city's poorer districts. Consequently, to control growth one must control the matter that makes it flourish; it is the 'double nature' of filth, as Cohen writes, that it is both 'dangerously polluting and bounteously providing'.[60] Hannay keeps waste in its place, preventing it crossing the threshold into public space, nipping anarchic growths in the bud, marshalling and expelling energies antithetical to civilization.

By comparison, McCunn's engagement with municipal waste management in *Huntingtower* is limited. In the first stages of his walking holiday he observes in the village of Kirkmichael that 'even the sanitary cart seemed a picturesque vehicle',[61] as a traditional mode of life creates harmony from even the most insalubrious of tasks. Yet, set against this quaint but harmonious system, images of waste focus on a different aspect of 1920s foment. The modernist poet Heritage explains the sources of his literary inspiration to McCunn:

> Poetry's everywhere, and the real thing is commoner among drabs and pot-houses and rubbish heaps than in your Sunday parlours. The poet's business is to distil it out of rottenness and show that it is all one spirit, the thing that keeps the stars in their place ... I wanted to call my book *Drains*, for drains are sheer poetry carrying off the excess and discards of human life to make the fields green and the corn ripen. But the publishers kicked. So I called it *Whorls*, to express my view of the exquisite involution of all things.[62]

Heritage's identification of the poetry of waste is a complex moment. On the one hand his unsavoury interests may be read as an attack by Buchan on what he described in *Memory Hold-the-Door* as a post-war 'deterioration in literary manners' against which he remained, like McCunn, sturdily traditional.[63] Summarizing his own place in literature Buchan commented, 'My taste was for things old and shabby and unpopular, and I regarded with scepticism whatever was proclaimed as the Spirit of the Age. I was born to be always out of fashion'.[64] Fashionable new verse to Buchan was mere 'unmelodious journalism',[65] a judgement that Gertrude Himmelfarb takes in her discussion of Buchan as the 'last Victorian' to be a direct reference to Eliot, though, in *Huntingtower* Heritage's sympathy with the working man strikes a different note to Eliot's association with right-wing politics.[66] Even if Heritage does not correspond directly with Eliot, he still cuts an Eliotic figure, his name ironically capturing the modernist iconoclastic spirit and his interest in drains chiming with Eliot's sordid cityscape of bodily and environmental of wastes and leakages, the rat 'Dragging its slimy belly on the bank';[67] the concupiscent attentions of the 'young man carbuncular'[68] or Lil's chemical abortion.[69]

The opposition between old and new literary cultures is most clearly illustrated at a low point for Heritage. He sits alone and freezing in the ruined keep of a castle with the Bolshevik foe approaching the coast in a Danish brig. He takes a resolutely practical but symbolically charged decision:

> He put on his waterproof, and turned his attention to the fire. It needed re-kindling, and he hunted in his pockets for paper, finding only the slim volume lettered *Whorls*.
>
> I set it down as the most significant commentary on his state of mind. He regarded the book with intense disfavour, tore it in two, and used a handful of its fine deckle-edged leaves to get the fire going.[70]

Heritage's burning of his book is a crucial aspect of the development of his character during the novel, from a cocky, ill-mannered know-it-all who rubs McCunn up the wrong way, to a heroic figure prepared to sacrifice all for a noble cause. The intrusion of a first-person narrative voice into the third person narration emphasises the importance of his action as, in his new 'state of mind', he embraces romance and consigns modernism to the flames, adding another metaphor to Buchan's programme of cultural and political hygiene.

While it may be tempting to read Buchan's symbolism of hygiene as a sweeping disapprobation of waste, modernism and political extremism, Heritage's *Drains* is crucially associated with the landscapes Buchan's heroes seek to uphold in *Huntingtower* and *The Three Hostages*. The green fields and ripening corn he imagines at the drains' outflow suggest the georgic harmony that McCunn and Hannay cherish, rather than the sinister excess of anarchism that they might potentially nourish. The alternative title, *Whorls*, with its 'exquisite involution of all things' expresses an interconnectedness of decay and growth, incontestable at an ecological level, which indicates the fundamental necessity of waste for all life. Heritage, then, while alluding to a gloomy Eliotic vision of life's underside, moves beyond *The Waste Land's* pessimism to imagine a rural alternative to the post-war urban nightmare absent from Eliot's poem. In this waste management deploys rather than destroys waste, channelling it to where it may be useful, or at least benign. Furthermore, a cycle of death and rebirth is central to the Christian narrative of redemption, a reference that may underpin Buchan's situation of Palmyra Square in Gospel Oak. While waste fertilises tropical excess, other, nobler plants may also rely on the same processes.

The significance of waste as both pollution and the organic basis for life evokes a wider interest in doubleness in Buchan's work that is most prominently figured in *The Three Hostages* in the striking similarity of the novel's hero and villain. As men of comparable stature and interests yet of antithetical ideological positions Hannay and Medina form a Manichean couple that argues the intimacy of civilization and barbarism or even the psychoanalytic coexistence of conscious and unconscious. As Hannay is exposed to Medina's hypnotic wiles he hears his enemy unwittingly vocalize their closeness: 'You are Richard Hannay ... Repeat, "I am Richard Hannay"'.[71] This doubling of the civilized Hannay and barbaric Medina is the human equivalent of the ecological interdependence of waste and life that exemplifies John Scanlon's argument that 'garbage is civilisation's double'.[72] Furthermore, beyond Buchan's interest in sewage and suburban litter, this theme is also applied to more rarefied forms of cultural production. When Hannay enters the curiosity shop he finds it 'full of rubbish' but also discovers among the dross a secret entrance to a more sophisticated residence with 'some fine Italian plaques [and] a set of green Chinese jars which looked like the real thing'.[73] Duality, then, operates in a number of arenas and suggests a degree of complexity and ambivalence rarely associated with Buchan's ostensibly normative political agenda. For Buchan things are seldom one thing or the other but rather a little bit of both, or at least haunted by the other: the hero's touch of savagery or the garbage surrounding art's magnificence.

This dialectic of self and other is a key constituent of the romance mode that Buchan embraced in his 'shockers', and a significant aspect of the environmental configurations that romance requires. As McCunn, approaching Dalquharter, observes the moor dropping 'down to green meadows, and the mystery of the dark woods beyond',[74] the juxtaposition of the bright and the dark, the known and the secret, sets the tone for the adventures to come and emphasises the necessity of ecological contrast. To some extent the wasteland in both *Huntingtower* and *The Three Hostages* serves the function of the wild land into which the romance hero voyages, but in the wider logic of Buchan's environmentality this move constitutes an ironic compromise. Writing once again in *Memory Hold-the-Door* Buchan describes a world in which science 'has gained all its major victories' and facilitated an inexorable development of the planet:

> In my nightmare I could picture such a world ... There was no corner of the globe left unexplored and unexploited, no geographical mysteries to fire the imagination. Broad highways crowded with automobiles threaded the remotest lands, and overhead great air-liners carried week-end tourists to the wilds of Africa and Asia. Everywhere there were guest-houses and luxury hotels and wayside camps and filling stations. What once were the savage tribes of Equatoria and Polynesia were now in reserves as an attraction to trippers, who bought from them curios and holiday mementoes.[75]

Buchan's portrayal of a world without mystery is a significant summary of developments in his own lifetime that also reads as a remarkably prescient account of twenty-first century globalized economies, overexploited land and homogenized experience that offers only the dismal consolation of ecotourism as an ersatz, degraded simulation of romance. If the growth of Fosse's woods and borders during the war represents a weakening of sanctities, this surely comprises another: a relentless march of utilitarian land-use that leaves the romancer with only a few ruined gardens to feed the imagination. Clearly, to seize on this romantic investment in ecology as a template for environmentalism would be deeply problematic in terms of environmental and social justice, not least in the reinvigoration of a colonial aesthetic: land kept wild for the benefit of the white adventurer (an intention that in fact has much to do with the early history of national parks in Africa and Asia). Neither does Buchan's discomfort at *natura maligna* sit comfortably with a green political agenda: the malignant wilds of Canada and Central Africa are, after all, among the world's most important remaining enclaves of biodiversity. But perhaps it is exactly this ambivalence in Buchan that provides the most telling contribution of his political ecology: the contrary impulses to prune and contain nature in making a home in the world alongside the desire for a broader imaginative home beyond the confines of habitation, depicting the ongoing, urgent negotiation of the human place in the biosphere.

17 TRACING THE THIRTY-NINE STEPS

Tony Williams

Published in 1915 and still in print almost one hundred years later, *The Thirty-Nine Steps* is the novel most identified with John Buchan, and represented as much of a challenge to its author as the fictional challenges facing Richard Hannay.[1] Begun at a time when Buchan suffered from ill-health and was unable to join the army, *The Thirty-Nine Steps* represented the second version of his attempt at writing a 'shocker' begun by *The Power-House* (first published in *Blackwood's Magazine* in December 1913) as well as a further exploration of themes from his first contemporary novel *The Half-Hearted* (1900). Like *The Half-Hearted*, *The Thirty-Nine Steps* appeared in the context of a threatening world stage where the Great Game took on more ominous overtones.

Buchan's most celebrated work is as much concerned with the problems of citizenship and masculinity as it is with the Great Game. At the end of *The Half-Hearted*, its hero Lewis Haystoun dies a heroic death, having overcome debilitating character flaws defined by the title of the novel. In the concluding sentence of *The Thirty-Nine Steps*, Richard Hannay expresses personal satisfaction for his role in solving the enigma within the novel's title. 'But I had done my best service, I think, before I put on khaki.'[2] Hannay had served his country impeccably, but he had also served himself by bringing out the better qualities of his nature and overcoming negative features within his own personality.

The Thirty-Nine Steps is a highly accomplished novel. In film studies it is generally cited to emphasize the distinctive features of its most celebrated cinematic adaptation by Alfred Hitchcock, rather than for its literary merit.[3] Hitchcock borrowed from Buchan the theme of a 'wrong man' unjustifiably accused of a crime, thrust into a world of chaos far removed from his everyday existence until balance becomes restored at the end. In *The Thirty-Nine Steps*, Buchan repeats the paradox of *The Power-House* in which Sir Edward Leithen struggles to escape his pursuers in the normal surroundings of a familiar London by placing most of the pursuit in Scotland. Richard Hannay becomes 'a stranger in a strange land being hunted by an unseen enemy, but in countryside familiar to many of his readers'.[4]

Buchan's novel has undergone three film adaptations.[5] The 1959 Ralph Thomas and 1979 Don Sharp versions have generally been regarded as inferior to the original novel and the 1935 Hitchcock adaptation. The chapter-based structure of Buchan's novel may be more appropriate for a ten-episode television series than a ninety-minute film version. However, every literary, cinematic and television text often reveals the presence of different cultural codes. Each version follows the original source in certain ways and departs from it in others, which often have to do with contemporary cultural influences.

According to Christopher Orr, each text represents the influence of certain competing cultural discourses. The literary original represents just one of a number of conflicting texts within any cinematic adaptation.

> By placing the notion of adaptation within the theory of intertextuality, we can describe the literary source as one of a series of pre-texts which share some of the same narrative conventions as the film adaptation. This description obviously does not exhaust the film's intertextual space, which also includes codes specific to the institution of cinema as well as codes that reflect the cultural conventions under which the film was produced.[6]

John Buchan embodies the cultural and social codes of his particular class that naturally influenced his own particular narrative. Later values also affect the three film versions made during different historical periods. *The Thirty-Nine Steps* represents the first-person narrative of a now extinct species of gentleman-adventurer tale that would soon disappear after the First World War, although the concept remained popular during the interwar years and beyond. However, different types of adaptations also occur as a result of new cultural codes and conventions influencing changed reading receptions. It is important to understand the nature of these influences arising from the different contexts and not merely dismiss them from feelings of infidelity, either to the original literary version or what the most successful cinematic version *ought* to be.

Any film version needs to depart from the literary original in order to confront the different challenges inherent to changed social circumstances influencing each production. Yet, at times, 'tracings' do occur, which function like a palimpsest embodying faint echoes of the original text. John Buchan's *The Thirty-Nine Steps* and its three film versions represent key examples of this tendency. 'Tracings' of the original literary text inhabit each version but exist in a tense relationship with different elements that enter the text during each adaptation. Although it is tempting to privilege the literary text above its cinematic successors, or choose the 'best' film, it is more challenging to attempt to define the particular nature of these tensions and what they represent in terms of different cultural eras.

The plot developments of *The Thirty-Nine Steps* deserve greater recognition in order to understand the deceptive complexity of the novel. At this point a detailed description of the narrative is necessary so that the reader may recognize the significant components of this novel. Opening on a May afternoon in London, in 1914, Buchan's first-person narrative describes his hero as a Scottish colonialist from Bulawayo eager to return to the veld following his disillusionment with the 'Old Country'. Citing the fact that he 'had no real pal to go about with', Richard Hannay describes himself as 'yawning my head off all day' and 'the best bored man in the United Kingdom'.[7] He fears becoming like the jaded upper-class figures he has mixed with on his return to England, and secretly admires the lower classes, of whom he can never be part. 'The crowd surged past me on the pavements, busy and chattering, and I envied the people for *having something to do*. These shop-girls and clerks and dandies and policemen *had some interest in life that kept them going*' (emphasis added).[8] Returning from a music-hall show, he gives money to a beggar 'because I saw him yawn; he was a fellow-sufferer'.[9]

These comments represent the first of many dualities present within *The Thirty-Nine Steps* suggesting Hannay's yearning for something exciting to happen in his life.[10] However, a Southern gentleman from Kentucky will fill that need in ways Hannay never considered. Described as a 'slim man, with a short brown beard and small, gimlety blue eyes',[11] Scudder involves Hannay within his own, fantasy, version of the Great Game, involving 'a big subterranean movement' engineered by very dangerous people such as Jews and businessmen. As the reader learns later, Scudder had embellished his own narrative. The authority figure Sir Walter Bullivant contradicts Scudder's fictional construction, revealing to the reader that these anti-Semitic feelings are not shared by either Buchan or Richard Hannay.[12] As Bullivant tells Hannay, he believed Scudder to be 'too romantic. He had the artistic temperament, and wanted a story to be better than God meant it to be. He had a lot of odd biases, too. Jews, for example, made him see red. Jews and the high finance'.[13] Despite initial disbelief, Hannay twice describes his interest in both the teller and tale. Mixing another drink for his unexpected guest, Hannay 'was getting interested in the beggar'.[14]

Scudder also displays his mastery of disguises, something Hannay will later appropriate. He takes on a new identity, 'Captain Theophilus Digby of the 40th Gurkhas but only his gimlety, hungry eyes were the same'.[15] By contrast, Scudder's adversary is an 'old man with a young voice who could hood his eyes like a hawk'.[16] This eye imagery links both men, and is a discreet instance of the fragile line dividing civilization from the world of chaos.[17] Hannay notes that Scudder was 'nursing his nerves back to health',[18] anticipating the very actions he will perform after his guest's murder. Like Scudder, Hannay will discover that he is 'no slouch at disguises'.[19]

After discovering the body, Hannay posthumously bonds with Scudder. Despite describing himself as 'an ordinary sort of fellow', Hannay decides to 'play the game in his place',[20] and welcomes the challenge of engaging in both contemplation *and* action as an escape from his boredom. Deciding to flee to Scotland rather than risk capture in a city before he can inform the authorities about the assassination plot, Hannay engages in his first act of disguise by clipping his moustache to parallel Scudder's own clean-shaven look. Leaving his apartment, Hannay encounters a milkman with an 'ill-nourished moustache' quite different from his own 'long and drooping' facial hair, whom he persuades to change identities, in order to escape Scudder's murderers waiting outside.[21] Hannay leaves, 'imitating the jaunty swing of the milkman', paralleling Scudder's earlier successful impersonation of a British officer in front of Hannay's man-servant Paddock.[22]

After leaving a Scottish train on his journey north, Hannay notices the effect that his new odyssey has on his spirits: he actually feels 'light-hearted'.[23] Despite earlier feelings of being more secure in the open countryside, he is pursued by a monoplane, an element that Hitchcock would later reuse in *North by Northwest*. Hannay also encounters another alter ego in the form of a literary innkeeper forced to take over his father's business despite his yearning 'to see life ... and write things like Kipling and Conrad'.[24] He too feels trapped in an unfamiliar environment but immediately becomes stimulated by Hannay's narrative, in the same way as Hannay had been fascinated by Scudder's tale. 'By God ... it is all pure Rider Haggard and Conan Doyle'.[25] The choice of authors is not accidental. Like a Haggard hero, Hannay experiences his own version of a great adventure, but at home and not abroad. He will later use the deductive powers of Sherlock Holmes in his successful victory against the Black Stone espionage ring.

Unlike the film versions of *The Thirty-Nine Steps*, there is no heroine in Buchan's narrative, in contrast with the presence of Mary Lamington and Janet Raden, for example, in the later novels,[26] a fact often leading to suggestions of the author's fear of female desire or used to dismiss the novel as a juvenile example of a Boy's Own narrative. However, this is not entirely true. The female presence represents a 'structured absence', a crucial feature of the structure in *The Thirty-Nine Steps*, inhabiting the narrative as a ghostly presence as dangerous to the hero as the sinister, effeminate presence of Marmaduke Jopley later in the novel. Hilda von Einem will not appear until *Greenmantle* (1916) nor will Hannay's late-life romantic ideal Mary until *Mr. Standfast* (1919). However, the unseen figure of 'Julia Czechenyi' represents an earlier version of both Hilda von Einem's femme fatale and Lucie Mannheim's Annabella Smith from Hitchcock's *The 39 Steps*. Scudder earlier describes 'Julia' as the female decoy designed to get Karolides out of the care of his guards to facilitate his assassination. 'Julia' is the keyword to Scudder's code in his diary, which enables Hannay to discover the plot. A hidden female presence thus aids Hannay in his quest.

Although fidelity school critics condemn the film versions for introducing female presences into Buchan's narrative, this insertion actually goes back to Buchan's original novel. Far from being present due to the logic of masculine desire, Julia's presence within Buchan's narrative represents fear of the deadly feminine presence, suggesting a sexual threat to male control.[27] When Hannay deciphers the code, he reports that he was 'reading with a whitish face and fingers that drummed on the table'.[28] These drumming fingers appear unusual in isolation but they are significant within the context of the novel. Hannay later recognizes his adversary when he notes 'his fingers tapping on his knees ... the movement I remembered when I had stood before him in the moorland farm with the pistols of his servants behind me'.[29] It is a Freudian slip, an error which would normally be associated with a careless female rather than an accomplished male player in the Great Game. In *The 39 Steps* Annabella plays this role, while Madeleine Carroll's Pamela represents the other version of a non-threatening female for Hitchcock. Julia embodies Buchan's castration complex. Debilitated by ill-health during the first months of the First World War, Buchan may have felt feminized by his confinement[30] and may have subconsciously written his demasculinization as Julia, and as the fop Marmaduke Jopley. Scudder's appearance in Hannay's life and the call to adventure save him from such fears. By rising to the challenge, Hannay will certainly not become identified with the 'weaker sex' as Jopley is,[31] nor will he become subject to the 'ladylike nerves' of intellectual doubt,[32] although he becomes perilously close to this in his final encounter with the Black Stone espionage group. Male control and resolution are indispensable for any male player in the Great Game. Any doubt leads to loss of masculine control.

Hannay engages enthusiastically with the performance aspects of the Great Game, whose theatrical overtones would also become a key element of Hitchcock's cinema.[33] As well as shaving, he recreates Scudder by selecting a blue serge suit 'which differed most conspicuously from my former garments',[34] and takes on Scudder's mission. After hijacking and terrorizing Marmaduke Jopley, the 'offence to creation',[35] Hannay becomes exhilarated by his new role. 'My spirits had risen and I was beginning to enjoy this crazy game of hide and seek'.[36] Hannay then walks into his opponent's lair. He avoids their headquarters fortified by the 'remembrance of little Scudder',[37] and also escapes their further scrutiny by living out his disguise as a roadmender. He adds to his theatrical roles by recreating himself as 'the living image of the kind of Scotsman you see in the illustrations to Burns's poems',[38] and later a 'not unpersonable young man'[39] when he reaches the safety of Sir Walter Bullivant's house. He has returned to his social world: 'I felt a free man once more, for I was now up against my country's enemies only and not my country's law'.[40] He is no longer an early version of Hitchcock's 'wrong man'.

Hannay's final masquerade is as Bullivant's chauffeur. He again feels frustrated at being out of the action and feels a desire to 'have a vulgar scrap'[41] with his antagonists. His lower-class performative role allows him to exercise physical action rather than the intellectual solving of clues that he does in higher levels of society. His desires become fulfilled in an unexpected manner. Jopley makes a second appearance in the novel enabling Hannay to avoid further feelings of emasculation and finally achieving his desire by knocking 'Marmie's imbecile face'[42] into the gutter. Returning to high society, he now resumes his former mode of intellectual combat. Hannay fulfills the literary innkeeper's desire for an action-hero version of Conan Doyle's Sherlock Holmes, using Holmes's deductive powers to solve the enigma of the thirty-nine steps and discover his enemies' location.

It is now Hannay's turn to attempt to penetrate his enemies' theatrical performances in their seaside bungalow. He is at first confused. 'These men might be acting; but if they were, where was their audience?'.[43] Hannay recognizes that he is out of his depth because he cannot understand 'the great comfortable, satisfied middle-class world ... He doesn't know how they look at things, he doesn't understand their conventions'.[44] Hannay begins to doubt himself and fears becoming like Jopley, 'the laughing stock of Britain',[45] if he fails in the final quest of the adventure. During his earlier encounter with the leader of the Black Stone, Hannay had also feared emasculation. 'I had felt a strong impulse to throw myself on his mercy and offer to join his side, and if you consider the way I felt about the whole thing you will see that the impulse must have been purely physical, the weakness of a brain mesmerized and mastered by a stronger spirit'.[46] However, this momentary risk of losing masculine identity, one of the strongest in the novel, soon passes. Hannay unmasks his enemy, whose eyes had not only been 'hooded like a bird of prey', but also representing 'the terrible thing I had been up against. This man was more than a spy; in his foul way he had been a patriot'.[47] Hannay had 'done his best service' not only to his country three weeks before the First World War, but also to himself by overcoming a threat to his own masculine identity. *The Thirty-Nine Steps* is a significant achievement as a suspense novel but also as a work of sublimated masculine crisis.

Later film versions of Buchan's novel only borrow elements lending themselves to cinematic adaptation. Hitchcock borrows the theme of an innocent man on the run, but jettisons both the original historical context and the significance of the thirty-nine steps. The director's interest lies elsewhere, namely the antagonistic arena of sexual politics that Buchan represses in his own narrative. As with the novel, a description of the key moments in Hitchcock's film version now follows enabling the reader to trace the similarities and differences with Buchan's original ideas.

Hitchcock's Hannay is still Colonial but Canadian, and enters a world of the music hall ('silly show, all capering women and monkey-faced men'[48]) to witness a performance by Wylie Watson's Mr Memory that is disrupted by violence within the audience and the firing of a gun. Hannay's encounter with the spy begins earlier than in Buchan, in the rush to the music-hall exit, and the spy is a woman. Annabella entices Hannay to take her to his apartment, thus casting Hannay 'to play a role in some scenario'.[49] She is an actress, and introduces Hannay into a theatrical scenario involving adventure and sexuality far removed from the worlds of Conan Doyle and Rider Haggard. She mentions that the leader of the spies has a missing finger and passes on a map of Scotland which gives his location, and then she dies. This is a cinematically more efficient reason for Hannay fleeing to Scotland than those given by Buchan. 'My notion was to get off to some wild district, where my veldcraft would be of some use to me, for I would be like a trapped rat in a city. I considered that Scotland would be best, for my people were Scotch and I could pass anywhere as an ordinary Scotsman'.[50]

Several critics have noted the presence of changing intertextual codes influencing Hichcock's film version.[51] It is set in the middle of the Depression whose world is evoked by the vulgar comments made by the audience in the music hall as well as the sudden outburst of violence between commissionaire and working-class man. Robert Donat's Hannay and Madeleine Carroll's Pamela play the antagonistic couple from an American screwball comedy who perpetually reconcile their differences before battle resumes once more.[52]

Perhaps the most notable difference between novel and Hitchcock's film involves the issue of disguise. Both Hannay and his antagonist disguise themselves beyond recognition, both externally and by thinking themselves into the role, a tactic attributed by Buchan's Hannay to Peter Pienaar, who will appear in later Hannay novels. When Hannay suffers his worst crisis of masculinity in the bungalow on the Kent coast, Peter's words reoccur to give him the key to cracking his enemy's disguise. 'A fool tries to look different: a clever man looks the same and *is* different ... If you are playing a part you will never keep it up unless you convince yourself that you are *it*'.[53] Hannay and his antagonist play different parts by plunging themselves into the roles and become character actors rather than recognized stars. Such a strategy is impossible in terms of the cinematic medium, and not merely because of a star system necessitating audience identification with a hero. Robert Donat is the star of *The 39 Steps*. Although he plays the roles of milkman and serial killer (the latter performance detected by Pamela), he cannot adopt successfully the disguised identities of Buchan's Hannay. Despite the well-known axiom of 'the camera cannot lie', the filmgoer's gaze can penetrate most forms of theatrical disguise, which often work much better on stage rather than screen. Although Pienaar's axiom does not appear in Hitch-cock's film version, the director implicitly uses it as a 'tracing' element from the original novel to make his work plausible, and not embarrass his actors by mak-ing them fools who try to look different.

Instead, Hitchcock elaborates the performance aspects of the original novel rather than attempt reproducing disguise mechanisms that work much better on the page rather than the screen. He does this by integrating performance within the context of his changed narrative. For example, as in the novel, Hannay dis-guises himself as a milkman. Buchan's character describes it as a bet and a member of the lower classes readily agrees 'not to spoil a bit of sport'.[54] Hitchcock's Han-nay attempts to tell the truth to his milkman who is disbelieving, so Hannay performs a different type of theatrical performance by identifying himself as an adulterer who has spent the night with a married woman and needs to evade her husband's agents. The milkman readily assents. Ironically, Donat's Hannay has allowed a mysterious woman to stay overnight at his apartment, and by doing so has broken one of his culture's contemporary moral codes. The *femme fatale* has also been punished by death, while the hero escapes. Donat does not imitate 'the jaunty swing of the milkman'[55] since he is star of the film. He makes no attempt to deceive the perceptive lens of the camera.

When Hitchcock's Hannay first meets his enemy, Professor Jordan (God-frey Tearle), he encounters an English gentleman perfectly at home and blending with his environment, as did the three spies in the concluding scene of the novel. However, it is the Professor who 'unmasks himself in a stunning theatrical gesture', inviting Hannay 'to acknowledge that his place is in the Professor's audience'.[56] Despite differences between novel and film, both episodes where the adversar-ies meet involve key elements of theatrical performance. Hitchcock has used an indirect tracing of elements within Buchan's text for his own authorial purposes. The film concludes by following the classical Hollywood narrative structure of the end echoing the beginning.[57] Hannay returns to a theatrical environment, but the London Palladium (Mr Memory has moved on from the music halls) echoes that 'comfortable, satisfied, middle-class world'[58] that Buchan's hero was uneasy with. The film ends with Hitchcock's discordant interpretation of the unity of the romantic couple: 'although the handcuffs no longer bind the couple, they are still dangling from Hannay's wrist'.[59] The objects may represent Hitch-cock's 'fear of femininity',[60] but they also denote John Buchan's fear of a shadowy female figure who inhabits the text of *The Thirty-Nine Steps*.

As seen in its title, *The 39 Steps* (1959), the Ralph Thomas version scripted by Frank Harvey, is little more than an attempt to remake the 1935 Hitchcock version. Producer Betty E. Box and Thomas had earlier collaborated on *Doctor in the House* (1954), featuring Kenneth More in the type of comedic role he had begun in *Genevieve* (1953). More had achieved effective dramatic performances in *The Deep Blue Sea* (1955) and *Reach for the Sky* (1956), and his return to a jaunty comedy performance probably represented light relief after his serious roles. When More first appears in Regents Park sporting a middle-class cloth cap and wielding a walking stick like a golf club, Ambrose Cleverhouse of *Genevieve* was playing Richard Hannay.

Hitchcock's version is openly referenced: both the milkman and More whistle Mr Memory's music-hall theme. More's Hannay, as did Donat's, also seizes each moment to change his character, and evade detection, as in his spontaneous action of kissing a newly-wed bride on the station platform, and fooling a policeman by kissing Miss Fisher (Taina Elg) in the railway carriage. When More arrives at St Catherine's School for Girls to give an unexpected lecture, which replaces the political meetings in the novel and 1935 film version, he has to masquerade as a botanist. But rather than attempting to play a role he is not suited for, he engages in another type of music-hall performance by telling jokes and making puns about a weed to the delighted schoolgirls. Nanny Robinson (ex-Annabella Smith, ex-Scudder) describes her adversary as somebody who is 'continually changing his way of life', and so does More's Hannay. When he escapes from the police on the Forth Bridge, he performs the same type of acrobatics as the performers in Hitchcock's music-hall sequence.

Thomas's version extends Hitchcock's vaudeville elements to encompass the entire film. British slapstick comedy traditions occur in the police pursuit of Hannay on the train as Sam Kydd's waiter spills food over an irate customer. Midway through the film, Hannay gets a lift from truck driver Percy, played by a pre-*Carry On* Sidney James. Convicted spiritualist Nellie Lumsden (Brenda de Banzie) represents the naughty middle-aged lady, approaching Hannay with lustful desires. As the landlady of The Gallows Inn and Café she also evokes Hitchcock's dark connections between the opposing worlds of murder and sexuality.

As with Hitchcock's version, sexuality is never far from the surface. Replacing the corset salesmen on the Scottish train, a group of giggly schoolgirls speculate about the private life of their netball teacher Miss Fisher, who is the 1959 version of Madeleine Carroll's Pamela. The 1935 handcuffs and stocking scenes remain intact but with two significant changes. This time Miss Fisher demands a whisky, and does not slap a sandwich into Hannay's hand to occupy his attention while she removes her stockings.

Some traces do exist in Thomas's film of Buchan's world. Unlike Robert Donat, Kenneth More's apartment displays artefacts from Africa and the Far East. He describes himself as involved in 'political warfare',[61] and immediately recognizes that 'Boomerang' is a code word for ballistic missile. Like Buchan's original, More's Hannay has to use his versatility and intelligence to escape his pursuers. He too spins the milkman the yarn of being an adulterer to borrow the milkman's outfit, but in this version More actively copies the milkman's walk and becomes the character, according to Peter Pienaar's rules. Although Macdonald believes that the film makes an original contribution to an interpretation of Buchan's ideas as to how a fugitive would hide by showing the hero's participation in a cycle rally,[62] More's Hannay is too middle-aged to cycle up a hill. He also looks ridiculous wearing shorts: he cannot infiltrate his personality into the costume in the same way that Buchan's Hannay easily did.

By contrast, Don Sharp's 1978 film contains more tracings of Buchan than Hitchcock. But it does so less by attempting a faithful version of the literary original, and more by using components of the novel for a different type of narrative. Influenced by contemporary British society's fascination with a past era, Michael Robson's screenplay retained the literal interpretation of the thirty-nine steps from Buchan's novel and the 1959 film version but extracted and reworked elements from the original text in several formations. Reverting to the novel's full title, this version set Buchan's story within its original time period and retained Hannay's profession as a mining engineer from South Africa and his Boer War experience. Bored with London society, he is planning a visit to his homeland of Scotland when Scudder intervenes into his life. Powell's Hannay is approximately the same age as Buchan's character.[63] He first appears in a safari jacket and carrying a hunting rifle. No hunting trophies appear on the wall of his apartment as in the 1959 version, but like his literary and cinematic predecessors, he becomes a man on the run seeking to establish his own innocence and countering the plans of a group of Prussian spies.

Despite its period setting in 1914, Buchan's novel has undergone radical changes. The film version employs an entirely different narrative. Scudder is now an elderly retired intelligence agent played by John Mills attempting in vain to warn the British establishment about the existence of a group of moles securely established within British society until they receive a coded message 'Let the sleepers awake'. These spies have more in common with the world of John Le Carré than their counterparts in Buchan's novel, and their long infiltration of British society has given them sufficient time to play their roles in the way that mystifies Hannay in the concluding chapter of *The Thirty-Nine Steps*. They too have blended with their surroundings, speak with perfect English accents and act like British gentlemen. These gentlemen do not need 'dyed hair and false beards and childish follies'.[64] The one time that David Warner's chief spy dons a false moustache and wig he looks incongruous, but when he impersonates Sir Walter Bullivant (George Baker) to gain access to government secrets, Sharp's use of lighting techniques makes the masquerade plausible. The character's name, Appleton, is borrowed from Buchan's character but rather than being a retired stockbroker as in the book, Warner's character is 'a successful businessman, a friend of half the members of the British Cabinet, who has shot grouse with

King George'. These German spies are British in all but name, mix with high society, and undoubtedly parallel those establishment figures forced from high office by the anti-German press campaign of May 1915.[65]

As in the novel, Hannay and Appleton engage in their own forms of masquerade. Powell's Hannay impersonates a parson, a tramp, an establishment chap donning the guise of a tramp for a 500-guinea wager, the mute invalid Mr Murchison, Scudder and a corpse on the train to London. As well as being an accepted member of the British establishment, Appleton masquerades as an invalid at a Scottish resort, Sir Walter Bullivant (rather than the First Sea Lord in the original novel) and finally wears the uniform of a Thames Valley river policeman before his eventual arrest. Echoing Hannay's amazement at his adversary's patriotism from the original novel, Appleton also identifies himself in the same manner: 'Remember, Hannay, I'm a patriot. I will do my duty, however distasteful'. This gang's plot is not the theft of naval plans, but to explode a bomb during a speech in the House of Commons by Greek Premier Karolides. The role of the shadowy Julia Czechenyi occurs indirectly in a different guise. A suffragette demonstration functions as a decoy for Appleton to set up an assassination, and this echoes Julia's role in Scudder's assassination in the original novel. Like Buchan's text and the 1958 version, the 1978 interpretation of the thirty-nine steps is literal. As in the novel, the *Ariadne* is a German ship anchored off the coat of Kent waiting to transport the three spies back to Germany following the success of their mission.

Despite the attempt to return to Buchan's world Sharp did succumb to Hitchcock's influence. Scudder is stabbed in the back in a scene resembling the United Nations assassination in *North by North West*. Like Roger Thornhill, Hannay is immediately identified as the guilty man. Ironically, a nun who looks as if she has emerged from the concluding scene of *Vertigo* (1958), accuses Hannay of murder and he has to flee. Like Hitchcock's Annabella Smith, Scudder speaks twice to Hannay beyond the grave to remind him of vital information. An aeroplane looks for Hannay in the novel, but only in this film does it pursue Hannay with strong associations from *North by Northwest*.[66]

By choosing Big Ben for the admittedly successful suspense finale when Hannay stops the clock reaching the fatal moment of 11.45 a.m., this sequence ironically evokes the world of Alfred Hitchcock. Big Ben is a familiar landmark of British society, paralleling those recognizable climactic Hitchcock set-pieces such as the British Museum in *Blackmail* (1929), the Statue of Liberty in *Saboteur* (1942) and Mount Rushmore in *North by Northwest*, the last two films also involving the dangling of the hero from a high object. Once Hannay achieves his heroic goal of preventing the minute hand reach its fatal destination a group of Londoners watching from below applaud his efforts like the audiences in the music hall and theatres of previous film versions.

Despite its differences from the original novel, Alfred Hitchcock's version is undoubtedly the most successful of all three film versions. Although he departed radically from Buchan's novel and added new characters and situations, the director was a great fan of the writer and managed to transfer many aspects from the original novel, such as performance and theatricality in innovative ways.[67] The 1959 version exists under the shadow of Hitchcock. But like Hitchcock's version and the later 1978 film, it contains intermingling elements of intertexuality that both engage with the original novel in a hybrid manner. All three versions contain key elements of period detail emerging from the different historical periods conditioning each. However, Hitchcock's influence remains the dominant factor influencing each particular version. This is perhaps as it should be. John Buchan and Alfred Hitchcock were strong authorial figures in the different worlds they operated within. They cast shadows on each succeeding text in terms of influence. Rather than bemoan each film version's departure from an original text that may be impossible to reproduce entirely, it is far more important to examine every successor in terms of its own distinctive approach and evaluate the changes it makes without undue prejudice. In this manner, the reader will not only appreciate the importance of the original novel but also the significant traces it leaves on each successive film adaptation both in terms of similarities and differences.

NOTES

Introduction

1. A. C. Turner, *Mr. Buchan, Writer* (Toronto: Macmillan, 1949); J. Adam Smith, *John Buchan: A Biography* (London: Rupert Hart-Davis, 1965); and A. Lownie, *John Buchan: The Presbyterian Cavalier* (London: Constable, 1995).
2. J. D. Mack, 'John Buchan in Print: A Bibliography of the Published Writings and Addresses of John Buchan, First Baron Tweedsmuir' (MA thesis, Lehigh University, 1949; published by Diebold in 1952); A. Hanna, *John Buchan, 1987–1940: A Bibliography* (Hamden, CT: Shoestring Press, 1953); R. G. Blanchard, *The First Editions of John Buchan. A Collector's Bibliography* (Hamden, CT: Archon Books, 1981). Blanchard was updated in 2008 by K. Hillier (ed.), *The First Editions of John Buchan: A Collector's Bibliography* (Bristol: Avonworld Ltd, 2008).
3. See K. Macdonald, *John Buchan: A Companion to the Mystery Fiction* (Jefferson, NC: McFarland & Co, 2009) for a comprehensive survey of the critical work on Buchan to date.

1 Greig, John Buchan and Calvinism

1. J. Buchan, *Memory Hold-the-Door* (London: Hodder & Stoughton, 1940), p. 35.
2. For a useful outline of the relevance of Calvinism for Buchan see D. Daniell, *The Interpreter's House: A Critical Assessment of the Works of John Buchan* (London: Thomas Nelson & Sons, 1975), pp. 125–30.
3. Buchan's first novel, *Sir Quixote of the Moors* (1895; Kansas City: Valancourt Press, 2008), also uses the 'Killing Times', as a backdrop to the main plot.
4. See, for example, J. Buchan, *Montrose* (London: Thomas Nelson & Sons, 1928), p. 41.
5. See also H. Waddell, *The Wandering Scholars* (London: Pelican Books, 1932), 1954), pp. 36–7; also W. Smith and H. Wace (eds), *A Dictionary of Christian Biography, Literature, Sects and Doctrines, being a Continuation of 'The Dictionary of the Bible'*, 4 vols (London: John Murray, 1877–87) vol. 4, s.v., p. 749ff.
6. Buchan, *Memory Hold-the-Door*, pp. 207f. Also Buchan, 'Montrose on Sovereign Power' in *Montrose*, p. 396ff.
7. J. Buchan, *Oliver Cromwell* (London: Hodder & Stoughton, 1934), p. 68.
8. This short story was reprinted in 1899 in *Grey Weather* as 'The Moor-Song', and in 1912 in *The Moon Endureth* as 'The Rime of True Thomas'.

9. There are strong connections with Matthew Arnold's poem 'The Scholar Gypsy' (1853), and Stevenson's *An Inland Voyage* (1878) as well.

10. Adam Smith, *John Buchan*; also A. Buchan, *A Scrap Screen*, (London: Hamish Hamilton Ltd, 1979), p. 136f. Buchan's mother was applying an Old Testament reference to 'the House of Rimmon' (2 Kings 5:18) to non-Presbyterian denominations, and specifically to the Anglican communion, with which she feared her children might have to come into contact – as he did when at Oxford. (The context of the Old Testament passage might be taken to be no stronger than her natural anxiety for her son's spiritual welfare.) Whether she realized that Calvinism had at times *some* force in Anglican thinking remains to be seen. Her husband must surely as a divinity student have been at least slightly aware of this.) See also Lownie, *John Buchan*.

11. Theology and literary developments are often closely intertwined. The distinction between them is in this context irrelevant.

12. Buchan, *Memory Hold-the-Door*, pp. 118–20. The rigid Boer family of Andrew du Preez in 'The Green Wildebeest' (1928; *The Watcher by the Threshold*, ed. B. Roden and C. Roden (Ashcroft, BC: Ash-Tree Press, 2005), pp. 226–39), may owe something to this experience.

13. Cf. the reference to a conical tower, with 'green doves', relating to Ashtaroth/Astarte: J. C. G. Greig (ed.), *John Buchan: Supernatural Tales*, (Edinburgh: B&W Publishing, 1997), p. xvi, p. xxv n. 10, and pp. 230, 222–4 and 232.

14. A. E. MacRobert, 'Muckle John Gib', *John Buchan Journal*, 37 (Autumn 2007), pp. 18f.

15. Romans 12:19.

16. J. Buchan, *Sick Heart River* (Oxford: Oxford University Press, 1994), p. 113.

17. The text is reproduced in the *John Buchan Journal*, 9 (Winter 1989), pp. 2–8. The body referred to has grown to be part of the World Alliance of Reformed Churches.

18. J. Buchan, *The Three Hostages* (Oxford: Oxford University Press, 1950, pp. 8–9.

19. Buchan, *Memory Hold-the-Door*, pp. 117f. and 130. Buchan reports on the several times he met Cecil Rhodes, the South African statesman, in England, who told him, 'You can make your book with roguery, but vanity is incalculable – it will always let you down'. In *The Three Hostages* Dominick Medina is Buchan's exemplar of *vanity*.

20. Buchan, *Memory Hold-the-Door*, pp. 35–6.

21. Ibid., pp. 257–61.

22. Ibid.

23. D. K. McKim (ed.), *Encyclopedia of the Reformed Faith*, (London: John Knox Press and Saint Andrew Press, 1992), p. 27f., s.v. Barth.

24. A. Buchan [O. Douglas], *Unforgettable, Unforgotten*, (London: Hodder and Stoughton, 1945).

25. Buchan, *Memory Hold-the-Door*, p. 247.

26. He had been Professor of Systematic Theology there from 1930 till then.

27. J. Calvin, *Institutes of the Christian Religion*, trans. J. Allen, 2 vols (London: J. Clarke & Co, 1935), vol. 2 (Book III, xxii) esp. p. 224.

28. McKim (ed.), *Encyclopedia of the Reformed Faith*, p. 28.

29. Cf. K. Barth, *The Epistle to the Romans* , trans. E. C. Hoskyns (Oxford: Oxford University Press, 1933, pb 1968), p. 422: 'in Christ Jesus […] the predicate, *Deus revelatus* has as its subject *Deus absconditus*'; and also pp. 360, 411, 415, 417, 421 and 401 ('Rejection is no more than the shadow of election') etc. In his *Kirchiche Dogmatik* (e.t. Curch Dogmatics) Barth further expanded his view of predestination – usefully summarized, for example, in H. Gollwitzer, *Karl Barth, Kirchliche Dogmatik* (Fischer Bücherei: Frank-

furt am Mainz & Hamburg, 1957), p. 115f. (Present writer's use of italics for Barth's 'Sperrdruck' typography.)

30. Buchan, *Memory Hold-the-Door*, pp. 306f.
31. Cf. C. Harvie, 'Introduction', in J. Buchan *The Thirty-Nine Steps* (Oxford: Oxford University Press, 1993), p. vii and pn p. 86.
32. Barth in this period, perhaps before Buchan knew much about him, was on the same appropriate moral high ground.
33. M. Lindsay, *History of Scottish Literature*, 2nd (revised) edn (London: Robert Hale Limited, 1992), p. 263: 'In spite of the narrative fluency, it was rather the dogmatic intolerance of its virtuous characters which ensured its popularity for more than two centuries, even among readers to whom the concept of prose fiction was positively sinful'.
34. Cf. W. Buchan, 'Introduction', in J. Buchan, *Mr Standfast* (Oxford: Oxford University Press, 1993), pp. vii–xxii.
35. *John Buchan's Collected Poems*, ed. Lownie and Milne (Aberdeen: Scottish Cultural Press, 1996), p. 67ff.
36. Several of Barth's similarly-minded contemporary theologians came to be known as promoting a so-called 'dialectical theology', or 'neo-orthodoxy'. Its roots go back to Kierkegaard and should not be confused with Hegel's use of the term dialectic (which in turn differs from what we find said of Socrates' approach). The Kierkegaardian emphasis is on *paradox*, and this Barth takes up repeatedly in his commentary on *Romans*. (We may usefully also note in passing that Buchan's father was 'a good classical scholar, and he remained a voracious reader', Buchan, *Memory Hold-the-Door*, p. 257. Buchan can say this despite his awareness of his father's theological limitations previously mentioned.)
37. J. Buchan, 'Wood Magic', in *The Moon Endureth* (London: Thomas Nelson, 1910), pp. 225–6, p.226.
38. See also Haslett and Haslett, this volume, pp. 17–27.
39. A. Biéler, *Calvin's Economic and Social Thought (La pensée économique et sociale de Calvin)* (Geneva: World Council of Churches/World Alliance of Reformed Churches, 2005), pp. 423–54 and ff.
40. S. Tweedsmuir (ed.) *John Buchan by His Wife and Friends*, (London: Hodder and Stoughton, 1947), pp. 289–91: 'He [Buchan] had developed to a high degree the virtue which the Greeks called Sophrosyne [*sic*]: an inner harmony which "saves the individual from extravagance of thought and word, the arrogance that exaggerates his capacities, and the ambition that overleaps itself". From this spiritual restraint (and restraint it was, for the Scots like the Greeks are an intemperate people) sprang a force so warm and positive that it charged the air around him'.

2 Haslett and Haslett, Buchan and the Classics

1. This essay is a development of a series of articles by Isobel and Michael Haslett, and in particular of a survey of Buchan's classical quotations by Isobel Haslett. Thanks are due to the *John Buchan Journal*, and also to Donald Smith and Ron Hargreaves.
2. His father's modest stipend was a powerful incentive to Buchan, from the age of seventeen, to find a way of paying his way through university, with bursaries, scholarships, prizes, journalism and literary earnings.
3. J. Buchan 'Mr Caddell: An Appreciation', *John Buchan Journal* (1999). 20, pp. 2–3.

4. Buchan's 'Mods' consisted of translations into and from Greek and Latin (three papers), four papers on four set authors (Homer, Horace, Virgil and Demosthenes) and three papers on three chosen authors (Theocritus, Horace and Tacitus), all requiring very extensive reading of their works. The examination also required a paper on Logic, a paper on Latin poetry and a General Paper.

5. 'Greats' consisted of papers on Greek History, Roman History and both Ancient and Modern Philosophy. Able candidates were allowed to take a paper on a special subject, which the candidate had to choose out of forty or so subjects selected by the examiners. Buchan probably chose 'The procedure in private and public trials under the Republic', at the suggestion of Greenidge.

6. Buchan, *Memory Hold-the-Door*, p. 49.

7. Adam Smith, *John Buchan*, p. 70.

8. F. W. Bussell, 'Lord Tweedsmuir', *The Brazen Nose* (1940), VII:2, pp. 40–2.

9. G. P. Gooch, *History and Historians in the Nineteenth Century* (London: Longmans Green and Co, 1952), pp. 472–3.

10. Buchan, *Memory Hold-the-Door*, p. 35.

11. J. Buchan, *Homilies and Recreations* (London: Hodder and Stoughton, 1939), p. 235.

12. Buchan, *Memory Hold-the-Door*, pp. 41–2.

13. J. Buchan *Nine Brasenose Worthies* Brasenose College Quatercentenary Monographs (Oxford: Clarendon Press, 1909), Volume II XIV 2, p. 29.

14. Buchan, *Memory Hold-the-Door*, p. 42.

15. Adam Smith, *John Buchan*, p. 41.

16. Buchan, *Memory Hold-the-Door*, p. 41.

17. R. Dumesmil and J. Barsen; 'Flaubert, Gustave', *Encyclopaedia Britanica* (London: Enclyclopaedia Britannica, 1992), p. 823.

18. I. Haslett and M. Haslett, 'Buchan and the Classics, part 3; John Buchan's *The Law Relating to the Taxation of Foreign Income* (1905)', *John Buchan Journal* 26 (Spring 2002), pp. 8–16.

19. A. L. Rowse, 'John Buchan at Elsfield', in Tweedsmuir (ed.) *John Buchan by his Wife and Friends*, pp. 174–87, p. 179.

20. Buchan, *Homilies*, p. 236.

21. Ibid., pp. 286–98.

22. J. Buchan, *The House of the Four Winds* (London: Hodder & Stoughton, 1935), p. 35.

23. The silentiaries formed a group close to the Emperor, of up to thirty officials, so that a fictitious member would not be easily detected.

24. 10 November 1895, quoted in Adam Smith, *John Buchan*, p. 51.

25. Buchan, *Memory Hold-the-Door*, p. 38.

26. J. Buchan, 'Plato', *The Collected Poems of John Buchan*, ed. Lownie and Milne p. 18.

27. Ibid., p. 21.

28. Ibid., p. 22.

29. Ibid.

30. Ibid.

31. Ibid., p. 37.

32. Ibid., p. 131 and p. 136.

33. J. Buchan *Witch Wood* (Edinburgh: Canongate, 1988), p. 258–9.

34. J. Buchan 'The Wind in the Portico', in *The Watcher by the Threshold*, ed. B. Roden and C. Roden (Ashcroft, BC: Ash-Tree Press, 2005), pp. 285–301, p. 293.

35. Ibid.

36. J. Buchan *The Blanket of the Dark* (Edinburgh: B&W Publishing, 1993), p. 6.
37. Ibid., p. 23.
38. Ibid., p. 153.
39. J. Buchan, *The Magic Walking Stick* (Edinburgh: Canongate, 1985), p. 58.
40. J. Buchan, *The King's Grace* (London: Hodder & Stoughton, 1935), p. 234.
41. J. Buchan, *Men & Deeds* (London: Peter Davies, 1935), p. 275.
42. M. Haslett and I. Haslett, 'Buchan and the Classics part 2; The Classics in Buchan's Work', *John Buchan Journal*, 25 (Autumn 2001), pp. 8–25, p.17.
43. J. Buchan 'The Watcher by the Threshold', in *The Watcher by the Threshold* (London: William Blackwood & Sons, 1915), pp. 149–224, p. 175.
44. Ibid., p. 173.
45. Procopius, *The Anecdota or Secret History*, trans. H. B. Dewing (London: Heinemann, 1935), ll. 12, 18–28, p. 151.
46. Ibid., ll. 12, l3, 23, p. 149.
47. J. Buchan 'The Kings of Orion', in *The Moon Endureth*, pp. 251–86, p. 260–1.
48. J. Buchan, *A Lodge in the Wilderness* (London: Thomas Nelson & Sons, 1916), p. 185–6.
49. Buchan, *The Magic Walking-Stick*, p. 59.
50. Adam Smith, *John Buchan*, p. 177.
51. Ibid., p. 265.
52. Asquith was a close second in the Hertford scholarship examination in his first year, and later won the Craven and the Ireland scholarships.
53. Bussell 'Lord Tweedsmuir', p. 40–2.
54. Marilyn Deegan, the editor of the Oxford University Press World's Classics edition of *The Dancing Floor*, was the first to demonstrate the extent of Buchan's debt (M. Deegan, 'Introduction', in J. Buchan, *The Dancing Floor* (Oxford: Oxford University Press, 1997), pp. vii–xxix, p. 226–7).
55. Lownie, *John Buchan*, p. 166. See also Chapter 9, this volume, pp. 103–16.
56. Buchan, *The Dancing Floor*, p. 29.
57. M. Haslett and I. Haslett, '*The Dancing Floor*: Places and Sources', *John Buchan Journal* 20 (Spring 1999), pp. 6–19, p. 16.
58. Buchan, *The Dancing Floor*, p. 78.
59. Ibid.
60. J. Harrison, *Themis* (London: Merlin Press, 1912, 1925), p. 7.
61. Ibid., p. 203.
62. Ibid.
63. Buchan *The Three Hostages*, p. 65.
64. Buchan, *Memory Hold-the-Door*, p. 90.
65. F. H. Lawson, *The Oxford Law School* (Oxford: Oxford University Press, 1968), p. 254.
66. The legal references in *Augustus* were probably supplied by Roberto Weiss, a recent Oxford law graduate cited in the Preface to that work.
67. cited in Lownie *The Presbyterian Cavalier*, p. 189.
68. Buchan, *Memory Hold-the-Door*, p. 209.
69. R. Syme, *The Roman Revolution* (Oxford: Clarendon Press, 1939). Last was barely on speaking terms with Syme and would have had no inkling of the contents of Syme's book before it was published. See also Anthony Birley's obituary of Syme, *Independent* (7 September 1989).
70. Lownie, *The Presbyterian Cavalier*, p. 76.

71. Buchan, *Memory Hold-the-Door*, p. 175.

3 Goldie, 'Twin Loyalties': John Buchan's England

1. H. MacDiarmid, *Contemporary Scottish Studies*, ed. A. Riach (Manchester: Carcanet, 1995), p. 8.
2. J. Buchan, *Midwinter: Certain Travellers in Old England* (Edinburgh: B&W Publishing, 1993), p. 2.
3. J. Buchan, *Mr Standfast* (Oxford: Oxford University Press, 1993), pp. 14–15.
4. R. Williams, *The Country and the City* (London: The Hogarth Press, 1993), pp. 281–2.
5. Lownie, *John Buchan*, pp. 145–6.
6. Buchan, *Homilies*, p. 375.
7. Buchan, *Memory Hold-the-Door*, p. 35.
8. J. Buchan, 'No-Man's Land', in *The Watcher by the Threshold* (London: William Blackwood & Sons, 1915), pp. 3–102, p. 6.
9. J. Buchan, 'The Green Glen', in *The Moon Endureth: Tales and Fancies* (London: Thomas Nelson & Sons, 1923), pp. 291–327, p. 299.
10. J. Buchan, 'Ho! The Merry Masons' (1933), in *The Watcher by the Threshold*, ed. B. Roden and C. Roden (Ashcroft, BC: Ash-Tree Press, 2005), pp. 238–50, contains a particularly strong example of a murderous house haunted by masonic ghosts.
11. J. Buchan, *Midwinter*, p. 21.
12. Ibid., p. 116.
13. Buchan, *The Blanket of the Dark*, p. 9.
14. Ibid., p.12.
15. Buchan, *Witch Wood*, p. 3.
16. For a discussion of the influence of Grahame's paganism on Buchan, see Adam Smith, *John Buchan*, pp. 93–4.
17. R. Kipling, 'A Pict Song', *Puck of Pook's Hill* (London: Penguin, 1987), p.165.
18. R. Kipling, 'Dymchurch Flit', Ibid., pp. 181–93.
19. For the influence of Newbolt on Buchan, see M. Redley, 'Henry Newbolt and John Buchan: A Literary Friendship?', *John Buchan Journal*, 28 (Spring 2003), pp. 26–7.
20. P. Wright, *On Living in an Old Country: The National Past in Contemporary Britain* (London: Verso, 1985), pp. 81–7.
21. J. Buchan, *The Free Fishers* (Edinburgh: B&W, 1994), p. 74.
22. Ibid., p. 80.
23. Ibid., p. 125.
24. Ibid., p. 145.
25. Ibid., p. 174.
26. Ibid., p. 275.
27. Buchan, *Midwinter*, p. 147.
28. Ibid., p. 232.
29. G. G. Smith, *Scottish Literature: Character and Influence* (London: Macmillan, 1919), p. 4.
30. T. C. Smout, 'Perspectives on the Scottish Identity', *Scottish Affairs*, 6 (Winter 1994), pp. 101–13.
31. See G. Morton, *Unionist-Nationalism: Governing Urban Scotland, 1830–1860* (East Linton: Tuckwell Press, 1999).

32. See W. Scott, *The Letters of Malachi Malagrowther* (Edinburgh: William Blackwood, 1981), pp. 143–4.

33. J. Ker, *Scottish Nationality: and Other Papers* (Edinburgh: Andrew Elliot, 1887), p. 5. See also, J. Ker 'Sir Walter Scott as Patriot', *Scotia*, 1:3 (Lammas 1907), pp. 204–7, J. Ferguson, 'Scottish Patriotism and Imperial Duty', *Scotia*, 2:3 (Lammas 1908), pp. 145–8, and D. Goldie, 'The British Invention of Scottish Culture: World War One and Before', *Review of Scottish Culture*, 18 (2006), pp. 128–48.

34. See D. Schreuder, 'The Making of the Idea of Colonial Nationalism, 1898–1905', in J. Eddy and D. Schreuder (eds), *The Rise of Colonial Nationalism* (London: Allen & Unwin, 1988), pp. 63–93.

35. J. Buchan, *A Lodge in the Wilderness*, p. 79.

36. J. Buchan, 'Tendebant Manus', in *The Watcher by the Threshold*, ed. B. Roden and C. Roden (Ashcroft, BC: Ash-Tree Press, 2005), pp. 274–84, p. 276.

37. J. Buchan, *Canadian Occasions: Addresses by Lord Tweedsmuir* (London: Hodder & Stoughton, 1940), pp. 82–3.

38. *Memoirs of Sir Walter Scott*, ed. J. G. Lockhart, 5 vols (London: Macmillan, 1900), vol. 4, p. 483.

39. *Parliamentary Debates*, 272 H.C.Deb. 5 s., cols 266–7.

4 Glassock, Buchan, Sport and Masculinity

1. J. Lowerson, 'Sport and British Middle-Class Culture: Some Issues of Representation and Identity before 1940', *International Journal of the History of Sport*, 21:1 (January 2004), pp. 34–49; see also C. Hilliard, 'Modernism and the Common Writer', *Historical Journal*, 48:3 (2005), pp. 769–87.

2. See J. A. Mangan, *Athleticism in the Victorian and Edwardian Public School: The Emergence and Consolidation of an Educational Ideology* (Cambridge: Cambridge University Press, 1981). Any consideration of athleticism and the links between the public schools and Empire must begin with Mangan's work. His studies are erudite, balanced and immensely readable.

3. See J. Tosh, *Manliness and Masculinities in Nineteenth-Century Britain*, (Harlow: Pearson Education Limited, 2005), pp. 197–9 and Mangan, *Athleticism in the Victorian and Edwardian Public School*, pp. 138–9

4. Anon., 'A College Tutor', Letter to the Editor, *The Times*, Saturday 3 January 1903, p. 6.

5. 'J. C. B', Letter to the Editor, *The Times*, Saturday 11 January 1902, p. 11.

6. W. J. Locke, Letter to the Editor, *The Times*, Saturday 11 January 1902, p. 11.

7. 'A.S', Letter to the Editor, *The Times*, Wednesday 15 January 1902, p. 12.

8. M. Kane, *Modern Men: Mapping Masculinity in English and German Literature, 1880–1930* (London: Cassell, 1999), p.120, p. 82; see also P. Henshaw, 'John Buchan and the Invention of Post-Colonial Literature', *John Buchan Journal*, 32 (Spring 2005), pp. 35–40 and P. R. Deslandes, *Oxbridge Men: British Masculinity and the Undergraduate Experience, 1850–1920* (Bloomington, IN and Indianapolis, IN: Indiana University Press, 2005)

9. Kane, *Modern Men*, p.67.

10. See M. Green, *Dreams of Adventure, Deeds of Empire*, (London: Routledge and Kegan Paul, 1980), for a detailed discussion of the place of adventure writing in British literary and social history, especially pp. 3–65.

11. The Boers were portrayed in some quarters as the peaceful victims of a corrupt Imperialism driven by greedy Rand lords (G. R. Searle, *A New England? Peace and War 1886–1918* (Oxford: Oxford University Press, 2004), pp. 287–8). See also Tosh, *Manliness and Masculinities*; J. Nauright, 'Sport, Manhood and Empire: British Responses to the New Zealand Rugby Tour of 1905', *International Journal of the History of Sport*, 8:2, September 1991, pp. 239–55; and P. A. Vaile, Letter to the Editor, *The Times*, Tuesday 10 October 1905, p.15.

12. E. C. Selwyn, Letter to the Editor, *The Times*, Wednesday 15 January 1902 p. 12; and H. H. Almond, Letter to the Editor, *The Times*, Wednesday 15 January 1902, p. 12.

13. See Kane, *Modern Men* and Tosh, *Manliness and Masculinities*.

14. J. Richards, 'Passing the Love of Women: Manly Love and Victorian Society', in J. A. Mangan, and J. Walvin (eds) *Manliness and Morality: Middle Class Masculinity in Britain and America, 1800–1940*. (New York: St Martin's Press, 1987), p. 96.

15. Kane, *Modern Men*, p. 116

16. For a discussion of the Apostles, see J. A. Taddeo, 'Plato's Apostles: Edwardian Cambridge and the "New Style of Love"', *Journal of the History of Sexuality*, 8:2 (October 1997), pp. 196–228.

17. L. Pykett, *Engendering Fictions: The English Novel in the Early Twentieth Century* (London: Edward Arnold, 1995).

18. Hilliard, 'Modernism and the Common Writer', p. 772.

19. S. Cole, 'Modernism, Male Intimacy, and the Great War', *ELH*, 68 (2001), p. 471.

20. Pykett, *Engendering Fictions*, p. 11

21. Taddeo, 'Plato's Apostles', p. 198.

22. Ibid., p. 204.

23. Ibid., p. 228.

24. Kane, *Modern Men*, p.113; Taddeo, 'Plato's Apostles', p. 204.

25. Buchan, *Memory Hold-The-Door*, p. 49.

26. The 'Kindergarten' acquired its nickname because of the youthful precocity of its members and their loyalty to Milner. Richards has commented that 'At the heart of Victorian culture and administration were tightly knit all-male groups: Milner's "kindergarten", Wolsely's "ring", Kitchener's "cubs", the Cambridge apostles and Henley's "regatta"' (Richards, 'Passing the Love of Women', p.107).

27. Buchan, *Memory Hold-The-Door*, p. 183

28. Ibid., p. 30

29. While Buchan was a pupil at Hutcheson's the only organized physical activities were drill, sword charge and optional swimming, though in the 1890s association football began to be played and an Athletics Club, Rambling Club and Cycling Club were founded. See A. D. Dunlop, *Hutcheson's Grammar: The History of a Glasgow School* (Glasgow: Hutcheson's Educational Trust, 1992), pp. 72–5

30. Buchan, *Memory Hold-The-Door*, p. 30

31. See R. D. Anderson, 'Sport in the Scottish Universities, 1860–1939', *International Journal of the History of Sport*, 4:2 (1987), pp. 177–88, and Adam Smith, *John Buchan*, p. 30.

32. Buchan, *Memory Hold-The-Door*, p. 33–4

33. A graduate of Glasgow University might have been expected to apply for a Snell scholarship at Balliol College but Buchan's Latin and Greek were not strong enough and he was advised to apply to Brasenose. I. Haslett and M. Haslett, 'Buchan and the Classics: School and University', *John Buchan Journal*, 24 (March 2001), pp. 30–40; M. Haslett

and I. Haslett, 'Buchan and the Classics part 2; the Classics in Buchan's work', *John Buchan Journal*, 25 (Autumn 2001), pp. 8–25.

34. Buchan, *Memory Hold-The-Door*, pp. 33–4. Mangan cites an undergraduate of 1896 reporting of the university that 'The Reign of Athletics is at Hand' (Mangan, *Athleticism in the Victorian and Edwardian Public School*, pp. 125–6).

35. Buchan, *Canadian Occasions*, p. 170.

36. Buchan, *Memory Hold-The-Door*, p. 52. See also pp. 48–9 for the full range of Buchan's acquaintance at Oxford.

37. Buchan, *Memory Hold-The-Door*, p. 48.

38. Adam Smith, *John Buchan*, p. 59.

39. Ibid., pp. 59–60.

40. J. Buchan, *University of Oxford College Histories: Brasenose College* (London: F. E. Robinson, 1898), p. 76. By contrast, Buchan recalled that at Glasgow he 'acquired the corporate spirit only at a rectorial election' (*Memory Hold-The-Door*, p. 33).

41. Lowerson, 'Sport and British Middle-Class Culture', p. 46.

42. Cricket, athletics, beagling and boxing are also mentioned in Buchan's popular novels but references to rugby predominate.

43. J. Buchan, *Prester John* (Oxford: Oxford University Press, 1994), p. 18.

44. J. Buchan, *The Power-House*, in *The Power-House & The Thirty-Nine Steps* (Edinburgh: B&W Publishing, 1999), p. 78.

45. J. Buchan, *Mr Standfast* (Oxford: Oxford University Press, 1993), p. 12.

46. Ibid., p. 155.

47. J. Buchan, *Comments and Characters by John Buchan*, ed. W. Gray (London: Nelson, 1940), p. 276.

48. Buchan, *Memory Hold-The-Door*, p. 134.

49. Buchan, *Comments and Characters*, p. 277.

50. Ibid., p.284.

51. Aristotle, *The Ethics of Aristotle: The Nichomachean Ethics* (London: Penguin Books, revised edition 1976); Aristotle, *The Politics* (London: Penguin Books, Reprinted with revised bibliography 1992).

52. J. E. C. Welldon, 'The Training of an English Gentleman in the Public Schools', *Nineteenth Century*, 60 (September 1906), pp. 396–413, p. 399.

53. Cited in Lowerson, 'Sport and British Middle-Class Culture', p. 46.

54. J. Buchan, *The Island of Sheep* (Oxford: Oxford University Press, 1996), p. 13.

55. Ibid., p. 225.

56. J. Buchan, *Huntingtower* (Oxford: Oxford World's Classics, 1996), pp. 23–9; pp. 207–8

57. Buchan, *Mr Standfast*, p. 222.

58. J. Buchan, *The Courts of the Morning* (Edinburgh: B&W Publishing Ltd, 1993), pp. 121–2; pp. 243–4; pp. 368–9; p. 378; p. 383

59. See J. Buchan and H. Newbolt (eds), *Days to Remember: The British Empire in the Great War* (London: Thomas Nelson and Sons, 1923) and J. Buchan, *The History of the Royal Scots Fusiliers* (London: Thomas Nelson and Sons, 1925).

60. Buchan, *Memory Hold-The-Door*, p. 180.

61. Ibid., p.181.

62. Ibid., p.145.

63. Ibid., p. 183.

64. Pykett, *Engendering Fictions*, p. 7.

65. Hilliard, 'Modernism and the Common Writer'.
66. J. Rose, *The Intellectual Life of the British Working Classes*, (New Haven, CT: Yale University Press, 2001) cited in Hilliard, 'Modernism and the Common Writer', p. 11, p. 780.
67. Buchan, *Memory Hold-The-Door*, p. 186.
68. Ibid., p. 185.
69. Ibid., p. 180. In addition, contrast the attitudes to male friendship and intimacy expressed in Buchan's popular fiction with those of the modernist writers analysed by Cole in 'Modernism, Male Intimacy, and the Great War', pp. 469–500.
70. Buchan, *Memory Hold-The-Door*, p. 184
71. Ibid., p.184.
72. Buchan, *Canadian Occasions*, p. 134.
73. Buchan, *Memory Hold-The-Door*, p. 87.

5 Nasson, John Buchan and the Creation of the Springbok Warrior

1. Buchan, *Memory Hold the Door*, p. 46.
2. B. Nasson, 'John Buchan's South African Visions', *John Buchan Journal*, 26 (2002), pp. 29–33; P. Rich, 'Milnerism and a Ripping Yarn: Transvaal Land Settlement and John Buchan's novel, Prester John, 1901–1910', in B. Bozzoli (ed.), *Town and Countryside in the Transvaal: Capitalist Penetration and Popular Response* (Johannesburg: Ravan, 1983), pp. 415–21; M. Redley, '"Administrative Archangel ?": John Buchan in South Africa, 1901–03' (unpublished seminar paper, Department of Historical Studies, University of Cape Town, July 2008).
3. D. G. Wright, 'The Great War, Government Propaganda and English "Men of Letters", 1914–1916', *Literature and History*, 7 (1978), pp. 83–100.
4. S. Badsey and P. Taylor, 'Images of Battle: The Press, Propaganda and Passchendaele', in P. H. Liddle (ed.), *Passchendaele: The Third Battle of Ypres* (London: Leo Cooper, 1997), pp. 371–89.
5. J. Buchan, *The History of the South African Forces in France* (London: Thomas Nelson & Sons, 1920), p. 5.
6. B. Nasson, *Springboks on the Somme: South Africa in the Great War 1914–1918* (Johannesburg: Penguin, 2007), p. 207.
7. Buchan, *The History of the South African Forces in France*.
8. Anon., 'Cause and Conscience', *Rand Daily Mail* (17 November 1920), p.14; Anon., 'From the Recent War', *Natal Witness* (21 November 1920).
9. P. van der Byl, *Top Hat to Veldskoen* (Cape Town: Timmins, 1973), p. 64.
10. Anon., 'A Great Soldier of the Great War', *Selbornian*, 21 (1922), p. 12.
11. Anon., 'A Gift for our Age', *Bloemfontein Sun* (28 November 1925), p. 16.
12. A solitary effort at a comprehensive chronicle of the Union's contribution to the Allied cause was the 1924 General Staff publication of an *Official History: Union of South Africa and the Great War*, a wordy compilation of leaden prose, banal detail and numerous appendices. Other wartime and interwar works with a more restricted geographical reach came not from historians but from army officers, war correspondents and other journalists, laying out a mostly formulaic narrative of war events and fostering approval of the government position. These included the standard chronicle of the German South West Africa invasion, J. J. Collyer's *The Campaign in German South West Africa, 1914–15* (1937), and earlier expositions, such as J. P. Kay Robinson's *With Botha's Army* (1916) and W. Whittall's *With Botha and Smuts in Africa* (1917).

13. See B. Willan, 'The South African Native Labour Contingent, 1916–1918', *Journal of African History*, 19:1 (1978), pp. 68–92.

14. *Official History: Union of South Africa and the Great War* (Pretoria: Government Printer, 1924), Appendix X, pp. 218–19.

15. Tosh, *Manliness and Masculinities*, pp. 193–4.

16. Anon., 'Nasionale Strijders', *De Zuid Afrikaan* (16 September 1914), p. 8.

17. N. G. Garson, 'South Africa and World War 1', *Journal of Imperial and Commonwealth History*, 8:1 (1979), pp. 83–108.

18. J. Rickard, *Australia: A Cultural History* (Harlow: Longman, 1996), p. 123. See also, A. Thomson, *Anzac Memories: Living with the Legend* (Melbourne: Oxford University Press, 1994), pp. 142–56.

19. Anon., 'Ons Kinders', *Zwartlander* (12 October 1914), p. 9; Anon., 'Disloyal Patriotism', *Pretoria Friend* (24 April 1915), p. 17.

20. Buchan, *The History of the South African Forces in France*, p. 11.

21. Ibid., p. 12.

22. Ibid., p. 13.

23. Ibid., p. 14.

24. Ibid., p. 13.

25. P. G. Halpern, 'The War at Sea', in H. Strachan (ed.), *The Oxford Illustrated History of the First World War* (Oxford: Oxford University Press, 1998), pp. 108–9.

26. Buchan, *The History of the South African Forces in France*, p. 13.

27. Ibid., p. 14.

28. K. Macdonald, 'Writing "The War"', *The Times Literary Supplement*, 10 August 2007, p. 15.

29. Buchan, *The History of the South African Forces in France*.

30. Ibid., p. 16.

31. Ibid., p. 15.

32. Ibid., p. 18.

33. Ibid., p. 18.

34. D. Cannadine, *History in Our Time* (London: Penguin, 2000), p. 242.

35. Buchan, *The History of the South African Forces in France*, p. 17.

36. N. Orpen, *The Cape Town Highlanders, 1885–1985* (Cape Town: Purnell, 1986), pp. 6–7. See, also, J. Hyslop, 'Cape Town Highlanders, Transvaal Scottish: Military "Scottishness" and Social Power in Nineteenth and Twentieth Century South Africa', *South African Historical Journal*, 49 (2003), pp. 25–42; B. Nasson, 'John Buchan, the Great War and Springbok Achievement', *John Buchan Journal*, 28 (2003), pp. 19–21.

37. Buchan, *The History of the South African Forces in France*, p. 18.

38. Ibid., pp. 260–1.

39. Ibid., p. 29.

40. Ibid., p. 41.

41. Ibid., p. 48.

42. Ibid., p. 73.

43. Anon., 'Springbok Heroism in Europe', *Cape Times* (23 October 1926), p. 6.

44. Buchan, *The History of the South African Forces in France*, p. 256.

45. Ibid., p. 260.

46. Ibid., p. 73.

47. Ibid., pp. 260–1.

48. Ibid., p. 261.

49. Ibid., p. 261.
50. Redley, "'Administrative Archangel?'", pp. 20–1.
51. K. Grieves, '*Nelson's History of the War*: John Buchan as Contemporary Military Historian, 1915–22', *Journal of Contemporary History*, 28:2 (1993), p. 544.
52. H. Baker, *Architecture and Personalities* (London: Country Life, 1944), p. 91.
53. Buchan, *The History of the South African Forces in France*, pp. 262–3.

6 Redley, John Buchan and the South African War

1. Buchan to William Buchan, 7 October 1901; Buchan to Charles Dick, 8 October 1901.
2. Milner's Diary, 5 October 1901.
3. Buchan, *Memory Hold-the-Door*, p. 96. 'Furth fortune and fill the fetters' is the motto of the Murray clan, which may be read as 'Fierceness in the fight, fortune in battle and bring home the booty'.
4. Buchan to Strachey, 11 October 1901.
5. Buchan to Charles Dick, 20 September 1902.
6. J. Buchan, 'The Edinburgh on South Africa', *Spectator* (26 January 1901), pp. 131–2; J. Buchan, 'The Debate on the Refugee Camps', *Spectator* (22 June 1901), pp. 905–6.
7. Buchan to Lady Mary Murray, 26 August 1901.
8. *W. Nimocks,* Milner's Young Men: the Kindergarten in Edwardian Imperial affairs *(Durham, NC: Duke University Press, 1970), ch. 4–8.*
9. M. Redley 'Origins of the Problem of Trust: Propaganda During the First World War', in V. Bakir and M. Barlow (eds), *Communications in the age of suspicion: trust and the media* (Basingstoke, 2007), pp. 28–9 & 31.
10. Buchan to Murray, 16 November 1902.
11. Buchan, *Memory Hold-the-Door*, pp. 124–5.
12. Milner to Buchan, 18 August 1901. Gerald Craig-Sellar, Clerk to the Executive Council, got £600, and Lionel Curtis, Town Clerk of the Johannesburg, £1,000. Hugh Wyndham, who got his place by political influence, was unpaid.
13. Buchan to Strachey, 11 October 1901.
14. Buchan to William Buchan, 7 October 1901.
15. Evidence that the poem is by Buchan is in his letter to Strachey, 28 January 1902.
16. J. Saxon Mills [J. Buchan], 'The Little Englander', *Spectator* (18 January 1902), p. 86.
17. Milner's Diary, 20 April 1902. There are seventy-two such entries over the two years of Buchan's time in South Africa.
18. Buchan's book of essays reflecting his experiences in South Africa, *The African Colony*, is dedicated to Hugh Wyndham, 'in memory of our African housekeeping'. For another view of their relationship and different views of South Africa, see I. Van der Waag, 'Hugh Wyndham, Transvaal Politics and the Attempt to Create an English Country Seat in South Africa, 1901–1914', *Journal of Imperial and Commonwealth History*, 31:2 (May 2003), pp. 136–57, pp. 139–40.
19. Interview with Lord Leconfield, 1 March 1959; postscript on Buchan to Milner, 9 February 1903.
20. Interview with Lord Leconfield, 1 March 1959.
21. Redley, 'Origins', pp. 33–4.
22. Adam Smith, *John Buchan*, pp. 114–15.

23. Milner to Chamberlain, 19 November 1901.

24. Maxwell [Military Governor Pretoria] to Buchan, 25 March 1902; Private Secretary Land Board to Provost Marshall, 2 May 1902; Buchan to Strachey, 12 March 1902, SLSP s/3/2/10: HLRO. A paragraph describing how the census of needs would also provide information on land 'in excess of the needs of its Boer population, and therefore open to us for our British settlement' was excised by Milner from a despatch drafted by Buchan (Despatch no 192, 25 April 1902).

25. Secretary to Land Board ORC to Officer Commanding, Durban, 15 May 1902; APM Natal to Officer Commanding, Durban, 21 May 1902; Superintendent, Jacobs Camp 2 June 1902 (enclosing cutting from *Natal Mercury*, 30 May 1902).

26. Buchan to O/C Orange Free State Camps, 4 March 1902; Secretary Land Board ORC to APS to Milner, 25 December 1901.

27. Secretary Land Board to Provost Marshall, 2 May 1902; Redley, 'Origins', pp. 29–30.

28. Despatch SA110, 25 January 1902.

29. Buchan to Strachey, 13 October 1901 and 28 December 1901; 'Soldier Settlement for South Africa', *The Spectator* (16 November 1901), pp. 750–1.

30. 'British Settlements in the New Colonies', *Blackwood's Magazine* CLXXI (January 1902), pp. 145–158; 'The Reconstruction of South Africa – Land Settlement', *National Review*, 230 (April 1902), pp. 316–36. The evidence that they are by Buchan is contained in his correspondence with Strachey.

31. For example, Assistant Resident Magistrate Krugersdorp to ACS, 2 October 1902.

32. Buchan to AG, 7 & 10 June 1902; AG to Buchan 12 August 1902; Draft by Buchan headed 'Barberton Commission: Letter defining terms of reference'.

33. Private Secretary to Milner to Campbell, 30 May 1902.

34. Buchan to Stair Gillon, 23 November 1902.

35. Buchan, *Memory Hold-the-Door*, p. 111.

36. Buchan to Director of Public Works Department, 9 December 1902. For circulars and private correspondence as Acting Secretary of the Land Department, see collection of his personal papers concerned with South Africa: Mss Afr.s. 2210: Rhodes House Library Oxford (RHO).

37. Buchan to CS Transvaal, 25 February 1903.

38. Transvaal Consolidated Land and Exploration Co Ltd: Report on Agricultural Prospects in the Transvaal, 30 January 1903, Mss Afr s. 2210/2 f14/2; Buchan to Milner, 9 February 1903.

39. Interview with Lord Leconfield, 1 March 1959.

40. Buchan to his mother, 7 December 1902.

41. W. S. Worsfold, *The Reconstruction of the New Colonies under Lord Milner*, 2 vols (London: Kegan Paul, Tench Trubner, 1913), vol 2, pp. 91–112.

42. F. D. Smith to Basil Williams, 17 July 1904 and 11 December 1904.

43. Adam Smith, *John Buchan*, p. 213.

44. Buchan to his mother, 7 December 1902.

45. Buchan to Strachey, 20 May 1903.

46. Buchan to Strachey, 10 January 1903; Buchan to Anna Buchan, 17 November & 21 December 1902.

47. Milner's Diary, 28 July 1903; F.J. Henley to Milner, 17 August 1903.

48. 'Land Settlement in the Transvaal', paragraph headed 'Class of Settler Required'; Buchan to Strachey, 10 June 1902..

49. H. A. Lawrence to Lord Milner, 13 April 1903.

50. 'The Close of the Transvaal Labour Commission', *Spectator* (24 October 1903), pp. 640–1.

51. Buchan to Strachey, 22 February 1903; J. Buchan, '*Transvaal Problems* by Lionel Phillips' [book review], *Times Literary Supplement* (24 November 1905), p. 402.

52. Buchan to Strachey, 22 February 1903.

53. J. Buchan *The African Colony: Studies in the Reconstruction* (Edinburgh: William Blackwood and Sons, 1903), p. 291 & p. 295.

54. Buchan to Strachey, 22 February 1903.

55. Buchan to Strachey, 20 May 1903.

56. Buchan to Strachey, 22 February 1903.

57. Buchan to Walter Blackie, 25 June 1905.

58. Buchan to Strachey, 17 July 1903; D. Denoon, *A Grand Illusion: The Failure of Imperial Policy in the Transvaal Colony During the Period of Reconstruction, 1900–1906* (London: Longman, 1973), p. 58.

59. J. Buchan, Introduction to *A Lodge in the Wilderness*, pp. ix–x.

60. Cutting from the *Scotsman*, 16 January and 5 December 1904; M. Redley, 'John Buchan and East Africa', *John Buchan Journal*, 27 (Autumn 2002), pp. 23–33, pp. 26–9.

61. J. Buchan, 'The Mountain'; Ecclesiastes 4: 1.

62. For example J. Buchan, 'Leopold Amery's *The 'Times' History of the War in South Africa, 1899–1902*, volumes 6 and 7' [book review], *Spectator* (10 July 1909), pp. 57–8; J. Buchan, 'Basil Worsfold's *The Reconstruction of the New Colonies under Lord Milner*' [book review], *Times Literary Supplement* (20 November 1913), p. 549.

63. J. Buchan, 'Violet Markham's *The South African Scene*' [book review], *Times Literary Supplement* (4 December 1913), p. 583.

64. J. Buchan, 'South African Native Race Committee (ed.), *The South African Native: Progress and Present Condition*' [book review], *Times Literary Supplement* (4 February 1909), p. 38.

65. J. Buchan, 'The Native Peril in South Africa', *Spectator* (17 February 1906), pp. 246–7.

66. P. Rich, 'Milnerism and a Ripping Yarn'.

67. J. Buchan, 'Olive Schreiner, *Thoughts on South Africa*' [book review], *Times Literary Supplement* (21 June 1923), p. 411.

68. Buchan to Strachey, 6 November 1901.

69. Hobhouse to Milner, 11 November 1901.

70. Milner to Buchan, 27 April 1921.

71. Buchan to Ferris Greenslet, 19 May 1925.

72. J. Buchan, 'A Lucid Interval', in *The Moon Endureth: Tales and Fancies* (London: Thomas Nelson & Sons, 1923), pp. 55–97. On Chinese labour in South Africa, see A. M. Gollin, *Proconsul in Politics: A Study of Lord Milner in Opposition and in Power* (London: Anthony Blond, 1964), ch. 3–4.

73. Milner to Buchan, 8 February 1910.

74. M. Redley 'Making Democracy Safe for the World: a Note on John Buchan's Political Career', *John Buchan Journal*, 17 (Autumn 1997), pp. 32–4.

75. Buchan to Strachey, 3 August 1902.

76. Buchan, *The African Colony*, p. 290.

77. Milner to Buchan, 16 November 1910; Redley 'Making Democracy Safe', pp. 34–5.

7 Strachan, John Buchan and the First World War: Fact into Fiction

1. J. Buchan, *A History of the Great War*, 4 vols (London: Thomas Nelson & Sons, 1921–2), vol. 3, p. 436.
2. D. L. George, *War Memoirs of David Lloyd George*, 2 vols (London: Odhams Press, 1938), vol. 1, pp. 886–7.
3. D. French, 'Sir James Edmonds and the Official History: France and Belgium', in B. Bond (ed.), *The First World War and British Military History* (Oxford: Clarendon Press, 1991), p. 77.
4. K. Macdonald, 'The Fiction of John Buchan with Particular Reference to the Richard Hannay Novels' (PhD thesis, University College London, 1991), p. 11, pp. 352–7.
5. K. Grieves, 'Early Historical Responses to the Great War: Fortescue, Conan Doyle, and Buchan', in Bond (ed.), *The First World War and British Military History*, pp. 29–37.
6. Buchan, *Memory Hold-the-Door*, pp. 165–6.
7. Lownie, *John Buchan*, pp. 132–3.
8. J. Buchan, *These for Remembrance* (privately printed, 1919), p. 36.
9. J. Buchan, *Nelson's History of the War*, 24 vols (London: Thomas Nelson & Sons, 1915–19), vol. 12, pp. 133–46.
10. Buchan, *A History of the Great War*, vol. 1, p. viii.
11. J. Buchan (ed.), *The Nations of To-day: A New History of the World* (London: Thomas Nelson & Sons, 1923), pp. v–vi.
12. J. Charteris, *At G.H.Q.* (London: Cassell, 1931), pp. 147, 149, 153, 170.
13. Oliver to Buchan, 8 February 1917, quoted in P. Buitenhuis, *The Great War of Words: Literature as Propaganda 1914–18 and After* (London: Batsford, 1989; first published 1987), p. 133.
14. For the organization of propaganda, see M. L. Sanders and P. Taylor, *British Propaganda* (London: Macmillan, 1982), p. 55–97; on Buchan in this period, see Adam Smith, *John Buchan*, pp. 193–218, and Lownie, *John Buchan*.
15. H. Strachan, *The First World War, Volume 1, To Arms*, (Oxford: Oxford University Press, 2001), pp. 694–814. In 1917, British agents were actively working within German socialism to spread war weariness and defeatism (M. Occleshaw, *Armour against Fate: British Military Intelligence in the First World War* (1988; London: Columbus, 1989), pp. 288–324).
16. Both versions are reprinted in J. Buchan, *The Complete Short Stories, Volume 3*, ed. A. Lownie; 'The loathly opposite' was first published in the *Pall Mall Gazette* in October 1927, and then incorporated in *The Runagates Club* (1928).
17. But see W. Buchan, *John Buchan: A Memoir* (London: Buchan & Enright, 1982), p. 141, for his father's recollection of receiving spies' reports in the Café Royal during the war, as 'Captain Stewart'.
18. S. Glassock, '*Greenmantle* in its Time', *John Buchan Journal*, 36 (spring 2007), pp. 7–17.
19. Buchan, *History of the Great War*, volume 1, p. viii.
20. M. Redley, 'Origins', p. 32.
21. J. Buchan, 'Hysteria and the Press', *Scottish Review* (19 March 1908), reprinted in Buchan, *Comments and Characters*, p. 267.
22. J. Buchan, 'The Old Journalism and the New' (16 January 1908), in ibid., pp. 260–1.
23. Macdonald, 'Writing The War'.

24. B. Millman, *Managing Domestic Dissent in First World War Britain* (London: Frank Cass, 2000), pp. 230–4; the discussion in this paragraph is also influenced by the arguments of Sanders and Taylor, *British Propaganda*.

25. Sanders and Taylor, *British Propaganda*, pp. 70–6, 147; Buitenhuis, *The Great War of Words*, pp. 133–4.

26. Buchan, *History of the Great War*, vol. 2, p. 65.

27. Buchan, *Nelson's History of the War*, vol. 18 (1917), p. 137.

28. Buchan, *History of the Great War*, vol. 2, pp. 63, 68; 4, pp. 161–3.

29. Haig's diary, 27 September 1916, cited in R. Blake (ed.), *Private Papers of Douglas Haig 1914–1919* (London: Eyre & Spottiswode, 1952), pp. 167–8; Buchan, *Memory Hold-the-Door*, p. 176.

30. Buchan, *Mr Standfast*, p. 198.

31. Buchan, *Nelson's History of the War*, vol. 20, p. 113.

32. Buchan to Liddell Hart, December 1916, Liddell Hart papers, Liddell Hart Centre for Military Archives (LHCMA), King's College London, LH 1/124/1.

33. Buchan to Liddell Hart, 19 February 1935, LHCMA, LH 1/124/60; see Buchan, *The King's Grace*, pp. 236–7, and for a fuller judgment on Haig, Buchan, *Memory Hold-the-Door*, pp. 175–9.

34. Buchan, *The Dancing Floor*, p. 35.

35. Ibid., p. 39.

36. Buchan, *These for Remembrance*, p. 26

37. A. Buchan [O. Douglas], *Unforgettable, Unforgotten* (London, 1945), p. 146. Alastair Buchan was twenty-three when he died.

38. J. Buchan, *A Prince of the Captivity* (Edinburgh: B&W Publishing, 1996), p. 66–7.

39. Ibid., p. 123.

40. Buchan, *History of the Great War*, vol. 4, p. 443; see also p. 437.

41. J. Buchan, 'The Problem of Defence', *Scottish Review* (4 July 1907), reprinted in Buchan, *Comments and Characters*, pp. 8–11.

42. Buchan, *History of the Great War*, vol. 2, pp. 58–9.

43. Buchan, 'Sweet Argos' (1916), in *John Buchan's Collected Poems*, p. 140.

44. Ibid., p. 142

45. See also N. Waddell, 'Buchan and the Pacifists', this volume, pp. 91–101.

46. Buchan, *History of the Great War*, vol. 1, pp. 8–9

47. Buchan, *History of the Great War*, vol. 1, pp. 239, 244. *Nelson's History*, vol. 2, pp. 192 and 217.

48. Buchan, *Memory Hold-the-Door*, p. 279

49. Buchan, *History of the Great War*, vol. 4, pp. 156–7, 443.

50. This was a symposium written with his wife in 1919 (and not to be confused with the novel of the same title, published in 1936).

51. J. Kruse, *John Buchan and the Idea of Empire: Popular Literature and Political Ideology* (Lewiston: Edwin Mellen Press, 1989), 111–14.

52. Buchan, *History of the Great War*, vol. 4, pp. 442–3.

53. Buchan, *Sick Heart River*, pp. 186–7.

54. Buchan, *Memory Hold-the-Door*, p. 1

8 Waddell, Buchan and the Pacifists

1. Buchan, *Mr Standfast* (Oxford: Oxford University Press, 1993), p. 317. My thanks to Andrzej Gasiorek and Alice Reeve-Tucker, who kindly read and commented on earlier drafts of this chapter.
2. Ibid., p. 324.
3. R. J. Q. Adams and P. P. Poirer, *The Conscription Controversy in Great Britain, 1900–18* (Basingstoke: Macmillan, 1987), pp. 140–1.
4. For two good discussions of such typecasting, see: L. Bibbings, 'State Reaction to Conscientious Objectors', in I. Loveland (ed.), *Frontiers of Criminality* (London: Sweet, 1995), pp. 57–81; T. C. Kennedy, 'Public Opinion and the Conscientious Objector, 1915–1919', *Journal of British Studies*, 12:2 (1973), pp. 105–19.
5. Quoted in J. Rae, *Conscience and Politics* (London: Oxford University Press, 1970), p. 35.
6. Buchan, *Mr Standfast*, p. 308.
7. For readings of Wake, see: C. Harvie, *The Centre of Things: Political Fiction from Disraeli to the Present* (London: Unwin, 1991), p. 151; J. Idle, 'The Pilgrim's Plane Crash: Buchan, Bunyan, and Canonicity', *Literature and Theology*, 13:3 (1999), pp. 249–58, at p. 252; Kruse, *John Buchan (1875–1940) and the Idea of Empire*, p. 108; Lownie, *John Buchan*, p. 142–3; Macdonald, *John Buchan*, p. 188; D. Nabers, 'Spies Like Us: John Buchan and the Great War Spy Craze', *Journal of Colonialism and Colonial History*, 2:1 (2001); J. P. Parry, 'From the Thirty-Nine Articles to the Thirty-Nine Steps: Reflections on the Thought of John Buchan', in M. Bentley (ed.), *Public and Private Doctrine: Essays in British History Presented to Maurice Cowling* (Cambridge: Cambridge University Press, 1993), pp. 209–35, at p. 213 n. 19; P. Webb, *A Buchan Companion: A Guide to the Novels and Short Stories* (Stroud: Sutton, 1994), p. 114.
8. Anders Nygren gives a classic account of *agapē* in his *Agape and Eros* (1930–6), trans. P. S. Watson (London: Society for Promoting Christian Knowledge, 1953).
9. J. Buchan, 'Count Tolstoi and the Idealism of War' (1904), in *Some Eighteenth Century Byways* (Edinburgh: William Blackwood, 1908), pp. 294–300, p. 298.
10. On this issue, note Tolstoy's numerous claims that a policy of non-violent resistance in fact amounted to a radical trans-valuation of struggle against war and conflict, one that was far more effective than spilling blood, however virtuously, in the name of peace. See, for example, 'A Letter to a Hindu' (1908), in *Tolstoy Centenary Edition*, 21 vols (London: Humphrey Milford, 1928–37), vol. 21, pp. 413–32, p. 428.
11. Buchan, 'Count Tolstoi', p. 298.
12. Ibid., p. 297.
13. W. James, 'The Moral Equivalent of War' (1910), in *Memories and Studies* (London: Longmans, 1911), pp. 265–96, at pp. 276, 275. For a fascinating reading of James's contribution to the pacifist debate see Daniel Pick's excellent *War Machine: The Rationalisation of Slaughter in the Modern Age* (New Haven, CT: Yale University Press, 1993), pp. 13–18.
14. James, 'The Moral Equivalent of War', p. 277.
15. Buchan, 'Count Tolstoi', p. 296.
16. Ibid., p. 299.
17. Compare this with Wilfred Wellock's almost precisely contrary claim just over a decade later: 'By participating in war, civilized man debases himself, affirms what is not true, viz., that intellectual, moral, and spiritual forces are not stronger than physical and material

forces' (W. Wellock, *Pacifism: What it is and What it is Capable of Doing* (Manchester: Blackfriars, 1916), p. 9).

18. Buchan, 'Count Tolstoi', p. 297.
19. Ibid.
20. Ibid., p. 296, pp. 296–7.
21. Ibid., p. 296.
22. Ibid., pp. 299–300.
23. For an interesting account of Buchan's response to one such effort, see: M. Redley, 'John Buchan and *The Great Illusion*', *John Buchan Journal*, 37 (2007), pp. 30–5.
24. *War Speeches by British Ministers: 1914–1916* (London: Unwin, 1917), p. 347. See also Castor's view in Buchan's *The Courts of the Morning* (1929) that it is '"governments, not peoples, that offend"' (Buchan, *The Courts of the Morning*, p. 59).
25. J. Buchan, *Greenmantle* (1916), (Oxford: Oxford University Press, 1993), pp. 117, 184.
26. J. Buchan, *The Purpose of War* (London: Dent, 1916), p. 14.
27. Buchan, *Nelson's History of the War*, vol. 8 (1915), p. 117, and vol. 11 (1916), p. 71.
28. Ibid., vol. 14 (1917), p. 91.
29. Ibid., pp. 88–9.
30. Ibid., 14, p. 88.
31. Ibid.
32. David Boulton has argued that the first work centre established by the Home Office Committee for the Employment of Conscientious Objectors outside the village of Dyce in Aberdeenshire 'was a prototype concentration camp' (D. Boulton, *Objection Overruled* (London: MacGibbon, 1967), p. 211).
33. Buchan, *Nelson's History*, vol 18 (1917), p. 144.
34. A. F. Brockway, *Socialism for Pacifists* (Manchester: National Labour Press, 1916), p. 11.
35. Buchan, *Memory Hold-the-Door*, p. 165.
36. R. Ferguson, *The Short Sharp Life of T. E. Hulme* (London: Allen Lane, 2002), p. 256.
37. Anon., 'Conscientious Objectors', *The Times*, 4 January 1919, p. 8.
38. R. Macaulay, *Non-Combatants and Others* (London: Methuen, 1986), p. 164.
39. Buchan, *Mr Standfast*, p. 8.
40. Ibid., pp. 29, 30.
41. Ibid., p. 30.
42. For this link see Buchan, *Mr Standfast*, p. 336, n. 24. Intriguingly, Letchworth was home to The Temple Press, which printed Buchan's *The Purpose of War* (see *The Purpose of War*, p. 15).
43. Quoted in D. Hardy, *From Garden Cities to New Towns: Campaigning for Town and Country Planning, 1899–1946* (London: Spon, 1991), p. 54.
44. Buchan, *Mr Standfast*, p. 26. Buchan was largely critical of literary modernism. Note that in Lawrence's text the similarly-named Ursula (Brangwen) portrays herself as an uninterested romantic who finds soldiers, and the wars they represent, insufferable (D. H. Lawrence, *The Rainbow* (1915), ed. J. Worthen (London: Penguin, 1981), p. 357).
45. Buchan, *Mr Standfast*, p. 34.
46. Ibid., p. 31.
47. Ibid., p. 33.
48. Ibid., p. 267.
49. Ibid., p. 277.
50. Ibid., p. 41.
51. Ibid., p. 63.

52. Buchan, 'The True Danger of Socialism' (1907), in W. F. Gray (ed.), *Comments and Characters by John Buchan* (London: Thomas Nelson & Sons, 1940), pp. 173–6, at pp. 175, 173.
53. Ibid., p. 42.
54. Ibid., p. 64.
55. Ibid., p. 65.
56. Buchan, *The Purpose of War*, p. 15.
57. J. B. Glasier, *The Peril of Conscription* (London: Independent Labour Party, 1915), p. 4.
58. Buchan, *Mr Standfast*, p. 62.
59. Ibid., p. 55.
60. Ibid., p. 49.
61. Ibid., p. 54.
62. Adam Smith, *John Buchan*, p. 260.
63. B. Russell, *The Philosophy of Pacifism* (London: Headley Brothers, 1915), p. 4.
64. M. R. Ridley, *Second Thoughts: More Studies in Literature* (London: J. M. Dent, 1965), p. 7.
65. A. V. Dicey, 'The Conscientious Objector', *Nineteenth Century and After*, 88 (1918), pp. 357–73, at p. 372.
66. Buchan, *Mr Standfast*, p. 173.
67. Ibid., p. 324.
68. Ibid., p. 100.
69. L. Bibbings, 'Images of Manliness: The Portrayal of Soldiers and Conscientious Objectors in the Great War', *Social Legal Studies*, 12:3 (2003), pp. 335–58, p. 352. However, note that her claim on the same page which reads Wake as a homosexual is unsubstantiated.
70. P. Rajamäe, 'John Buchan's Heroes and The Chivalric Ideal: Gentlemen Born' (Ph.D. dissertation, University of Tartu, Estonia), pp. 208–15.
71. Rajamäe, 'John Buchan's Heroes', pp. 208, 212–3, 214–5.
72. Buchan, *Mr Standfast*, p. 222.
73. Ibid., pp. 306–7.
74. George Parfitt is simply wrong, I think, in claiming that 'the extent to which Buchan continues to be read with approval defines the extent to which we, like Buchan himself, have failed to learn either from *Pilgrim's Progress* or the Great War', but there is some truth in his assertion that *Mr Standfast's* 'simplifications reinforce prejudice', even if that prejudice cannot easily be mapped onto Buchan's thought more generally (G. Parfitt, *Fiction of the First World War: A Study* (London: Faber and Faber, 1988), p. 20).
75. Buchan, *Mr Standfast*, p. 324.
76. Ibid., p. 307.
77. L. E. Roller, *In Search of God the Mother: The Cult of Anatolian Cybele* (Berkeley, CA: University of California Press, 1999), pp. 253–4.
78. J. Buchan, 'The Grove of Ashtaroth', *The Moon Endureth: Tales and Fancies* (London: Thomas Nelson & Sons, 1923), pp. 187–224, p. 214. See also K. Macdonald, 'Artemis and Aphrodite', Chapter 9 of this volume, pp. 103–15.
79. Buchan, *Mr Standfast*, p. 221.
80. A. T. Fitzroy [R. Allatini], *Despised and Rejected* (1917), intro. J. Cutbill (London: Gay Men's Press, 1988), p. 194.
81. Buchan, *Mr Standfast*, p. 317.
82. Ibid., p. 221.

9 Henshaw, John Buchan, America and the 'British World', 1904–40

1. M. Redley, 'John Buchan at Milton Academy', *John Buchan Journal*, 22 (2000), pp. 22–32. The title of this article is misleading. It actually provides an excellent overview and analysis of Buchan's ideas about America and his activities in promoting Anglo–American relations. It includes many ideas and details which usefully supplement my chapter.
2. For a discussion of Buchan's wartime activities, see: Lownie, *John Buchan*, ch. 8, pp. 119–44; and Adam Smith, *John Buchan*, ch. 8, pp. 193–217. M. A. Pudlo, 'John Buchan's Americanism in the First World War', *John Buchan Journal*, 17 (1997), pp. 38–45.
3. For overviews of Buchan's wartime histories, see: K. Macdonald, 'Translating Propaganda: John Buchan's Writing During the First World War', in M. Hammond and S. Towheed (eds), *Publishing in the First World War: Essays in Book History* (London: Palgrave Macmillan, 2007), pp. 181–201; and Grieves, '*Nelson's History of the War*'.
4. Adam Smith, *John Buchan*, pp. 194–6.
5. *Nelson's History of the War*, vol. 1 (1914), preface, pp. 5–8. A large part of Rosebery's preface was quoted in Anon., 'Rosebery Sees Blessings in War', the *New York Times* (23 Jan 1915), p. BR 452; and in Anon., 'Frederick Palmer's View of the War', the *New York Times* (21 November 1915), BR 452.
6. Anon., 'Rosebery Sees Blessings in War'; Anon., 'Frederick Palmer's View of the War'.
7. Ibid.
8. In March 1916, Buchan spoke to the National Liberal Club on comparisons between the First World War and the American Civil War. For an American report of this speech see: Anon., 'American Civil War lessons for Britain', *Christian Science Monitor* (20 March 1916), p. 3. American newspapers also reported the comparisons with the Civil War which Buchan made in *Nelson's History*. See J. L. Balderston, 'Grant and Lee Invented "New" Trench Warfare', *Duluth News-Tribune* (27 August 1916), p. 2. For some of Buchan's other references to the Civil War see Grieves, '*Nelson's History of the War*', p. 536; *Nelson's History of the War*, vol. 19 (1918), p. 99; and vol. 21 (1918), p. 228–9.
9. Anon., 'Frederick Palmer's View of the War'.
10. Anon., 'Conan Doyle's History of the War', the *New York Times* (21 January 1917), p. BR 2.
11. T. B. Wells, 'Publishers in Khaki, Office "Boys" in Skirts', the *New York Times*, (11 Feb. 1917), p. SM 4.
12. Anon., 'British Role in Allies' Advance on West Front', *Christian Science Monitor* (25 October 1915), p. 2; and Anon., 'British Success in West Discussed', *Christian Science Monitor* (26 October 1915), p. 2.
13. Anon., 'American Civil War Lessons for Britain', *Christian Science Monitor* (20 March 1916), p. 3.
14. Unpublished speech at the National Liberal Club, 14 November 1917, quoted in Adam Smith, *John Buchan*, p. 203.
15. Ibid.
16. Anon., 'With authors and publishers', *New York Times* (20 January 1918), p. 56.
17. Macdonald, 'Translating Propaganda', p. 192.
18. Grieves, '*Nelson's History of the War*', p. 550, n. 38.
19. *Stars and Stripes* [US Army, France] (5 May 1918), p. 6. The Nelson's advertisement in *Stars and Stripes* advised that *The History* and other book from Nelson's were: 'on sale all over France, at all booksellers and railway bookstalls'.
20. Wells, 'Publishers in Khaki, Office "Boys" in Skirts'.

21. Blanchard, *The First Editions of John Buchan*, pp. 29–42.
22. For examples of advertising for *The Thirty-Nine Steps* see *New York Times* (10 October 1915), and San Jose *Evening News* (6 October 1916); *The Powerhouse, Hartford Courant* (7 October 1916); *Greenmantle, New York Times* (17 February 1917); and *Mr Standfast, New York Times* (17 August 1919). For multiple novels, see *Stars and Stripes* (9 August 1918). For a favourable review of *Greenmantle, Hartford Courant* (5 March 1917); *Salute to Adventurers, New York Times* (11 November 1917); *Mr Standfast, New York Times* (17 August 1919); *The Powerhouse, Greenmantle* and *Mr Standfast* were all actively advertised and well-received by reviewers in America.
23. *The Thirty-Nine Steps* was serialized in the San Jose *Evening News*, in October 1916. *Mr Standfast* was serialized in the *Popular Magazine*, January–February 1919.
24. The *Boston Daily Globe* advertised *Greenmantle* as one of its 'Best Sellers of the Week' on 3 March 1917, p. 2. The *Atlanta Constitution* listed *Greenmantle* as being 'among the best sellers in fiction of 1917', (10 March 1918), p. 8F.
25. Buchan, *Greenmantle*, p. 24.
26. Ibid., p. 20–1.
27. In its preface, *Salute* also makes reference to Buchan's interest in the American Civil War, with a dedication to his uncle who joined the staff of a Northern general during the war, and with a reference to General Lee as being 'the greatest of the great'.
28. On the subject of America as model for South African unification and British imperial federation, F. S. Oliver's biography of Alexander Hamilton is credited with crystallizing the thinking of Milner's Kindergarten, including its members who went on to form the Round Table movement. The Kindergarten included Robert Brand, Lionel Curtis, and Philip Kerr (who, as Lord Lothian, was British ambassador in Washington from 1939 to 1940. A. May, 'Milner's Kindergarten', *ODNB*. R. Davenport-Hines, 'Frederick Scott Oliver', *ONDB*).
29. For Buchan's own account see Buchan, *Memory Hold-the-Door*, ch. 11, 'My America', pp. 259–74. *Memory Hold-the-Door* was also published in America as *Pilgrim's Way* by Houghton Mifflin.
30. Adam Smith, *John Buchan*, pp. 269–71.
31. Review of F. S. Oliver, *Alexander Hamilton: An Essay on American Union*, (London: Constable, 1906), *Spectator* (14 July 1906), pp. 58–60.
32. Adam Smith, *John Buchan*, p. 153.
33. J. Buchan, 'America Today', review of A.R. Colquhoun, *Greater America, Spectator* (2 July 1904), pp. 16–18. J. Buchan, 'The American People', review of H. Munsterberg, *The American* (London: Williams and Norgate), *Spectator*, (17 June 1905), pp. 894–5.
34. J. Buchan, 'The American Experiment in Imperial Reconstruction', *Spectator* (27 February 1904), pp. 323–4. J. Buchan, 'The United States and Cuba', *Spectator* (22 September 1906), pp. 391–2.
35. J. Buchan, 'Britain and the United States', *Spectator*, (26 January 1907), p. 128.
36. J. Buchan, 'The American Civil War', review of J.K. Hosmer, *The American Civil War, Spectator* (14 February 1914), pp. 267–8.
37. J. Buchan, 'Abraham Lincoln', review of F. Fisher Browne, *The Everyday Life of Abraham Lincoln, Spectator* (18 July 1914), p. 94.
38. Buchan, 'The American Civil War', p. 268.
39. Ibid., p. 269.
40. Buchan, 'Abraham Lincoln', p. 94.

41. Buchan, 'Two Ordeals of Democracy', in J. Buchan, *Homilies and Recreations* (London: Hodder and Stoughton, 1939), pp. 89–119. A. S. Will review of *Two Ordeals of Democracy*, *New York Times* (3 May 1925), p. BR 3. Redley, 'John Buchan at Milton Academy'.
42. Buchan, 'Two Ordeals of Democracy', p. 89.
43. Ibid., pp. 118–19.
44. Quoted in Adam Smith, *John Buchan*, p. 331.
45. Anon., 'Today on the Radio', *New York Times* (30 November 1934), p. 17. Anon., 'Columbia Opens Its New Library; Buchan Outlines Role for Colleges', *New York Times* (1 December 1934), p. 15.
46. Anon., 'JB at Yale, 1938', *John Buchan Journal*, 15 (1996), pp. 20–2.
47. Adam Smith, *John Buchan*, pp. 446–7.
48. Ibid., pp. 444–5.
49. Anon., 'Hail Tweedsmuir with Capital Pomp', *New York Times* (31 March 1937), p. 3.
50. Adam Smith, *John Buchan*, p. 446.
51. Ibid., p. 447.
52. Ibid., p. 449.
53. Ibid., p. 454–7.

10 al-Rawi, Islam and the East in John Buchan's Novels

1. J. H. Rose, A. P. Newton, and E. A. Benians (eds), *The Cambridge History of the British Empire, Volume II* (Cambridge: Cambridge University Press, 1940), p. v.
2. See Daniell, *The Interpreter's House*; Lownie, *John Buchan*; and Adam Smith, *John Buchan*.
3. Buchan, *A Lodge in the Wilderness*, p. x.
4. Rose et al. (eds), *The Cambridge History of the British Empire, Vol. II*, p. vi.
5. E. Byers, *The British Empire: Its Origin and Destiny* (Ottawa: James T. Pattison, 1922),pp. 8 and 13.
6. G. Ellison, *An Englishwoman in a Turkish Harem* (London: Methuen & Co. Ltd., 1915), p. vii.
7. R. MacDonald, *The Language of Empire: Myths and Metaphors of Popular Imperialism, 1880–1918* (Manchester: Manchester University Press, 1994), p. 21.
8. N. Daniel, *Islam, Europe and Empire* (Edinburgh: University Press, 1962), p.154.
9. Lownie, *John Buchan*, p. 116.
10. Adam Smith, *John Buchan*, p. 177. See also J. Buchan, 'Romancers: John Buchan and T. E. Lawrence', *T. E. Notes*, 4:1 (January 1993), p. 2. But James Buchan was in error when citing the visit in 1912 instead of 1910.
11. Buchan, *The African Colony*, pp. 289–90.
12. G. L. Bell, *The Desert and the Sown* (London: William Heinemann, 1907), pp. ix–x
13. Buchan, *A Lodge in the Wilderness*, p. 33.
14. Ibid., pp. 34–5.
15. Buchan, *Prester John* (Oxford: Oxford University Press, 1994), p. 197–8.
16. Buchan, *The Island of Sheep*, p. 13.
17. J. Buchan, *The Half-Hearted* (London: Hodder and Stoughton, 1920), p. 113.
18. B. P. Smith, *Islam in English Literature* (New York: Caravan Books, 1977), p. 16.
19. M. Basha Al-Makhzumi, *The Impressions of Jamal Al-Deen Al-Afghani: Including a Comprehensive Account of his Attitudes, Ideas, Thoughts About the People of the East and*

the West in Moral, Political, and Social Aspects* (In Arabic) (Beirut: Al-A'almia Printing House, 1931), pp. 52–3. English translation of quotation by the present author.

20. Buchan, *The Half-Hearted*, p. 49. The 'crooked knife' is a reference here to the Khanjar, a dagger used by Muslims. Buchan's choice of 'crooked' (rather than, say, 'curved') carries derogatory associations, since it is a synonym for 'illegal', 'dishonest' and 'devious'.

21. Ibid., p. 252.

22. Ibid., p. 253.

23. Ibid.

24. Ibid. A similar romantic image of the East can be seen in Buchan's poem 'From the Pentlands Looking North and South' where he refers to the 'far gates of Samarkand' picturing it as a faraway exotic land. The poet invites the reader to come to 'the dusky East, / And share the Caliph's secret feast'. See J. Buchan, 'From the Pentlands Looking North and South', in *The Moon Endureth: Tales and Fancies* (London: Thomas Nelson & Sons, 1923), p. 10.

25. Buchan, *The Thirty-Nine Steps* (Oxford: Oxford University Press, 1993), p. 7.

26. J. Buchan, *The Path of the King*, (London: Thomas Nelson & Sons, 1924), p. 241.

27. Buchan, *The Half-Hearted*, p. 253. The Edwardian poetry of Buchan's later close friend and associate Sir Henry Newbolt gives the wider context for this highly romantic conception of 'the East', and in 'He Fell Among Thieves' in particular the romance is aligned with cruelty and implacable hate.

28. Buchan, *The Dancing Floor* (Oxford: Oxford University Press, 1997), p. 45.

29. Macdonald, *John Buchan*, p. 90.

30. Buchan, *The Half-Hearted*, p. 229.

31. Ibid., p. 228. In *Greenmantle*, Buchan emphasizes the same point saying that one has to remember 'the old torrential raids which crumpled the Byzantine Empire and shook the walls of Vienna?' See Buchan, *Greenmantle*, p. 12.

32. See Macdonald, *John Buchan*, pp. 167–8.

33. Buchan, *The Half-Hearted*, p. 228.

34. Lownie, *John Buchan*, pp. 70–85.

35. See for instance MacDonald's *The Language of Empire*, P. Brantlinger's *Rule of Darkness: British Literature and Imperialism* (1988), and C. Smith, 'Every Man Must Kill the Thing He Loves: Empire, Homoerotics, and Nationalism in John Buchan's *Prester John*', *NOVEL: A Forum on Fiction*, (Winter, 1995).

36. Buchan, *Prester John*, p. 23.

37. C. Darwin, *The Descent of Man and Action in Relation to Sex* (New York: Clarke, Given and Hooper, Publishers, 1874), see in particular pp. 156 7.

38. D. A. H. Aljubouri, 'The Medieval Idea of the Saracen, as Illustrated in English Literature, Spectacle and Sport' (PhD Dissertation, University of Leicester, 1972), p. 26. See also I. R. Whitaker, 'An Historical Explanation of the Asiatic Myth of Prester John', *Asiatic Review*, 48 (1952), pp. 74–9.

39. Buchan, *The African Colony*, p. 21.

40. E. Bar-Yosef, 'The Last Crusade: British Propaganda and the Palestine Campaign, 1917–18', *Journal of Contemporary History*, 36:1 (January 2001), pp. 93, 95.

41. G. A. Mann, 'John Buchan (1875–1940) and the First World War: A Scot's Career in Imperial Britain' (Ph.D. Dissertation, University of North Texas, 1999), p.8.

42. The title of the story is taken from John Dryden's poem 'Macflecknoe' where the poet says: 'But Shadwell never deviates into sense. / Some beams of wit on other souls may fall/ Strike through and make a lucid interval'. Dryden's lines are linked to the story because it

deals with the magical drug that leads to the loss of wit and sense like Shadwell's natural stupidity. See J. Buchan (ed.), *English Literature, Volume II* (Edinburgh: New University Society), p. 129.

43. J. Buchan, 'A Lucid Interval' in *The Moon Endureth: Tales and Fancies,* p. 58.
44. Ibid.
45. The danger is also suggested to lie outside the Empire, as the Foreign Secretary leaves the dinner declaring his intentions to put a flea in the ear of the German Chancellor. The political tension in Western Europe only four years before the First World War is clearly suggested here.
46. Buchan, 'A Lucid Interval', p. 72.
47. Ibid., p. 86.
48. See L. Hopkins, 'The Irish and the Germans in the Fiction of John Buchan and Erskine Childers', *Irish Studies Review* 9:1 (2001), pp. 69–80.
49. Buchan, *The Three Hostages,* p. 88.
50. Ibid., p.122.
51. Ibid., p. 113.
52. Ibid., p. 119.
53. Ibid, p. 123.
54. Ibid., p. 202–3.
55. Ibid., p. 123.
56. Ibid., p. 118.
57. A. K. Al-Rawi, 'Manipulating Muslims in John Buchan's *Greenmantle* and A. J. Quinnell's '*The Mahdi*: A Pattern of Consistency', *John Buchan Journal*, 36 (Spring 2007), p. 23.
58. For more details, see C. J. Burnett and H. Bennett, *The Green Mantle: A Celebration of the Revival in 1687 of the Most Ancient and Most Noble Order of the Thistle.* National Museums of Scotland, 1989.
59. Buchan, *Greenmantle,* p. 26.
60. Buchan, *Memory Hold-the-Door*, p. 32.
61. W. Scott, *The Talisman* (London: A. Glasgow Collins' Clear Type Press, 1832), p. 410.
62. W. Scott, *Redgauntlet* (London: Whittaker & Co., 1832), p. 223.
63. Ibid., p. 236.
64. There are other conections between Lilias, whose name is close to Lilith, a demon, and Hilda von Einem.
65. See for instance C. S. Hurgronje, *The Holy War: 'Made in Germany'* (New York: G. P. Putnam & Sons, 1915), and C. S. Hurgronje, *Mohammedanism: Lectures on its Origin, its Religious and Political Growth, and its Present State* (New York, G. P. Putnam & Sons, 1916).
66. Buchan, *Greenmantle*, p. 12.
67. Ibid., p. 54.
68. Ibid., p. 14.
69. Ibid., p. 181.
70. Ibid., p. 272.
71. Buchan, *The Three Hostages*, p. 63.
72. Ibid.
73. Buchan, *Greenmantle*, p. 182.
74. Ibid., p. 23–4.
75. Buchan, *The Three Hostages*, p. 241.

11 Taylor, Conquistadors: Buchan's Businessmen

1. M. J. Wiener, *English Culture and the Decline of the Industrial Spirit, 1850–1980* (Cambridge: Cambridge University Press, 1981). Wiener links E. M. Forster to a generalized yearning for mythic rural bliss, but he offers no examples of post-Victorian British novelists making an explicit critique of business or industry as a major theme.

2. W. D. Rubinstein, 'Cultural Explanations for Britain's Economic Decline: How True?', in B. Collins and K. Robbins (eds), *British Culture and Economic Decline* (London: Weidenfeld and Nicolson, 1990), pp. 78–9; W. D. Rubinstein, *Capitalism, Culture and Decline in Britain, 1750–1990* (London: Routledge, 1994), pp. 60–4.

3. '"Gentlemen and Players" Revisited: the Gentlemanly Ideal, the Business Ideal and the Professional Ideal in English Literary Culture', in N. McKendrick and R. B. Outhwaite (eds), *Business Life and Public Policy, Essays in Honour of D.C. Coleman* (Cambridge: Cambridge University Press, 1986).

4. Shaw, Wells, Bennett, Forster, Lawrence.

5. N. McKendrick 'The Enemies of Technology and the Self-Made Man', General Introduction to R.Church, *Herbert Austin* (London: Europa, 1979), p. xx, and p. xxv.

6. Ibid., p.xxxv.

7. N. McKendrick, 'Literary Luddism and the Businessman', General Introduction to P.N. Davies, *Sir Alfred Jones* (London, Europa, 1978). Disengagement from business themes is also emphasized by John McVeagh in *Tradefull Merchants: The Portrayal of the Capitalist in Literature* (London, Routledge & Kegan Paul, 1981), pp. 160–92.

8. Buchan, *A Lodge in the Wilderness*; Adam Smith, *John Buchan*, p. 136. Unlike Rhodes, but in common with others of Buchan's businessmen, Carey's strong suit was copper.

9. Buchan, *A Lodge in the Wilderness*, p. 12.

10. Ibid., p. 25. Carey's voice was borrowed from Rhodes.

11. Buchan, *Greenmantle*, p. 67; Buchan, *The Three Hostages*, pp. 146–50.

12. Buchan, *The Thirty-Nine Steps*, p. 7.

13. The Hannay of *The Three Hostages* is another matter. By then, however, it is not his business efforts but four years of secret service and soldiering that have claimed their reward.

14. Buchan, *The Thirty-Nine Steps*, p. 55.

15. Buchan, *Greenmantle*, p. 22.

16. Buchan, *Mr Standfast*, pp. 41–2; Buchan, *The Courts of the Morning*, p. 77.

17. Buchan, *The Courts of the Morning*, p. 2.

18. Buchan, *Mr Standfast*, p. 210.

19. S. Smiles, *Self-Help* (1859; London: John Murray, 1897), p.266. Sense is the characteristic of another of Buchan's businessmen, the retired Glasgow grocer Dickson McCunn. 'He was a big business man in Glasgow – but he's retired now. I never met his equal for whinstone common sense. You've only to look at him to see that what he thinks about forty million others think also' (J. Buchan, *Castle Gay* (London: Dent, 1983), p. 94). As Buchan concentrates on his romantic retirement, rather than his past status as a businessman, McCunn falls outside the scope of this study.

20. Buchan, *Mr Standfast*, p. 211.

21. Ibid., p. 210.

22. Buchan, *Sick Heart River*, p. 17.

23. J. Buchan, *John Macnab* (Oxford: Oxford University Press, 1994).

24. F. M. L. Thompson, *Gentrification and the Enterprise Culture* (Oxford: Oxford University Press, 2001), p. 97.

25. Macdonald, *John Buchan*, p. 66. Editor of the non-conformist *British Weekly*, Nicoll (1851–1923) 'disliked fresh air and always had a fire blazing in his study' (*DNB*). Rothermere (1868–1940) ran a pro-Hungarian campaign in the *Daily Mail* from 1927.

26. Buchan, *The Courts of the Morning*.

27. Ibid., pp. 95–6.

28. Ibid., p. 95.

29. A. D. Chandler, *The Visible Hand* (Cambridge, MA: Harvard University Press, 1977).

30. Ibid., pp. 6–12; A. D. Chandler, *Scale and Scope: Dynamics of Industrial Capitalism* (Cambridge, MA: Harvard University Press, 1990), p. 8.

31. 'Mr. Durant had been able to operate the corporation in his own way, as the saying goes, "by the seat of his pants". The new administration was made up of men with very different ideas about business administration. They desired a highly rational and objective mode of operation.' A. P. Sloan, *My Years With General Motors* (London: Sidgwick and Jackson, 1965), p. 52).

32. Chandler, *Scale and Scope*, pp. 389–92. For the rationalization movement see L. Hannah, *The Rise of the Corporate Economy* (London: Methuen, 1983), pp. 27–40, and J. F. Wilson, *British Business History, 1720–1994* (Manchester: Manchester University Press, 1995), pp. 133–64.

33. Buchan, *The Courts of the Morning*, p. 98.

34. Ibid.

35. Ibid., p. 96.

36. In 1929 Shell employed 2,156 Europeans and 56,983 Asians in the Dutch East Indies. J. L. Van Zanden, S. Howarth, J. Jonker, and K. Sluyterman, *A History of Royal Dutch Shell*, 3 vols (Oxford: Oxford University Press, 2007), vol. 1, p. 307.

37. Chandler, *Scale and Scope*, pp. 298–304.

38. An internal Shell communication of the period is suggestive in this respect: 'The whole question of [national] control is very largely nonsense. It is a matter of sentiment, but if by transferring control to the Hottentots we could increase our security and our dividends I don't believe any of us would hesitate for long.' (Sir R. Waley Cohen, 27 Dec. 1923). Quoted by G. G. Jones, 'The British Government and the Oil Companies 1912–1924: the Search For An Oil Policy', *The Historical Journal*, 20:3 (1977), pp. 647–72. Deterding's autobiography contains the sinister condition 'If I were dictator of the world...' H. Deterding, *An International Oilman* (London: Ivor Nicholson and Watson, 1934), p. 114.

39. Buchan, *The Courts of the Morning*, pp. 375–6.

40. Buchan, *The Island of Sheep*.

41. Buchan indulges in a good deal of snobbery at Beryl Lombard's expense, but fails to notice her quality of heroic self-restraint. How many other women would have permitted their husbands to turn down a knighthood, and the title of Lady Lombard with it, for obscure reasons of corporate sensitivity? (Buchan, *The Island of Sheep*, p. 15).

42. Buchan, *Sick Heart River*, pp. 19–25.

43. Ibid., p. 18.

44. Ibid., pp. 40–1.

45. This was not necessarily a romantic fantasy, and Buchan was early in identifying an actual problem. D. C. Coleman points out that 'in Courtaulds in the 1930's for example, it was the "practical men", at board and managerial level, who were ... least willing to recognize

trades unions or the need for change in the face of labour unrest'. D. C. Coleman, 'Gentlemen and Players', *Economic History Review*, 2nd ser., 26 (1973), p. 113.

46. Insofar as Shell served as a reference for the Gran Seco Company, Buchan would have approved its later lines of human resource development. After the pro-Nazi Deterding was eased out in 1939, a collegiate-style oligarchy of managing directors emerged. 'The consensus-oriented business culture may also have contributed to Shell people becoming, in Spaght's words, "kind to a fault" rather than hard-nosed'. (Luiten van Zanden et al., *A History of Royal Dutch Shell*, vol. 2, p. 147, quoting Monroe E. Spaght, Managing Director of Royal Dutch 1965–70).

47. According to Professor Wiener, 'My original idea for the book was "English Culture and the Containment of Industrialism". I was persuaded, partly by the publisher, to change it because "decline" grabs readers more...'. M. Wiener interview in R. English and M. Kenny (eds) *Rethinking British Decline* (London: Macmillan, 2000), p. 35.

48. Buchan, *The Courts of the Morning*, p. 380; Buchan, *Sick Heart River*, p. 17.

12 Kerr, 'A Fraud Called John Buchan': Buchan, Joseph Conrad and Literary Theft

1. Buchan, *The Island of Sheep*, p. 212.

2. J. Conrad, *Victory* (London: Dent, 1948), p. 329.

3. J. Conrad to W. Blackwood, 8 November 1899. *The Collected Letters of Joseph Conrad: Volume 2, 1898–1902*, ed. F. R. Karl and L. Davies (Cambridge: Cambridge University Press, 1986), 2: p. 216 [Cited as *CL*].

4. J. Conrad to Edward Garnett, 9 November 1899 (*CL* 2: p. 218).

5. J. Buchan, 'The Far Islands', *The Watcher by the Threshold* (London: William Blackwood & Sons, 1915), pp. 103–48, p. 139.

6. Ibid., p. 144.

7. Confusingly, Haggard himself was repeatedly accused of plagiarism. As Joseph Bristow notes, in one instance *Allen Quatermain* was charged by a reviewer with extensive borrowing from a travel narrative by E. F. Smith, and later a story by Smith 'was criticized by one commentator for abstracting large parts of *Allen Quatermain*' (J. Bristow, *Empire Boys: Adventures in a Man's World* (London: Harper Collins, 1991), p. 146).

8. Classics of the nineteenth-century fascination with heredity include Charles Darwin's *The Descent of Man* (1871) on human physical ancestry, Cesare Lombroso's *L'Uomo Delinquente* (1876) on inherited criminal tendencies, and J. G. Frazer's *The Golden Bough* (1890) on the mythic genealogies of religion.

9. A. Sandison, *The Wheel of Empire* (London: Macmillan, 1967); Kruse, *John Buchan and the Idea of Empire*, pp. 96–106.

10. Z. Najder, *Joseph Conrad: A Chronicle* (Cambridge: Cambridge University Press, 1983), p. 205.

11. P. Mallios, 'An Interview with Edward Said', in C. M. Kaplan, P. Mallios and A. White (eds), *Conrad in the Twenty-First Century: Contemporary Approaches and Perspectives* (New York: Routledge, 2005), pp. 283–303, p. 286.

12. See H. Epstein, '*Victory*'s Marionettes: Conrad's Revisitation of Stevenson', in K. Carabine, O. Knowles and P. Armstrong (eds), *Conrad, James and Other Relations* (Boulder, CO: Social Science Monographs; Lublin: Maria Curie-Skłodowska University, 1998), pp. 189–216; O. Knowles, 'Conrad, Anatole France, and the Early French Romantic

Tradition: Some Influences', *Conradiana*, 11 (1979), pp. 41–61; and I. Watt, *Conrad in the Nineteenth Century* (London: Chatto and Windus, 1980); and the essays collected in G. M. Moore, O. Knowles and J. H. Stape (eds) *Conrad: Intertexts and Appropriations: Essays in Memory of Yves Hervouet* (Amsterdam: Rodopi, 1997).

13. Watt, *Conrad* p. 50.
14. Y. Hervouet, 'Why Did Conrad Borrow So Extensively?', *Conradian* 9:2 (November 1984), pp. 53–68, 50.
15. F. R. Karl, *Joseph Conrad: The Three Lives* (London: Faber and Faber, 1979), pp. 537–8.
16. Hervouet, 'Extensively', p. 63.
17. Ibid., p. 64. I call these two works parasitic on the 'already-written' for slightly different reasons. Shakespeare's *Hamlet* is known to be a reworking of an earlier play which already had a performance history, and Fielding's *Joseph Andrews* appropriates and parodies Richardson's hugely successful *Pamela*.
18. L. Hutcheon, 'Literary Borrowing ... and Stealing: Plagiarism, Sources, Influences, and Intertexts', *English Studies in Canada*, 12:2 (June 1986), pp. 229–39, p. 234.
19. G. Genette, *Palimpsests: Literature in the Second Degree,* trans. Channa Newman and Claude Doubinsky (Lincoln, NE: University of Nebraska Press, 1997), pp. 3–7, 5.
20. Ibid., *Palimpsests* p. 6.
21. H. Bloom, *A Map of Misreading* (Oxford: Oxford University Press, 2003), pp. 85–105.
22. Buchan, *The Courts of the Morning*, p. 30.
23. Kruse, *John Buchan and the Idea of Empire*; P. E. Ray, 'The Villain in the Spy Novels of John Buchan', *English Literature in Transition*, 24:2 (1981), pp. 81–90.
24. Buchan, *The Courts of the Morning*, pp. 309–10.
25. Genette, *Palimpsests* p. 213.
26. J. Conrad, *Almayer's Folly* (London: Dent, 1946), p. 147. This is, as a matter of fact, possibly the most important and intriguing sentence in Conrad. It features frequently in *A Personal Record* as the point at which Conrad abandoned the writing of *Almayer's Folly*, his first novel, whose composition is the central motif of this autobiographical work. The sentence is the point at which Conrad's career as a writer almost foundered, more than once. *Konrad Wallenrod*, from which the words are plagiarized (or appropriated), was the great poem of romantic Polish nationalism, a thoroughly patriarchal text for Joseph Conrad, besides bearing his own name.
27. Hervouet, 'Extensively' p. 57.
28. N. Frye, *Anatomy of Criticism* (Princeton, NJ: Princeton University Press, 1957), pp. 186–206.
29. Buchan, *The Island of Sheep*, p. 14.
30. Ibid., p. 17.
31. Ibid., p. 224.
32. Ibid., p. 33.
33. Another explanation is that, like Heyst, and like their common hypotextual ancestor Hamlet the Dane, he suffers under 'the dominant influence' of his absent father.
34. Buchan, *The Island of Sheep*, p. 221.
35. Buchan, *Island*, p. 222.
36. Conrad, *Victory*, p. 329.
37. Buchan, *The Island of Sheep*, p. 169.
38. Ibid., p. 88.
39. With some inevitability, Richard Hannay finds his sanctuary in a country retreat, Fosse, named after a defensive fortification.

13 Macdonald, Aphrodite Rejected: Archetypal Women in Buchan's Fiction

1. Buchan wrote to his sister Anna about the heroine of her new novel *The Setons* (1926), 'you draw a wonderful picture of a woman (a thing I could as much do as fly to the moon)': Adam Smith *John Buchan*, p. 248.

2. The added ending for the American edition of *Sir Quixote* added a few lines which sent the hero back to Anne. This was apparently a 'pirated' edition (D. Daniell, *The Interpreter's House*, p. 70, and it is not known if Buchan wrote the lines, or even knew of the edition until too late. See also K. Macdonald 'Afterword', J. Buchan, *Sir Quixote of the Moors* (Kansas City: Valancourt Press, 2008), pp. 81–3.

3. E. Showalter, *Sexual Anarchy: Gender and Culture at the Fin de Siècle* (London: Bloomsbury, 1990), 78–9; and see also S. Jones, 'Into the Twentieth Century: Imperial Romance from Haggard to Buchan' in Corinne Saunders (ed.) *A Companion to Romance: From Classical to Contemporary* (Oxford: Blackwell Publishing, 2007), pp. 406–23.

4. P. Keating, *The Haunted Study. A Social History of the English Novel, 1875–1914* (London: Martin, Secker & Warburg, 1997), p. 179.

5. In 1910 Buchan was advising Wells not to proceed with an action for damages against the *Field* for their review of *Ann Veronica*, describing the novel as 'indefensible'. K. Macdonald, 'Wells' correspondence with John Buchan', *The Wellsian*, 13 (1990), pp. 43–8.

6. Buchan is generally absent from biographies of contemporary literary figures, such as Ford Madox Ford, Joseph Conrad (except in passing), or E. Nesbit.

7. Keating, *The Haunted Study*, p. 181.

8. Showalter, *Sexual Anarchy*, p. 78, and see also M. Dekoven, *Rich and Strange: Gender, History and Modernism* (Princeton, NJ: Princeton University Press, 1991); Pykett, *Engendering Fictions*; M. Beetham, *A Magazine of her Own? Domesticity and Desire in the Woman's Magazine 1800–1914* (London: Routledge, 1996).

9. J. E. Miller, *Rebel Women: Feminism, Modernism and the Edwardian Novel* (London: Virago Press, 1994), pp. 29–30.

10. J. E. Miller, *Rebel Women*, p. 3.

11. Ibid., p. 4 and p. 38.

12. C. Baldick, *The Oxford English Literary History, vol 10, 1910–1940; The Modern Movement* (Oxford: Oxford University Press, 2004), p. 284.

13. See also Haslett and Haslett, this volume, pp. 17–27.

14. A. J. Greimas, *Semantique Structurale* (Paris: Larousse, 1966).

15. V. Propp, *A Morphology of the Folk Tale*, trans. L. Scott (Austin, TX: University of Texas Press, 1968). Propp first published his work in Russian in 1928, and it was not translated into English until 1958. However, Propp was contemporary with Buchan, in the sense that both men would have been familiar with a corpus of mythic material from the same historical period, if from different cultures.

16. L. Hébert, 'The Actantial Model', in L. Hébert (ed.), *Signo* [online] (Quebec: Rimouski, 2006), http://www.signosemio.com.

17. J. G. Frazer, *The Golden Bough. A Study in Magic and Religion* (abridged edition) (London: Macmillan, 1925), p. 411.

18. Harrison, *Themis*, p. 494.

19. Those which do not appear in Buchan are the unfaithful wife, the stepdaughter, the sister, the supernatural spouse, the godmother and the stepmother.

20. C. P. Estés, *Women who Run with the Wolves. Myths and Stories of the Wild Woman Archetype* (New York: Ballantine Books, 1992).

21. See, for example, Mary Lamington, Princess Saskia, Janet Raden, Jacqueline Armine, Araminta Troyos, and Anna Haraldsen.

22. Although given in Deuteronomy I:4 *passim* as an Old Testament location, here Ashtaroth is the plural of Ashtoreth, the Hebrew name for Astarte (J. C. G. Greig, 'Introduction' to J. Buchan, *Supernatural Tales* (Edinburgh: B&W Publishing, 1997), pp. vii–xxvi, xvi), and Aphrodite was her Greek name.

23. Deegan, 'Introduction', in Buchan, *The Dancing Floor*.

24. The Misses Wymondham from *Mr Standfast*; for example, and the Hallward great-aunts, of 'A Ship to Tarshish'.

25. Lady Manorwater for Alice Wishart, the Misses Wymondham for Mary Lamington, the Duchess of Queensberry for Lady Norreys, Mollie Nantley for Koré Arabin and for her own daughters, Grizel Saintserf for Katrine Yester and Harriet Westwater for her niece Alison.

26. J. Cannan, 'Novels of Character', *The Bookman*, 84:503 (August 1933), p. 260.

27. A. C. Turner, 'John Buchan' (PhD dissertation, University of California, 1952), and Turner, *Mr. Buchan, Writer*, contain the fullest descriptions.

28. This was the name Buchan used for his autobiographical character in *A Lodge in the Wilderness* (1906).

29. See Turner, *Mr Buchan, Writer*.

30. Buchan, *Mr Standfast*, pp. 217–18.

31. It is significant that in John Prebble's screenplay for the 1978 BBC TV version, Mary is brought to centre-stage without any change in her actions precisely because Hannay's first-person narration has been lost, and the narrative is reported through the third person. Hannay smothered his wife's potential.

32. H. E. Taylor, 'John Buchan's *The Three Hostages*', *The Salisbury Review*, 26:2 (Winter 2007), p. 33.

33. This story was first published in *Macmillan's Magazine* in 1897 as 'The Song of the Moor' and in *Grey Weather* (1899), where it was given the alternate title of 'The Moor-Song'. For its appearance in *The Moon Endureth* (1912), Buchan renamed the story again, as 'The Rime of True Thomas, The Tale of the Respectable Whaup and the Great Godly Man'.

34. Anna did go on to become the successful and very popular novelist 'O. Douglas', but the heroines of her fiction also reflect this sense of the sister left at home while the brother explores the wide world. She was also her widowed mother's companion until her mother's death.

35. Lownie, *John Buchan*, ch. 4.

36. Buchan, *John Macnab*, p. 156.

37. Women were first allowed to stand for election to the British Parliament in 1918, and Countess de Markievicz was the first British woman to be elected as a Member of Parliament, but did not take her seat. The American Nancy Astor was the first serving woman Member of Parliament (1919–45).

38. A fifth woman opposing Adam, and Britain, is the cardboard villain 'Rosa Klebb'; only mentioned in passing, and not included in this discussion.

39. See also Rudyard Kipling's short stories 'A Habitation Enforced' (in *Actions and Reactions*, 1909), and 'My Son's Wife' (in *A Diversity of Creatures*, 1917), which address the same issues.

40. He bought his own Oxfordshire country house in 1919, but his wife was from an aristocratic background.

41. Buchan, *A Prince of the Captivity*, p. 165.

42. Ibid., p. 166

43. Ibid., p. 122. Interestingly, Buchan also describes Utlaw, her husband, in the same terms (p. 172).

44. Op cit, p. 208.

45. See also Haslett and Haslett, this volume, pp. 17–27.

46. The woman's version of the hero on a quest for adventure would be created by novelists such as Una L Silberrad in *The Good Comrade* (1907), and, much later, by Hilary Bailey in *Hannie Richards, or, The Intrepid Adventures of a Restless Wife* (London: Virago, 1986).

47. G. Uden, 'Books I Have Never Read: Confessions of Certain Bookmen', *Bookman* 83:493 (October 1932), p. 21.

48. Buchan, *Mr Standfast*, p. 16.

49. J. Buchan, *The Gap in the Curtain* (London: Thomas Nelson & Sons, 1934), p. 196.

14 John Buchan: Politics, Language and Suspense

1. L. MacNeice, 'To posterity', in *Collected Poems* (London: Faber and Faber, 1979), p. 443.

2. A. Smith, 'The Running Man', *Scotland on Sunday Review Supplement* (28 December 2008), pp. 8–9.

3. Buchan, *The Thirty-Nine Steps*, p. 107.

4. Ibid., p.103.

5. Ibid., p.103.

6. Ibid., p.108.

7. Ibid., p.109.

8. Ibid., p.112.

9. J. Buchan, *The Last Secrets: The Final Mysteries of Exploration* (London: Thomas Nelson, 1923), pp. 33–4.

10. J. L. Mitchell, *Hanno; or, the Future of Exploration* (London: Kegan Paul, Trench, Trubner & Co., 1928).

11. R. B. C. Graham, 'Might, Majesty and Dominion', in *Success and Other Sketches* (London: Duckworth, 1902), pp.81–5.

12. O. D. Edwards, 'John Buchan: Novelist, Publisher & Politician', in A. Reid and B. D. Osbourne (eds), *Discovering Scottish Writers* (Hamilton & Edinburgh: Scottish Library Association & Scottish Cultural Press, 1997), p.16.

13. M. Pittock, 'Scotland, empire and apocalypse: from Stevenson to Buchan', in *The Edinburgh Companion to Twentieth-Century Scottish Literature* (Edinburgh: Edinburgh University Press, forthcoming 2009).

14. Buchan *The Three Hostages*, p.62.

15. M. Walker, *Scottish Literature since 1707* (London and New York: Longman, 1996), p. 242.

16. J. Buchan, 'Some Scottish Characteristics', in *The Scottish Tongue: A Series of Lectures on the Vernacular Language of Lowland Scotland* (London: Cassell & Co., 1924), pp. 47–88.

17. E. Morgan, 'Buchan, John (1875–1940): Sick Heart River (1941)', in *Twentieth-Century Scottish Classics* (Glasgow: Book Trust Scotland, 1987), p. 3.
18. D. Gifford, S. Dunnigan, B. Dickson, A. MacGillivray (eds), *Scottish Literature in English and Scots* (Edinburgh: Edinburgh University Press, 2002), p.705.

15 Grant, Buchan's Supernatural Fiction

1. Daniell, *The Interpreter's House*, p. 40.
2. P. Haining (ed.), *Clans of Darkness: Scottish Stories of Fantasy and Horror* (New York: Taplinger Publishing, 1971), p. 156. *Watcher* contains five stories, four of which can safely be classified as supernatural; the exception is 'Fountainblue'.
3. Buchan's novels and short stories share many themes. The paganism present in 'The Outgoing of the Tide', for example, drives the plot of *Witch Wood*, 'The Far Islands' prefigures *A Prince of the Captivity*, and *The Dancing Floor* is foreshadowed by 'Basilissa'. Further cross-pollination is evidenced by the fact that characters like Richard Hannay and Edward Leithen appear in both the novels and the short stories.
4. Haining, *Clans of Darkness*, p. 156.
5. In chronological order: *The Far Islands and Other Tales of Fantasy*, ed. J. Bell (West Kingston, RI: D.M. Grant, 1984); *The Best Supernatural Stories of John Buchan*, ed. P. Haining (London: Robert Hale, 1991); *Supernatural Tales*, ed. J. C. G. Greig (Edinburgh: Black and White Publishing, 1997); *The Watcher by the Threshold*, ed. B. and C. Roden; *Supernatural Buchan: Stories of Ancient Spirits, Uncanny Places and Strange Creatures* (London: Leonaur Press, 2007).
6. H. P. Lovecraft, *Supernatural Horror in Literature* (1927; New York: Ben Abramson, 1945), p. 15. As S. T. Joshi notes, 'weird' was 'used consistently by Lovecraft as an umbrella term for the field as a whole' (S. T. Joshi, *The Weird Tale* (Austin: University of Texas Press, 1990), p. 1). Although Joshi has reservations about the way Lovecraft equates supernatural horror with the weird tale, he thinks Lovecraft provides 'as satisfactory a definition of the weird tale as any' (p. 6).
7. Lovecraft, *Supernatural Horror in Literature*, p. 17. Poe's belief that the short story should convey a single, overpowering emotional effect seems to be at the root of these remarks. Lovecraft devotes a chapter of his study to Poe, the writer who is perhaps closest to him in spirit. Buchan was also a fan of Poe, and expressed his admiration in his introduction to the Nelson Library Series edition of the latter's *Tales of Mystery and Imagination* (1911).
8. Lovecraft, *Supernatural Horror in Literature*, p. 79. Lovecraft's praise for *Witch Wood* would have pleased Buchan, who considered it the 'best' of his novels (Buchan, *Memory Hold-the-Door* (London: Hodder and Stoughton, 1940), p. 196).
9. Lovecraft, *Supernatural Horror in Literature*, p. 79.
10. Lovecraft devotes even less space to other Scots who have tackled supernatural themes. He singles Stevenson out for praise, calling 'Markheim', 'The Body Snatcher' and *Strange Case of Dr Jekyll and Mr Hyde* 'permanent classics' (*Supernatural Horror in Literature*, p. 43). He also cites Burns' 'Tam O' Shanter', acknowledges the 'ghostly charm' of Hogg's *Kilmeny*, and praises Scott, 'whose respect for the supernatural was always great' (op. cit., p. 23), and whose *Letters on Demonology and Witchcraft* he calls 'one of our best compendia of European witch-lore' (op. cit., p. 40).
11. Buchan, *Memory Hold-the-Door*, p. 13.
12. Ibid., p. 15.

13. Ibid., p. 16.
14. Daniell, *The Interpreter's House*, p. 49.
15. Buchan, *Memory Hold-the-Door*, p. 28.
16. Ibid., p. 120.
17. See, for example, 'The Moor Song', in *The Watcher by the Threshold*, ed. B. Roden and C. Roden, pp. 36–42; 'No-Man's-Land'; 'The Watcher by the Threshold'; 'The Outgoing of the Tide', in op. cit., pp. 225–64; 'The Grove of Ashtaroth'; 'The Green Glen'; 'The Green Wildebeest', in op. cit., pp. 226–39; 'Basilissa', in op. cit., pp. 240–51; 'Fullcircle', in op. cit., pp. 252–63; 'The Wind in the Portico', in op. cit., pp. 285–301; 'Skule Skerry', in op. cit., pp. 302–12.
18. Dedication to Stair Gillon, *The Watcher by the Threshold*.
19. Buchan, 'The Grove of Ashtaroth', *The Moon Endureth*, p. 211.
20. J. Bell, Introduction, *The Far Islands and Other Tales of Fantasy* (West Kingston, RI: D.M. Grant, 1984), pp. 16–17. Bell incorrectly substitutes the term 'fantasy' for 'supernatural.'
21. Daniell, *The Interpreter's House*, p. 22.
22. Lovecraft, *Supernatural Horror in Literature*, p. 40.
23. Smith describes 'The Outgoing of the Tide' as being 'in the tradition of Burns' 'Tam O' Shanter', Scott's 'Wandering Willie's Tale' and Stevenson's 'Thrawn Janet' (Adam Smith, *John Buchan*, p. 102). This opens the door to discussions on Buchan's place within a tradition of Scottish supernatural fiction, which would require a separate article to address. Daniell, like Smith, sees Buchan as part of a 'Scottish tradition' (p. xviii) 'in the line of Scott and Stevenson' (p. xii), while Haining sees Buchan as 'a master of the supernatural tale along the line of Poe and Stevenson by way of Bram Stoker and M. R. James to today's hugely successful exponents such as Ray Bradbury and Stephen King' (*Best Supernatural Tales*, p. 24). Buchan's admiration for Burns, Scott and Stevenson is a matter of record, but the influence of their supernatural fiction on his work is speculative. In his study on Scott's use of the supernatural, Coleman O. Parsons briefly discusses Buchan's supernatural texts, but he does not draw any comparisons with Scott's work in the genre. Like Lovecraft, Parsons praises *Witch Wood*, Buchan's depiction of evil, and his settings, but believes that his 'hasty composition and desire for moral clarity' lead him to oversimplify his characters, who as a result become 'champions of civilisation' battling 'apostles of chaos' (C. Parsons, *Witchcraft and Demonology in Scott's Fiction, with Chapters on the Supernatural in Scottish Literature* (Edinburgh: Oliver and Boyd, 1964), p. 317).
24. J. Buchan, 'A Journey of Little Profit', in *The Watcher by the Threshold*, ed. B. Roden and C. Roden, pp. 3–10, p. 10.
25. J. Buchan, 'No-Man's Land', pp. 3–102, p. 45.
26. See, for example, Buchan, 'A Journey of Little Profit'; 'The Herd of Standlan', in *The Watcher by the Threshold*, ed. B. Roden and C. Roden, pp. 11–20; 'The Moor Song', 'The Far Islands', 'Space', 'The Green Glen', 'Skule Skerry', 'Ho! The Merry Masons'.
27. Lovecraft, *Supernatural Horror in Literature*, p. 17.
28. J. Buchan, 'Skule Skerry', p. 304.
29. Ibid., p. 309.
30. Ibid.
31. Ibid., p. 310.
32. Ibid., p. 307.
33. Ibid., p. 311.
34. Ibid., p. 312.

35. Bell, 'Introduction', p. 74.
36. Lovecraft, *Supernatural Horror in Literature*, p. 15.
37. J. Buchan, 'Space', in *The Moon Endureth*, pp. 131–59, p. 139.
38. Ibid., p. 141.
39. Ibid., p. 145.
40. Ibid., p. 149.
41. Ibid., p. 150.
42. Ibid., p. 155.
43. Ibid., p. 158.
44. Lovecraft, *Supernatural Horror in Literature*, p. 12.
45. Buchan, 'The Green Wildebeest', p. 231.
46. Buchan, 'The Wind in the Portico', p. 300.
47. Buchan, 'Basilissa', p. 240.
48. Ibid., p. 241.
49. Ibid., p. 242.
50. Ibid., pp. 242–3.
51. Ibid., p. 248.
52. Haining, 'Introduction', *Best Supernatural Stories*, p. 9.

16 Miller, The Anarchist's Garden: Politics and Ecology in John Buchan's Wastelands

1.   T. S. Eliot, *The Waste Land*, *Selected Poems* (London: Faber and Faber, 1954), pp. 49–67, l. 1.
2.   Buchan, *The Three Hostages*, p. 7.
3.   Ibid.
4.   Eliot, *The Waste Land*, ll. 19–20.
5.   Ibid., ll. 71–2
6.   Buchan, *Memory Hold-the-Door*, p. 182.
7.   Ibid., p. 13.
8.   Ibid., p. 28.
9.   Buchan, *The Three Hostages*, p. 9.
10. Ibid., p. 116.
11. Ibid., p. 31.
12. Eliot, *The Waste Land*, l. 2.
13. M. North, *Reading 1922* (Oxford: Oxford University Press, 1999), p. 3.
14. Ibid., p. 7.
15. Cited in I. B. Nadel, *The Cambridge Introduction to Ezra Pound* (Cambridge: Cambridge University Press, 2007), p. viii.
16. Cited in Lownie, *John Buchan*, p. 169.
17. Buchan, *Huntingtower*, p. 14.
18. North, *Reading 1922*, p. 3.
19. Buchan, *Huntingtower*, pp. 34–5.
20. Buchan, *The Three Hostages*, p. 7.
21. Ibid., p. 23.
22. G. Garrard, *Ecocriticism* (Abingdon: Routledge, 2004), p. 108.
23. Buchan, *The Three Hostages*, p. 8.

24. Ibid., p. 21.
25. A later Conservative Member of Parliament for the Scottish Universities (elected 1927), he had stood unsuccessfully as a Unionist candidate in 1911 in Peebles.
26. Buchan, *The Three Hostages*, p. 8.
27. Ibid., p. 222.
28. Ibid., p. 23.
29. Buchan, *Huntingtower*, p. 68.
30. Buchan, *The Three Hostages*, p. 46.
31. Buchan, *Huntingtower*, p. 35.
32. Ibid., p. 61.
33. Ibid., p. 62.
34. Ibid., p. 64.
35. Buchan, *The Three Hostages*, p. 110.
36. For a full discussion of Islam and the East in Buchan's work see al-Rawi in this volume, pp. 117–28.
37. Buchan, *The Three Hostages*, p. 77.
38. Buchan, *Memory Hold-the-Door*, p. 46.
39. Ibid., pp. 13–14.
40. Buchan, *Sick Heart River*, p. 38.
41. Buchan, *The Three Hostages*, p. 77.
42. The trope of the urban jungle was well-established in writing about London either side of the war: the Salvation Army's General Booth's 1889 reimaging of Stanley's African explorations *In Darkest Africa* in his gloomy reportage of Britain's urban decline *In Darkest London* providing perhaps its most noted version.
43. To further accentuate the novel's complex geographical references the principal threat in *The Three Hostages* is from the Irish Medina rather than any tropical force.
44. Buchan, *The Power-House*, p. 33. The first articulation of this idea by Buchan in his fiction is in 'Fountainblue' (J. Buchan, 'Fountainblue', *The Watcher by the Threshold* (London: William Blackwood & Sons, 1915), pp. 265–334, p. 286).
45. Buchan, *Huntingtower*, p. 116.
46. Buchan, *The Three Hostages*, p. 13.
47. For an account of Saturn and Saturnalia see G. Shipley, J. Vanderspoel, D. Mattingley, L. Foxhall (eds), *The Cambridge Dictionary of Classical Civilization* (Cambridge: Cambridge University Press, 2006), p. 789.
48. Another example of Buchan's engagement with *Natura Maligna* appears in *Sick Heart River* particularly in Leithen's journey in a plane above 'a treacherous deathly waste, pale like a snake's belly, a thing beyond humanity and beyond time' (p. 52).
49. Buchan, *Memory Hold-the-Door*, p. 116.
50. Buchan, *The Power-House*, p. 38.
51. Ibid., p. 49.
52. Buchan, *The Three Hostages*, p. 171.
53. Ibid., p. 21.
54. Ibid., p. 72.
55. Ibid., p. 39.
56. Ibid., p. 229.
57. For an earlier version of Buchan's connection of hygiene and politics see *The Power-House*, at the beginning of which Leithen is discovered at work on legal briefs concerning a 'new

drainage scheme in West Ham' (p. 13) as his ensuing battle against Lumley's anarchists is similarly framed by the exigencies of urban waste management.

58. W. A. Cohen, 'Introduction', in W. A. Cohen and R. Johnson, (eds), *Filth: Dirt, Disgust and Modern Life* (Minneapolis, MN: University of Minnesota Press, 2005), pp. vii–xxxvii, p. xxi.

59. D. L. Pike, 'Sewage Treatments' in Cohen and Johnson (eds), *Filth: Dirt, Disgust and Modern Life*, pp. 51–77, p. 52.

60. Cohen, 'Introduction', p. xvii.

61. Buchan, *Huntingtower*, p. 29.

62. Ibid., p. 27.

63. Buchan, *Memory Hold-the-D*oor, p. 186.

64. Ibid., p. 150.

65. Ibid., p. 201.

66. G. Himmelfarb, *Victorian Minds* (London: Weidenfield and Nicolson, 1968), p. 255.

67. Eliot, *The Waste Land*, l. 188.

68. Ibid., l. 231.

69. Ibid., l. 158–9.

70. Buchan, *Huntingtower*, p. 167.

71. Buchan, *The Three Hostages*, p. 67.

72. J. Scanlon, *On Garbage* (London: Reaktion, 2005), p. 179.

73. Buchan, *The Three Hostages*, p. 175.

74. Buchan, *Huntingtower*, p. 32.

75. Buchan, *Memory Hold-the-D*oor, pp. 283–4.

17 Williams, Tracing *The Thirty-Nine Steps*

1. Adam Smith, *John Buchan*, p. 192.

2. Buchan, *The Thirty-Nine Steps*, p. 111.

3. See M. Yacowar, *Hitchcock's British Films* (Hamden, CT: Archon, 1970; R. Wood, *Hitchcock's Film Revisited* (New York: Columbia University Press, 1988); W. Rothman, *Hitchcock: The Murderous Gaze* (Cambridge, MA: Harvard University Press, 1982), and C. Barr, *English Hitchcock* (Moffatt: Cameron & Hollis, 1999), as representative examples of this tendency.

4. Macdonald, *John Buchan*, p. 171.

5. Although a fourth film version, made by BBC TV and broadcast on 28 December 2008, was in preparation at the time of this writing, it has not been possible to include this version in this study.

6. C. Orr, 'The Discourse on Adaptation', *Wide Angle*, 6:2 (1984), pp. 72–3.

7. Buchan, *The Thirty-Nine Steps*, p. 7.

8. Ibid., p. 8.

9. Ibid.

10. These are feelings later shared by Hitchcock characters such as Fred and Em in *Rich and Strange* (1932), Young Charlie in *Shadow of a Doubt* (1943), and Roger Thornhill in *North by North-West* (1959)

11. Buchan, *The Thirty-Nine Steps*, p. 8.

12. Scudder's Kentucky background implicitly suggests Ku-Klux Klan influence as well as upper-class prejudice. Coincidentally, D. W. Griffith's *The Birth of a Nation* (credited with reviving the fortunes of the Klan) was released in the same year as *The Thirty-Nine*

Steps. As several critics note, it is important to maintain a distinction between Buchan's own attitudes and those of his fictional characters. See especially Parry, 'From the Thirty-Nine Articles to the Thirty-Nine Steps'; Macdonald, *John Buchan*, pp. 40–4.

13. Buchan, *The Thirty-Nine Steps*, p. 81.
14. Ibid., pp. 11 & 12.
15. Ibid., p. 15.
16. Ibid., p. 17
17. This trope was used by Buchan in most of his fiction, first in his short story 'Fountain-blue' in 1901.
18. Buchan, *The Thirty-Nine Steps*, p. 16.
19. Ibid., p. 13.
20. Ibid., p. 20.
21. Ibid., p. 22.
22. Ibid., p. 24.
23. Ibid., p. 26. Like Roger Thornhill in *North by North-west* (1959) who tells Eve 'I never felt more alive' after his own reluctant involvement in a later version of the Great Game.
24. Buchan, *The Thirty-Nine Steps*, p. 26.
25. Ibid., p. 33.
26. See K. Macdonald 'Artemis and Aphrodite', Chapter 9 of this volume.
27. For this concept see J. Bergstrom, 'Alternation, Segmentation, Hypnosis: Interview with Raymond Bellour', *Camera Obscura*, 3:4 (1979), pp. 87–93, also cited by T. Ryall, 'One Hundred and Seventeen Steps towards Masculinity', in P. Kirkham and J. Thumim (eds), *You Tarzan: Masculinity, Movies and Men* (London: Lawrence and Wishart, 1993), p. 88. A. Devas also notes that Hitchcock 'takes a classic imperial text and re-invents it as a modernist one, combining tropes of the adventure story with aestheticised technology, comedy, and a narrative which includes the feminine sexuality which is so determinedly absent from the novel', (A. Devas, 'How to be a Hero: Space, Place and Masculinity in *The 39 Steps* (Hitchcock, UK, 1935), *Journal of Gender Studies* 14:1 (2005), pp. 45–6). By contrast, I believe that Julia and Marmaduke represent different versions of this fear of the feminine.
28. Buchan, *The Thirty-Nine Steps*, p. 34.
29. Ibid., p. 109. Buchan's contemporary, 'Sapper', gives the knee-tapping giveaway to his evil mastermind Carl Peterson in his four Bulldog Drummond novels (1920–6).
30. Where his wife nursed him, wrote and signed his letters for him (to dictation), and ran the household (which apart from John Buchan was herself and their daughter, a burgeoning matriarchy).
31. Buchan, *The Thirty-Nine Steps*, p. 55.
32. Parry, 'From The Thirty-Nine Articles to the Thirty-Nine Steps', p. 228.
33. See Rothman, *Hitchcock*, especially pp. 11–14, 59–67, 71–4, 93–102, 157–60.
34. Buchan, *The Thirty-Nine Steps*, p. 42.
35. Ibid., p. 55.
36. Ibid., p. 57.
37. Ibid., p. 67.
38. Ibid., p. 73.
39. Ibid., p. 78.
40. Ibid., p. 81.
41. Ibid., p. 86.
42. Ibid., p. 87.

43. Ibid., p. 102.
44. Ibid., p. 104.
45. Ibid., p. 107.
46. Ibid., p. 64.
47. Ibid., p. 111.
48. Ibid., p. 8.
49. Rothman, *Hitchcock*, p. 118.
50. Buchan, *The Thirty-Nine Steps*, p. 21.
51. Tom Ryall has noted the different cultural contexts influencing the novel and each film version ('One Hundred and Seventeen Steps', pp. 153–4). The question asked frequently by the henpecked husband in the Hitchock film, 'What causes pip in poultry?', has sexual overtones. 'Pip' 'is also a slang term for venereal disease and the link between subversion and sexuality that is initiated here runs throughout the film. The power play that is at the heart of the story – one nation seeking to weaken, dominate and control another – is paralleled in everyday sexual relationships, including that of the timid husband who dares to ask this question and the wife who so swiftly rebukes him' (M. Glancy, *The 39 Steps* (London: I.B. Tauris, 2003), pp. 43–5). This also represents another significant extension of Julia's 'structured absence ' from novel to film.
52. As in Howard Hawks's *Twentieth Century* (1934)
53. Buchan, *The Thirty-Nine Steps*, p. 103.
54. Ibid., p. 23.
55. Ibid., p. 24.
56. Rothman, *Hitchcock*, p. 127 & p. 145.
57. T. Kuntzel, 'The Film Work 2' *Camera Obscura*, 5 (1980), pp. 7–72.
58. Buchan, *The Thirty-Nine Steps*, p. 104.
59. Wood, *Hitchcock's Film Revisited*, p. 283.
60. See T. Modleski, *The Women who Knew Too Much: Hitchcock and Feminist Theory* (New York: Routledge, 1989).
61. This also suggests the type of intelligence work that Buchan engaged in during the First World War two years after *The Thirty-Nine Steps* was published
62. Macdonald, *John Buchan*, pp. 175–6.
63. Although Robert Powell repeated the role in the 1988–9 Thames Television series *Hannay*, none of the episodes bore any relation to any Buchan story. However, BBC TV adapted *The Three Hostages* twice. A 1952 six-episode version featured Patrick Barr as Hannay while a 1977 teleplay starred Barry Foster in the same role. See T. Vahmagi (ed.), *British Television: An Illustrated Guide* (New York: Oxford University Press, 1996), 316.
64. Buchan, *The Thirty-Nine Steps*, p. 102.
65. Harvie, 'Introduction' to Buchan, *The Thirty-Nine Steps*.
66. D. Daniell, 'At the Foot of the Thirty-Ninth step', *John Buchan Journal*, 10 (1991), pp. 15–26.
67. F. Truffaut, *Hitchcock* (New York: Touchstone, 1984), p. 95, p. 307, p. 308.

WORKS CITED

Works by John Buchan

Since the editions of Buchan's works cited in the essays in this book are in a mixture of modern and older editions, it was felt to be more convenient to the reader to order these alphabetically by title (excepting definite articles and the like) as a separate section of the Bibliography. Dates of original publication are given as well as the date of the edition.

'Abraham Lincoln', review of F. Fisher Browne, *The Everyday Life of Abraham Lincoln*, *Spectator* (18 July 1914), p. 94.

The African Colony: Studies in the Reconstruction (Edinburgh: William Blackwood and Sons, 1903).

'The American Civil War', review of J.K. Hosmer, *The American Civil War (London: Harper and Brothers)* in *The Spectator* (14 Feb 1914), pp. 267–8.

'The American Experiment in Imperial Reconstruction', *Spectator* (27 February 1904), pp. 323–4.

'The American People' [review of H. Munsterberg], *The American, Spectator*, (17 June 1905), pp. 894–5.

'America Today' [review of A.R. Colquhoun, *Greater America*], *Spectator* (2 July 1904), pp. 16–18.

Augustus (1937; London: Hodder and Stoughton, 1941).

'Basil Worsfold's *The Reconstruction of the New Colonies under Lord Milner*' [book review], *Times Literary Supplement* (20 November 1913), p. 549.

'Basilissa', *The Watcher by the Threshold*, ed. B. Roden and C. Roden (1914; Ashcroft, BC: Ash-Tree Press, 2005), pp. 240–51.

The Best Supernatural Stories of John Buchan, ed. P. Haining (London: Robert Hale, 1991)

The Blanket of the Dark (1931; Edinburgh: B&W Publishing, 1993).

Brasenose College: University of Oxford College Histories (London: F. E. Robinson, 1898).

'Britain and the United States', *The Spectator*, (26 Jan. 1907), p. 128.

'British Settlements in the New Colonies', *Blackwood's Magazine* CLXXI (January 1902), pp. 145–58.

Canadian Occasions: Addresses by Lord Tweedsmuir (London: Hodder & Stoughton, 1940).

Castle Gay (1930; London: Dent, 1983).

'The Close of the Transvaal Labour Commission', *The Spectator* (24 October 1903), pp. 640–1.

'Count Tolstoi and the Idealism of War', in *Some Eighteenth Century Byways* (1904; Edinburgh: William Blackwood, 1908), pp. 294–300.

The Courts of the Morning (1929; Edinburgh: B&W Publishing, 1993).

The Dancing Floor (1926; Oxford: Oxford University Press, 1997).

'The Debate on the Refugee Camps', *The Spectator* (22 June 1901), pp. 905–6.

'The Edinburgh on South Africa', *Spectator* (26 January 1901), pp. 131–2.

'The Far Islands', in *The Watcher by the Threshold* (1899; London: William Blackwood & Sons, 1915), pp. 103–48.

'Fountainblue', *The Watcher by the Threshold* (1901; London: William Blackwood & Sons, 1915), pp. 265–334.

The Free Fishers (1934; Edinburgh: B&W Publishing, 1994).

'From the Pentlands Looking North and South', *The Moon Endureth: Tales and Fancies* (1912; London: Thomas Nelson & Sons, 1923), pp. 9–12.

'Fullcircle', *The Watcher by the Threshold*, ed. B. Roden and C. Roden (1920; Ashcroft, BC: Ash-Tree Press, 2005), pp. 252–63.

The Gap in the Curtain (1932; London: Thomas Nelson & Sons, 1934).

'The Green Glen', *The Moon Endureth: Tales and Fancies* (1912; London: Thomas Nelson & Sons, 1923), pp. 291–327.

Greenmantle (1916; Oxford: Oxford University Press, 1993).

'The Green Wildebeest', in *The Watcher by the Threshold*, ed. B. Roden and C. Roden (1927; Ashcroft, BC: Ash-Tree Press, 2005), pp. 226–39.

'The Grove of Ashtaroth', *The Moon Endureth: Tales and Fancies* (1910; London: Thomas Nelson & Sons, 1923), pp. 187–224.

The Half-Hearted (1900; London: Hodder & Stoughton, 1920).

'The Herd of Standlan', in *The Watcher by the Threshold*, ed. B. Roden and C. Roden (1899; Ashcroft, BC: Ash-Tree Press, 2005), pp. 11–20.

A History of the Great War, 4 vols (1933; London: Thomas Nelson & Sons, 1921–2).

The History of the Royal Scots Fusiliers (1926; London: Thomas Nelson & Sons, 1925).

The History of the South African Forces in France (London: Thomas Nelson & Sons, 1920).

'Ho! The Merry Masons', in *The Watcher by the Threshold*, ed. B. Roden and C. Roden (1933; Ashcroft, BC: Ash-Tree Press, 2005), pp. 238–50.

Homilies and Recreations (1926; London: Hodder and Stoughton, 1939)

The House of the Four Winds (London: Hodder & Stoughton, 1935).

Huntingtower (1922; Oxford: Oxford University Press, 1996).

'Hysteria in the Press' (1908), in *Comments and Characters by John Buchan*, ed. W. Gray (London: Nelson, 1940), pp. 267–71.

The Island of Sheep (1936; Oxford: Oxford University Press, 1996).

John Macnab (1925; Oxford: Oxford University Press, 1994).

'A Journey of Little Profit', in *The Watcher by the Threshold*, ed. B. Roden and C. Roden (1896; Ashcroft BC: Ash-Tree Press, 2005), pp. 3–10.

Julius Caesar (London: Peter Davies, 1938).

The King's Grace (London: Hodder and Stoughton, 1935).

'The Kings of Orion', in *The Moon Endureth: Tales and Fancies* (1906; London: Thomas Nelson & Sons, 1923), pp. 251–86.

The Last Secrets: The Final Mysteries of Exploration (London: Thomas Nelson & Sons, 1923).

'Leopold Amery's *The 'Times' History of the War in South Africa, 1899–1902*, volumes 6 and 7' [book review], *The Spectator* (10 July 1909), pp. 57–8.

'The Little Englander', *Spectator* (18 January 1902), p. 86 [under the pseudonym J. Saxon Mills].

A Lodge in the Wilderness (1906; London: Thomas Nelson & Sons, 1916).

'Lord Tweedsmuir's Address', *John Buchan Journal*, 9 (Winter 1989), pp. 2–8.

'A Lucid Interval', *The Moon Endureth. Tales and Fancies* (1910; London: Thomas Nelson & Sons, 1923), pp. 55–97.

The Magic Walking Stick (1932; Edinburgh: Canongate, 1985).

Memory Hold-the-Door (London: Hodder & Stoughton, 1940).

Men and Deeds (London: Peter Davies, 1935).

Midwinter: Certain Travellers in Old England (1923; Edinburgh: B&W Publishing, 1993).

Montrose (London: Thomas Nelson & Sons, 1928).

'Montrose on Sovereign Power' in *Montrose* (London: Thomas Nelson & Sons, 1928), pp. 361–70.

The Moon Endureth. Tales and Fancies (1912; London: Thomas Nelson & Sons, 1923)

'The Moor Song', in *The Watcher by the Threshold*, ed. B. Roden and C. Roden (1897; Ashcroft, BC: Ash-Tree Press, 2005), pp. 36–42.

'Mr Caddell. An appreciation', *John Buchan Journal*, 20, pp. 2–3.

Mr Standfast (1919; Oxford: Oxford University Press, 1993).

'The Native Peril in South Africa', *The Spectator* (17 February 1906), pp. 246–7

Nelson's History of the War, 24 vols (London: Thomas Nelson & Sons, 1915–19).

Nine Brasenose Worthies, Brasenose College Quatercentenary Monographs (Oxford: Clarendon Press, 1909), Volume II XIV 2.

'No-Man's Land', in *The Watcher by the Threshold* (1899; London: William Blackwood & Sons, 1915), pp. 3–102.

'The Old Journalism and the New', (1908), in *Comments and Characters by John Buchan*, ed. W. F. Gray (London: Nelson, 1940), pp. 260–1.

'Olive Schreiner, *Thoughts on South Africa*' [book review], *Times Literary Supplement* (21 June 1923), p. 411.

Oliver Cromwell (London: Hodder & Stoughton, 1934).

'The Outgoing of the Tide', *The Watcher by the Threshold* (1902; London: William Blackwood & Sons, 1915), pp. 225–64.

The Path of the King (1921; London: Thomas Nelson & Sons, 1924).

The Power-House, in *The Power-House & The Thirty-Nine Steps* (1913; Edinburgh: B&W Publishing, 1999).

Prester John (1910; Oxford: Oxford University Press, 1994).

A Prince of the Captivity (1933; Edinburgh: B&W Publishing, 1996).

'The Problem of Defence' (1907), in *Comments and Characters by John Buchan*, ed. W. F. Gray (London: Nelson, 1940), pp. 8–11.

The Purpose of War (London: Dent, 1916).

'The Reconstruction of South Africa – Land Settlement', *National Review* 230 (April 1902), pp. 316–36.

'Romancers: John Buchan and T. E. Lawrence', *T. E. Notes*, 4:1 (January 1993), p. 2.

The Scottish Tongue: A Series of Lectures on the Vernacular Language of Lowland Scotland (London: Cassell & Co., 1924).

Sick Heart River (1941; Oxford: Oxford University Press, 1994).

Sir Quixote of the Moors (1895; Kansas City: Valancourt Press, 2008).

'Skule Skerry', in *The Watcher by the Threshold*, ed. B. Roden and C. Roden (1928; Ashcroft, BC: Ash-Tree Press, 2005), pp. 302–12.

'South African Native Race Committee (ed.), *The South African Native: Progress and Present Condition*' [book review], *Times Literary Supplement* (4 February 1909), p. 38.

'Space', *The Moon Endureth. Tales and Fancies* (1911; London: Thomas Nelson & Sons, 1923), pp. 131–59.

Supernatural Buchan: Stories of Ancient Spirits, Uncanny Places and Strange Creatures (London: Leonaur Press, 2007).

Supernatural Tales, ed. J. C. G. Greig (Edinburgh: B&W Publishing, 1997).

'Tendebant Manus', in *The Watcher by the Threshold*, ed. B. Roden and C. Roden (1927; Ashcroft, BC: Ash-Tree Press, 2005), pp. 274–84.

These for Remembrance (privately printed, 1919).

The Thirty-Nine Steps (1915; Oxford: Oxford University Press, 1993).

The Three Hostages (1924; Oxford: Oxford University Press, 1995).

'*Transvaal Problems* by Lionel Phillips' [book review], *Times Literary Supplement* (24 November 1905), p. 402.

'The True Danger of Socialism' (1907), ed. W. F. Gray, *Comments and Characters by John Buchan*, (London: Nelson, 1940), pp. 173–6.

'Two Ordeals of Democracy', in *Homilies and Recreations* (1925; London: Hodder and Stoughton, 1939), pp. 89–119.

'The United States and Cuba', *The Spectator*, (22 September 1906), pp. 391–2.

University of Oxford College Histories: Brasenose College (London: F.E. Robinson, 1898).

'Violet Markham's *The South African Scene*' [book review], *Times Literary Supplement* (4 December 1913), p. 583.

'The Watcher by the Threshold', *The Watcher by the Threshold* (1900; London: William Blackwood & Sons, 1915), pp. 149–224.

'The Wind in the Portico', in *The Watcher by the Threshold*, ed. B. Roden and C. Roden (1928; Ashcroft, BC: Ash-Tree Press, 2005), pp. 285–301.

Witch Wood (1927; Edinburgh: Canongate, 1988).

'Wood Magic', in *The Moon Endureth* (London: Thomas Nelson, 1912), pp.225–6.

John Buchan's Collected Poems, ed. A. Lownie and W. Milne (Aberdeen: Scottish Cultural Press, 1996).

The Complete Short Stories, Volume 3, ed. A. Lownie (London: Thistle Publishing, 1997).

Works Edited by John Buchan

English Literature, Volume II (Edinburgh: New University Society, 1923).

The Nations of To-day: A New History of the World (London: Thomas Nelson & Sons, 1923).

With Sir Henry Newbolt (eds), *Days to Remember: The British Empire in the Great War* (London: Thomas Nelson & Sons, 1923).

Correspondence (ordered chronologically)

Milner to Buchan, 18 August 1901, CT 288/JL55/03: National Archives of South Africa (NASA).

Buchan to Lady Mary Murray, 26 August 1901, Gilbert Murray Papers (GMP), mss 126: Bodleian Library Oxford (BLO).

Buchan to William Buchan, 7 October 1901, John Buchan Papers (JBP), Queens University (QU) mff 303: National Library of Scotland (NLS).

Buchan to Charles Dick, 8 October 1901, Charles Dick Papers (CDP): University Library Edinburgh (ULE).

Buchan to Strachey, 11 October 1901, St Loe Strachey Papers(SLSP) s/3/2/1: (House of Lords Record Office) HLRO.

Buchan to Strachey, 13 October 1901, SLSP s/3/2/2: HLRO.

Buchan to Strachey, 6 November 1901, SLSP, s/3/2/5:HLRO.

Hobhouse to Milner, 11 November 1901, in Despatch 994 (Despatches Transvaal and Orange River Colony), CO510 (National Archives UK).

Milner to Chamberlain, 19 November 1901, CO 545/11/140948: NAUK.

Secretary Land Board ORC to APS to Milner, 25 December 1901, Gov 505/583301: NASA.

Buchan to Strachey, 28 December 1901, SLSP s/3/2/5: HLRO.

Despatch SA110, 25 January 1902, Gov 505/4799: NASA.

Buchan to Strachey, 28 January 1902, SLSP 8/3/2/8: HLRO.

Buchan to O/C Orange Free State Camps, 4 March 1902: John Buchan Mss, Brown University, Rhode Island.

Buchan to Strachey, 12 March 1902, SLSP s/3/2/10: HLRO.

Maxwell [Military Governor Pretoria] to Buchan, 25 March 1902, Gov 498/4500.

Despatch no 192, 25 April 1902, Gov 507/2373: NASA.

Private Secretary Land Board to Provost Marshall, 2 May 1902, MPO 59/4121/02: NASA.

Secretary Land Board to Provost Marshall, 2 May 1902, PMO 59/PM4141: NASA.

Secretary to Land Board ORC to Officer Commanding, Durban, 15 May 1902, PMO41/PM2774/01: NASA.

APM Natal to Officer Commanding, Durban, 21 May 1902, PMO41/PM2774/01: NASA.

Private Secretary to Milner to Campbell, 30 May 1902, PMO 57/3931/02: NASA.

Superintendent, Jacobs Camp 2 June 1902 (enclosing cutting from *Natal Mercury*, 30 May 1902), Gov 498: NASA.

Buchan to AG, 7 June 1902, LD 82/AG 3583B

Buchan to AG, 10 June 1902, LD 82/AG 3583B

Buchan to Strachey, 10 June 1902, SLSP s/3/2/13: HLRO.

Buchan to Strachey, 3 August 1902, SLSP, s/3/2/14: HLRO.

AG to Buchan 12 August 1902: Gov 484/PS 129/02: NASA.

Buchan to Charles Dick, 20 September 1902: JBP QUmss 310: NLS.

Assistant Resident Magistrate Krugersdorp to ACS, 2 October 1902, CS 144/11865: NASA.

Buchan to Murray, 16 November 1902, JBP QUmff 303: NLS.

Buchan to Anna Buchan, 17 November 1902: JBP QUmff 303: NLS.

Buchan to Stair Gillon, 23 November 1902 (wrongly located with papers for November 1901), JBP QUmff 303: NLS.

Buchan to his mother, 7 December 1902, JBP QUmff 303: NLS.

Buchan to Director of Public Works Department, 9 December 1902, PWD 56/4901/02: NASA.

Buchan to Anna Buchan, 21 December 1902: JBP QUmff 303: NLS.

Buchan to Strachey, 10 January 1903, SLSP s/3/2/7 (number wrongly attributed): HLRO.

Buchan to Milner, 9 February 1903, LTG 91/9619: NASA.

Postscript on Buchan to Milner, 9 February 1903, LTG 91/9619: NASA.

Buchan to Strachey, 22 February 1903, SLSP, s/3/2/19: HLRO.

Buchan to CS Transvaal, 25 February 1903, CS191/10156/02: NASA.

H. A. Lawrence to Lord Milner, 13 April 1903, G481: NASA.

Buchan to Strachey, 20 May 1903, SLSP, s/3/2/21: HLRO.

Buchan to Strachey, 17 July 1903, SLSP, s/3/2/22:HLRO.

F.J. Henley to Milner, 17 August 1903, LMP 74 & 253: BLO.

F.D. Smith to Basil Williams, 17 July 1904, Mss Afri S.132, vol. 3 (Basil Williams Papers): RHO.

F.D. Smith to Basil Williams, 11 December 1904, Mss Afri S.132, vol. 3 (Basil Williams Papers): RHO.

Buchan to Walter Blackie, 25 June 1905, Blackie Papers, Ms2641: NLS.

Milner to Buchan, 8 February 1910, JBP, Acc 6975: NLS.

Milner to Buchan, 16 November 1910, JBP, Acc 6975: NLS.

Buchan to Liddell Hart, December 1916, Liddell Hart papers, Liddell Hart Centre for Military Archives (LHCMA), King's College London, LH 1/124/1.

Milner to Buchan, 27 April 1921, JBP, Acc 6975:NLS.

Buchan to Ferris Greenslet, 19 May 1925, Houghton Mifflin Papers, bMs Am1925, Houghton Library, Harvard University.

Buchan to Liddell Hart, 19 February 1935, LHCMA, LH 1/124/60.

Interview with Lord Leconfield, 1 March 1959, Janet Adam Smith Papers: NLS.

Manuscript Sources

Milner's Diary, 5 October 1901, Lord Milner Papers (LMP) 71: BLO.

Draft by Buchan headed 'Barberton Commission: Letter defining terms of reference', Gov 483/PS 129/0 vol 4: NASA.

'Land Settlement in the Transvaal', June 1902, Mss Afr s. 2210/7: RHLO.

Transvaal Consolidated Land and Exploration Co Ltd: Report on Agricultural Prospects in the Transvaal, 30 January 1903, Mss Afr s. 2210/2 f14/2; RHLO.

Cutting from the *Scotsman*, 16 January & 5 December 1904, JBP, QUmff 317.

J. Buchan, 'The Mountain', JBP, QUmss 324:NLS.

Main Bibliography

Anon., Review of F.S. Oliver, *Alexander Hamilton: An Essay on American Union*, (London: Constable, 1906), *Spectator* (14 July 1906), pp. 58–60.

—, 'Nasionale Strijders', *De Zuid Afrikaan* (16 September 1914), p. 8.

—, 'Ons Kinders', *Zwartlander* (12 October 1914), p. 9.

—, 'Rosebery sees Blessings in War', *New York Times* (23 January 1915), p. BR 452.

—, 'Disloyal Patriotism', *The Pretoria Friend* (24 April 1915), p. 17.

—, 'British Role in Allies' Advance on West Front', *Christian Science Monitor* (25 October 1915), p. 2.

—, 'British Success in West Discussed', *Christian Science Monitor* (26 October 1915), p. 2.

—, 'Frederick Palmer's View of the War', *New York Times* (21 November 1915), p. 2.

—, 'American Civil War Lessons for Britain', *Christian Science Monitor* (20 March 1916), p. 3.

—, 'Conan Doyle's History of the War', *New York Times* (21 January 1917), p. BR 2.

—, 'With Authors and Publishers', *New York Times* (20 January 1918), p. 56.

—, 'Conscientious Objectors', *The Times* (4 January 1919), p. 8.

—, 'Cause and Conscience', *Rand Daily Mail* (17 November 1920), p. 14.

—, 'From the Recent War', *Natal Witness* (21 November 1920), p. 10.

—, 'A Great Soldier of the Great War', *Selbornian*, 21 (1922), pp. 12–13.

—, 'A Gift for our Age', *Bloemfontein Sun* (28 November 1925), p. 16.

—, 'Springbok Heroism in Europe', *Cape Times* (23 October 1926), p. 6.

—, 'Today on the Radio', *New York Times* (30 November 1934), p. 17.

—, 'Columbia Opens Its New Library; Buchan Outlines Role for Colleges', *New York Times* (1 December 1934), p. 15.

—, 'Hail Tweedsmuir with Capital Pomp', *New York Times* (31 March 1937), p. 3.

—, 'A College Tutor', Letter to the Editor, *The Times* (3 January 1903), p. 6.

—, 'JB at Yale, 1938', *John Buchan Journal*, 15 (1996), pp. 20–2.

Adam Smith, J., *John Buchan: A Biography* (London: Rupert Hart-Davis, 1965).

Adams, R. J. Q., and P. P. Poirer, *The Conscription Controversy in Great Britain, 1900–18* (Basingstoke: Macmillan, 1987).

Aljubouri, D. A. H., 'The Medieval Idea of the Saracen, as Illustrated in English Literature, Spectacle and Sport' (Ph.D. dissertation, University of Leicester, 1972).

Almond, H. H., 'Letter to the Editor', *The Times* (15 January 1902), p. 12.

Anderson, R. D., 'Sport in the Scottish Universities, 1860–1939', *International Journal of the History of Sport*, 4:2 (1987), pp. 177–88.

Aristotle, *The Ethics of Aristotle: The Nichomachean Ethics* (London: Penguin, revised edition, 1976).

—, *The Politics* (London: Penguin, revised edition, 1992).

Arnold, Matthew, 'The Scholar Gypsy', ed. C. B. Tinker and H. F. Lowry, *The Poetical Works of Matthew Arnold* (London: Oxford University Press, 1955), pp. 255–62.

J. C. B., 'Letter to the Editor', *The Times* (11 January 1902), p. 11.

Badsey, S. and P. Taylor, 'Images of Battle: The Press, Propaganda and Passchendaele', in P. H. Liddle (ed.), *Passchendaele: The Third Battle of Ypres* (London: Leo Cooper, 1997), pp. 371–92.

Bailey, H., in *Hannie Richards, or, The Intrepid Adventures of a Restless Wife* (London: Virago, 1986)

Baker, H., *Architecture and Personalities* (London: Country Life, 1944).

Balderston, J. L., 'Grant and Lee Invented "New" Trench Warfare', *Duluth News-Tribune* (27 August 1916), p. 2.

Baldick, C., *The Oxford English Literary History, vol 10, 1910–1940; The Modern Movement* (Oxford: Oxford University Press, 2004).

Barr, C., *English Hitchcock* (Moffatt: Cameron & Hollis, 1999).

Barth, K., *The Epistle to the Romans*, trans. Sir E. C. Hoskyns (Oxford: Oxford University Press, 1933, pb 1968).

Bar-Yosef, E., 'The Last Crusade: British Propaganda and the Palestine Campaign, 1917–18', *Journal of Contemporary History*, 36:1 (January 2001), pp. 93, 95.

Beetham, M., *A Magazine of her Own? Domesticity and Desire in the Woman's Magazine 1800–1914* (London: Routledge, 1996).

Bell, G. L., *The Desert and the Sown* (London: William Heinemann, 1907).

Bell, J., ed. *John Buchan's The Far Islands and Other Tales of Fantasy* (West Kingston, RI: D. M. Grant, 1984).

Bell, J., 'Introduction', in J. Buchan, *The Far Islands and Other Tales of Fantasy*, J. Bell (ed.), (West Kingston, RI: D. M. Grant, 1984), pp. 16–17.

Bergstrom, J., 'Alternation, Segmentation, Hypnosis: Interview with Raymond Bellour', *Camera Obscura*, 3:4 (1979), pp. 87–93.

Bibbings, L., 'State Reaction to Conscientious Objectors', in I. Loveland (ed.), *Frontiers of Criminality* (London: Sweet, 1995), pp. 57–81.

—, 'Images of Manliness: The Portrayal of Soldiers and Conscientious Objectors in the Great War', *Social Legal Studies*, 12:3 (2003), pp. 335–58.

Biéler, A., *Calvin's Economic and Social Thought* (*La pensée économique et sociale de Calvin*) (Geneva: World Council of Churches/World Alliance of Reformed Churches, 2005).

Birley, A., 'Sir Ronald Syme', *Independent* (7 September 1989), p. 35.

Blake, R. (ed.), *Private Papers of Douglas Haig 1914–1919* (London: Eyre & Spottiswode, 1952)

Bloom, H., *A Map of Misreading* (Oxford: Oxford University Press, 2003).

Boulton, D., *Objection Overruled* (London: MacGibbon, 1967).

Brantlinger, P., *Rule of Darkness: British Literature and Imperialism* (Ithaca, NY: Cornell University Press, 1988).

Bristow, J., *Empire Boys: Adventures in a Man's World* (London: Harper Collins, 1991).

Brockway, A. F., *Socialism for Pacifists* (Manchester: National Labour Press, 1916).

Burnett, C. J., and H. Bennett, *The Green Mantle: A Celebration of the Revival in 1687 of the Most Ancient and Most Noble Order of the Thistle* (Edinburgh: National Museums of Scotland, 1989).

Buchan, A., *A Scrap Screen* (London: Hamish Hamilton Ltd, 1979).

Buchan, A [O. Douglas], *Unforgettable, Unforgotten* (London: Hodder and Stoughton Ltd, 1945).

Buchan, J., 'Romancers Entwined: John Buchan and T. E. Lawrence', *T. E. Notes,* IV: 1 (January 1993), pp. 13–14.

Buchan, W., 'Introduction', in J. Buchan, *Mr Standfast* (Oxford: Oxford University Press, 1993), pp. vii–xxii.

—, *John Buchan: A Memoir* (London: Buchan & Enright, 1982).

Buitenhuis, P., *The Great War of Words: Literature as Propaganda 1914–18 and After* (London: Batsford, 1989).

Bussell, F. W., 'Lord Tweedsmuir', *The Brazen Nose*, 7:2 (1940), pp. 40–2.

Byers, E., *The British Empire: Its Origin and Destiny* (Ottawa: James T. Pattison, 1922).

Calvin, J., *Institutes of the Christian Religion,* trans. J. Allen, 2 vols (London: J. Clarke & Co, 1935),

Cameron, A., *Procopius and the Sixth Century* (London: Routledge, 1996).

Cannadine, D., *History in Our Time* (London: Penguin, 2000).

Cannan, J., 'Novels of Character', *The Bookman*, 84:503 (August 1933), p. 260.

Chandler, A. D., *The Visible Hand* (Cambridge, MA: Harvard University Press, 1977).

—, *Scale and Scope: Dynamics of Industrial Capitalism* (Cambridge, MA: Harvard University Press, 1990).

Charteris, J., *At G.H.Q.* (London: Cassell, 1931)

Cohen, W. A., 'Introduction', in W. A. Cohen and R. Johnson, (eds), *Filth: Dirt, Disgust and Modern Life* (Minneapolis, MN: University of Minnesota Press, 2005), pp. vii–xxxvii.

Cole, S., 'Modernism, Male Intimacy, and the Great War', *ELH*, 68 (2001), pp. 469–500.

Coleman, D. C., 'Gentlemen and Players', *Economic History Review*, 2nd ser., 26: 1 (1973), p. 92–116.

Conrad, J., *Almayer's Folly* (London: Dent, 1946).

—, *Victory* (London: Dent, 1948).

—, *The Collected Letters of Joseph Conrad: Volume 2, 1898–1902*, ed. F. R. Karl and L. Davies (Cambridge: Cambridge University Press, 1986).

Daniel, N., *Islam, Europe and Empire* (Edinburgh: University Press, 1962).

Daniell, D., *The Interpreter's House: A Critical Assessment of the Works of John Buchan* (Edinburgh: Thomas Nelson & Sons, 1975).

—, 'At the Foot of the Thirty-Ninth step', *John Buchan Journal*, 10 (1991), pp. 15–26.

Darwin, C., *The Descent of Man and Action in Relation to Sex* (New York: Clarke, Given and Hooper, Publishers, 1874).

Davenport-Hines, R., 'Frederick Scott Oliver', *Oxford Dictionary of National Biography* Oxford University Press, Sept 2004; online edn, Jan 2008 [http://www.oxforddnb.com/view/article/35305, accessed 19 Nov 2008].

Deegan, M., 'Introduction', in John Buchan, *The Dancing Floor* (Oxford: Oxford University Press, 1997), pp. vii–xxix.

Dekoven, M., *Rich and Strange: Gender, History and Modernism* (Princeton, NJ: Princeton University Press, 1991).

Denoon, D., *A Grand Illusion: The failure of imperial policy in the Transvaal Colony during the period of reconstruction, 1900–1906* (London: Longman, 1973).

Deslandes, P. R., *Oxbridge Men: British Masculinity and the Undergraduate Experience, 1850–1920* (Bloomington, IN and Indianapolis, IN: Indiana University Press, 2005).

Deterding, H., *An International Oilman* (London: Ivor Nicholson and Watson, 1934).

Devas, A., 'How to be a Hero: Space, Place and Masculinity in *The 39 Steps* (Hitchcock, UK, 1935)', *Journal of Gender Studies* 14:1 (2005), pp. 45–6.

Dicey, A. V., 'The Conscientious Objector', *Nineteenth Century and After*, 88 (1918), pp. 357–73.

Dumesmil, R., and J. Barsen, 'Flaubert, Gustave', *Encyclopaedia Britannica* (London: Encyclopaedia Britannica, 1992), p. 823.

Dunlop, A. D., *Hutcheson's Grammar: The History of a Glasgow School* (Glasgow: Hutcheson's Educational Trust, 1992).

Edwards, O. D., 'John Buchan: Novelist, Publisher & Politician', in A. Reid and B. D. Osbourne (eds), *Discovering Scottish Writers* (Hamilton & Edinburgh: Scottish Library Association & Scottish Cultural Press, 1997), p. 16.

Eliot, T. S., 'The Waste Land', *Selected Poems* (London: Faber and Faber, 1954), pp. 49–67.

Ellison, G., *An Englishwoman in a Turkish Harem* (London: Methuen & Co. Ltd., 1915).

English, R. and M. Kenny (eds), *Rethinking British Decline* (London: Macmillan, 2000).

Epstein, H., '*Victory*'s Marionettes: Conrad's Revisitation of Stevenson', in K. Carabine, O. Knowles and P. Armstrong (eds) *Conrad, James and Other Relations* (Boulder, CO: Social Science Monographs; Lublin: Maria Curie-Skłodowska University, 1998).

Estés, C. P., *Women who Run with the Wolves. Myths and Stories of the Wild Woman Archetype* (New York: Ballantine Books, 1992).

Ferguson, J., 'Scottish Patriotism and Imperial Duty', *Scotia*, 2:3 (Lammas 1908), pp. 145–8.

Ferguson, R., *The Short Sharp Life of T. E. Hulme* (London: Allen Lane, 2002).

Fitzroy, A. T. [R. Allatini], *Despised and Rejected* (1917), intro. J. Cutbill (London: Gay Men's Press, 1988).

Frazer, J. G., *The Golden Bough. A Study in Magic and Religion*, abridged edition (London: Macmillan, 1925).

French, D., 'Sir James Edmonds and the Official History: France and Belgium', in B. Bond (ed.), *The First World War and British Military History* (Oxford: Clarendon Press, 1991).

Frye, N., *Anatomy of Criticism* (Princeton, NJ: Princeton University Press, 1957).

Garrard, G., *Ecocriticism* (Abingdon: Routledge New Critical Idiom, 2004).

Garson, N. G., 'South Africa and World War 1', *Journal of Imperial and Commonwealth History*, 8, 1 (1979), pp. 83–108.

George, D. L., *War Memoirs of David Lloyd George*, 2 vols (London: Odhams Press, 1938).

Genette, G., *Palimpsests: Literature in the Second Degree*, trans. C. Newman and C. Doubinsky (Lincoln, NE: University of Nebraska Press, 1997).

Gifford, D., S. Dunnigan, B. Dickson, A. MacGillivray (eds), *Scottish Literature in English and Scots* (Edinburgh: Edinburgh University Press, 2002).

Glancy, M., *The 39 Steps* (London: I.B. Tauris, 2003).

Glasier, J. B., *The Peril of Conscription* (London: Independent Labour Party, 1915).

Glassock, S., '*Greenmantle* in its time', *John Buchan Journal*, 36 (Spring 2007), pp. 7–17.

Goldie, D., 'The British Invention of Scottish Culture: World War One and Before', *Review of Scottish Culture* 18 (2006), pp. 128–48.

Gollin, A. M., *Proconsul in Politics: A study of Lord Milner in Opposition and in Power* (London: Anthony Blond, 1964).

Gollwitzer, H., *Karl Barth, Kirchliche Dogmatik* (Fischer Bücherei: Frankfurt am Mainz & Hamburg, 1957)

Gooch, G. P., *History and Historians in the Nineteenth Century* (London: Longmans Green and Co, 1952).

Graham, R. B. C., *Success and Other Sketches* (London: Duckworth, 1902).

Gray, W. F. (ed.), *Comments and Characters by John Buchan* (London: Thomas Nelson & Sons, 1940).

Green, M., *Dreams of Adventure, Deeds of Empire* (London: Routledge and Kegan Paul, 1980).

Greig, J. C. G., 'Introduction' to John Buchan, *Supernatural Tales* (Edinburgh: B&W Publishing, 1997), pp. vii–xxvi.

Greimas, A. J., *Semantique Structurale* (Paris: Larousse, 1966).

Grieves, K., 'Early historical responses to the Great War: Fortescue, Conan Doyle, and Buchan', in B. Bond (ed.), *The First World War and British Military History* (Oxford: Clarendon Press, 1991), pp. 29–37.

—, '*Nelson's History of the War*: John Buchan as Contemporary Military Historian', *Journal of Contemporary History*, 28: 3 (1993), pp. 533–51.

Haining P. (ed.), *Clans of Darkness: Scottish Stories of Fantasy and Horror* (New York: Taplinger Publishing, 1971).

Halpern, P. G., 'The War at Sea', in H. Strachan (ed.), *The Oxford Illustrated History of the First World War* (Oxford: Oxford University Press, 1998), pp. 108–9.

Hanna, A., *John Buchan, 1987–1940: A Bibliography* (Hamden, CT: Shoestring Press, 1953).

Hannah, L., *The Rise of the Corporate Economy* (London: Methuen, 1983).

Hardy, D., *From Garden Cities to New Towns: Campaigning for Town and Country Planning, 1899–1946* (London: Spon, 1991).

Harrison, J., *Themis* (London: Merlin Press, 1912, 1925).

Harvie, C., *The Centre of Things: Political Fiction from Disraeli to the Present* (London: Unwin, 1991).

—, 'Introduction' to John Buchan, *The Thirty-Nine Steps* (Oxford: Oxford University Press, 1993), pp. vvii–xxii.

Haslett, I. and M. Haslett, 'Buchan and the Classics: School and University', *John Buchan Journal*, 24 (March 2001), pp. 30–40.

—, 'Buchan and the Classics, part 3; John Buchan's *The Law Relating to the Taxation of Foreign Income* (1905)', *John Buchan Journal*, 26 (Spring 2002), pp. 8–16.

Haslett, M. and I. Haslett, '*The Dancing Floor*: Places and Sources', *John Buchan Journal* 20 (Spring 1999), pp. 6–19.

—, 'Buchan and the Classics part 2; The Classics in Buchan's work', *John Buchan Journal*, 25 (Autumn 2001), pp. 8–25.

Hébert, L., 'The Actantial Model', in L. Hébert (ed.), *Signo* (Quebec: Rimouski, 2006), http://www.signosemio.com.

Henshaw, P., 'John Buchan and the Invention of Post-Colonial Literature', *John Buchan Journal*, 32 (Spring 2005), pp. 35–40.

Hervouet, Y., 'Why Did Conrad Borrow So Extensively?', *Conradian* 9:2 (November 1984), pp. 53–68.

Hilliard, C., 'Modernism and the Common Writer', *Historical Journal*, 48:3 (2005), pp. 769–87.

Hillier, K. (ed.), *The First Editions of John Buchan: A Collector's Bibliography*, (Hamden, CT: Archon Books, 1981), (Bristol: Avonworld Ltd, 2008).

Himmelfarb, G., *Victorian Minds* (London: Weidenfield and Nicolson, 1968).

Hopkins, L., 'The Irish and the Germans in the fiction of John Buchan and Erskine Childers', *Irish Studies Review* 9:1 (2001), pp. 69–80.

Hurgronje, C. S., *The Holy War: 'Made in German'* (New York: G. P. Putnam & Sons, 1915).

—, *Mohammedanism: Lectures on its Origin, its Religious and Political Growth, and its Present State* (New York: G. P. Putnam & Sons, 1916).

Hutcheon, L., 'Literary Borrowing … and Stealing: Plagiarism, Sources, Influences, and Intertexts', *English Studies in Canada*, 12:2 (June 1986), pp. 229–39.

Hyslop, J., 'Cape Town Highlanders, Transvaal Scottish: Military "Scottishness" and Social Power in Nineteenth and Twentieth Century South Africa', *South African Historical Journal*, 49 (2003), pp. 25–42.

Idle, J., 'The Pilgrim's Plane Crash: Buchan, Bunyan, and Canonicity', *Literature and Theology*, 13:3 (1999), pp. 249–58.

James, W., *Memories and Studies* (London: Longmans, 1911).

Jones, G. G., 'The British Government and the Oil Companies 1912–1924: the Search For An Oil Policy', *The Historical Journal*, 20:3 (1977), pp. 647–72.

Jones, S., 'Into the Twentieth Century: Imperial Romance from Haggard to Buchan' in C. Saunders (ed.) *A Companion to Romance: From Classical to Contemporary* (Oxford: Blackwell Publishing, 2007), pp. 406–23.

Joshi, S. T., *The Weird Tale* (Austin, TX: University of Texas Press, 1990).

Kane, M., *Modern Men: Mapping Masculinity in English and German Literature, 1880–1930* (London: Cassell, 1999).

Karl, F. R., *Joseph Conrad: The Three Lives* (London: Faber, 1979).

Keating, P., *The Haunted Study: A Social History of the English Novel, 1875–1914* (London: Martin, Secker & Warburg, 1997).

Kennedy, T. C., 'Public Opinion and the Conscientious Objector, 1915–1919', *Journal of British Studies*, 12: 2 (1973), pp. 105–19.

Ker, J., *Scottish Nationality: and Other Papers* (Edinburgh: Andrew Elliot, 1887).

—, 'Sir Walter Scott as Patriot', *Scotia* 1: 3 (Lammas 1907), pp. 204–7.

Kerr, D., 'Stealing *Victory*?: The Strange Case of Conrad and Buchan', *Conradiana* 40: 2 (Summer 2008), pp.147–63.

Kipling, R., 'A Pict Song', *Puck of Pook's Hill* (London: Pan, 1975), p. 175.

—, 'Dymchurch Flit', *Puck of Pook's Hill* (London: Pan, 1975), pp. 199–217.

Knowles, O., 'Conrad, Anatole France, and the Early French Romantic Tradition: Some Influences', *Conradiana*, 11 (1979), pp. 41–61.

Kruse, J., *John Buchan and the Idea of Empire: Popular Literature and Political Ideology* (Lewiston: Edwin Mellen Press, 1989).

Kuntzel, T., 'The Film Work 2', *Camera Obscura*, 5 (1980), pp. 7–72.

Lawrence, D. H., *The Rainbow* (London: Penguin, 1981).

Lawson, F. H., *The Oxford Law School* (Oxford: Oxford University Press, 1968).

Lindsay, M., *History of Scottish Literature*, 2nd (revised) edn (London: Robert Hale Limited, 1992).

Locke, W. J., 'Letter to the Editor', *The Times* (11 January 1902), p. 11.

Lovecraft, H. P., *Supernatural Horror in Literature* (New York: Ben Abramson, 1945).

Lowerson, J., 'Sport and British Middle-Class Culture: Some Issues of Representation and Identity before 1940', *International Journal of the History of Sport*, 21:1 (January 2004), pp. 34–49.

Lownie, A., *John Buchan: The Presbyterian Cavalier* (London: Constable, 1995).

Macaulay, R., *Non-Combatants and Others* (London: Methuen, 1986).

Macdonald, K., 'Wells' correspondence with John Buchan', *The Wellsian*, 13 (1990), pp. 43–8.

—, 'The Fiction of John Buchan with Particular Reference to the Richard Hannay Novels' (PhD thesis, University College London, 1991).

—, 'Translating Propaganda: John Buchan's Writing During the First World War', in M. Hammond and S. Towheed (eds), *Publishing in the First World War: Essays in Book History* (London: Palgrave Macmillan, 2007), pp.181–201.

—, 'Writing "The War"', *The Times Literary Supplement*, 10 August 2007, p. 15–16.

—, 'Afterword', John Buchan, *Sir Quixote of the Moors* (Kansas City, KC: Valancourt Press, 2008), pp. 81–3.

—, *John Buchan: A Companion to the Mystery Fiction* (Jefferson, NC: McFarland & Co, 2009).

—, 'Introduction', to John Buchan, *The Thirty-Nine Steps* (New York: Barnes & Noble, 2009), p. vii–xiv.

MacDiarmid, H., *Contemporary Scottish Studies* (Manchester: Carcanet, 1995).

MacDonald, R., *The Language of Empire: Myths and Metaphors of Popular Imperialism, 1880–1918* (Manchester: Manchester University Press, 1994).

Mack, J. D., 'John Buchan in Print: A Bibliography of the Published Writings and Addresses of John Buchan, First Baron Tweedsmuir' (MA thesis, Lehigh University, 1949; published by Diebold in 1952)

MacNeice, L., *Collected Poems* (London: Faber and Faber, 1979).

MacRobert, A. E., 'Muckle John Gib', *John Buchan Journal*, 37 (Autumn 2007), pp. 18–19.

Al-Makhzumi, M. B., *The Impressions of Jamal Al-Deen Al-Afghani: Including a Comprehensive Account of his Attitudes, Ideas, Thoughts About the People of the East and the West in Moral, Political, and Social Aspects* (in Arabic) (Beirut: Al-A'almia Printing House, 1931).

Mallios, P., 'An Interview with Edward Said', in C. M. Kaplan, P. Mallios and A. White (eds) *Conrad in the Twenty-First Century: Contemporary Approaches and Perspectives* (New York: Routledge, 2005), pp. 283–303.

Mangan, J. A., *Athleticism in the Victorian and Edwardian Public School: The Emergence and Consolidation of an Educational Ideology* (Cambridge: Cambridge University Press, 1981).

Mann, G. A., 'John Buchan (1875–1940) and the First World War: A Scot's Career in Imperial Britain' (PhD dissertation, University of North Texas, 1999).

May, A., 'Milner's Kindergarten (*act.* 1902–1910)', *Oxford Dictionary of National Biography*, online edn (Oxford: Oxford University Press, 2005) [http://www.oxforddnb.com/view/theme/93711, accessed 19 Nov 2008].

McKendrick, N., 'Literary Luddism and the Businessman', in P. N. Davies, *Sir Alfred Jones* (London: Europa, 1978).

—, 'The Enemies of Technology and the Self-Made Man', in R. Church, *Herbert Austin* (London: Europa, 1979).

—, '"Gentlemen and Players" revisited: the gentlemanly ideal, the business ideal and the professional ideal in English literary culture', in N. McKendrick and R. B. Outhwaite (eds), *Business Life and Public Policy, Essays in Honour of D.C. Coleman* (Cambridge: Cambridge University Press, 1986).

McKim, D. K. (ed.), *Encyclopedia of the Reformed Faith* (London: John Knox Press and Saint Andrew Press, 1992)

McVeagh, J., *Tradefull Merchants: The Portrayal of the Capitalist in Literature* (London: Routledge & Kegan Paul, 1981).

Miller, J. E., *Rebel Women: Feminism, Modernism and the Edwardian Novel* (London: Virago Press, 1994).

Millman, B., *Managing Domestic Dissent in First World War Britain* (London, 2000)

Mitchell, J. L., *Hanno; or, the Future of Exploration* (London: Kegan Paul, Trench, Trubner & Co., 1928).

Modleski, T., *The Women who Knew Too Much: Hitchcock and Feminist Theory* (New York: Routledge, 1989).

Moore, G. M., O. Knowles and J. H. Stape (eds), *Conrad: Intertexts and Appropriations: Essays in Memory of Yves Hervouet* (Amsterdam: Rodopi, 1997).

Morgan, E., 'Buchan, John (1875–1940): *Sick Heart River* (1941)', in *Twentieth-Century Scottish Classics* (Glasgow: Book Trust Scotland, 1987), p. 3.

Morton, G., *Unionist-Nationalism: Governing Urban Scotland, 1830–1860* (East Linton: Tuckwell Press, 1999).

Nabers, D., 'Spies Like Us: John Buchan and the Great War Spy Craze', *Journal of Colonialism and Colonial History*, 2:1 (2001), [http://muse.jhu.edu/journals/cch/v002/2.1nabers.html, accessed 19 November 2008].

Nadel, I. B., *The Cambridge Introduction to Ezra Pound* (Cambridge: Cambridge University Press, 2007).

Najder, Z., *Joseph Conrad: A Chronicle* (Cambridge: Cambridge University Press, 1983).

Nasson, B., 'John Buchan's South African Visions', *John Buchan Journal*, 26 (2002), pp. 29–33.

—, 'John Buchan, the Great War and Springbok Achievement', *John Buchan Journal*, 28 (2003), pp.19–21.

—, *Springboks on the Somme: South Africa in the Great War 1914–1918* (Johannesburg: Penguin, 2007).

Nauright, J., 'Sport, Manhood and Empire: British Responses to the New Zealand Rugby Tour of 1905', *International Journal of the History of Sport*, 8:2 (September 1991), pp. 239–55.

Nimocks, W., *Milner's Young Men: the Kindergarten in Edwardian Imperial affairs* (Durham, NC: Duke University Press, 1970).

North, M., *Reading 1922* (Oxford: Oxford University Press, 1999).

Nygren, A., *Agape and Eros*, trans. P. S. Watson (London: Society for Promoting Christian Knowledge, 1953).

Occleshaw, M., *Armour against Fate: British Military Intelligence in the First World War* (London, 1989)

Official History: Union of South Africa and the Great War (Pretoria: Government Printer, 1924).

Orpen, N., *The Cape Town Highlanders, 1885–1985* (Cape Town: Purnell, 1986).

Orr, C., 'The Discourse on Adaptation', *Wide Angle* 6.2 (1984), pp. 72–3.

Parfitt, G., *Fiction of the First World War: A Study* (London: Faber and Faber, 1988).

Parliamentary Debates, 272 H. C. Deb. 5 s., cols 266–7.

Parry, J. P., 'From the Thirty-Nine Articles to the Thirty-Nine Steps: Reflections on the Thought of John Buchan', in M. Bentley (ed.), *Public and Private Doctrine: Essays in British History Presented to Maurice Cowling* (Cambridge: Cambridge University Press, 1993), pp. 209–35.

Parsons, C. O., *Witchcraft and Demonology in Scott's Fiction, with Chapters on the Supernatural in Scottish Literature* (Edinburgh: Oliver and Boyd, 1964).

Pick, D., *War Machine: The Rationalisation of Slaughter in the Modern Age* (New Haven, CT: Yale University Press, 1993).

Pike, D. L., 'Sewage Treatments' in W. A. Cohen and R. Johnson, (eds.), *Filth: Dirt, Disgust and Modern Life* (Minneapolis: University of Minnesota Press, 2005), pp. 51–77.

Pittock, M., 'Scotland, Empire and Apocalypse: from Stevenson to Buchan', in *The Edinburgh Companion to Twentieth-Century Scottish Literature* (Edinburgh: Edinburgh University Press, forthcoming 2009).

Procopius, *The Anecdota or Secret History*, trans. H. B. Dewing (London: Heinemann, 1935).

Propp, V., *A Morphology of the Folk Tale*, trans. L. Scott (Austin, TX: University of Texas Press, 1968).

Pudlo, M. A., 'John Buchan's Americanism in the First World War', *John Buchan Journal*, 17 (1997), pp. 38–45.

Pykett, L., *Engendering Fictions: The English Novel in the Early Twentieth Century* (London: Edward Arnold, 1995).

Rae, J., *Conscience and Politics* (London: Oxford University Press, 1970).

Al-Rawi, A. K., 'Manipulating Muslims in John Buchan's *Greenmantle* and A. J. Quinnell's *The Mahdi*: A Pattern of Consistency', *John Buchan Journal*, 36 (Spring 2007), pp. 18–32.

Rajamäe, P., 'John Buchan's Adventurers and The Chivalric Ideal: Gentlemen Born' (PhD dissertation, University of Tartu, 2007).

Ray, P. E., 'The Villain in the Spy Novels of John Buchan', *English Literature in Transition* 24.2 (1981), pp. 81–90.

Redley, M., 'Making Democracy Safe for the World: a Note on John Buchan's Political Career', *John Buchan Journal*, 17 (Autumn 1997), pp. 31–7.

—, 'John Buchan at Milton Academy', *John Buchan Journal*, 22 (2000), pp. 22–32.

—, 'John Buchan and East Africa', *John Buchan Journal*, 27 (Autumn 2002), pp. 23–33.

—, 'Henry Newbolt and John Buchan: A Literary Friendship?', *John Buchan Journal*, 28 (Spring 2003), pp. 25–42.

—, 'Origins of the Problem of Trust: Propaganda During the First World War', in V. Bakir and M. Barlow (eds), *Communications in the age of suspicion: trust and the media* (Basingstoke, 2007).

—, 'John Buchan and *The Great Illusion*', *John Buchan Journal*, 37 (2007), pp. 30–5.

—, '"Administrative Archangel?": John Buchan in South Africa, 1901–03' (unpublished seminar paper, Department of Historical Studies, University of Cape Town, July 2008).

Rich, P., 'Milnerism and a Ripping Yarn: Transvaal Land Settlement and John Buchan's novel, Prester John, 1901–1910', in B. Bozzoli (ed.), *Town and Countryside in the Transvaal: Capitalist Penetration and Popular Response* (Johannesburg: Ravan, 1983), pp. 415–21.

Richards, J., 'Passing the Love of Women: Manly Love and Victorian Society', in J. A. Mangan and J. Walvin (eds), *Manliness and Morality: Middle Class Masculinity in Britain and America, 1800–1940* (New York: St Martin's Press, 1987).

Ridley, M. R., *Second Thoughts: More Studies in Literature* (London: J. M. Dent, 1965).

Rickard, J., *Australia: A Cultural History* (Longman, Harlow, 1996).

Roden, B. and C. Roden, eds. *The Watcher by the Threshold* (Ashcroft BC: Ash-Tree Press, 2005).

Roller, L. E., *In Search of God the Mother: The Cult of Anatolian Cybele* (Berkeley, CA: University of California Press, 1999).

Rose, J., *The Intellectual Life of the British Working Classes* (New Haven CT: Yale University Press, 2001).

Rose, J. H., A. P. Newton, and E. A. Benians (eds), *The Cambridge History of the British Empire, Volume II* (Cambridge: Cambridge University Press, 1940).

Rosebery, Lord, 'Preface' in J. Buchan, *Nelson's History of the War*, vol. I, *From the Beginning of the War to the fall of Namur* (Edinburgh: Thomas Nelson and Sons, 1915), pp. 5–8.

Rothman, W., *Hitchcock: The Murderous Gaze* (Cambridge MA: Harvard University Press, 1982).

Rowse, A. L., 'John Buchan at Elsfield', in ed. S. Tweedsmuir, *John Buchan by his Wife and Friends* (London: Hodder & Stoughton, 1947), pp. 174–87.

Rubinstein, W. D., 'Cultural Explanations for Britain's Economic Decline: How True?', in B. Collins and K. Robbins (eds.), *British Culture and Economic Decline* (London: Weidenfeld and Nicolson, 1990), pp. 78–9.

—, *Capitalism, Culture and Decline in Britain, 1750–1990* (London: Routledge, 1994).

Russell, B., *The Philosophy of Pacifism* (London: Headley Brothers, 1915).

Ryall, T., 'One Hundred and Seventeen Steps towards Masculinity', in P. Kirkham and J. Thumim (eds), *You Tarzan: Masculinity, Movies and Men* (London: Lawrence and Wishart, 1993).

A S, 'Letter to the Editor', *The Times* (15 January 1902), p. 12.

Sanders, M. L., and P. Taylor, *British Propaganda during the First World War, 1914–18* (London: Macmillan, 1982).

Sandison, A., *The Wheel of Empire* (London: Macmillan, 1967).

Scanlon, J., *On Garbage* (London: Reaktion, 2005).

Schreuder, D., 'The Making of the Idea of Colonial Nationalism, 1898–1905', in J. Eddy and D. Schreuder (eds), *The Rise of Colonial Nationalism: Australia, New Zealand, Canada and South Africa Assert their Nationalities, 1880–1914* (London: Allen & Unwin, 1988), pp. 192–226.

Scott, W., *The Letters of Malachi Malagrowther* (Edinburgh: William Blackwood, 1981).

—, *Redgauntlet* (London: Whittaker & Co., 1832).

—, *The Talisman* (London: A. Glasgow Collins' Clear Type Press, 1832).

—, *Memoirs of Sir Walter Scott*, 5 vols (London: Macmillan, 1900).

Searle, G. R., *A New England? Peace and War 1886–1918* (Oxford: Oxford University Press, 2004), pp. 287–8.

Selwyn, E. C., 'Letter to the Editor', *The Times* (15 January 1902), p. 12.

Shipley, G., J. Vanderspoel, D. Mattingley, L. Foxhall (eds), *The Cambridge Dictionary of Classical Civilization* (Cambridge: Cambridge University Press, 2006).

Showalter, E., *Sexual Anarchy: Gender and Culture at the Fin de Siècle* (London: Bloomsbury, 1990).

Sloan, A. P., *My Years with General Motors* (London, Sidgwick and Jackson, 1965).

Smiles, S., *Self-Help* (1859; London: John Murray, 1897).

Smith, A., 'The Running Man', *Scotland on Sunday Review Supplement*, 28 December 2008, pp. 8–9.

Smith, B. P., *Islam in English Literature* (New York: Caravan Books, 1977).

Smith, C., 'Every Man Must Kill the Thing He Loves: Empire, Homoerotics, and Nationalism in John Buchan's *Prester John*', *NOVEL: A Forum on Fiction*, 28:2 (Winter 1995), pp. 173–202.

Smith, G. G., *Scottish Literature: Character and Influence* (London: Macmillan, 1919).

Smout, T. C., 'Perspectives on the Scottish Identity', *Scottish Affairs*, 6 (1994), pp. 101–13.

Smith, W., and H. Wace (eds), *A Dictionary of Christian Biography, Literature, Sects and Doctrines, being a Continuation of 'The Dictionary of the Bible'*, 4 vols (London: John Murray, 1877–87).

'Soldier Settlement for South Africa', *The Spectator*, 16 November 1901, pp. 750–1.

Stars and Stripes [US Army, France] (5 May 1918), p. 6.

Strachan, H., *The First World War, Volume 1, To Arms*, (Oxford, 2001)

Syme, R., *The Roman Revolution* (Oxford: Clarendon Press, 1939).

Taddeo, J. A., 'Plato's Apostles: Edwardian Cambridge and the "New Style of Love"', *Journal of the History of Sexuality*, 8:2 (October 1997), pp. 196–228.

Taylor, H. E., 'John Buchan's *The Three Hostages*', *The Salisbury Review*, 26:2 (Winter 2007), p. 33.

Thompson, F. M. L., *Gentrification and the Enterprise Culture* (Oxford: Oxford University Press, 2001).

Thomson, A., *Anzac Memories: Living with the Legend* (Melbourne: Oxford University Press, 1994), pp.142–56.

Tolstoy, L., 'A Letter to a Hindu', in *Tolstoy Centenary Edition*, 21 vols (London: Humphrey Milford, 1928–37), vol. 21, pp. 413–32.

Tosh, J., *Manliness and Masculinities in Nineteenth-Century Britain: Essays on Gender, Family and Empire* (Harlow: Longman, 2005).

Turner, A. C., 'John Buchan', (PhD dissertation, University of California, 1952).

—, *Mr. Buchan, Writer* (Toronto: Macmillan, 1949).

Tweedsmuir, S. (ed.), *John Buchan by His Wife and Friends* (London: Hodder and Stoughton Ltd, 1947).

Truffaut, F., *Hitchcock* (New York: Touchstone, 1984).

Vahmagi, T. (ed.), *British Television: An Illustrated Guide* (New York: Oxford University Press, 1996).

Uden, G., 'Books I Have Never Read: Confessions of Certain Bookmen', *Bookman* 83:493 (October 1932), p. 21.

Vaile, P. A., 'Letter to the Editor', *The Times* (10 October 1905), p. 15.

Van der Byl, P., *Top Hat to Veldskoen* (Cape Town: Timmins, 1973).

Van der Waag, I., 'Hugh Wyndham, Transvaal Politics and the Attempt to Create an English Country Seat in South Africa, 1901–1914', *Journal of Imperial and Commonwealth History*, 31:2 (May 2003), pp. 136–57.

Van Zanden, J. L., S. Howarth, J. Jonker, and K. Sluyterman, *A History of Royal Dutch Shell* (Oxford: Oxford University Press, 2007).

Waddell, H., *The Wandering Scholars* (London: Constable, 1932).

Walker, M., *Scottish Literature since 1707* (London and New York: Longman, 1996).

War Speeches by British Ministers: 1914–1916 (London: Unwin, 1917).

Watt, I., *Conrad in the Nineteenth Century* (London: Chatto and Windus, 1980).

Webb, P., *A Buchan Companion: A Guide to the Novels and Short Stories* (Stroud: Sutton, 1994).

Welldon, J. E. C., 'The Training of an English Gentleman in the Public Schools', *Nineteenth Century*, 60 (September 1906), pp. 396–413.

Wellock, W., *Pacifism: What it is and What it is Capable of Doing* (Manchester: Blackfriars, 1916).

Wells, T. B., 'Publishers in Khaki, Office "Boys" in Skirts', *The New York Times* (11 February 1917), p. SM 4.

Whitaker, R., 'An Historical Explanation of the Asiatic Myth of Prester John', *Asiatic Review,* 48 (1952), pp. 74–9.

Wiener, M. J., *English Culture and the Decline of the Industrial Spirit, 1850–1980* (Cambridge: Cambridge University Press, 1981).

Will, A. S., Review of John Buchan, *Two Ordeals of Democracy, The New York Times* (3 May 1925), p. BR 3.

Williams, R., *The Country and the City* (London: The Hogarth Press, 1993).

Willan, B., 'The South African Native Labour Contingent, 1916–1918', *Journal of African History,* 19:1 (1978), pp. 68–92.

Wilson, J. F., *British Business History, 1720–1994* (Manchester: Manchester University Press, 1995).

Wood, R., *Hitchcock's Film Revisited* (New York: Columbia University Press, 1988).

Worsfold, W. S., *The Reconstruction of the New Colonies under Lord Milner*, 2 vols (London: Kegan Paul, Tench Trubner, 1913).

Wright, D. G., 'The Great War, Government Propaganda and English "Men of Letters", 1914–1916', *Literature and History,* 7 (1978), pp. 83–100.

Wright, P., *On Living in an Old Country: The National Past in Contemporary Britain* (London: Verso, 1985).

Yacowar, M., *Hitchcock's British Films* (Hamden, CT: Archon, 1977).

INDEX

protagonists, 153, 155
Protestant; see also Presbyterian, 12, 13, 63, 73
Proust, Marcel, 134
Prussianism, 36, 57, 88, 98, 106, 216
psychology, 15, 81, 85, 91, 92, 99, 101, 142, 146, 151, 178, 186, 188
purity, 125, 160, 162, 178
The Purpose of War, 94

quest, 13, 14, 154, 156, 160, 168, 180, 194, 198, 211, 212

race, 3, 55, 56, 66, 70, 73, 118, 119, 121, 122, 123, 124, 127, 144, 150, 179
Raden, Janet, 153, 157, 159, 161, 165, 167, 168, 210
rationalism, 49, 127, 185, 186, 187, 189
readership, 41, 50
realism, 43, 130, 145, 154
reconciliation, 181
Red Cross, 91, 100
redemption, 48, 98, 138, 149, 203
rehabilitation, 148, 149
regeneration, 42, 150
regression, 121
revolution, 57, 80, 147, 148, 176, 194, 195
religion, 7, 13, 14, 15, 19, 23, 24, 117, 118, 122, 125, 127, 155
repatriation, 68, 70
resistance, 5, 94, 126, 151, 179, 196, 201
responsibility, 48, 71, 72, 83, 91, 114, 119, 139, 196
retrogression, 126
Rhodes, Cecil, 49, 130, 138
ridicule; see also satire, 169
'The Riding of Ninemileburn', 157
the Right, 202
Roman Catholicism, 11, 36, 63, 166
the romance, 63, 130, 138, 139, 142, 144, 149, 150, 151, 153, 154, 168, 175, 195, 203–5, 209
the Romans, 9, 12, 13, 16, 17, 20, 22, 25, 26, 31–4, 63, 150, 200
Roosevelt, Franklin D, 112, 114
Rosebery, Lord, 67, 104, 105
Rowse, A. L., 19
Royal Flying Corps, 56, 85

Roylance, Sir Archie, 47, 85, 165, 194
rugby; see also football, 45, 46, 47, 84
The Runagates Club, 21
the rural, 10, 35, 70, 86, 109, 129, 185, 194–7, 199, 203
Russell, Bertrand, 43, 98, 99
Russia, 47, 80–2, 118, 120, 121, 176, 194, 195

sacrifice, 93, 101, 178, 181
Saki (H. H. Munro), 138
Salute to Adventurers, 6, 11, 106, 108, 157
Sapper (H. C. McNeile), 130
Sappho, 21
Satan; see also the devil, 14, 124, 186
satire; see also ridicule, 75, 122, 133, 166, 167, 168
savagery, 34, 120, 142, 150, 188, 204
schizophrenia, 10
scholars, 138, 185
the scholar gypsy, 44, 164
the schoolboy, 44
schools, 41–8, 55
Schreiner, Olive, 74
scientists, 135, 185, 186, 188, 189
Scotland, 29, 31–3, 63, 108, 142, 175, 179, 184, 185, 207, 210, 213
the *Scotsman,* 81
Scots, 3, 7, 10, 36, 47, 60, 61, 105, 107, 110, 121, 126, 145, 178, 184, 186
Scott, Michael, 25
Scott, Sir Walter, 37, 38, 125, 177, 186, 192, 195
the *Scottish Review,* 6, 29, 46, 81
the Second Boer War; see the Boer War
the Second World War, 88, 89, 114, 180
secret service, 164
Seneca the Elder, 21, 25
Seneca the Younger, 21
servant, 162, 163, 211
servitude, 164
settings, 4
the settler, 3, 41, 57, 68, 70, 103, 107, 108, 109, 110, 130
sexuality; see also homosexuality, 162, 163, 168, 213, 215
Sharp, Don, 5, 208, 216
shellshock, 85